(((REAL MEN DON'T SING)))

REFIGURING AMERICAN MUSIC

A series edited by Ronald Radano and Josh Kun

Charles McGovern, contributing editor

REAL MEN DON'T SING

CROONING IN AMERICAN CULTURE

(((Allison McCracken)))

Duke University Press   Durham and London   2015

© 2015 Duke University Press
All rights reserved
Printed in the United States of America
on acid-free paper ∞
Interior design by Mindy Basinger Hill
Cover design by Heather Hensley
Typeset in Whitman by Westchester Publishing Services

Library of Congress Cataloging-in-Publication Data
McCracken, Allison, [date] author.
Real men don't sing : crooning in American culture / Allison McCracken.
pages cm—(Refiguring American music)
Includes bibliographical references and index.
ISBN 978-0-8223-5917-3 (hardcover : alk. paper)
ISBN 978-0-8223-5936-4 (pbk. : alk. paper)
ISBN 978-0-8223-7532-6 (e-book)
1. Crooning. 2. Male singers—United States. 3. Popular music—
United States—1921–1930—History and criticism. 4. Popular
music—United States—1931–1940—History and criticism. I. Title.
II. Series: Refiguring American music.
ML3477.M37 2015
782.42164'0811—dc23
2015010107

FRONTISPIECE: Bing Crosby, publicity still for his first film short, *I
Surrender, Dear* (1931). This shot demonstrates the way that crooners
of the time were simultaneously represented both as romantic
catalysts for heterosexual couples and as potential competition for
women's affections. Author's collection.

COVER ART: Rudy Vallée with megaphone and saxophone, *Vanity
Fair*, July 1929. Photo by George Hoyningen-Huené. © Condé Nast
Archive / CORBIS.

CONTENTS

ACKNOWLEDGMENTS

When I began this project, I did not anticipate the way it would personally speak to me, and of me, and how much its long gestation process would teach me about feeling historical connection as well as tracing historical change. I have been so fortunate and learned so much from having these crooning voices in my head these many years, but it took me a surprisingly long time to realize that they were just pulling on and extending parts of me that were already there. It took me a long time to acknowledge that the purposes these voices served for their audiences in the increasingly conservative, heteronormative, masculinist late 1920s and early 1930s were the same purposes such voices had served for me growing up as an alienated feminist, queer, working-class Irish Catholic girl in a conservative, ferociously middle-class midwestern town in the 1980s.

In fact I grew up during one of the heydays of the romantic crooner in American culture. Since the 1920s crooners have always been present in some form, those vulnerable young men who undermined masculine codes with their pretty faces, soft hair, and sweet, pleading voices longing for love. At the time I didn't grasp the incongruity that the most macho decade in American history was set to popular songs by the Smiths, Depeche Mode, wham, Phil Collins, Air Supply, Culture Club, and Tears for Fears, and what were tellingly referred to as "power ballads" by "soft" rock bands such as Chicago, REO Speedwagon, Foreigner, and Journey. But my allies and I responded to these songs because their lyrics spoke of our own desire for connection and community. Songs such as "Don't You Forget about Me," "I Want to Know What Love Is," "Lay Your Hands on Me," "People Are People," and "How Soon Is Now" were representative of our feelings of difference, frustration, and marginalization.

While these songs were widely enjoyed, they were especially resonant for nascent feminist, gay, and queer-coded "theater" kids like us. Their wistfulness and pain suggested mourning for the more progressive, inclusive world that had existed in the 1960s and 1970s. Like fans of the early 1930s who resisted socially conservative changes and championed romantic crooners as their cultural representatives when other avenues of pleasure and protest were closed to them, romantic crooners represented values and desires very much at odds with our contemporary social condition. Our world was suffused by the Reagan era's macho masculinity and its feminist backlash, by the hateful misogynist, homophobic rhetoric and activity of the religious right, by the arms race and the ever-present threat of nuclear war, and by the constant fear and sadness of the AIDS crisis. Identifying as a feminist or being perceived as queer (often conflated in our town) made one a target for bullying at school and suspicion at home. Crooners gave us a source of identification for desires that we couldn't name and dare not try, their closeted pain embodying the thwarted sexual revolution that we had missed out on. And unlike other commercial genres such as masculine-coded rock, heavy metal, and rap, these haunted, tender songs by gender-queer, most often un-American, emotionally vulnerable and intense young men collapsed differences between masculine and feminine, affirmed female and queer desires, addressed women with love and sensitivity, and affirmed a world outside of our narrow national borders. For us, therefore, their music contained more culturally transgressive elements than many other popular culture products, both in their acknowledgment of profound loss and in their constant desire for that better world in which they—and we—could feel included and be loved.

My first thanks for this project, therefore, must go to the groups that shared this struggle and these songs with me and helped me both survive and remain human: Sylvia Mae Langworthy's Young People's Theater, and our high school group: Stef, Jewel, Chris, Paul, Tat, and Becky.

THERE HAVE BEEN SO MANY PEOPLE, over many years, who helped make possible the words and pictures on these pages. When I was an undergraduate, Ann Jones taught me how to be a feminist writer and critic, Dan Czitrom taught me how to study U.S. cultural history, and Frank Krutnik introduced me to film theory and cultural studies. These teachers indulged my frequently unorthodox approaches to course materials and gave me the freedom to write what I pleased. The English Department at Mount Holyoke College supported me in every possible way, including helping to fund my graduate education.

At the University of Iowa, I was fortunate to have dissertation cochairs who reflected my interdisciplinary commitments to both media studies and American studies, Rick Altman and Lauren Rabinovitz. This project began when Rick suggested I look into the history of microphone technology for his sound seminar class; instead I found Rudy Vallée, and my life was forever changed. Rick's boundless knowledge, intellectual enthusiasm, and commitment to me and to this project have never wavered; he will also always be my favorite singing partner because of the unironic joy he takes in songs from the old musicals we both love. Lauren's expert editing skills and high standards, as well as the model of her own exemplary feminist reception work, have shaped this project in innumerable ways.

My peers and colleagues during my time as a graduate student made it the most stimulating period of my life. I extend my gratitude to Taylor Harrison, John Raeburn, Eric Rothenbuhler, Corey Creekmur, Kathleen Farrell, Doris Witt, Allen Steinberg, and Chrys Poff. John Durham Peters has not only been an intellectual mentor and pedagogical model but is one of the most humane people I have ever known. I want to particularly thank Melanie Nash, Martti Lahti, and Clark Farmer for their insights and for organizing the queer theory and whiteness studies reading groups that were invaluable to this project.

Beyond Iowa, I want to thank my fellow media studies scholars from the University of Wisconsin–Madison who were so supportive of this Iowa girl, especially Elana Levine, and all my radio studies peers, especially Matthew Murray, Jason Loviglio, and Alex Russo. Jean Retzinger at UC-Berkeley and Miles Orvell at Temple were extraordinary mentors. John Burton skillfully guided my tenure process at DePaul. Robert Walser shepherded my first article on this subject in American Music, and Pam Wojcik and Arthur Knight included a version of this work in their book Soundtrack Available. Portions of my conclusion appeared in the online journal Antenna, and I am grateful to its overlords, Jonathan Gray and Myles McNutt, for being so flexible and accommodating. In addition, many friends have provided a variety of assistance and creature comforts while I was "finishing the hat," including Josh Miles, Ann and Walter Burk, Nancy Belbas, Lindsay Giggey, Jennifer Gordon, Gene Combs, Traci Schlesinger, Kathleen Frederickson, Meheli Sen, and Ellie June Navidson. Samantha Holland and Amy Newton, especially, have been close friends as well as intellectual allies. Carolyn Fairbanks's unwavering support has been a blessing for thirty-five years.

I am an enthusiastic researcher and have enjoyed the aid of equally engaged archivists. At Duke University I want to thank Ellen Gartrell, her family, and the staff at the John W. Hartman Center for Sales, Advertising and Marketing History. The staffs of the State Historical Society of Wisconsin, the UCLA Film and Television Archive, and the Margaret Herrick Library have all been wonderfully helpful. I have asked the most of the staff of the Rudy Vallée Collection at the American Library of Radio Archives, and they have often gone above and beyond to help me over these many years, including providing me with scans of the photos that have so enriched this book; my enormous gratitude to Brad Bauer, Jeanette Berard, and especially Klaudia Englund for their unflagging effort and encouragement. My greatest debt in this regard is to Eleanor Vallée, Rudy Vallée's widow, for having faith in my project from its earliest days. She shared her personal memories with me and granted me unfettered access to her late husband's personal papers, letters, and photos. This project could not exist as it does without her help and trust.

My editors at Duke University Press have been nothing short of outstanding. Ken Wissoker originally championed this project from an untested scholar, and Courtney Berger has brought it home. I am so grateful to Courtney for her immense patience, understanding, tenacity, and encouragement. Courtney's assistant, Erin Hanas, has endured my many queries with remarkable grace. My project editor, Liz Smith, has been extraordinarily kind and helpful. I was also greatly helped in the development of this project by a Seashore-Ballard Dissertation Fellowship from the University of Iowa and by two grants from DePaul University's Council for Faculty Research that covered the costs of travel, some illustrations, and indexing.

Interdisciplinary projects rely on the expertise of others. My interviews with sound engineer and mixer Jim Webb and linguistics scholar Ron Smyth were crucial to this work, and both were exceptionally generous with their time. Will Straw, Jennifer Myers Visscher, Ron Gregg, Toby Miller, Shawn VanCour, Christopher Petro, Claire Brandt, and Rae Votta shared their own research and knowledge with me at key moments. Paige Harding's always meticulous and thoughtful research was invaluable. Some of my excellent DePaul American studies undergraduates provided further research and editorial assistance, including Steve Ritchey, Katherine Paris, and the late James Wilson. Bristol Cave-LaCoste has always been in a class by herself; her insightful comments on this manuscript began with "you need to make it sexier," and I have done my best.

Over the years many people have read draft portions of this manuscript, often multiple times, and each time improved it, including Steve Cohan, Heather Hendershot, Francesca Royster, Christina Simmons, Allen F. Davis, and Duke's anonymous readers. Michele Hilmes has been a scholarly role model, cheerleader, and incredibly generous colleague from the beginning of my graduate career; I am fortunate to have had her input on this project many times over the years. Jay Beck has provided much-needed friendship and technological expertise since day one. Norma Coates shared her expertise and her home with me during difficult times; her daughter, Isabelle Nagel, supplied both key research and vital moments of joy. My dear friend Joe Wlodarz's sensibilities and pleasures are closest to mine; he has always known what I'm trying to say better than I know myself, and I am grateful every day for his presence in my life. I am very lucky that Kristen Hatch was simultaneously working on the popular culture of the 1920s and 1930s and that we shared such similar viewpoints; she became an invaluable collaborator, and our many conversations during shared writing retreats gave this project—and me—some much-needed breathing room.

Finally this project would not exist without the efforts of two people. Clark Farmer's unconditional love, humanity, and intellectual gifts have done so much to shape my life and this work; he gave me the place and the space to write, endlessly talked through ideas with me, and thoughtfully read every draft. Lucas Hilderbrand is my best friend, my most valued colleague, and my family. He has never faltered in his enthusiasm for this project and his belief that I could accomplish it, even at my lowest moments. He continually affirmed that what I was trying to say was intellectually valuable, and, just as significant, he acted on this conviction by regularly prodding me, encouraging me, helping me to trust my instincts, proofing my work even when he was very busy, cutting as needed, and, at last, helping me to "let it go." There are debts we can never repay in kind, and mine to him is one of them.

Given that this is a project about the often life-sustaining functions of mass-media figures for their grateful fans, I want to acknowledge those whose work regarding the cultural meanings of popular songs, voices, and female/queer reception has most influenced me: Dennis Potter, Wayne Koestenbaum, Terrence Davies, Todd Haynes, and Mx Justin Vivian Bond. I have also been inspired daily in this project by the creative work of Joss Whedon (and everyone he knows), Johnny Weir, Chris Colfer, and Darren Criss. Finally, I am so, so thankful for the insights and warmth of my fan communities: the Bronzers, the Gleeks, and the Klainers. At every stage of this process, I have been amazed by the similarities between today's fans and those of Rudy Vallée from nearly a century ago, and I have been equally moved and enlightened by all of them. Being able to give voice to some of these fans in this book has been, for me, its greatest joy.

I began and end here with my own childhood. I am the first person in my immediate family to attend college, the first woman in my extended families. Most of the women in my family started working at fourteen or sixteen in the 1910s, late 1940s, and 1950s. They were secretaries, bookkeepers, saleswomen, telephone operators, receptionists, and catalogue models. Many did not marry or have children. The mass media allowed them to express emotion safely in otherwise unstable environments and provided them with daily companionship and pleasure in ways that did not compromise their autonomy. Their intense responses to media did not change with age; indeed my mother, Helen, still yells her head off at Neil Diamond concerts. Two of these women were my biggest fans, my grandmother Rita Murphy and my aunt Mary McCracken; both died while I was writing this book. I dedicate it to their memory, and to my mother, and to all the fans like them, and like me, then and now.

INTRODUCTION

The musical power of the disenfranchised—whether youth,
the underclass, ethnic minorities, women or gay people . . . resides in
their ability to articulate different ways of construing the body, ways that
bring along in their wake the potential for different experiential worlds.
And the anxious reactions that so often greet new musics from
such groups indicate that something crucially political is at issue.
—Susan McClary, "Same as It Ever Was," 1994

Extraordinary how potent cheap music is.
—Noel Coward, *Private Lives*, 1930

"The voice of New York is effeminate!" Such was the horrified announcement of the syndicated columnist Gilbert Swan in newspapers across America in December 1931. Swan reported that a research engineer, Dr. William
Baird White, had come to this disturbing conclusion after systematically recording the radio voices in capital cities around the globe. The sound waves
of Manhattan, he found, were "slightly hysterical and falsetto . . . a combination of [crooner] Morton Downey in his more falsetto moments, [crooner]
Rudy Vallée in the process of calling a moose and [boxer] Jack Dempsey in his
usual talking voice." In contrast London's "voice" was "pleasantly masculine:
a good, deep baritone with a bass quality." Swan was appalled: "Here was
New York, prideful of strength and he-man qualities of survival, pictured as a
giant of tremendous vitality! And then the embarrassing discovery that the
giant had a piping tenor voice!"[1]

Swan's alarm, however tongue-in-cheek, was nonetheless an acknowledgment of the growing public anxiety surrounding the popularity and influence
of crooners such as Downey and Vallée, whose electronically amplified,

high-pitched, quavering, and yearning voices had recently transformed popular music. But the couching of White's critique of "effeminate" voices in terms of competing national identities suggests just how much was at stake to America's cultural gatekeepers. The 1930s was a period of new cultural nationalism in the United States, the result of mass-media consolidation and technological standardization most obviously represented by national radio networks and the Hollywood film industry. Corporate America's commitment to a for-profit rather than state-owned media had permitted low culture to eclipse high culture as the national brand, both at home and abroad. The most popular American cultural commodities were more entertaining than educational, the products of ethnic, religious, racial, and sexual minorities, made popular by an increasingly influential female audience. America's cultural elite feared that this new national culture no longer represented their Anglo-American social values.

Just who were these public menaces, these men-who-were-not-real-men, responsible for emasculating New York City? It would seem hard to imagine a less threatening figure than the crooner. Crooners were mostly young men who softly sang love songs into microphones, most popularly over the radio; they gave crooning its modern and still current meaning, "to sing popular, sentimental songs in a low, smooth voice, especially into a closely-held microphone."[2] Their melodies were catchy and familiar, and their lyrics were generally innocuous and inoffensive. Their songs contained no explicit social agenda and were far less ribald than typical vaudeville fare. The top stars were either Irish or Italian American, and although predominantly Catholic, they were all "white" in the increasingly ethnically assimilated and racially segregated urban entertainment landscape of the time. They hailed from middle-class or working-class families. They did not consider themselves cutting-edge artists but rather commercial properties, working for profit. And they generated a lot of money at a time when the economy really needed it. They made millions of dollars for the sheet music industry, were widely acknowledged as having saved the record industry from total collapse in the wake of the Depression, and proved the capacity of radio's new commercial network system to deliver massive national audiences to advertisers. Although largely forgotten or marginalized in popular music history, Rudy Vallée, Russ Columbo, Gene Austin, Morton Downey, Nick Lucas, and the young Bing Crosby were not merely the most popular singers in the nation between the late 1920s and the early 1930s; they were the most popular singers there had *ever* been. They capitalized on the exposure and promotion offered them by an integrated mass media of network radio, sound film, the recording industry, syndicated newspapers and tabloid coverage, national vaudeville and movie house appearances, and sheet music covers. Their intimate address and passionate, sensitive personae made them America's first modern singing stars.

But great commercial success often comes with unexpected social consequences. Until the rise of the romantic crooning star, the idea that New York had one dominating voice, or even that a vocal identity could exist independently of a masculine body, undermining that body's appearance of "he-man" strength and "tremendous vitality," had not been a topic of consideration for the guardians of popular culture. No one had been concerned about high-voiced men, either as singers or as speakers (such as the prizefighter Jack Dempsey), so long as those performers remained within their own particular lowbrow cultural venues, to be reviewed or quoted but otherwise silent. No one anticipated the transformative effects of microphone technology, which put soft-voiced singers on equal footing with classically trained singers and Broadway belters, nor the profound social impact of combining these amplified voices with radio's expansive reach. When Rudy Vallée became a local phenomenon in New York City singing radio love songs in 1928, crooners were still thought of only as novelties. But nationwide network access plus millions of adoring fans quickly made romantic crooning voices the norm rather than the exception in popular performance. By the end of 1931 such voices were everywhere. Public address systems and loudspeakers made crooners inescapable even to those who didn't choose to listen to them; their voices poured out of department stores, storefronts, hotel lobbies, movie and vaudeville theaters, park stadiums, and bandstands. The playwright Noel Coward remarked on "the potency" of such "cheap music" in his play *Private Lives*, a huge hit in London's West End and on Broadway in 1930–31. Clearly, cultural authorities had fallen dangerously behind advancing technologies and a nationalized mediascape. Now that the voices of mass culture dominated both the public and private spheres of every class, it was becoming ever more apparent that no consistent criteria existed to standardize or police them.

Leading figures in the fields of religion, education, psychology, engineering, and science thus turned anxious ears to crooners, whom they quickly and uniformly condemned as unfit representatives of American manhood. Crooners showed an unseemly degree of ardent emotion and vulnerability for white men, and they used microphones and amplifiers to artificially enhance their soft, trembling, often sensually breathy sounds. In addition, crooners were able to address listeners directly and intimately within their own homes, allowing unprecedented public penetration into private space. Worse yet, crooners privileged their female listeners, addressing them as beloved individuals and offering them nothing less than an alternative masculine idol and ideal, one who served their desires and was available to them at the flick of a switch. Most frustrating to professional authorities, though, was that there seemed no easy way to regulate crooners' access to their audiences or their listeners' access to them. Singers of color, by contrast, could be and were easily policed and segregated by mass-media industries, and the emotionality in their voices was perceived as being of a piece with their racial inferiority. White men in the public spotlight, however, were expected to be representatives of the dominant culture and to uphold the values of white supremacy through recognizably active, productive masculine behavior. Charles Lindbergh, for example, that other idol of the late 1920s, had proved his masculine mettle by flying solo across the Atlantic Ocean. There was nothing conclusively masculine about the crooner, conversely, beyond the fact of his sex and sexual preference for women, although even this trait was so overstated that it became part of the problem. Men were supposed to love women, but not too much; crooners instead publicly embraced their dependence on women as mothers and lovers. As an anxious Dr. White points out, crooners not only exposed the fact that American national culture had no set criteria for masculine vocalizing, but they had actually established a new standard, one that reflected the gender blurring and loosened social and sexual mores of the New York popular performance world. As authorities feared, Vallée and his ilk were merely the tip of the iceberg.

In *Real Men Don't Sing*, I argue that the popularity of early crooners instigated the imposition, for the first time, of masculine norms for voices on a mass scale in American society. The upper classes had long held such norms to distinguish their own vocal production, but enforcing them on popular entertainers and their audiences was a radical shift, although one that had been a long time coming. Contrary to their radio press, crooners did not simply emerge out of the ether. As this book demonstrates, the sudden stardom of the romantic icon Rudy Vallée was in fact the result of a convergence of forces representing fifty years of change in society and urban entertainment: the growing inclusion and influence of female consumers in popular entertainment; the rise of increasingly homogenized, nationalized mass-media industries concentrated in New York City; the development of modern audio technologies that enabled new forms of intimacy between per-

FIG. I.1. This clipping is representative of the many news stories of the era that portrayed women as dupes for falling in love with radio's romantic singers. The prevalence of such stories also suggests, however, new cultural anxieties about the "magic powers" of radio's voices to generate such intense emotional attachments. Rupert Hughes column, *New York American*, 28 July 1929. Courtesy of Rudy Vallée Collection, American Radio Archives.

formers and their audiences; the privileging of individual, generic romantic desires over other kinds of affective relationships (class, ethnic, familial) in both dominant social discourses and consumer products; and a thriving New York performance culture of social outsiders (immigrants, queers, people of color) that helped to fuel an increasingly sophisticated, socially diverse, and sexually expressive modern urban culture. Crooners were hardly an anomaly in the 1920s performance world, where vocal variety and gender play thrived against the illicit backdrop of Prohibition, but their ubiquity made them representatives of a popular culture out of control. As a result cultural authorities targeted crooners as obvious examples of the need to identify and codify an "American culture" in the early 1930s, a standardizing move that would not just affect the content of arts and popular culture but also broadly impact social norms.[3]

While gender concerns were the most publicized aspect of the crooner problem, the complaints about crooners reveal a cornucopia of related anxieties. In addition to effeminacy, crooners were subject to a range of contradictory descriptors, including being immoral, immature, sensuous, base, coarse, profane, imbecilic, primitive, untalented, abnormal, insincere, artificial, pretentious, and corrupting of the nation's youth. As this torrent of adjectives indicates, the crooner controversy crossed boundaries of class, race, religion, and aesthetics and was diagnosed in often conflicting and contradictory ways. To the moral leaders and high-cultured of society, crooners were primitive and sensuous, terms usually associated with racial others and the lower classes, while to mass-media producers, reeling in response to these attacks from above, crooners were publicized and became viewed as pretentious, elitist, and artificial, terms associated with the upper class. To the primarily male representatives of both highbrow and lowbrow culture, however, crooners' high voices, their privileging of emotional vulnerability, and their association with female audiences devalued them artistically *and* suggested a lack of manliness that, as acceptable gender behavior narrowed in the early 1930s, increasingly came to be associated with homosexual identity.[4] The conflation of the crooner with the homosexual, especially as represented by the gay "pansy" characters highly visible in the popular culture of the time, was to prove the most damning and long-lasting accusation against them. "Why do they fall for that pansy?" moans the newspaper columnist Lee Tracy about the crooner Bunny Harmon's (Dick Powell) large female following in the 1932 film *Blessed Event.* Tracy was echoing his real-life counterparts, who were vigorously reinforcing the association of crooners with homosexuality and effeminacy that would soon be taken for granted.

Although other nations made similar shifts against the cultural feminine in the 1930s, the United States established norms of masculinity that were particularly narrow and enduring. The concern over the proper gendering of voices in the early 1930s, exemplified by the crooning controversy, resulted in the establishment of codes and standards through which institutional leaders high and low sought to enforce gender behavior and public responses by continually connecting high-pitched, emotionally vulnerable, and romantic male voices with either the immaturity of youth or the dangers of effeminacy. But the negotiation among high culture's standards, mass culture's commercial needs, and audiences' desires took some time to be fully realized. Crooning thus continued to appear irredeemable (although highly profitable) until changes in Bing Crosby's crooner persona enabled the development of an acceptably "masculine" national crooner standard. Crosby had risen to fame as a romantic crooner and had been widely criticized as such, but key changes in microphone technology helped distance the baritone Crosby from his tenor brethren, and he worked hard to distinguish himself from his peers by diversifying his recordings, toning down their emotional intensity, emphasizing his happy marriage and family life, and identifying himself with the "common man" of Depression America. In this rehabilitation process, the visibility of Crosby's active masculine body was essential, and Hollywood consistently provided it. His early films do much to mitigate the warmth in the sound of his voice through the disciplined physical activity of his body and the modern "cool" emotional detachment of his manner. By the mid-1930s Crosby's masculine crooner persona was in place, identified with traditional tropes of white masculinity (normative gender roles, property ownership and procreation, religious practice, racial supremacy) that conveniently bypassed and erased the urban melting pot and vocal variety of the 1920s. While the crooner persona would continue to remain unstable, Crosby's position as "America's Crooner" effectively established a hegemonic masculine standard for male popular singing against which other singers could be compared and judged. These restrictive standards reverberated beyond the music world and throughout the larger culture, resulting in damaging social stigmas for generations of men and boys whose voices deviated from the new normal.

THE CULTURAL CONSTRUCTION
OF VOCAL AESTHETICS

This book recovers the story of early crooners, focusing on their fundamental, largely unacknowledged role in the development of American music and American culture as we know it today. Although there has been some significant scholarly attention to mass media's voices, such work still represents a small fraction of the work on raced and gendered bodies, most of which does not include or even acknowledge a vocal component.[5] Indeed there remains much to be done on the historical development of vocal aesthetics, especially the way "white" voices have been culturally produced, employed, and essentialized. Ironically, the most commercial, mainstream figures in American culture often have been the least seriously examined, even when, like crooners, their popularity has had massive structural, institutional, and cultural impact.[6] Part of the reason for this neglect is that white voices have tended to remain unmarked and monolithic in mainstream American culture and thus have rarely been examined according to their own racial and historical specificity. However, the cultural meanings of white voices have frequently altered in relation to the social politics of their time, perhaps never more significantly than during the years of this study.

The primary reason early crooners in particular have been marginalized, I suggest, lies in the fact that the norms for white masculine singing that were developed in the early 1930s to counter crooning's cultural dominance and authority largely succeeded and are still in place. These 1930s norms first established the now standard crooner paradigm in which crooners as a group (with rare individual exceptions) became associated with artistically devalued commercial cultural forms and nonnormative gender and sexual behaviors, and their primary audiences were characterized as female or feminized, immature and emotionally needy, and lacking in both taste and judgment. This paradigm has persisted because it drew from aesthetic hierarchies, categories of social difference, and nationalist ideals that themselves were being codified during these years and that were further reinforced in the early 1930s by technological changes. New microphones engineered in 1931–32 enhanced midrange male voices and gave them more warmth and fullness; these mics became the default industrial standard, making any sound recorded before this period seem high, tinny, distant, and less warm to our ears. For all these reasons crooners before 1934 came to be considered frivolous, embarrassing kitsch with a less familiar microphonic sound rather than the transformative figures they actually were. We have thus tended to overlook what their story reveals about the origins of crooning and its critical role in the development of vocal norms in American culture.[7] By examining the boom and backlash surrounding male crooners, *Real Men Don't Sing* presents a cultural history not just of a key period in pop music but of the social construction of the masculine American voice more generally. I argue that pitch, intonation, affect, technological mediation, address, narrative content, and other aspects of vocal production became key indicators of newly rigid notions of gender, race, sexuality, and class.

The vocal codes developed to segregate and police popular music during this time have become so culturally entrenched that it is difficult to imagine that before the 1930s, vocal delivery styles in popular culture were actually not essentialized, neither raced nor gendered. Recordings, performance reviews, promotional materials, and other documents from the time reveal that, unlike the classification of bodies, there were no firm, cultural divisions between "black" vocal sounds and "white" vocal sounds, nor was there any such thing as exclusively "masculine" or "feminine" singing styles in 1920s popular performance. While the highbrow entertainment opera had rejected the gender ambiguities of its castrato stars and instituted gendered vocalizing by the nineteenth century, popular entertainments had not followed suit.[8] Voices thus remained socially fluid. In such an environment, a broad vocal versatility and the ability to perform what *Variety* termed "vocal tricks" like scatting and yodeling were highly prized and praised in all performers. Singers constantly exposed the way men's and women's voices do, in fact, overlap more than they do not by singing each other's songs in the same ranges. Indeed vocal musical culture fostered porous communities in which men and women of varied races and ethnicities performed torch songs, scatted, warbled, yodeled, crooned, and sang the blues.[9] The blues singer Ethel Waters famously learned her breakthrough song, "St. Louis Blues," from a female impersonator, Charlie Anderson.[10] Promotional materials and reviews commonly employed compound descriptives such as "blues crooning" and "crooning jazz" and described popular performers as "male altos" or "female baritones." Crooning singing and jazz dancing were the two biggest musical vogues of the 1920s, two sides of the same coin, and equally popular among urban immigrants, white collegiate youth, and people of color. Musicologists have already demonstrated how racial and class lines in performance styles were redrawn industrially and culturally in the mid-1920s; this book shows how gendered divisions soon followed in the early 1930s.[11] While everybody crooned in the 1920s, only white men would come to be criticized for it, a reflection of the increasingly rigid cultural boundaries on vocalizing initiated during this era.

Because the stigmas surrounding male pop singing have existed for so long, it's easy to forget that singing was a traditional, widely accepted part of male culture, cutting across classes, races, religions, and ethnic groups. Male performers far outnumbered women in the popular culture of the 1920s, and most were singers of some stripe; chorus boys, singing waiters, speakeasy performers, band singers, vaudeville belters, and cabaret confidential tenors were staples of urban nightlife (many hired for their youth and attractiveness as much as for their vocal abilities). Singing suffused social life and was an important agent of homosocial bonding among men. Eddie Cantor wistfully recalled his neighborhood "gang" singing around the stoop, and F. Scott Fitzgerald's 1920s novels revere the camaraderie of male singing collegians. The crooning star Gene Austin found great pleasure as a child singing along with cowboys on Texas trails and, later, singing with other soldiers in his military unit during World War I and with his fellow ragtime pianists in Paris and Harlem. Businessmen likewise sang around the pianos at their gentlemen's clubs as well as in their parlors and places of worship, while their working-class peers sang in saloons, community theaters, and their religious centers. Boy singers were particularly highly valued and mentored as singers in their churches and synagogues. Both high-pitched, emotionally intense male vocal performances and men's equally emotional responses to them were regular occurrences, completely naturalized and unstigmatized; adult men,

RUDY'S FANS FIGHT FOR A PHOTOGRAPH

PAUL ASH | MERRY MAD GANG | SOPHOMORE | SOPH

Photo or Evening Journal Staff Photographer.

This crowd—both men and women—milled about the lobby of the Brooklyn Paramount Theatre in an effort to receive an autographed photograph of Rudy Vallee from the hands of the entertainer. Special police of the theatre assisted by traffic officers dispersed the crowd when it assumed the aspects of a five o'clock subway rush at Times Square. A newspaper photographer's camera was broken during the melee.

FIG. I.2. This news report of the "melee" of fans fighting for Vallée's autograph during an appearance at the Brooklyn Paramount is indicative of his tremendous initial appeal. The caption notes that the crowd was composed of "both men and women," an unusual admission of Vallée's mixed fan base by the popular press, but the photo made it self-evident. The caption also notes that theater security had to work with traffic officers to disperse the crowd. Rudy Vallée fans at the Brooklyn Paramount, *New York Evening Journal*, 8 August 1929. Courtesy of Rudy Vallée Collection, American Radio Archives.

for example, regularly and unashamedly wept listening to adolescent boys sing about their love for their mothers.

In this environment, muscular, energetic "he-men" regularly sang in falsetto voice, countertenor, or high tenor; in fact the higher a man could sing, the more he was celebrated by popular audiences, and it had been that way for decades. Male performers spent years developing their falsettos and high tenor or countertenor voices *because* they were so popular and thus more commercially valuable than other vocal registers. Audience preferences for high-pitched male voices continued through the 1920s; New York City radio listeners, for example, chose Will Oakland, a longtime Irish countertenor recording star, as their favorite radio voice in 1925.[12]

Real Men Don't Sing demonstrates that the very identification of high pitch or emotional vulnerability as a stigmatizing factor (a literal black mark) in the evaluation of white male popular singing was new in the mass culture of the early 1930s and that such distinctions served the purposes of establishing vocal norms that enforced race, class, gender, and sexual divisions and hierarchies. The very fact that men of color with high-pitched or emotionally expressive voices were not similarly labeled as too feminine or homosexual during the attacks on crooning makes it very clear that the association between pitch and gender or sexuality was a way for the dominant cultural authorities to narrow the qualifications for white masculine performance in the mass media (and beyond). Given their decades of previous popularity, the fairly swift suppression of these voices in the early 1930s is remarkable, as is their consequent erasure from music history. And yet rapid changes in the audio landscape were also characteristic of this period, as evidenced by microphone crooning's initial, mercurial ascent. Although we live in a commercial music culture that the early crooners did much to shape, the aesthetic and related social changes their unprecedented popularity initiated are still largely unknown, misrepresented, or devalued.

I argue that crooners from 1925 through the early 1930s transformed popular music, initiating the dominance of the commercial "pop" microphone sound in both live and recorded entertainment. For the music industry, crooners offer the best evidence of the enormous impact of microphone technology, electrical recording, and amplification; indeed, crooning is the first song-delivery style created specifically by the microphone. In the chronology of popular music, crooners are particularly important because they bridge a longer history of mass entertainment forms—including minstrelsy, vaudeville, song-slide presentations, Tin Pan Alley sheet music production, and gramophone recording—with new, technically enabled forms of romantic and intimate expression. They were commercial and comforting and registered with listeners as *sincere*, the template for pop singing ever after.[13] In fact the trade journal *Variety* began employing the term *pop* to describe the vocal delivery style of these singers as a group, whereas previously the term had been used to designate any kind of cheaply priced, commercial entertainment.[14] Crooning song pluggers became the nation's first pop singers, and in 1929 Rudy Vallée became America's first pop idol.

Not only did early crooners dominate radio, records, and sheet music for years, their popularity also spurred the reorientation of both popular music recording and live jazz band performance away from star instrumentalists to star singers, creating the first band lead singers. These singers further introduced the concept of the slow dance in nightclubs and tea dances, a new form of intimacy in which couples clung to each other, barely swaying to music rather than following steps. Crooners helped popularize the "confidential tenor" table singer for the cabaret audience, and their success shifted the dominant site of popular music sales and singing stardom from vaudeville to radio and movie houses (where crooners performed in live "presentations" before and between film screenings). As a result, crooning singers led the larger aesthetic shift in vocal popular culture from vaudeville's variety, in which success depended on the singer's mastery of myriad characterizations and styles as well as projection abilities, to the intimate aesthetic of the microphone performer, in which success depended greatly upon the singer's perceived sincere presentation of his own feelings and his involvement in the song's romantic narrative.

This intimate aesthetic closely resembled that of the Hollywood films and tabloids of the time because it depended on the audience's affective immersion in the romantic narrative, but radio crooning proved to be an especially—and unexpectedly—potent mode of delivery of romantic feeling.[15] Although crooners were broadly popular across sexes, ages, classes, regions, races, and ethnicities—a fact that was continually underreported even during the peak of their popularity—they most visibly took over the mantle of the "matinee idol" for American youth, especially women, beginning with the unprecedented intensity of fan response to Vallée in 1929. Vallée's first public New York City concerts in 1929 drew such tremendous, fervent, and demonstrative crowds that police had to be called to contain them. The crooning-song lover and his enthralled fan have become such familiar figures in the decades since that it is difficult to appreciate how unusual such visceral responses to and mass adoration of a radio singer actually were. Before Vallée only certain film stars, Broadway actors, and opera singers had provoked similar kinds of impassioned, love-struck, swooning crowds; after Vallée, however, such extreme devotional displays would be associated *primarily* with young male pop singers.[16] Vallée sparked a new phase of celebrity vocal culture that media industries swiftly exploited; from 1929 to 1933 legions of romantic singers flooded the radio, recording, and film industries. Crooning singers would soon establish the sincere male singer as a film character and remained central to the Hollywood film musical for decades, in addition to their already integral role in Americans' lived experience in popular musical performances of every kind, from jazz band performances to wedding receptions.

Real Men Don't Sing reappraises early crooners' role in American culture. I take the view that there is no one determining factor in American cultural production, that culture has always comprised multiple agents engaged in continual negotiation. I therefore contend that crooners' importance cannot be understood without taking into account the various overlapping influences during this period that made them possible, popular, and ultimately threatening: technological changes; major developments in the radio, print, music, and film industries; the growth and commercial impact of mass audiences; new masculinist definitions of modern culture and taste that explicitly devalued the cultural feminine and female audiences; a new emphasis on cultural authenticity that reified a larger turn toward fixed, "natural" identities; and increasing nationalist fervor marked by white immigrant assimilation, the segregation of nonwhites, and the continuing influence of eugenics.

The dominant social and mass-media discourses of the late 1920s and early 1930s, when the romantic crooner emerged, focused on sex, gender, and consumption as subjects of primary significance for Americans, a reflection of the critical ideological shifts regarding marriage, gender norms, and sexual behavior and identity that were taking place: the growing influence of Freudian psychology and human developmental "norms," the acknowledgment of women as sexual beings outside of their maternal role, the rise of an exclusive sexual identity (tied to gender behavior) as the core of modern selfhood, the unprecedented growth of consumer culture (especially in relation to sexual subjects), and the accompanying surge in consumer response and activism. The groundswell of nuanced, interdisciplinary scholarship about this historical period in recent years—particularly in the fields of sound and media studies; musicology; nationalism and consumerism; American studies; and race, gender, and sexuality studies—has been essential to this study in helping to determine the specific ways enduring social norms were shaped at this time. I draw on all this recent work to offer an intersectional history of the crooning voice in American popular culture and its political and affective importance in the 1920s and 1930s.

Early crooners caused such anxiety because they occupied a cultural position across the aesthetic and social divisions that authorities were attempting to impose, exposing and undermining them to such a degree that they had to be publicly denounced by a broad spectrum of institutional leaders. Crooners conflated masculine and feminine, live and canned entertainment, authenticity and artificiality, the sentimental and the sophisticated, Victorian high romanticism and modern sensuality, adult and adolescent, the body and the machine. They were broadly popular across gender, race, class, and religious lines. Their brand of modern sound undercut dominant masculine, scientific definitions of modernity by restoring the uncontrollable body to the new vocal technology. Their whiteness too closely echoed the racially suspect desires and affiliations of their working-class and immigrant forebears rather than their Anglo leaders at a time when differences between whites were being homogenized in favor of a clearer black/white binary. They likewise blurred gender lines at a time when gender distinctions and behaviors were being newly emphasized, narrowed, and policed, and their willingness to be both vulnerable subjects and objects of desire for their audiences made their manhood suspect at the very moment of the creation of the heterosexual/homosexual divide.

During this period of increased nationalism, white assimilation, and gender normativity, newly white Americans were pressured to continue to ensure racial dominance through marriages and reproduction with equally physically and psychologically "fit" partners. In the mountain of popular discourses devoted to marriage advocacy that characterizes this period, racial, class, and other cultural differences were implied rather than spoken about directly; instead, as the historian Julian Carter has shown, cultural authorities and consumer culture producers addressed their target audiences not as members of immigrant or raced or political groups but as psychologically distinct, gendered individuals.[17] They similarly influenced their audiences' personal behaviors through discourses of romantic love, idealized marriage, and sexual pleasure (in that order). The correct choice of gender behavior and romantic object thus assumed enormous cultural weight during this time—perhaps more than it ever had before in American history. And because of the intensified cultural stakes surrounding appropriate heterosexual pairings, crooners' popularity—specifically their status as icons of romantic love and models of idealized white masculinity—represented a genuine threat to a number of related, intersecting hierarchies.

Part of the challenge in telling this story of the crooner's origins and cultural meaning is that this history is rooted in an America that is unfamiliar, a world that was still, both visibly and audibly, in the process of becoming nationalized and uniform but remained remarkably regional and heterogeneous. This was particularly true of New York City, the focus of much of this study, which at the time—although not for much longer—was the cultural capital of the country, where national live performance tours originated and where much of the mass media was located. In reimagining the vital, diverse, and complex vocal performance world from which early crooners emerged, I have relied on a multitude of primary source materials in addition to interdisciplinary scholarship. Most significantly I have had the very good fortune to be able to draw from the vast personal archive—including fan letters and media coverage—of Rudy Vallée, a central figure in this history. In addition, I have depended on the detailed descriptions of vocal performances in the trade papers of the time, particularly *Variety*, as well as critical and fan responses to crooners in local and nationally syndicated newspapers and magazines.[18] I have also examined anticrooning discourses in popular social science and psychology tracts, music publications, educational materials, and industrial assessments. And I have analyzed as many original audio and video recordings of crooning performances as I could find, in addition to the numerous popular novels, plays, films, and songs about crooners that abounded during this period. This process has further convinced me of the riches and rewards of a more intersectional approach to the study of vocal culture and politics; the remainder of this introduction points to the ways in which telling the story of crooning's changing historical meanings and ideological complexity illuminates the larger cultural significance—and devastating social consequences—of "masculinizing" the American voice.

CROONING, GENDER, AND THE EVOLUTION OF MODERN MICROPHONE SINGING

The 1920s was a transformative era in audio experience for Americans: radio, electric recording, microphone technologies, sound film, loudspeakers, and public address systems were introduced and constantly evolving. Although historians disagree about precisely when mass commercial culture came to dominate Americans leisure time, if one privileges sound over visual culture the 1920s stand out as the key transitional decade. As for other social and cultural innovations of the decade, the primary descriptive term for these new sound technologies was *modern*. Although the definition of *modernity* was contradictory and flexible in the era and has remained so since, cultural commentators and professionals at the time defined a modern sound as the product of science and technology—and connotatively rational, clear, direct, efficient, controlled, productive, and, most significant, *masculine*. As sound studies scholars such as Emily Thompson and Jonathan Sterne have

suggested, "man's mastery of his environment" was one of the key characteristics of modern culture, and sound technologies represented "the promise
of science, rationality and industry and the power of the white man to co-
opt and supersede domains of life that were previously considered to be magical."[19] The radio crooner complicated this discourse. Although the microphone
crooner marked an inarguable technological and cultural transition between
modern and premodern vocalizing, this study demonstrates how these early
crooners epitomized modern technological achievement while continuing
to evoke the premodern etymological and social associations of crooning.
Crooners disrupted the cultural hierarchies—of masculine/feminine,
mechanical/natural, mind/body, artificial/authentic—on which dominant
conceptions of modern sound depended, helping to incite both intense
fandom and anxious forms of regulation.

Although microphones were new, *crooning* as a descriptor for a particular
type of vocal expression was not; the term had long been affiliated with the
uncivilized underside of Western culture. *Crooning* was a term of the colo-
nized, not the colonizers, its origins rooted in the mystical and the romantic. Originally a Scottish vernacular term derived from the Low German
croyn, *crooning* dates back to the fifteenth century, when it meant "to utter
a low murmuring sound; to sing (or speak) in a low murmuring tone." Beginning in the sixteenth century it was also regularly used to describe the
tolling of a bell, "a low, deep sound," or the "bellow of a bull." *Crooning* was
used to describe not only the human voice but, more often, the sounds made
by animals or mythic figures like devils and witches; a crooning voice was
low and insinuating, somewhere between the bucolic and the otherworldly.
An additional meaning, "to make murmuring lament or wail," developed in
the nineteenth century, imbuing the term with the potential for pathos that
American minstrels, early blues singers, and radio crooners would exploit.[20]

Crooning reached North American shores through blackface minstrelsy;
minstrels first popularized the term in the nineteenth century as a descriptor
for the loving, protective murmurs of the black slave woman singing to her
infant charge. The minstrel mammy's sound was, like her persona, natural,
nurturing, emotionally driven, considered at once primal and magical. This
was the romantic age; Irish and Scottish folk melodies—the basis of much
minstrel music—and slave spirituals had begun to be more appreciated by
upper-class white audiences for their perceived naturalism, authenticity
of expression, and spiritual purity.[21] During this period, however, the minstrel performers themselves were considered racially apart from their Anglo

audiences. The popular Irish melodies on which crooning songs were most often grafted were part of an oral tradition and were initially considered, like the low-class, uneducated Irish themselves, "novel, wild, irregular, even barbaric" in the music culture of their time; their singers frequently traveled beyond the standard European pentatonic scale, their voices sliding between and around notes as their emotions dictated.[22] As well as being racially inassimilable, crooning singers were also considered unthreatening because their audiences (especially women) were heavily policed, and the affective structure of reception was different, such that songs that would be perceived as romantic or even erotic a century later were often interpreted by cultural authorities and many audience members as spiritual and uplifting.[23]

In terms of content, mammy crooning songs were also identifiably Victorian and premodern because their subject was often mothers and mothering. Of all the female characters in popular songs of the late nineteenth and early twentieth centuries, mothers were the most revered. The "mother song" was a staple of popular song throughout the Victorian period (usually the property of Irish or Italian tenors) and reached its peak in the songs of the 1890s, when, as Sigmund Spaeth notes, Tin Pan Alley's "favorite assonance was rhyming 'mother' with 'love her.'"[24] These songs were predominantly sentimental ballads, many tinged with what might be interpreted today as romantic yearning. The Victorian cult of motherhood encouraged reverence for those women who performed their proper domestic functions well, but mother love was equally popular with immigrants new and old. Mother love was central to the cultural and religious identity of many immigrant groups, who celebrated their mothers as their primary champions and emotional supports. The crooning singers of the 1920s were the mollycoddled boys of the 1890s–1910s, and their songs reflected it.

As American society changed in the late nineteenth and early twentieth centuries, however, minstrelsy and crooning changed with it. The greater social diversity of urban spaces—the result of immigration, southern and rural migration, and women's greater presence as workers and consumers—combined to make possible the development of a more centralized, streamlined popular culture industry, one that targeted couples and families as its primary audiences and that offered a number of new venues for consumption, including vaudeville, burlesque, cabaret, and amusement parks. These changes were reflected in the content of popular entertainment in a number of ways that affected the public's larger understanding and reception of crooning. The rise of black minstrel troupes and female minstrels who directly embodied the crooning mammy, for example, changed the nature of the crooning song performance. These performers shifted the focus of the songs from the grown child to the loving, protective mother, concerned about the future of her black child in a white world and, increasingly, her own relationship with the men in her life. Female audiences responded strongly to such content and identified with the female stars who performed these songs (both black women and those in blackface, such as Sophie Tucker), helping to make popular entertainment a more star-driven industry in which female performers and audiences had a greater role in shaping content.

Concurrent with and related to changes in audience and performance was the consolidation of the sheet music industry in New York City around Tin Pan Alley. Its publishers and songwriters worked to broaden their nets by de-emphasizing specific racial, ethnic, and political song content and stressed instead universal and generic romantic courtship that could appeal across social categories. One strategy of the new industry was to redefine existing terms to broaden their meaning with the public; while *mammy* never lost its specific association with African Americans, *crooning* did. During the 1900s and 1910s, then, *crooning* took on an additional meaning in American music, as an expression of intimate affection between lovers as well as between mother and child. This is the songwriting moment when all those *moon, June,* and *spoon* rhymes became so popular as romantic idylls between young lovers. As American performance changed to foreground star performers singing love songs to mixed audiences, and entertainment culture increasingly drew on romantic narratives and star identification to sell products of all kinds, minstrel troupes declined and crooning became associated more with romantic than familial relationships.

The concept and practice of crooning as a physically and emotionally intimate behavior had thus existed, in varying forms, for several decades in American culture before the birth of the crooner, an entirely new kind of popular singer, who had to wait for modernity's microphone and radio broadcasting to give him life. Early radio microphones were too sensitive for the powerful voices of most trained singers and vaudevillians, but they responded well when vocalists sang softly and gently into them, a practice that technicians in the early 1920s dubbed *crooning* since it signified the intimate, unprojected singing that would be difficult to hear otherwise. Singers now had the ability to convey small, subtle variations in their deliveries. They could record songs with more lyrical and narrative complexity, closer harmonies, and a variety of other vocal effects. Commercial song promoters (known as pluggers) were radio's most prominent first crooners; the popularity of their "microphone sound" appalled music critics high and low, but the audience response to them was so strong that their delivery style prevailed and changed the musical landscape.

The emergence and popularity of radio crooners in American national culture most immediately disrupted the hierarchies of vocal production that had been established by the American professional classes in the late nineteenth and early twentieth centuries. These groups had felt the need to publicly articulate masculine vocal standards in order to differentiate their culturally enriching products from those produced by mass commercial entertainment industries and enjoyed by their pleasure-oriented immigrant consumers. While no gendered standards or stigmas existed for popular singers and their working-class audiences before the crooners' rise to popularity, such standards *were* employed by the middle and upper classes to police their own and had existed, in one form or another, for centuries. Concerns about singing's emasculating and sensual effects had long been known to the West's ruling elites. Singing has always been associated with the body, the suspiciously "feminine" side of culture, and the more a voice exposed the presence of a desiring body, the more troubling it was perceived to be.[25] Not surprisingly, because the discourses of modernity and masculinity were being produced and circulated by the same people (white, male, upper- or middle-class professionals), the social standards for professional vocalizing that emerged at the turn of the century echoed those of modernity more broadly, including its contradictions. And yet until the assimilation of immigrant whites and the concurrent massive national popularity of crooners across 1920s mass media, white middle-class cultural authorities had not felt the need to impose these standards on popular culture performers or their audiences.

The white professional classes defined proper vocal conduct narrowly, specifically in terms of masculinity and morality rather than profitability. Their directives reveal an anxious desire to contain the affective potential of singing on the singer and listener through professional education and controlled exhibition. According to the American Academy of Teachers in Singing in 1908—and widely recirculated in light of the crooning crisis in 1931—public singing was intended not primarily for self-enjoyment or as a means of personal expression but for the appreciation and erudition of others. It was to be the product of long-term study and professional training, where it could be carefully developed and monitored. Like other forms of masculine bodybuilding or self-discipline in vogue at the time, singing was supposed to be an *exercise* to make one mentally and physically healthy and morally good; it was a way to preserve one's physical and emotional well-being through the productive and controlled "release" of the singer's "pent up emotions." Manuals of the time describe singing as analogous to a sport, an activity that one could master and that would help develop "strong muscles."[26] Opera stars of the day concurred with singing instructors, emphasizing the years of hard work and self-control needed to develop a vocal instrument of sufficient power, strength, and size. The emotional excesses of commercial entertainments were not to be tolerated. If the voice is not properly conserved, explained the noted singer Bernice De Pasquali in 1921, the singer will "expend its capital before it has been able to earn any interest," an apt American analogy that also echoed public health tracts against the dangers of male masturbation (an analogy that would only gain momentum with the coming of crooners).[27]

In contrast to the strictly gendered, classed world of singing professionals, popular singers generally remained immune to public condemnation during this period, even though individual acts or stage appearances might receive local censorship (especially for language) and certain types of music, such as ragtime and jazz, were often subjects of moral outrage and their performers subject to segregation.[28] Their vocal transgressions, however, were not considered significant enough to warrant policing by their betters until crooners took over the airwaves. More important, until the advent of the microphone and amplification, all popular singing *had* to operate to some degree within the requirements of American masculinity, at least in terms of muscular requirements. Even the untrained, romantic singers in vaudeville houses had to rely on muscular projection to be heard by the audience; their performances were seen as hard physical labor. Making acoustic recordings was also a challenging physical ordeal for most singers, and the process favored trained voices for that reason. Table singers in cabarets might get away with whispering songs in patrons' ears as part of the expected intimacies of the performance space, but few could imagine a singer achieving mass popularity by doing little more than simply standing, unmoving, on a stage and singing so softly that one could barely hear him. As a result, when microphone crooning emerged as the unexpected by-product of modern audio technology, it seemed to turn the performance world on its head, obliterating established aesthetic and cultural hierarchies regarding vocal production and prowess.

Real Men Don't Sing focuses on the first two groups of microphone crooners: the earliest crooners of radio, recording, and film, who dominated popular music from the early 1920s to 1929, and the exclusively romantic crooner idols, whose reign from 1929 to 1933 cemented the association of the term with young white men and ensured that an intimate singing aesthetic would dominate American pop music from that moment on, even as these pioneer singers would themselves be largely forgotten. These early singers helped shape and define popular singing by continually asserting the presence of the body in the technology. The first group experimented with the microphone's potential to produce a variety of vocal effects. Echoing the original associations of crooning with the natural world, these singers whistled, whispered, cooed, stuttered, scatted, giggled, trilled, and made a variety of animal sounds, including meows, woofs, and bird trills. Others pushed the erotic possibilities of such vocal intimacy through breathiness, murmuring, and whispered words, vocal effects that romantic crooners would further enhance and refine. Romantic crooners, beginning with Vallée, added the affective engagement, sincerity of expression, vulnerability, and consistent direct address that would come to characterize the crooner as an icon in popular culture.

Enthusiastic audiences guaranteed the success of the microphone crooner, and fan letters of the time emphasize the bodily effects of microphone crooning on its listeners. "The microphone," noted Martin Hansen, a Vallée fan, "picks up something you can't hear, but you can feel."[29] Women wrote of the shivers they experienced listening to Vallée and of planning their evenings around his broadcast as if they were preparing for dates. Blind listeners were particularly devoted radio patrons, and their letters put into relief the physically affective power of the romantic crooning voice; one devoted blind *and deaf* listener noted that she had a special radio made for her so she could literally feel the vibrations made by Vallée's voice: "When I put my hand on it, for you . . . it is such a happy feeling . . . bound to repeat itself when your voice is broadcast."[30] The visceral intensity of the connection fans felt with microphone singers was unpredictable and profoundly troubling in a soundscape devoted to "scientific," "rational" technological production and reception, as well as stable cultural hierarchies.

Crooners' unsettling combination of the romantic and the sensual complicated the opposition between Victorian and modern in 1920s discourse. The sexual frankness of masculine modernity was generally perceived as a break with and refutation of the sentimentality, mysticism, moralizing, and romanticism associated at the time with the "feminine" culture of the Victorian era.[31] Crooners' disruption of this division led to a reinscription of Victorian-era moral codes by the very cultural authorities who were ostensibly committed to the rationalist modes and progressive promise of modernity. Even as such critics extolled a modern freedom of sexual expression, they were quick to police and scale back such freedoms if they proved too threatening to established gender, race, and class hierarchies, as romantic crooners' popularity did. In giving national prominence and social power to the tastes of a mass rather than class audience, particularly women, crooners offered the American public an alternative, competing definition of modernity that it would take an equally powerful effort to suppress.

HOW CROONING VOICES
BECAME WHITE AND QUEER

The attacks on crooners provide a valuable opportunity to trace how white middle-class gender and sexual norms were constituted and imposed on popular vocalists. Ironically, because crooners *were* white men and because the anxieties surrounding them were primarily expressed in terms of gender and sexual deviance, their role in the construction of a racially specific standard for white voices has gone unexamined. Voices were gendered at the same time that musical styles were raced, and these processes are inextricably linked. Musicologists Ronald Radano and Karl Hagstrom Miller have provided detailed analyses of how a black/white binary was culturally and industrially constructed out of interracial American musical practices and histories. In his analysis of southern musicians and the music industry, for example, Miller details how the recording industry and a variety of cultural authorities established a "musical color line" during the 1920s, associating raced and classed bodies with raced and classed market-created genres of music and promoting these genres as "authentic" cultural products of the musicians' racial heritage and regional affiliations. Vocal divisions operated along the same lines. Black performers became primarily affiliated with what the industry labeled "blues" singing, for example, and white, working-class southerners with "hillbilly" (nascent country) music, even though all popular singers could and did perform blues and country songs and styles, and southern music was just as varied and interracial as that of the New York performance world.[32]

Just as "black" musical sounds were becoming standardized and culturally distinct in the 1920s, so too were crooners' voices derided as "effeminate" or "emasculated" as gender standards narrowed and the concept of a discrete sexual identity achieved cultural dominance by the early 1930s. Historically the development of race norms and that of gender norms in music have been perceived as distinct from one another. Yet the terms used to attack crooners—*primitive, sensuous, degenerate, immoral*—reveal the way race and gender specifically intersected in performance culture and its regulation during the period this book covers. These words were employed by cultural authorities in the early to mid-1920s to object to "hot" jazz music associated most strongly with black performers, as well as, famously, the racially suspect and queerly marked persona of the Italian film idol Rudolph Valentino.[33] In the late 1920s and early 1930s, however, these previously racialized terms were used to denounce the perceived *gender* deviance of white crooners. Rather than conveying the performers' racial inferiority, these terms were applied to signal that crooners were insufficiently masculine and therefore unfit representatives of American manhood.

This change happened because radio crooners emerged as stars in the context of a major shift in the cultural and social meaning of whiteness in America. Matthew Frye Jacobson has identified the 1924 Johnson-Reed Act, which restricted new immigration along racial lines, and the Great Migration, in which African Americans migrated in large numbers to the North and West, as introducing a new era in which "whiteness was reconsolidated . . . as the unitary Caucasian race."[34] Prior to the 1920s all white Americans were not considered equal; public discourse separated them into races, and many considered themselves separate from Anglo-Saxons, identifying more with their cultural, class, national, or religious affiliations than with an American whiteness. By the mid-1920s, however, these groups, including their popular singers, had been largely assimilated, which served the interests of entertainment producers eager to broaden their audience base. Tin Pan Alley song publishers and recording labels standardized both their songs and their singers in the 1920s, carving out a dominant commercial "pop" sound that served as an unmarked standard against the "specialty" labels of, for example, racially or rurally constructed markets. The crooning stars of this era—most of whom were white singers who would have previously been promoted according to racial, ethnic, or regional affiliations (Irish, Latin, southern)—were promoted instead along the homogenizing patterns of the culture at large and offered to the public as generic romantic singers.

Yet even as their racial or ethnic or classed identities were increasingly redefined as white, early crooners' voices retained multiple traces of their once "othered" identities. The majority of crooning singers were products of social and class minorities, particularly immigrant groups: Irish and Italian

Catholics, Jews, working-class white southerners and midwesterners, and sexual minorities.[35] They also retained personal affiliations with the ethnic, gender, class, sexual, and racial others alongside whom they had developed as entertainers. Assimilating into whiteness required many of these newly white citizens to abandon the community values, political practices, gender behaviors, professional collaborations, and cultural traditions that they had long held dear. They also had different relationships to music than that of the Anglo-Saxon white middle classes. Many were young men raised in community singing environments that included churches, synagogues, schools, and neighborhood theatrical spaces (such as Yiddish theater and audience sing-alongs at the local nickelodeon); they were equally familiar with Tin Pan Alley's popular melodies of romance and sentiment and with more ribald vaudeville fare. Early crooners offered emotive and expressive rather than erudite performances, and their vocals favored a number of techniques to increase listener affect that would later become indicators of deviance.

By the late 1920s gender behavior—newly tied to sexual identity—had become a primary, public concern of cultural authorities as their quest to maintain social hierarchies shifted from thwarting the immigration of undesirable classes of people to reinforcing racial divisions within the U.S. population. In the 1920s, cultural authorities encouraged marriage and reproduction among the white middle classes by focusing on the importance of marital "compatibility," particularly romantic and erotic satisfaction, and psychological health according to new developmental norms.[36] This agenda was a particular challenge in the 1920s. The rise of youth culture and the enfranchisement of women had upended traditional sexual norms. White middle-class collegians and flappers began driving popular culture for the first time, and many enjoyed unprecedented degrees of gender and racial mixing: they showed a preference for dancing to hot jazz music, mingling with people of color in black-and-tan cabarets, dressing in androgynous fashions, engaging in petting and same-sex flirtations, and idolizing gender-deviant celebrities. Accordingly authorities intervened during these years to reset and reassert gender, race, and class divides by policing public social mixing, censoring the media, and advocating new standards of personal behavior for the nation's youth by guiding their interest in romance and sex toward the larger service of nation building rather than the pleasures associated with defying or overturning social categories.

At first romantic crooning singers' soft, intimate delivery seemed to perfectly suit the intentions of marriage advocates; many men, for example, wrote Vallée to thank him for helping them to set the mood in romancing their wives or sweethearts. Vallée himself seemed to exemplify the psychic rewards of consumer citizenship; he was the perfect conflation of the attentive lover idealized in marriage manuals and a widely accessible consumer product. Radio advertisers rushed to replicate his intimate, direct address and soft sound and were very successful in doing so.[37] At the same time, however, the intensity of desire for these singers made cultural authorities more and more uneasy. Romantic crooners' personae were marked by feminine-coded qualities that were not unusual for 1920s male stars, but they registered all the more strongly because of their youth, beauty, collegiate status, and easy accessibility. The crooner was at once seductive and vulnerable, indeed so seductive *because* he was vulnerable. The crooning body was young, open, impressionable, even submissive; he solicited care, protectiveness, empathy, and identification, as well as eroticization and objectification. Many crooners, especially Vallée, identified with and even privileged feminine-associated culture (mass media, personal grooming, dancing, fashionable dress, beach lounging), marking them as particular allies to women. Crooning's most fervent fans embraced and defended the very qualities that most violated gender norms and sexual hierarchies.

In response to these cultural subversions, institutional and cultural authorities singled out crooning singers for particular criticism as gender-deviant figures; although the mass public pushed back, the attacks proved especially resonant and enduring because of two intervening, related factors: the Great Depression and the new concrete association of sexual identity and gender behavior. The Depression's impact on popular entertainment was profound. The combination of economic and regulatory anxieties prompted entertainment producers to knuckle under to censorship, and the destabilization of gender roles caused by the loss of masculine status provoked the resentment of particular male celebrities who were perceived as insufficiently masculine. This concern about the crooner's gender identity was fueled by the middle class's growing investment in discrete sexual identities that tied gender variance to sexual deviance and psychosocial immaturity or pathology. This connection to maturity and mental illness was new, the product of Freudian-influenced psychiatry and other human sciences that dominated modern conceptions of sexuality and reflected the discourse of developmental norms that would become so central to social life and thought.[38]

Thus the romantic crooners who had been largely celebrated as ideal lovers, commercial blessings, and broadly popular American icons in 1929–30 were recoded in the conservative shift between 1930 and 1932 as social deviants, specifically homosexuals; the very act of crooning became a sign of effeminacy and therefore of homosexuality and pathology. As homosexuality moved from a behavior to a fixed identity, crooning followed suit, becoming the first song style specifically attached to a sexual identity. Crooning wasn't what you did; it was now who you *were*. In this newly binary culture, any indeterminacy of identity was pathologized; a crooner was not properly heterosexual, and therefore he must be homosexual. Although many critics considered crooners to be immoral, artistically lacking, cheaply commercial, and industrially toxic according to their own individual concerns, they anchored such objections in the language of gender and sexual deviance rather than race, class, or religion.

Crooning, accordingly, became representative of what a non-normative, emasculated, queer voice sounded like, and amid a normative cultural turn white male bodies were not supposed to emit queer sounds. A dominant white voice had to suggest a closed, commanding, classical body, the voice of cultural and patriarchal authority, not the soft, sobbing, exposed voice of the "gender in-between." Indeed critics often pointed to crooners' vocal indeterminacy and artificially amplified, inauthentic sound as proof of the singers' gender indeterminacy and unnaturalness, and thus their social threat. Crooners were "between a baritone and a tenor"; they did not hit notes "cleanly," but instead were accused of "sliding" and "scooping" between them; their use of vibrato was "uncontrolled," their sound "weak" and "effeminate."[39] Crooners' use of falsetto was specifically reviled since it employed a "half" rather than "full" voice and indicated a lack of proper vocal development and control; it also originated in the nasal passages and throat rather than the manly chest. In fact, romantic crooners' vocal delivery drew on a variety of popular (working class, religious, and non-Anglo) musics, and these same vocal characteristics would continue to figure in performances of blues, jazz, hillbilly, and gospel music. For the white middle-class males at the forefront of American culture, however, these characteristics were recoded as objectionably feminine. For them falsetto, high pitch, and "sliding" (glissando) notes became indicative of a greater pathology and had to be silenced.

By the mid-1930s, cultural authorities and cowed mass media industries fearful of regulation and boycotts had successfully established the romantic crooner archetype as artistically worthless, weak, effeminate, and sexually deviant, an arrested adolescent at best. As a result, the cross-cultural, and cross-class affiliations of crooning were erased for decades to come. Crooning's

FIG. 1.3. One of the publicity ads for the popular motion picture *Crooner*, a satire of Vallée's rise to fame. This ad reflects the popular media's attempts by 1932 to erode the romantic crooner's mass appeal by portraying him as a feminized narcissist who "fell in love with himself." By this point gender nonnormativity had become conflated with sexual "deviance" in cultural discourses, and ridicule of the crooner image thus generally depicted him with the prevailing "pansy" (homosexual) attributes: heavy makeup, long lashes, marcelled hair, and limp, cuffed wrist. *Crooner*, unknown newspaper, August 1932. Courtesy of Rudy Vallée Collection, American Radio Archives.

primary audiences, now constructed entirely as female, were likewise disdained as immature, silly, tasteless, and sometimes mentally ill. Growing media censorship and industry standardization, the increasing dominance of Freudian discourse, and the criminalization of gender deviance ensured that the socially conservative turn in modern culture that started during the Great Depression would continue to shape further generations. Bing Crosby would emerge in the mid-1930s as an acceptably masculine crooner, but his rehabilitation was not representative of his peers. They came to represent a threat to now hegemonic national standards of gender and sexual difference and they were largely erased from history.

CULTURAL NATIONALISM, PUBLIC MEMORY, AND BING CROSBY

Part of the larger project of this book is to document how, at this moment in history, a particular class of voices came to be labeled as not only socially deviant in their violation of gender norms but also specifically *un-American*. Thus I examine the role of nationalist ideology in the development, endurance, and social effects of new vocal norms that could be acceptably "American." Very few singers survived from the early 1930s, but those who did, most notably and successfully Bing Crosby, were able to "remasculinize" their voice and persona to fit the new norms while still serving the mass public's desire for the crooning male. This book's historical period ends in 1934, when Crosby's success as a major Hollywood star was assured and the new vocal norms had been securely established. By reexamining Crosby's emergence as a national icon, the production of masculine vocal standards that followed in the wake of the crooning crisis comes into clearer focus.

Cultural nationalism on a mass scale was new to America in the late 1920s and early 1930s. The political nationalism of World War I resulted in increased nativism in the postwar period, most notably exhibited in the unprecedented restrictions on immigration, and was accompanied by a new brand of cultural patriotism that Cecilia O'Leary has characterized as "defined by the ascendance of national power, shaped by the language of masculinity, infused with a martial spirit, and narrowed by the imposition of racialized and anti-radical criteria defined by Anglo-superiority and political intolerance."[40] These nationalist discourses affected all classes and races. New citizens and the leaders of every political and identity group scrambled to defend their patriotism and proclaim the Americanness of their particular group in order to ensure government resources and avoid persecution. Many leaders of minority groups especially worked to minimize their perceived difference by emphasizing singular "authentic" identities (for example, Italian American) and refusing more intersectional understandings of identity or community.[41] As this study will show, the Catholic Church became a particularly zealous advocate for both national censorship and self-policing, and crooners and their audiences were valuable public targets for Church leaders.

In this context of a narrowing but still widely contested popular culture landscape, Bing Crosby came to be considered a suitable crooner for national consumption—in the words of one critic of the time, he was "the almost bearable crooner."[42] Crosby provided a baritone variation on the crooning sound that audiences craved and a more acceptably masculine persona than many of his contemporaries. While he has been the subject of countless music appreciations and biographical studies, most of these are intent on proving his everyman qualities; in contrast I argue that Crosby's career is important because he was the exceptional crooner who became the rule. He became a national star as a romantic crooner in the Vallée vein, but he backed away from the style's emotional vulnerability in response to conservative attacks, and he adapted his singing and film career to align himself with the culture's masculinist turn. His star persona and voice ultimately fused masculine gender performance with national identity, creating a new, more narrow vocal norm for American pop singers. And he became the model on which subsequent male vocalists built their careers. For years young male singers were judged on the Crosby vocal spectrum, where they placed between a "high Crosby and a low Crosby."[43] Any other vocal placement was beyond the pale.

This new vocal norm had such enduring power because 1920s popular culture largely disappeared from American cultural memory until after the cold war. Technological, industrial, and ideological standards that consolidated in the mid-1930s were codified for generations. Educational authorities and social scientists advocated firing music teachers who taught crooning singing styles, broadcasting reduced its male crooners to supporting players and adolescent characters, and big bands largely replaced their crooning tenors with female altos. The film world in which Crosby became a top-ten box office star in 1934 was in many ways a different place from what it had been only a year or two before. The implementation of the Hollywood Production Code in 1934 shut the door, decisively, on the kinds of gender fluidity and range of sexual expression that had previously been common in American popular culture. The new gender standards dictated by the Code resulted in fundamental changes to film texts and a massive turnover in star players.[44] Men with high "feminine" voices were actively censored from Hollywood films, as were male singers who were deemed lacking in masculine appearance. Code practices had such impact, in part, because the Depression had largely wiped out Hollywood's live performance competition and helped drive the shift from New York to Los Angeles as the capital of the entertainment world.

Music critics and popular historians have perpetuated this masculinist discourse for decades. Again, Crosby's musical heritage is instructive. The terms most often used to describe Crosby's style and his success are *natural*, *average*, *ordinary*, and *American*. In contrast, critics and historians routinely dismiss early crooners as "effeminate tenors," "prissy aesthetes," and "drearily anemic" singers with "flaccid styles" who are "blandly" commercial, with no artistic or social significance and certainly no genuine emotional or erotic power.[45] They note approvingly that Crosby does not sing "in tenor and falsetto"; rather his voice is characterized as "robust," "full-bodied," and "virile," and as having "hair on it."[46] What's most revealing is the way Crosby's more "masculine" persona is naturalized in this narrative as not just *an* American sound but *the* American sound, signaling the ideological nature of the assessment. With Crosby as America's crooning icon, racial, gendered, and sexual hierarchies remain in place and are completely naturalized, with early crooners' high-pitched, passionate warbling dismissed as an aberration.

Thus I contend that early crooners have been stigmatized and neglected because their story threatens to undermine the accepted narrative of a whitened, classed, "natural," and "masculine" turn in popular vocal music and social norms in the early 1930s. This shift in American popular vocal performance is one aspect of a more general constricting and silencing of voices—for speakers as well as singers—in order to create a standard "American" sound, one that was certainly not, as popular historians have claimed, inclusive or uniformly embraced.

Addressing the larger social and psychic harm of maintaining these standards in any depth is beyond the scope of this book, but, as I discuss in more detail in the conclusion, the masculinist vocal norms set in the early 1930s established stigmas that have endured. Voices that were once the most beloved in American popular culture have all but disappeared. The association of certain vocal characteristics with a gay identity—and therefore social abnormality—was naturalized in medical and psychiatric discourse by World War II and has persisted for decades. This has been most obviously damaging for generations of boys and men who have been bullied and stigmatized by peers and pathologized by educators and speech pathologists who sought to correct their "vocal disorders." I hope this project helps expose how assessments of both vocal deviance and normativity in American culture are historically specific and constructed. They did not always exist on such a mass scale; rather they were created in the early 1930s to perpetuate national hierarchies of gender, sexuality, race, and class, and they have resonated in American music, popular culture, and social life since then.

THE CULTURAL LEGACY
OF RUDY VALLÉE'S AUDIENCES

As a result of these cultural stigmas and erasures, the historical importance of both early crooners and their audiences has largely been ignored, and this book seeks to restore the social significance and generative industrial power of that audience to the development of American popular culture. Because Vallée was a fan-produced star, I situate his rise in relation to his initial reception on local New York radio in order to trace how romantic crooning as commercial entertainment evolved in response to and in conjunction with his audience's desires and interests. *Real Men Don't Sing* details how Vallée's first audiences played a foundational role in the emergence of crooning as a new genre, a popular cultural phenomenon, and a source of genuine social anxiety, particularly in regard to gender and class. These audiences established an affective structure for the crooner's reception that is based in a critical cultural politics that has continued to endure *because* of—and despite—the alternative, maligned masculinities crooners have represented.

Foregrounding the early reception of crooning disproves many long-held cultural assumptions and biases about the audiences for crooning. Although today we still tend to associate displays of intense emotion for romantic singers with adolescent girls, there was a time when such responses were not publicly limited to any single type of audience member. Historians have long upheld masculinist views of popular culture that have devalued cultural products and tastes perceived as feminine and commercial; they have therefore viewed early crooners as culturally reactionary, insidious commercial forces who catered to "wasp or would-be wasp" audiences in what was otherwise a thriving and authentic urban entertainment environment.[47] Such accounts fail to acknowledge that crooners themselves were part of this heterogeneous urban popular culture, as was the majority of their audiences.

Crooning singers were popular in every type of urban entertainment. Vallée's fan letters, public appearances, and media coverage from this period reveal that his voice held affective power for male and female listeners of every age, class, religion, ethnicity, and race. Listeners expressed their own fervent, loving responses to him through a variety of overlapping frames that spoke to their particular cultural positions and investments, which included familial, national, spiritual, and aesthetic appreciation as well as romantic and erotic engagement. From 1929 to 1932 Vallée was widely celebrated as an "American" star; he received requests to sing for groups across the political spectrum and from organizations as varied as the Boy Scouts, the socialist *Jewish Daily Forward*, the all-black Brotherhood of Sleeping Car Porters union, and the U.S. Congress. The size and variety of his audience affirmed that the mass audience for popular singing had not yet begun to differentiate themselves according to the identity categories, gender divides, and taste hierarchies that industry leaders, cultural authorities, and much of Vallée's own highly contradictory media coverage would promote.

Indeed, Vallée's archive affirms that his audiences had not internalized the rigid hierarchies of gender, sexuality, and class that authorities were seeking to impose on them, especially in relation to popular voices, and they viewed any criticism of crooners as coming from cultural elites.[48] Like Vallée himself, his audiences often celebrated feminine-associated values and affinities, which were, in fact, just as integral to many working-class and immigrant communities as they were to the white middle class. His youth, emotionality, and high-pitched voice evoked the "mother songs" regularly performed by Irish, Italian, and Jewish boys that had dominated popular music for decades. Vallée's male fans also expressed no qualms about embracing his vocal production, and media coverage of male romantic crooning fans from this period confirms their overt enthusiasm for his loving, longing voice. Vallée's letters from male fans refuse binary understandings of his reception by them as either straight or homoerotic, and they are untroubled by any sense that their love for his voice signals deviance or degeneracy. When romantic crooners were attacked for their gender (and therefore sexual) deviance, there was significant opposition to their denigration among the public at large. Many working-class and middle-class people refused this new categorization of the crooner or his voice as deviant.[49] When interviewed about the controversy on the street by a *New York News* reporter, a machinist named Samuel Schurman commented, "It is true that [crooners] are not exactly the he-man type of masculinity, but they are not feminine either. I think they are a sort of compromise."[50] Other male fans felt close class ties to Vallée as a popular idol and rejected any idea of him as effete.

Vallée was particularly important to many women because he directly addressed them, and he privileged women at a time of narrowing sex roles, diminishing professional opportunities, and attacks on "feminine" culture. A new cultural focus on marriage affected women more than it did men; both men and women were newly discouraged from engaging in intimate relationships outside the immediate family, but women were more likely to be isolated by this advice.[51] They were also more directly constructed as modern consumer citizens who relied on consumer products to shape their social identities.[52] Vallée championed women's cultural interests, sang the songs they requested, welcomed their demonstrations of desire, and gave them emotional comfort and sexual pleasure outside of the confines of marriage. In soliciting active female desire and enhancing the erotics of male passivity and submissiveness, he inverted both gender and sex hierarchies, making him uniquely valuable as a transgressive figure for audiences and an increasingly threatening one for authorities.

As crooners' most visible target audience, many women responded defensively, recognizing attacks on romantic crooners as attacks on them. In a masculinist culture, the fates of women and gender or sexual transgressors are always intertwined; for many women in the 1930s (and since), loving romantic crooners was a form of self-determination and cultural validation. "You don't belong to yourself anymore, you are OURS, you belong to us, your Public," wrote Julia W. to Vallée from Chattanooga in 1931.[53] When advised by cultural authorities to view consumption as their primary civic duty, Vallée's fans chose him in an effort to preserve some cultural representation of the feminine and the feminist values they held dear. The fervency of their desire and advocacy for Vallée in the face of attacks against him and other crooners shows just how important—and at risk—those values were and suggests the growing paucity of other outlets through which to express them.

Even when the new vocal codes took hold, the romantic crooner's model of sensitive, vulnerable masculinity never disappeared entirely; his industrial influence was too profound, and the cultural desires he addressed were too formative and resonant across the generations. The affective framework that took shape in the 1920s was the result of cultural anxieties surrounding sexual freedom and gender hierarchies that have persisted through the decades.[54] Indeed crooning male pop stars today still register with their fans as sincerely devoted to them despite naysayers, and they often self-present and are embraced by fans as sites of androgyny, sexual nonnormativity, and female sexual agency. Although such affective appreciation by young, often straight-seeming women is dismissed as politically insignificant, such dismissals are themselves evidence of the continued marginalization of young women's desires for gender-transgressive male stars.

By paying serious attention to these audiences and their intense emotional investments in male crooners, we can identify ways that affective responses offer the potential to disrupt social norms or, at the very least, identify much-needed alternatives to them.[55] Affective investments are inspirational to their fan communities in part because they are *aspirational*; they offer them, as McClary suggests, the "potential for different experiential worlds." For the thousands of women who wrote Vallée letters and attended his concerts, there were millions who did not, who could not, but for whom Vallée represented hope for change, a material (living, breathing) alternative to the masculinist, heteronormative nationalism taking shape around them; it is not surprising that his fans so fervently defended the fantasy of masculinity that Vallée embodied. As Judith Butler has so aptly noted, "Fantasy is not the opposite of reality; it is what reality forecloses, and, as a result, it defines the limits of reality."[56]

The political efficacy of fantasy, the way it allows us to envision life beyond our institutional and cultural boundaries, can fuel our own survival and, in favorable circumstances, help inspire and promote larger social movements. Feminist historians have noted the specific convergence of affect and public activism most strongly in relation to Beatlemania, which many have pointed to as evidence of young women's push back against their sexual and political repression in the larger culture, "the first and most dramatic uprising of *women's* sexual revolution."[57] We need to recognize Vallée's fandom as one that anticipates and provides the affective basis for subsequent social critique and activism. The fact that such intense female and feminine desire for and the subsequent ridicule of youthful male singing stars from Frank Sinatra to David Cassidy to One Direction has not abated suggests that this revolution remains ongoing. Despite social change on many fronts, sexism, homophobia, and effemiphobia remain linked and deeply entrenched in the American cultural landscape.[58]

Real Men Don't Sing argues that the controversy that surrounded crooners in the late 1920s and early 1930s requires a rewriting of the accepted historical narratives, an acknowledgment of the suppressions, assumptions, and negotiations that continue to lie just beneath the surface of any discussion of male voices and that often still emerge when the subject is popular singing. The story of early crooners and their audiences is, in many ways, the story of the losers, those whose voices were largely silenced when new, narrow, vocal standards took hold and became representative of a "unified" national culture. Recovering and restoring these lost voices and recognizing their profound and continuing impact on American culture is the project of this book.

One

PUTTING OVER A SONG

Crooning, Performance, and Audience

in the Acoustic Era, 1880–1920

An excerpt from the 1884 song "Crooning to the Baby" conveys the way the word *croon* originally evoked a comforting maternal figure, typically the soothing black mammy of the antebellum South, and an idealized state of childhood:

> 'Cross de path of time I see her still
> Hush de piccaninny off to rest
> Still I hear her voice so soft and low
> Croon, croon, crooning to de baby
> Backward along de years I seem to go
> To de little cotton farm 'way West.[1]

Twenty years later the term connoted romantic vocal address:

> Each day they spoon to the engine's tune
> Their honeymoon will happen soon
> He'll win Lucile with his Oldsmobile
> And then he'll fondly croon:
> "Come Away with me Lucile
> In my merry Oldsmobile
> Down the road of life we'll fly
> Automo-bubbling you and I."[2]

Although in both cases *croon* describes singing within an intimate relation-ship, the term broadened from the exclusively nostalgic associations of min-strel shows to modern courtship. The industrial developments and social dynamics that enabled and accompanied crooning's evolution—changes in pop-ular song texts and publishing, performers and venues, and audiences—are the subject of this chapter.

Standard histories of popular music have addressed these developments in partial ways, through minstrelsy, ragtime, coon songs, jazz, and blues. Yet the evolution of popular crooning love songs has remained little more than a footnote, despite their great popularity. Minstrelsy, for example, is primarily known for its syncopated comic and dance songs, despite the importance of sentimental songs to its repertoire beginning in the 1830s. Likewise fe-male blackface singers of the 1890s are better remembered for their "coon shouting" than for their performances as crooning mammies. This emphasis is commonly attributed to the fact that crooning songs are not genuinely "American" music because they are based in European-derived musical tradi-tions. But all American popular music is fundamentally hybrid, the product of a variety of different stylistic, cultural, and social influences.[3] Mainstream love songs have been neglected historically because they are "feminine": sen-timental, emotional. American popular music is typically celebrated for its "masculine" energy, the rhythms that encourage listeners to dance, jump, and wail. In contrast, crooning songs activate passions that are more inter-nalized, focusing on private, intimate relations, whether between mother and child or two lovers, comforting listeners or inviting them to empathize. All these features—comfort, intimacy, privacy, emotionality—are associated with the cultural feminine; indeed what uniquely defines crooning songs is their grounding in gender difference. Perceived femininity, both real and representational, lies at the core of crooning, its significance in the history of American popular song, and its historical marginalization.

In the beginning the "women" were men. The story of crooning begins, as does so much of American popular music, with blackface minstrelsy. Min-strelsy was a product of northern, urban, white male working-class culture of the 1830s, but troupes dominated American popular culture generally from the 1840s through the rise of vaudeville in the 1880s and 1890s. Minstrel singers, overwhelmingly Irish, first employed the British-derived term *croon* in the 1870s to describe the soothing sound of a plantation mammy singing a lullaby to her charges. The mammy figure was primarily employed to com-fort white audiences unnerved by post–Civil War social change; she represented an idealized agrarian southern past in which social divisions of race, class, and gender were naturalized and harmonious. By the 1890s mammies were being regularly embodied by black and white *female* minstrel performers, known as "coon-shouters." Although the crooning mammy figure tells us little about the historical conditions of actual black women or their children, her growing popularity reveals the white male's need for reassurance amid anxieties in the postbellum world.

Between 1880 and 1920 the public sphere in northern American cities was transformed by rapid urbanization, an emergent mass culture, loosening sexual mores, and the increasing public presence of immigrants, independent working women, non-Anglos, and same-sex-oriented groups. The consumer products and targets of the new entertainment industries transgressed established Victorian divisions between high and low culture (with all the attached ethnic and racial hierarchies and assumptions) and between public male and private female cultures.[4] By contrast, prewar minstrelsy had worked within Victorian social conventions as their abject counterpoint: vulgar and erotic pleasures of the poor and socially marginalized. Because minstrels wore blackface and projected their transgressions onto society's others—primarily blacks and women—such performances preserved racial and gender hierarchies while still giving performers access to expressions of emotional intensity and sensuality. These qualities were still associated with many immigrant groups not yet considered white, such as the Irish, but blackface allowed Irish players to displace them onto other groups.[5] Minstrelsy had also been protected from criticism by the nature of its audience; particularly in urban areas, minstrelsy was largely a male preserve until the 1870s. Minstrels themselves, however, were never completely assimilable; their status as entertainers in working-class culture automatically put them beyond the pale of respectable middle-class society, in which actors of any kind were looked upon with suspicion.[6]

As popular culture became increasingly corporatized in the late nineteenth century, however, new leisure industries such as burlesque, musical comedy, the circus, vaudeville, and cabaret targeted a much broader audience that included wives and often children, thrived on novelty and variety, and allowed more social interaction between performers and audience members. Women's presence as performers exponentially increased beginning in the late 1800s, as did the presence of non-Anglos and gender variants, such as male and female impersonators and "sissy" characters. Vaudeville offered a variety of acts on a single bill, and replaced minstrelsy as the most popular entertainment form in America from the 1890s until the 1920s. Blackface began to fade by the 1910s and shifted from troupes to solo performers and duos as vaudeville and the music industry increasingly relied on the appeal of singular star personalities or teams to "put over" a song. While traditional minstrelsy made concessions to compete with these new family-friendly industries, minstrel songs continued to express disappointment with and resentment of social changes. The two dominant minstrel song styles of the era expressed feelings of both grief and anger: plantation songs focusing on the crooning mammy that wailed and waxed nostalgic for an idealized past and coon songs that ridiculed the public presence of freed blacks, immigrants, and women.[7]

Ironically, by the turn of the century minstrel songwriters often hailed from the very social groups critiqued in the songs. The rise of Tin Pan Alley centered the popular song business in multicultural New York City, where new immigrant songwriters, composers, and entrepreneurs, predominantly Jewish, spearheaded the modernization of popular song. Like many of the Irish minstrel immigrants a generation or two before them, discrimination and a lack of resources meant that Jewish men could work in only a very few industries, including entertainment. Tin Pan Alley writers drew on a variety of influences, both past and present, and often worked closely with black musicians. They created a new urban songscape that collapsed aspects of high and low, sentimental and sensual music in a standardized song form. The shift in performance from groups to individuals also shaped Tin Pan Alley songs, as writers moved to identify their songs with particular singers. The cultural meanings of coon and crooning songs became more complex and moved away from their racialized roots. Our concept of the modern pop song—its romanticism and intimacy, its standard form, and its association with a particular star or group—is a consequence of these song publishers, who broadened the appeal of crooning songs by moving away from racial, ethnic, or political content and instead stressed romantic narratives and emotional stakes.

This new emphasis on intimate relationships in popular music can also be attributed in large part to the new public presence of women as performers, consumers, and audience members. Female performers in burlesques and vaudeville remained disreputable throughout this period, yet their presence gave voice to female points of view. Popular singers such as the white Sophie Tucker and Mae Irwin and the black Bessie Gillam and Belle Davis were admired; their songs often critiqued male behavior and foregrounded female desires. While scholarship on these women has focused on their roles as coon-shouters in minstrel ragtime songs, they also reshaped the sentiments of crooning ballads, both as mammy figures and increasingly as pragmatic lovers. Beginning in the 1890s, female performers, both white and nonwhite, were the primary portrayers of the crooning mammy, and their renditions refocused attention from the child to the concerned parent. As crooning songs broadened to include lovers who crooned to each other, female points of view emphasized anxieties about fidelity and the desire for emotional intimacy that anticipated the blues, torch, and crooning singers of the 1920s.

Women had their greatest impact as visible, active audience members. They had always been the target audience for and the biggest consumers of sheet music, and the industry increasingly targeted them by selling music in both large department stores and neighborhood five-and-ten-cent shops. Although histories of popular amusements always acknowledge the way entrepreneurs "cleaned up" performance content in the late nineteenth century to attract middle-class women, less attention has been paid to how the desires of female audiences affected the content of popular entertainment and changed the social dynamics of performance, both literally and ideologically. Female audiences helped drive the rise of star culture, they identified with female singers and points of view, and they openly appreciated male singers as objects of desire. As a result this transitional era generated the context for the gendered tensions about male voices and female fandom that climaxed in the crooning controversies of the early 1930s. This chapter thus testifies to the actual cultural heft of what has always been considered the fluffiest of mainstream music.

MINSTRELS AND THEIR MAMMIES: THE PLANTATION CROON, 1890S–1910

Mammies were the first and best-known crooners in American popular song. The crooning mammy song was part of the "plantation song" tradition of late nineteenth-century blackface minstrelsy. Also known as the song of southern nostalgia, the plantation song was a staple of American minstrelsy from its earliest days on the New York City stages of the 1820s and 1830s because it appealed to a wide audience of uprooted groups, immigrants as well as migrants.[8] In these songs the South represented a romanticized version of the minstrels' rural childhood home, recalled and celebrated for an infantile state of happiness and simplicity.[9] While plantation songs faded during the

Civil War, the minstrels revived and revised them in the 1870s as a reaction to the social changes brought about by Reconstruction and urbanization, especially the public presence of women and free blacks. Faced with changes they could not control but could certainly comment on, minstrels took refuge in nostalgia. These working-class, white men promoted songs that contrasted the alienation and amorality produced by urban life with the comforting fictional world of the Old South as an example of a preindustrialized society with a secure social fabric.[10]

The postbellum minstrels developed new characters for the plantation songs of this era that represented this idealized white view of black lives under slavery, most prominently the "old darky" and the "mammy." The old darky is a freed male slave who has left the South but longs to return to his antebellum life on his master's plantation; James Bland's 1878 song, "Carry Me Back to Old Virginny" was one of the first big hits in this vein.[11] The character became a popular figure in minstrel shows well beyond the turn of the century, most famously in Al Jolson's impersonations of the 1910s and 1920s. Displaced migrant and immigrant audiences could enjoy their own memories of home through the old darky character, envying and enjoying his "carefree life of perpetual childhood" while continuing to feel safely racially superior to him.[12] While the old darky's longing for his master and the "old folks" dominated the plantation songs of the 1870s and 1880s, the mammy began to emerge as a specific object of his longing in the 1880s. By the mid-1890s she had become the central figure in plantation nostalgia and had been given her own voice; female minstrels largely replaced the male performers, directly impersonating the mammy character and singing lullabies onstage, often to black "pickaninny" dolls in cradles. The term *crooning* was first employed in relation to this mammy character as a descriptor for the soothing sound she made as she sang her lullaby to him. The word *croon* was also employed in a generic sense in song marketing as a way to distinguish these minstrel songs from white lullabies: "Darky Crooning Songs," "Southern Croons," and "Plantation Croons."

Both *mammy* and *croon* were of English, Scottish, and Irish derivation, like much minstrel music and many of the early minstrels themselves (the word *mammy* is still used by many Irish as a term for "mother"). While the iconic American mammy figure is a fictional creation of the postbellum period, a minstrel imagining of the ideal mother and nurse, the first appearance of a historical mammy is not precisely known. The *Oxford English Dictionary* places the first use of the British-derived term *mammy* in the United States in 1837 to connote "a black woman with the responsibility for the care of white children." References to devoted female house slaves called mammies emerge in southern writings from the same decade.[13] Between the seventeenth and nineteenth centuries in Scotland the term was commonly used to describe servant wet nurses, and it seems to have been first used in the southern United States to describe slave women, "wet mammies," who performed similar duties for white children. However, it is difficult to know precisely whether it was American slave owners or the minstrels singing about slaves who first began using the descriptor. Given that Irish and Scottish ethnic affiliations were almost as common among southern planters as among northern minstrels, the term could easily have been popularized by either group.

One of the mammy's defining characteristics was her crooning sound. The Scottish vernacular poet Robert Burns brought the word *croon* into the English language from the German *croyn*, meaning "murmur," in the late eighteenth century; Burns employed it to describe private, reflective moments in which individuals crooned to themselves or listened to their cattle or "the waters" croon.[14] Minstrels' use of the term to describe the mammy's sound identified her with an intimate, soft utterance and with the natural world, making her representative of stable racial and gender hierarchies and therefore a very comforting figure. The earliest minstrel mammy songs reference her soft crooning to children, and sheet music covers of mammies invariably picture them singing a lullaby to a child on their lap or in a crib.

As a racially inferior mother figure in a rural setting, the crooning mammy personified benevolent nature. Thus she was the least threatening of minstrel characters, since her sex, domestic duties, and location prevented her from any movement into public or urban life. Minstrel coon songs, crooning's more vicious cousins, warned specifically of the dangers represented by free urban black men, their syncopated ragtime rhythms replicating the urgent pulse of the city. The musicologist Ronald Radano views the rise of rhythmic black music in the 1890s as a metaphor for the actual movement of blacks into northern urban spaces, movement that minstrels and other whites found threatening.[15] Even the minstrel's comparatively benign male old darky character has roamed far and wide before turning back home. His mammy counterpart, in contrast, has never moved off the plantation.

The mammy became a central fixture of postbellum nostalgia by representing white men's desire to both rewrite the past and challenge the present. She erased the problematic mixed-race house servant and caretaker of slave days, whose sexual desirability would have been threatening to the white family, and replaced her with an asexual woman whose devotion to her white charges was total and whose place in the racial and gender hierarchy was unquestioned.[16] The importance of the mammy as an ideal rather than an accessible human being perhaps explains why male minstrels do not seem to have impersonated her *as a crooning singer* as they impersonated other female characters in their romantic and comic songs. (They did, however, impersonate mammy characters for comic effect.) Rather, in the earliest mammy songs the mammy figure seems to have been most often sung *about* by male soloists or quartets, with hushed reverence, as in "The Darkies Cradle Song" (1895) and "Kentucky Babe" (1896).[17]

Unlike the mythical antebellum mammy, the postbellum mammy had an obvious contemporary counterpart, as more and more black women began working as paid servants and nurses in white people's homes. The mammy persona showed black women how they should behave and helped shape white employers' expectations for black servants. Corporate America took its cue from minstrelsy and reinforced this comforting model, promoting the mammy as a born cook and nanny who existed only to dole out wholesome food to her employers and loving comfort to her charges.[18] The first use of the mammy for a branded product occurred in 1875, and Aunt Jemima, the most iconic incarnation, emerged in 1889. Aunt Jemima's pancake mix was a top-selling brand for decades to come, and in turn helped promote the vogue for mammy crooning songs at the turn of the century.[19] Male minstrels' passion and reverence for their idealized mammy also lasted long past the waning of minstrelsy generally; Al Jolson's old darky character ensured her mainstream popularity in song well into the Depression years. Indeed Jolson's success with one particular strain of the mammy song in the 1910s and 1920s has erased from public memory the much more complex and varied development of this genre from the 1890s through the 1910s; restoring this history is essential in order to appreciate how foundational a figure the crooning mammy was for 1920s male crooning idols and blues singers.

While the initial crooning mammy song, as performed by male minstrels, focused on an iconic, romanticized mammy figure, by the late 1890s these songs were primarily performed by female minstrels, both white and black, and much of the heavy minstrel dialect and crude characterizations began to fall away. The sentimental mammy crooning song, which originally served to provide a softer counterpoint to the aggressive, ridiculing coon song, developed into an alternative "feminine" space in which female performers could shine, black songwriters could experiment, and audiences could emotionally invest. In these ways mammy crooning songs helped to move popular song away from the predominantly male and masculine concerns of minstrelsy, linking family-friendly Victorian sentiment with an often intensely emotional delivery style that crooners, sans blackface and minstrel dialect, would replicate for their fans.

Mammy crooning songs have generally received little attention because of their lack of musical innovation and their sentimental content. Crooning songs were stylistically mixed, influenced both by classical lullabies of European derivation and the ragtime rhythms that emerged in the mid-1890s. Overall, like the lighter "sweet jazz" that formed the base of 1920s crooning songs, crooning mammy songs contained lighter syncopation than their coon counterparts, and some were even entirely classically based; the songwriter Hattie Starr's hit "Little Alabama Coon," for example, was written in the classical style and sung in concert settings.[20] While crooning mammy songs incorporated more ragtime rhythms as they increased in popularity, they maintained a more conservative musical palate, at least on the page, than other minstrel songs; this generic difference allied crooning songs with the genteel ballads marketed to middle-class women—more appropriate for singing around the family piano than coon songs but not as well respected musically by historians eager to chart innovations in American music.

Mammy songs were broadly popular during the late Victorian and early twentieth century in part because they were about mothering, and mother-loving was a central theme of popular song in this period. "Mother love" songs were popular across class, ethnic, and racial lines, and many were also deeply entwined with larger religious and cultural practices (for example, Catholicism and the Madonna figure, the Irish tenor tradition). While the mammy of crooning songs was part of minstrelsy's back-to-the-plantation agenda, her songs also shared many commonalities with reverential mother love songs, ensuring that when black and white women began regularly portraying her on the stage, she was generally written as a sympathetic, even heroic figure, in contrast to the black figures in coon songs.

By attributing intense emotionality to black characters, the mammy crooning song often provided a greater range of expression for its female performers than most mother songs. Through the mammy figure, women's concerns were vocalized: the responsibilities of parenting, a mother's love of and fears for her children, and the effects of absent fathers. Her inherently noble and sacrificing nature is often emphasized by her impoverished, abandoned, and desperate condition. These narratives called for performers to draw more strongly than ever before on the croon's secondary definition of "murmuring lament or wail," to offer their audiences intense expressions of both love and heartache. Mammy songs are frequently identified as "pathetic" in the sheet music of the time, meaning that they are intended to generate pathos for the listener, who is presumed to empathize with the vulnerable mother's desire to quiet a fretful infant:

De night am long an' de col' win' roar
Sleep, l'il chile, go sleep! (Mow'o-o!*)
Yo' pappy he doan' come home no more
Sleep, l'il chile, go sleep! Mow'o-o!
I wonder he see us all alone
Wif nuffin' to eat escept a bone
An' do he hear yo' mammy moan
Sleep, l'il chile, go sleep! Mow'o-o!
(*"Moaning Cry of Distress")[21]

Just as this mammy has no power to protect her children from the wind or hunger, she also has less power than white mothers in lullabies to protect them from embodied and disembodied threats. The mammy's refrain in "Mammy's Little Alligator Bait," for example, contains this caution to her child:

(refrain)
Shut yo' eye bye and bye, mam will whip yo' if yo' cry,
Someone am a-comin' in thro' de gate;
Go to sleep, don't yo' peep, listen to me tell yo',
yo's mammy's little alligator bait.[22]

The mother's concern here that "someone am a-comin' in thro' de gate" is echoed in other songs that characterize these looming figures more playfully as the bogeyman or the folktale character Br'er Fox. Yet the sense of vulnerability in mammy songs is underlined by the awareness of her racial and sexual positioning and by frequent nods to her consistently light-skinned children (possible products of either rape or illegal consensual sex with white men) in songs like "My Little 'Lasses Candy Coon" (1899), "Mammy's Little Yaller Gal" (1897), and "Mammy's Little Pumpkin Colored Coons" (1897). At times the mammy's lament does specifically indict the children's father for deserting his family, either reaffirming cultural stereotypes about feckless black men for white audiences or affirming white male exploitation of black women for black audiences. Either interpretation is possible, given that the

FIG. 1.1. The term *crooning* was first employed in the United States in relation to the devoted, selfless, crooning mammy of minstrelsy singing to her charges. This cover is typical of the many "plantation" mammy crooning songs that appeared in the post–Civil War era and peaked in popularity from the 1890s to the 1900s, during the height of the "mother" craze in popular song. Though the cover suggests an interpretation focusing on eliciting empathy ("pathetic"), the stage directions offer a satiric interpretation as well, suggesting the variety of ways such songs were being interpreted by the turn of the century. Sheet music, "Sleep L'il Chile: A Pathetic Mammy Song," 1900. Courtesy of Rare Book, Manuscript, and Special Collections Library, Duke University.

particular meaning of mammy crooning songs, like all popular music at this time, varied greatly depending on the composer, the performance space, and the musical interpretation of the genre by singers and audiences.

Because mammy crooning songs were composed and interpreted in multiple ways by a variety of musicians and performers, any single or totalizing narrative of their history or impact is misleading. For example, while crooning mammy songs generally appear on the page as standard declarations of motherly devotion, they were not necessarily performed that way. Minstrel and vaudeville performers frequently undercut the genteel moralism of the middle-class ballad form. The lightly syncopated accompaniment of a crooning song was easily further "ragged" by the musicians, allowing for more comic, satirical, or dramatic interpretations. The music and lyrics of "Sleep L'il Chile, Go Sleep" read on the page like a sincere cry of grief meant to evoke tears from the audience, but the accompanying stage directions suggest that the mammy's pathetic plight could also be used to "create amusement for the audience" by having the pickaninny figure "pop his head up from the cradle as mammy sings the cry of distress." Obviously the effect would be different when performed by white or black minstrels; for white performers and audiences, the satire could provoke ridicule of the mammy as a feminine or racialized figure, whereas black performers and audiences could enjoy lampooning the mammy as the creation of white minstrels. Both audiences could take pleasure in undercutting the pathos of the excessively sentimental, feminine genre that would soon go out of vogue and members of both could likewise resent this same ridicule.

By the end of the nineteenth century, black minstrel and musical-comedy troupes were, in fact, as plentiful and successful as white troupes, and black composers were scoring major popular song hits that included many mammy crooning songs. While all songwriters had to work within the limitations established by minstrel conventions and institutional racism and sexism, the interventions of these performers and songwriters ensured greater variety both in the songs themselves and in how performers interpreted them. Black performers and songwriting teams such as Bert Williams and George Walker, George Hillman and Sidney Perrin, Bob Cole and Rosamond Johnson, and Noble Sissle and Eubie Blake all penned mammy crooning songs and subtly changed aspects of them to make them less generic and caricatured; their efforts offered alternatives in this genre that helped promote a gradual shift from the more dialect-heavy, iconic portraits of mammy martyrs to more grounded, individualized, and humane ones.

The possibility of writing comforting or romantic crooning songs rather than coon songs had special appeal for these writers, many of whom lobbied against the more virulently racist aspects of coon songs, such as the monstrous caricatures of razor-wielding black men menacing and attacking whites. Unlike crooning songs, coon songs could incite race riots or attacks on black men; after one such incident in New York, the black songwriter Rosamond Johnson abandoned writing coon songs entirely and, like many of his peers, tried instead to revise the plantation song genre. Such artists carved out a new market for songwriters by developing songs that could be sold as more "authentically black" by incorporating street slang and vernacular language without the narrow, caricatured aspects of traditional minstrel dialect.[23] Bert Williams and George Walker, who rose to fame by billing themselves as "two real coons," likewise emphasized the authenticity of their crooning mammy song "Mammy's Little Pickaninny Boy" (1896) by advertising it on the sheet music cover as "A Plantation Slumber Song Introducing a Correct Mammy Croon" (fig. 1.2). In distinct contrast with the cartoon-like mammies decorating the covers of much crooning song sheet music, their cover portrayed a more lifelike drawing of the black mother and child.[24]

The next year the same young Tin Pan Alley publishing company, M. Witmark and Sons, published George Hillman and Sidney Perrin's "Mammy's Little Pumpkin Colored Coons: A Plantation Slumber Song," which proved to be one of the biggest hits of the genre. The song is exceptional for its lack of blackface dialect, its strong syncopation (it was described in Witmark's song list as "genteel but catchy"), and the presence of a hardworking father who adores his children and also sings to them after a hard day's work, shifting the crooning song from motherly love to familial love:

(verse #2)
Each evening after supper when his daily toil is o'er,
The Daddy of these cunning little coons
Takes each upon his knee from off the kitchen floor,
Their little eyes with laughter shine like moons
Then to amuse his little pets, 'till Mammy makes the bed
Dad sings to them some old familiar tunes
It nearly breaks his heart when from them he has to part
When Mammy puts to bed her little coons
(refrain)
Go to sleep Sh! my little pickaninies,

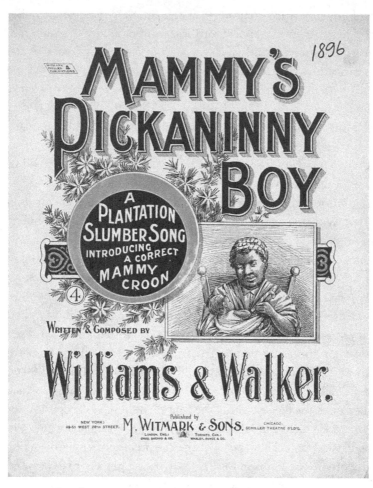

FIG. 1.2. The African American theatrical team of Bert Williams and George Walker capitalized on the vogue for "authenticity" at the turn of the century by promoting themselves as "two real coons." Like the many black popular song-writers of the era, however, they sought to move away from the inflammatory coon genre by writing variations on other genres, such as mammy and novelty songs, and they worked to make such songs less offensive to black audiences. This cover combines these two impulses, presenting a "correct mammy croon" in which the mammy figure is not cartoonish and is warmly comforting her own child. Sheet music, "Mammy's Pickaninny Boy," 1896. Music Division, New York Public Library for the Performing Arts, Astor, Lenox and Tilden Foundations.

Don't you weep or cry
If you don't, Mammy won't
Buy her babies anymore sweet 'lasses candy.
Shut your eyes, Sh! My little pickaninies,
Dad will be here soon.
Sh! don't cry By-a-by
Mammy's little pumpkin colored coons.[25]

This song is the earliest instance I have found of crooning in vernacular but
without dialect. The songwriters' suggestion that crooning did not necessarily have to be linked to racialized dialect would become the norm in popular
song by the 1920s. It is also the first but far from the only instance I have found
of black songwriters consciously revising the crooning song and helping to
disconnect it from minstrelsy. Not all their innovations would be adopted,
however; the presence of an intact black family was an ultimately less successful attempt at restructuring the genre (perhaps because the crooning
genre was so linked to solo female stars), as was Rosamond Johnson and
Bob Cole's attempt in "Mudder Knows" to reproduce the typical mammy-
pickaninny scenario without the word *mammy*. But even if some of these
innovations had more legs than others, the popularity of these songs among
whites and blacks is significant in suggesting the degree of variation permitted in the genre.

The performances of female minstrel stars also greatly shaped the reception of crooning songs for audiences and would directly influence the
first radio crooner, Vaughn De Leath. The term *coon-shouters* was used as
a descriptor for certain singers during the height of coon song popularity,
1896–1910; these were generally black or white women (and some men)
who had strong voices and vocal control but not the good looks required of
a minstrel leading lady, and the mammy was one of the few generic roles
that existed for such performers. Women like Clarice Vance, Artie Hall, May
Irwin, Maude Rockwell, Ma Rainey, Isadore Rush, Rosa Scott, Carrie Hall,
Adele Rowland, Sophie Tucker, and the young Bessie Smith offered a variety
of interpretations of coon and crooning songs, and period reviews indicate
that they performed both genres in similar quantity and in the same song
sets.[26] Black troupes' choice of crooning songs also helped promote the revisionist approach of black songwriters, helping to naturalize the erasure of
minstrel dialect. On 9 April 1898, for example, the black newspaper *Indianapolis Freeman* reported that coon-shouter Bessie Gillham, a member of

Wright's Colored Comedy Company, was singing "'Mammy's Pumpkin Colored Coons' to perfection nightly."[27]

The significance of having women, especially black women, perform *as* mammies rather than being sung *about* by white minstrel men cannot be underestimated. These songs allowed for identification with black female points of view, foregrounding domestic concerns in ways that minstrel songs up to that time had not. While the self-sacrificing mother is common to Victorian domestic ideology, the focus on female rather than male concerns as expressed by female performers in public arenas was an important step in mitigating minstrelsy's paternalism and misogyny. Additionally, having a black woman onstage singing about her black child substantially undercut the racially mediated context of the crooning songs themselves, actualizing the relationship of a black mother and child rather than using the song to represent white nostalgia. Conversely, black women likely also used this platform as an opportunity to satirize and critique the minstrel mammy. Indeed the pairing of black songwriters with black singers shows that these fairly generic songs could be tailored to particular audiences in ways that subverted their original minstrel context.

By 1910 coon songs, mother songs, and crooning mammy songs were all staple commodities of Tin Pan Alley's song-publishing machine, and they were performed in a variety of venues that served audiences of mixed genders, classes, and ethnicities. The insularity of the Victorian minstrels' world was ending, but their fears of social change would not be forgotten; the new popular songs reflected this cultural ambivalence by offering a variety of songs that addressed desires old and new. The minstrel's mammy would remain popular, but other uses of the term *croon* soon emerged, uses even more pointedly directed at pleasing and serving the desires of broader—especially female—audiences. Black songwriters would continue to help shift crooning away from its attachment to the mammy and expand the term's usage to romantic songs. The modernization of the croon during these years represented an American culture that would no longer be driven primarily by or for white male consumers nor adhere to Victorian moral standards. These shifts were made manifest in the development of the modern American song business through the rise of Tin Pan Alley.

TIN PAN ALLEY AND THE BIRTH
OF THE ROMANTIC CROONING SONG,
1900S–1920

In 1900 the poet Paul Lawrence Dunbar and the musician Will Marion Cook, both black, published a sweet, lively, and popular tune, "Down de Lover's Lane: A Plantation Croon." The song's first-person narrative focuses on a courtship: "Me an' Mandy han' in han' / Struttin' lak we owned de lan' / 'Long de Lover's Lane." "Down de Lover's Lane" was a departure from 1890s plantation songs. The songwriters recontextualized the word *croon* to indicate romantic feeling rather than the soothing mammy sound: "I whispahs low lak dis / An' my Mandy smile huh bliss." The plantation itself is reconfigured as a racially integrated space for all lovers, a country lane or park area.

Dunbar and Cook were ahead of their time. Lyrically and musically "Down de Lover's Lane" rejected many of the standard popular music practices and social mores of the nineteenth century and anticipated the twentieth. As a black poet, Dunbar believed that the minstrel song's dialect could be revised to better represent the vernacular of black people. The song is notable for the way the dialect is not employed to suggest the stupidity or inferiority of the narrator. The gradual abandonment, assimilation, and recontextualization of minstrel dialect and characters would come to characterize the dominant commercial model for popular songs of the 1910s and 1920s produced by leading New York publishing houses known collectively as Tin Pan Alley. These changes would modernize song characters and situations to reflect the more inclusive politics of the Progressive Era and promote a secular, modern approach to lovemaking. In "Down de Lover's Lane," the moralism and religious feeling endemic to the love songs of the nineteenth century are notably missing; the narrator of this song explicitly rejects religion for love, noting that if there isn't a lover's lane in the afterlife, "'Legion do look mighty blue." Musically, "Down de Lover's Lane" found its own middle ground, influenced by classical music, marching beats, and ragtime, resulting in a slow but sunny beat that anticipated the conflation of the syncopated novelty song with the romantic ballad in 1920s crooning love songs.

While classical and popular music had both been mainstays of middle-class homes since the mid-nineteenth century, by 1900 popular music clearly had begun to dominate. Tin Pan Alley publishers centralized, integrated, and streamlined the music business, consolidating their operations in Lower Manhattan. Their offices were song factories; their writers created standardized tunes that were both familiar and novel enough for mass appeal, and they used aggressive marketing efforts employing both known singing stars and young male song pluggers to promote their songs in every conceivable public arena. As the music historian Charles Hamm has argued, Tin Pan Alley largely invented the music we think of today as American popular song, dominating and determining national popular culture for decades.[28]

Before the rise of Tin Pan Alley, the music business had been the province of several powerful firms in urban areas, the biggest in Boston, New York, Philadelphia, Baltimore, and Chicago. The business was internally diversified as well; the top firms produced sheet music for both amateur and professional performance, not only popular songs but choral arrangements, chamber music, and pieces for varied instruments. In the 1880s a few New York firms had big successes with certain popular songs, convincing them that focusing solely on selling popular songs to a mass audience could be very profitable. Rather than depending primarily on professional sales, these publishers concentrated on selling sheet music for voice with piano accompaniment, establishing the amateur home performance market. Their strategy worked, sending piano and sheet music sales soaring.[29]

Tin Pan Alley publishers were so successful in part because of their lack of snobbery about popular tastes, their close ties with New York performers and exhibitors, and their factory-like production of standardized songs. By the 1890s New York was dominated by Jewish song publishers, theater owners, and performers.[30] Early on these publishers specialized in the immigrant urban culture that they knew, pushing out more established firms by offering rousing songs sung in local beer gardens and variety shows rather than those sung in more respectable domestic parlors. Once established, these publishers sought broader audiences, putting out widely accessible songs that appealed to youth in New York dance halls as well as families singing together in smaller communities. Typical Tin Pan Alley standards had memorable titles and thirty-two-bar structure with simple, repetitive AABA formats that foregrounded the choruses rather than the verses. Publishers wanted their songs to be catchy, simple, and easy to sing rather than complex creations that required a wide vocal range.[31] Cutting the number of verses and moving the melodic hook from the verse to the chorus made it more likely that audiences would remember the chorus's lyrics and tune.

Tin Pan Alley songwriting is often separated into roughly two eras, the first from the 1890s to the 1900s, and the second from the 1910s through the 1930s, "the golden era." A second generation of Jewish immigrants, often inspired by black musical production and working with black musicians, dominated the second era, replacing the midwestern-born songwriters of the first generation.[32] This second wave, led by Irving Berlin, had little connection to the genteel culture of the parlor song or any nostalgia for the plantation; they sought to represent the diverse and changing urban world around them. These writers modernized American popular song, blending aspects of the old and the new to create the standards still recognized today. The first generation's biggest successes were high-minded romantic ballads or sentimental songs, epitomized by Charles K. Harris's huge hit "After the Ball" (1892), that looked back wistfully to an idealized rural past, home, or lost love. In contrast the modern songs that dominate the second generation increasingly examined contemporary urban life, acknowledged technological progress (like automobiles and telephones), and looked forward to the future, often with a hard-won pragmatism. The Tin Pan Alley publisher Isadore Witmark aptly characterized his business as "a species of song-and-dance journalism, intimately bound up with the current trend of events."[33] For the historian, the richness of this music comes in part from its topicality.

The two eras are marked by a distinct turn in popular song content from rural to urban, romantic to sensual, spiritual to secular, and idealistic to pragmatic. Given the preponderance of immigrants, sentimental or nostalgic songs about the longing for home did not go completely out of style, but traditional "poetical" allusions largely gave way to more accessible language and timely references. Political subjects like racism, women's rights, and workers' views were woven into many popular songs. Coon songs had fallen out of favor by 1910, silenced by protests from the newly formed NAACP and the generally more progressive politics of the era, although certain common blackface terms like *baby* and *croon* became deracinated. The syncopated rhythms of coon songs, however, became ever more widely incorporated into popular music and dance. Within ten to fifteen years the European-influenced waltz-song that had dominated 1890s dance music gave way to syncopated songs that drew on the rhythms of marching bands and ragtime music.[34] By 1905 songs that were still in waltz time were often defensively labeled "timely waltzes," such as "In My Merry Oldsmobile," quoted at the beginning of this chapter. By the 1910s the remarkable variety of Tin Pan Alley offerings reflected the diversity of live performance styles in New York City: band songs, ragtime, operetta, musical comedy, Irish-inflected tenor solos, "Hawaiian" songs, patriotic songs, "musical geography" (songs about cities or states), comic novelty songs, blackface croon songs, "dialect" songs that satirized a variety of ethnic or racial groups (most prominently Jewish, Chinese, German, Irish, and Italian people), beer songs, English music hall songs, Yiddish songs, "syllabic nonsense songs," and of course romantic ballads. Tin Pan Alley songwriters churned out every type of song, from sentimental to sophisticated, with individual writers often taking on many different genres.[35]

The evolving use of the word *croon* reflected these modernizing shifts. Popular songs that still retained the narrative figure of the crooning mammy broke down into two thematic groups: topical lullaby mammy songs that referenced racial inequalities, popularized by female coon-shouters, and syncopated revivals of the nostalgic old darky blackface numbers, popularized by Al Jolson and his legion of imitators. While the crooning mammy survived as a key persona for female singers well into the 1910s and 1920s, the content of her lullabies reveals a new, politicized use of her soothing croon. The bogeymen of 1890s croons take on concrete forms in these 1910s songs, which openly address the pain of white racism. In fact the point of most of these lullabies is to soothe a black child who has experienced racism for the first time; the mammy's song reaffirms her love for her child and the child's worth. Here the infant has grown up; such songs feature a child who can articulate hurt, not just a crying baby. One of the earliest examples is "Mammy's Angel Chile: A Pickaninny Croon" (1911), in which the mammy reassures her child: "Don't yo' worry 'bout them Honey / Ev'rything will come out right / Mammy loves yo', don't she? Don't she?"[36] This song cycle remained prominent through the early 1920s. "Mammy's Sugar Plum" (1920) paints a poignant and detailed picture of the child's suffering:

(verse)
Pickanninny starts to play
White kids won't be near him
Nothin' seems to cheer him
All he does is cry the live long day
Soon his dear old mammy heaves a sigh
And again she sings this lullabye:
(chorus)
Mammy's little Sugar Plum
Mammy's little yum yum yum
Dry your chalky eyes it's time to go rest
Lay your little kinky head on mammy's breast
Don't cha mind what white folks say

They'll be sorry some sweet day

And tho' you may be black just like a crow

I couldn't love you more if you were white as snow.[37]

Although some songs appropriated the mammy's reassuring love for other uses—for example, to encourage blacks to enlist in World War I ("Mammy's Chocolate Soldier," 1918)—the NAACP context of these songs is apparent not only in their political content but in their "black is beautiful" rhetoric. (Many were by black songwriters.) "S'posin' all the flowers was colorless and white?" asks the mammy of "Angel Chile": "Why there wouldn't be no beauty in the world to make it bright." Unlike the pumpkin- and molasses-colored children that characterized mammy songs of the 1890s and 1900s, songs of this era explicitly value the dark skin of the child: "Mammy's Little Coal Black Rose" (1916), "Mammy's Little Pansy (Blackest Fl'r Dat Grows)" (1918), "Mammy's Lit'l Choc'late Cullud Chile" (1919).

These tributes to blackness were sung by the most famous coon-shouting stars of the era, including major star Sophie Tucker, as well as lesser-known vocalists such as the white Adele Rowland and the black Bessie Gillham and Marie Anderson; such singers were publicized as "up to date coon shouters" in the 1910s, and some would become more generally known as blues singers.[38] Often these songs were marketed with a particular star performer, a practice that Tin Pan Alley, like the film industry, began in earnest in the 1910s. The combination of these strong individual vocalists and their socially aware, fiercely protective mammy characterizations reflected the politically active New Woman of the 1910s and the effects of the civil rights movement.

This more progressive function of the mammy crooning figure in popular songs of the era has been largely eclipsed historically by her use in Jolson's famous songs. Jolson's blackface revival of old darky laments made him a star. Where women's performances offered a less jazzy sound with more modern sentiments, Jolson paired more modern music with reactionary sentiments. On "Tennessee, I Hear You Calling Me" (1914), "Rock a Bye Your Baby with a Dixie Melody" (1918), "My Mammy" (1920), and "Carolina Mammy" (1921), Jolson loudly and enthusiastically laments his separation from his mammy as a child. The lyrical expressions of these sentiments, however, employ modern vernacular language (not minstrel dialect) and are less reverent than their nineteenth-century forebears; Jolson's mammy songs are more fervent, reflecting both their jazzy accompaniment and the general shift in popular music from the spiritual to the sensual. The most famous of these songs

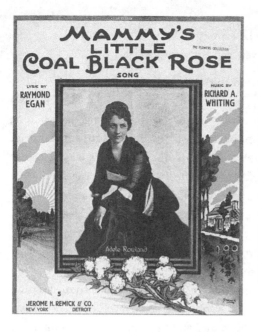

FIG. 1.3. This piece of sheet music represents the shift toward "black is beautiful" rhetoric in mammy crooning songs of the NAACP era, in which the child is explicitly valued by his mother for the blackness of his skin. Most crooning mammy singers no longer employed blackface in the 1910s; instead, like Adele Rowland pictured here, they sang a variety of ethnic and other "character" songs in a single vaudeville performance. Sheet music, "Mammy's Little Coal Black Rose," 1916. Courtesy of Rare Book, Manuscript, and Special Collections Library, Duke University.

is the 1918 hit "Rock a Bye Your Baby with a Dixie Melody," where Jolson promises "a million baby kisses" to the one who will "croon" like his mammy. The popular success of his songs was also tied to their deft fusion of melodic, sentimental singing with a syncopated accompaniment: his elongated notes drew from the sweeping emotionality of Irish and Italian ballads and the Jewish cantor's wails, but the accompanying music was ragged, both on the page and in performance.

Inspired by Jolson's success, contemporary songwriters attempted to modernize the mammy figure in a number of ways, yet Jolson's mammy has largely erased all other approaches in public memory. One of the more interesting of these was "Mammy o' Mine" (1919), which, as the title suggests, was written by an Irish-black songwriting team and presented by a black male duo, Billy Farrell and Ike Hatch of Hatch's Harlem Stompers. The music and lyrics are modern (no dialect), but the sentiment is almost entirely plantation pap: the old darky character longing for his southern mammy.[39] Yet the sheet music's cover shows a white man reaching out to his white mother (fig. 1.4), an attempt to broaden the meaning of the minstrel term *mammy* to represent mothers generally (and white mothers specifically). This approach was not limited to this particular example; the 1920 song "I'd Love to Fall

FIG. 1.4. This song represents a failed attempt by Tin Pan Alley songwriters and promoters to broaden the use of the term *mammy* beyond the black minstrel mammy—a failure likely due, in large part, to Al Jolson's tremendous success with the iconic mammy figure. The song was produced by an Irish and black songwriting team, attesting to the racially and ethnically mixed popular music culture of the time that would become much more segregated within the next decade. Sheet music, "Mammy o' Mine," 1919. Courtesy of Rare Book, Manuscript, and Special Collections Library, Duke University.

Asleep and Wake Up in My Mammy's Arms" portrays a white woman and child on its cover, while its lyrics are from the perspective of an old darky character.[40] These songs failed to represent mothers generally because Jolson's iconic black mammy and his revamped minstrel man were so powerful. His popularity represented part of the growing political backlash against the progressive forces of the period that would characterize the World War I and postwar periods.

Though the mammy could not be fully transplanted from minstrelsy, crooning itself proved much more assimilable. By the 1910s Tin Pan Alley had begun to cut its apron strings in earnest; a new breed of popular songs abandoned the chaste stance and often moralizing themes of romantic ballads to focus on modern definitions of love as emotional satisfaction and sensual connection. Thus "Crooning to the Baby" no longer called up images only of mother and child, as the slang term *baby*, commonly used only in minstrel coon songs of the 1890s and 1900s, began to serve as a generic term for *lover*, regardless of race or class. Following the example of "Down de Lover's Lane," the 1910s saw the popular broadening of the term *croon* as a way to express intimate romantic and erotic feelings. This new usage of the word in second-generation Tin Pan Alley songs soon would become standard in love songs and supplant public memory of the crooning mammy.

The romantic crooning songs of the 1910s and 1920s had their foundations in the ballad, a European-based, narrative song detailing a personal experience, romantic wish, or historical event in a verse-chorus form. There were two kinds of ballads sung within the family circle in the 1890s: the "high-class" ballad, tied to classical music, primarily performed by women, and conveying an intensely romantic, moralistic sentiment; and the "popular" ballad, based in vernacular (folk) music, sung by both men and women, and conveying a nostalgic sentiment. European art songs were the most important influence on the former style, and the early minstrel songs of Stephen Foster (themselves influenced by Irish and Italian melodies) on the latter. Initially ballads were separated from other song genres because of their association with white, Protestant values; characters in both high-class and popular ballads who transgressed moral boundaries were typically punished.[41] In line with Victorian singing standards, intense feelings were structurally contained in ballads by standard musical notation and the poetic language and conventional moralism of the lyrics. Because these songs were primarily aimed at and performed by women, they served in part as tracts meant to help regulate women's behavior, teaching them how to become good wives and mothers, and describing the unfortunate fate that awaited them if they did not behave. While female sexual desire was a frequent comedic subject in racialized coon songs, it was not considered suitable for ladies' sentimental songs.

Tin Pan Alley's second generation, however, brought out new ballads in the 1910s that erased many of the distinctions between high-class and popular ballads, moving ballads away from moralizing toward the sensibility and musical innovations of the novelty song. The novelty song developed in minstrelsy and the concert saloon and by the 1890s was the dominant song genre in vaudeville. Novelty songs drew on racial and ethnic stereotypes and comic characters, usually of African Americans and immigrant groups. Songs were sung in dialect or an accent to make the ethnic affiliations clear, since the same performer often took on multiple ethnic roles without changing costume (vocal drag replaced visual drag).[42] Unlike those of late Victorian ballads, the protagonists of novelty songs often went unpunished for immoral or transgressive behavior; their hedonism was of a piece with their ethnic otherness and low-class status. Musically novelty songs were rousing and energizing, influenced by popular marching band and ragtime syncopations that permitted more experimentation and variation in performance.

Novelty songs were incredibly popular with all audiences and, like all the songs discussed here, were culturally and musically more complex in actual performance than they appear today on the page. Nevertheless, the obviously racist base of many of the genre's songs, especially coon songs, made them the subject of increasing controversy in the Progressive Era and ultimately threatened to undercut Tin Pan Alley's profits.[43] As complaints mounted, songwriters started to transform novelty songs, reducing their racially and ethnically specific characteristics while retaining their more modern form and content, especially sexual directness. They also began to conflate the novelty song with the ballad in ways that would ultimately standardize popular songs and make the use of minstrel dialect and characterizations increasingly obsolete.

While Irving Berlin is not usually thought of as a sexually explicit songwriter, his early work was formative in introducing sexual content to Tin Pan Alley popular song. Charles Hamm's detailed analysis of the songwriter shows that Berlin began introducing variations on the ballad in 1910 by incorporating novelty song attitudes, modern rhythms, and slang. In Berlin's "novelty ballads," love can be taken lightly and enjoyed irreverently, which was quite a departure from the intense romanticism and earnestness of the high-class ballad. Similarly his innovative "rhythmic ballads" have their roots in syncopated ragtime and employ vernacular language, elisions (for example, "lovin'"), and terminology previously associated only with the black protagonists of coon songs. In "Stop! Stop! Stop! (Come Over and Love Me Some More)" (1910) Berlin erased most of the dialect of coon songs but kept the sex; the desires expressed in the song are erotic rather than romantic, and he employs the word *love*, Hamm notes, "as an active verb rather than an emotional state."[44] In addition, Berlin's early rhythmic ballads notably are all articulated from a female point of view. While sexually aggressive and strong-willed women were staples of ethnic novelty and coon songs (often as comic figures), Berlin's songs make an ethnically unmarked, presumably *white* woman's sexual desires central to the song.

While high-culture promoters and moralists would remain disdainful of popular songs like these, the mass audience largely embraced them. Indeed the absorption of novelty elements into the ballad would become commonplace by the late 1910s, as would the reverse; sentimental and romantic lyrics would be syncopated, most notably in the popular "fox trot ballads" of the 1920s. The ethnic novelty song itself would soon be entirely absorbed into a more generic musical form, in which its protagonists celebrated urban life and values but did not identify themselves with any immigrant or ethnic group. The early 1930s RKO movie musicals of Fred Astaire and Ginger Rogers include the best-known examples of this type of song.

Berlin and his fellow songwriters initiated the elimination of many explicit ethnic, racial, and class distinctions in popular song. They largely refocused the content of popular songs away from social differences, political affiliations, and community feeling, and replaced these with an almost total emphasis on individual psychology and romantic desire. The racial and ethnic differences and provocations of the 1910s were most often replaced in the songs of the 1920s and early 1930s by sexual sophistication and provocation. While female and queer audiences of all groups would embrace and benefit from this sexual variety in popular culture, this turn also limited the intersectionality of gendered expressions by gradually erasing ethnic and class markers from homogenized mainstream entertainment. This shift resulted in romantic songs assuming even more social significance and tremendous cultural weight.

The beginning of this transition is clear in crooning's evolution in the 1910s, in which the term shifted from a racially specific, familial context to one of generic (white by default), individual romantic desire. *Croon* was still an expression of love or longing and remained associated with intimate behavior between two people; devoted lovers, however, replaced doting moth-

FIG. 1.5. Although the term *mammy* could not be severed from its minstrel roots, *crooning* shifted easily from representing a mother's expression of love for a child to an expression of intimacy between lovers, as in this song. *Crooning's* shift in meaning was part of a larger industrial and cultural shift, clear by the 1920s, that privileged romantic love and lovers over any other kind of relationship or characters in American popular culture. Sheet music, "Crooning Lullabies," 1921. Author's collection.

ers. Most of these songs reflect the mix of modern and traditional approaches to love and romance that exemplified Tin Pan Alley's desire for broad appeal. The lover characters are sometimes hopeful for promised love, sometimes pining for past love, and sometimes actively desiring. Happy lovers, those of "Winter Garden Glide" (1916) and "Crooning Lullabies" (1921), croon to each other. The flavor of modern courtship rituals is clear in the sheet music covers of both these songs, which portray couples skating close together on the former and embracing on the latter (fig. 1.5):

> Moontime, tunetime,
> Birdland calls it croontime,
> Hear the skaters are singing it,
> How pleasing . . .
> Moontime, tunetime
> Why not call it spoontime?[45]

Although these songs seem very polite today, their employment of slang terms like *spooning* (a euphemism for kissing and caressing) indicate a sensual, unchaperoned closeness between lovers that was part of popular song's modern turn. Musically as well, many crooning songs moved away from waltz time to embrace a livelier sound, reflecting the dance craze for syncopated music. The lovers of "Winter Garden Glide," for example, refer to themselves as "ragtime skating" to a "soulful Ragtime number."[46]

Part of this shift in popular songs' portrayals of courtship was a more egalitarian approach to courting that acknowledged female desire and points of view as important factors in modern lovemaking. The wildly popular "In My Merry Oldsmobile" (1910) explicitly links crooning to the carnal when the male character whispers to his love, "You can go as far as you like with me, in my merry Oldsmobile." The physical proximity made possible by the two-seater car, which was of concern to cultural authorities, ties whispered crooning to physical intimacy in a modern context, and the man happily offers himself up to his partner's sensual preferences. Other songs highlight a modern young woman's dilemma: while she enjoys lovemaking, she worries about whether her beau will still love her tomorrow. In the Berlin song "Bring Me a Ring in the Spring" (1911), the female protagonist ultimately rejects further spooning until she gets a ring:

> Spooning and crooning they sit,
> Loving it quite a bit,
> Telling lies by the pack;
> See him steal a kiss . . .
> (chorus)
> Bring me a ring in the Spring,
> And I'll know that you love me,
> A simple band of gold,
> Just like your father gave your mother
> In the days of old.[47]

Although crooning songs of all types were sung in minstrel, vaudeville, and variety shows by both male and female singers throughout the period, performers and consumers increasingly favored romantic crooning songs. Syncopation and sensuality remained threatening to many cultural authorities, and yet these qualities were also broadly popular and became essential aspects of the crooner's repertoire in the 1920s and early 1930s. But the music industry's stylistic and content shifts were only part of the reason for romantic crooning's rapid rise; another primary factor was female audiences' growing consuming power and desire.

MALE PERFORMANCE AND FEMALE
CONSUMPTION IN POPULAR ENTERTAINMENTS

In his memoir of theatrical life in the mid- to late nineteenth century, the producer John J. Jennings recalled an incident that caused "a sensation": during a minstrel show, a well-dressed woman stepped out of her private box and onto the stage, grabbed the blackface performer, and exclaimed loudly, "You're the sort of man I like!"[48] This bawdy gesture from an apparently refined woman was extraordinary. Women's public expressions of desire were rare, as Victorian social mores demanded their public passivity.

Within a generation audience dynamics had changed as more women gained access to the public realm. Beginning in the 1880s producers saw female audiences as their way to access the pocketbooks of the respectable middle class, and they actively solicited women's expressions of desire and approbation.[49] While some historians have mourned the loss of working-class solidarity and rowdy audience activity that resulted from this shift, I argue that imbuing women with more social power and consumer agency moved social provocations from classed to gendered sites. In recruiting middle-class women, theater managers sought to associate their fare with moral respectability and good taste; while the plan largely worked institutionally, women increasingly could not be trusted to perform their assigned roles. Although the socially transgressive potential of women's desires was not always as obvious as that of working-class men's, the fact that women's desires were at the forefront of popular culture from the 1890s through the 1920s affected the entertainment world structurally, economically, socially, and culturally. Women's consuming power resulted in new possibilities for public expression of female pleasure and desire. The crooning controversy that erupted in the early 1930s had its roots in women's empowerment as consumers in the 1890s and in their preference for romantic love songs sung by attractive, witty young men and boys, a preference that would alter the economic and sexual politics of the performance world and reverberate far beyond it. Although young male singers had always been popular with men as well and would remain so, such desires would become increasingly presented as the result *entirely* of women's greater presence as consumers in both trade papers and critical discourses. The intrusion of "feminine tastes," as they were dubbed by the entertainment industry, represented a significant historical shift that decisively ended centuries of the male audience's domination of popular entertainment and, in turn, began the redefinition (and devaluation) of the popular culture consumer as female and feminine.[50]

Before the turn of the century, men had sung primarily for other men. Women were excluded from public religious singing and were regarded with suspicion in secular performances beyond opera.[51] In the United States men's singing was a central part of cultural life. Men ran singing schools and dominated vocal education; they sang as soloists and groups in churches and synagogues; they sang together in amateur choruses and barbershop quartets; soldiers sang in military camps; and singing waiters sang for their customers. Singing was not antithetical to normative masculinity: cowboys sang, neighborhood boys sang, coal miners sang, policemen sang, and many athletes, from baseball players to boxers, were also songwriters and performers.

Public audiences for popular song in the early to mid-nineteenth century were likewise overwhelmingly male, particularly in urban areas and the "uncivilized" West. Before the feminization of popular culture, men did not feel self-conscious weeping at a minstrel's romantic or nostalgic song. Minstrel fans and writers such as Mark Twain and William Makepeace Thackeray wrote movingly about the profound emotional effects sentimental minstrel songs had on them.[52] The avowal of such intense responses for another man's performance reflected an entertainment world that was almost exclusively male, where men regularly impersonated women for both comic and dramatic effects. Male soprano "prima donnas" such as Eugene and Francis Leon, who cross-dressed in high fashion as "mulatto" characters, were particular favorites in the 1860s and 1870s, often performing in all-male environments such as mining towns.[53] When this masculine world began to break down, not only including more women but also giving their preferences weight, a gendered divide developed in musical tastes that largely had not existed before. These upheavals in turn became the subject of intense public discussion and growing scrutiny.

Although women made up at least a portion of the audience for minstrel shows and other popular theatricals throughout the nineteenth century, their presence and influence were typically monitored and restricted. Many commercial entertainments, especially those catering primarily to the working classes, barred women entirely.[54] In large urban theaters, presumably disreputable women were relegated to the famous "third tier" reserved for prostitutes, while respectable women were shepherded into private boxes by watchful male guardians. In smaller venues, such as traveling minstrel shows, women's access to public entertainment depended even more on their association with male attendees.

Regulating women's attendance reflects the paternalistic Victorian rhetoric of the time, which posited that respectable white women were too delicate to withstand the more emotional, provocative aspects of popular music, especially that performed by black people or those (like minstrels) who claimed to represent the black experience. The unspoken fear, however, was not that women would be overwhelmed but that they would be activated, that popular performance would stir their passions in ways that would be socially disruptive. Dutiful middle-class women such as Mary Boykin Chesnut internalized this proscription and policed themselves in this regard. Chesnut, a respectable woman from Charleston, was so affected by a concert of slave spirituals in 1861 that she wept, noting in her diary, "It was devotional passion of voice and manner which was so magnetic. . . . It was a little too exciting for me. I would very much have liked to shout, too." She interpreted her reaction as spiritual passion—a common framework for interpreting strong feelings among such women in the mid-nineteenth century—but by the twentieth century many women would interpret similar sensations as erotic passion. Female desire unleashed would betray the Victorian charade of white middle-class sexual purity and passivity and, it was believed, would open the doors to a host of threats against the status quo, particularly miscegenation and class transgression.[55]

Nineteenth-century working-class minstrels were generally seen as prominent threats to female virtue. As a consequence they were isolated from respectable social circles, and thus minstrel troupes functioned as traveling all-male worlds; their participants often joined as youths and remained with various troupes all their lives. In his memoir of the period, the song publisher Edward Marks tellingly describes minstrels as "boys" who never grew up; they were skirt-chasers, alcoholics, and card players who usually squandered their earnings and died impoverished.[56] John J. Jennings notes that their dandified street dress also set them apart.[57] While today we can easily imagine many such men preferring the all-male companionship and escape from the monotony of industrial labor that minstrel life offered, these assessments underline the ways that these flashy, hedonistic "boys" were never considered fully mature and therefore were not capable of assimilation into a society defined by adherence to rigid social roles.

It is not surprising that minstrels' outsider status and privileging of pleasure would appeal to women who were themselves so restricted, nor that when respectable women *were* permitted to attend public performances of minstrel shows, they were closely supervised. Although historians record that male opera tenors and minstrel ballad singers were favorites of female audience members in the 1870s and 1880s, class conventions and women's narrowly defined public roles discouraged demonstrations of esteem.[58] Nevertheless, some women did send their favorite minstrels flowers and "mash notes" to convey their affection, but at some risk. One young woman, a theater watcher recalled, was so infatuated with a young tenor that she "used to spend all her pin money in buying presents and baskets of flowers for him. Her father received hint of it and she was sent to a convent."[59] It was the rare woman who followed through with her attachments, although some did; Jennings cites several cases in which women abandoned their families and respectable social circles to pursue relationships with minstrel singers.[60]

In the late nineteenth century, however, social and industrial changes fueled an increase in women's public presence and activity. Commuter trains made it possible for women to go between downtown and home more easily, and the department store emerged, taking advantage of women's new mobility and encouraging their public presence as consumers. Previously domestic middle-class women also began to take more public roles in politics, business, and social work; the term *New Woman* was applied to suffragette, office worker, and charity organizer alike. Mass entertainment industries joined Tin Pan Alley in targeting their popular magazines, gramophone recordings, and films at respectable female and family audiences in order to increase profits. Working-class women also benefited from this new attention, frequenting smaller-ticket amusements like dance halls and nickelodeons, often to the consternation of their immigrant parents.[61] These popular amusements foregrounded romantic narratives to attract women, and they also provided spaces where young men and women could interact without a chaperone.

The creation of vaudeville in the 1890s helped to inaugurate the era of feminized popular entertainment by consistently targeting a mixed audience. Three theater entrepreneurs in New York City, Tony Pastor, B. F. Keith, and Edward F. Albee II, sought to create performance venues that would be less bawdy than variety shows, the revue-style programs common in saloons that had been the province of working-class male audiences and disreputable female waitresses and performers.[62] In order to attract a more "respectable" (middle-class, female) audience, Pastor and Albee opened statelier theaters and cleaned up old ones; they also professionalized and streamlined vaudeville acts by creating circuits organized through central booking offices with preapproved, family-friendly content. Producers openly wooed women with promises of safe, clean environments and romantic song narratives, sometimes sung by opera singers.

The desire to please female audiences—and appeal to the wholesome, middlebrow taste they were seen to represent—ensured the shift from the minstrel show to vaudeville as the nation's most popular entertainment by the turn of the century. The variety of acts in vaudeville was impressive, even within the increasing constraints of the corporate circuit structure; novelty was highly valued, and vaudeville offered animal acts, acrobats, dancers, and singers of every stripe. In minstrel shows the entire troupe remained onstage throughout every performance, and the emphasis was squarely on troupe identity. In contrast, vaudeville relied on a series of acts that took the stage separately, and as a result individual celebrity acquired much more importance.

One way promoters wooed female audiences was by altering the structure of entertainment to feature the male solo singer and his ballads.[63] Men continued to dominate singing, but they started singing more openly to women, using whatever powers they had to convey strong feelings. Ballads dominated the 1890s music scene; Witmark characterized them as "sentimental tabloid novels" set to music.[64] Irish tenors remained the most sought after male soloists, but high-pitched minstrel soloists were also very popular. Even as minstrelsy criticized the New Woman, it increasingly served her desires. In place of technical or artistic achievement—masculine criteria for success—producers stressed the more "peculiar," "feminine" aspects of performance: the singer's ability to convey a compelling narrative and to make audiences cry. W. C. Handy, who joined a black minstrel troupe in the 1890s, recalled the "peculiar responsibilities" their tenor singers had: "Everyone knew that there were those who came to a minstrel show to cry as well as to laugh. Ladies of that mauve decade were likely to follow the plot of a song with much the same sentimental interest that their daughters show in the development of a movie theme nowadays. The tenors were required to tell the stories that jerked the tears. If he failed to do this, he was simply not first string by minstrel standards and could expect to be replaced by a better man."[65] Handy noted that minstrel tenors frequently sang in alto and soprano ranges, and many could "hit the top C like women."[66] Although Handy's troupe were entirely black, they usually performed for white audiences. In these socially sanctioned spaces, black men quite deliberately moved white women to tears. These female fans would be undisturbed by the increasing loss of blackface with its heavy, cartoon makeup, since their primary investment was in the singer's interior emotions, which could be conveyed more personally and "authentically" without it.

Women's identification with the sentiments of a song was often intensified by an attraction to the singer, and some minstrels openly courted the potential eroticism of this relationship by blatantly vamping during their performances. While it had been common in the 1870s and 1880s for prima donna minstrels to titillate male crowds by dressing as attractive "high yeller gals," theater memoirists of the 1880s and 1890s despairingly note that some minstrels also began openly appealing to the growing numbers of women in their audiences by wearing "trousers tight-fitting and showing every muscle," thereby "spreading conjugal dissent."[67] Women's admiration of the minstrels' singing talent, emotional exposure, and physical attractiveness made their male companions (including these memoirists) jealous or uncomfortable. Minstrel shows, once sites of male camaraderie, now became sites of male competition.

By the turn of the century male singers had also become more accessible as romantic partners, as minstrel troupes disbanded and their singers moved into a performance world that was more star-driven, heterogeneous, flexible, and socially integrated (particularly in New York) than ever before. Vaudeville's mixed audiences, corporate structure, and promise of regulated content made assimilation possible. Most minstrels abandoned the use of burnt cork (blackface)—and, with it, their anonymity. Instead they differentiated themselves by their ethnic, racial, and cultural affiliations: Italian, Irish, Jewish, and black. The Cornish countertenor Richard "Dick" Jose (1862–1941), the most famous of these singers, specialized in sentimental, romantic ballads, which he sang in an exceptionally high, full, and clear voice. Because few ballad singers were also accomplished countertenors, those who could master high notes were particularly prized performers, and Jose gave enormously popular solo concerts. He had a huge following among both sexes and, along with the Italian opera tenor Enrico Caruso, was one of the biggest acoustic recording artists of the early 1900s. Former minstrel tenor and countertenor stars were the primary song promoters for ballads, as Edward Marks notes: "They had a practiced quaver in their high, pure, almost soprano voices that served them for years."[68]

Most ex-minstrels went into vaudeville, where they remained popular until its demise in the 1920s.[69] Those who made the move increasingly leaned on romantic and novelty songs rather than other minstrel fare (comedy or dialect songs); those with vocal flexibility and adaptability became soloists or specialty acts, while one-trick minstrels settled for parts in male choruses or barbershop quartets. Vaudeville offered myriad opportunities for male singers, who continued to vastly outnumber females; besides the ever-popular ballad soloists, who ranged from Metropolitan Opera stars to "double-voiced" singers (singing in full voice and falsetto) and female impersonators, vaudeville also routinely offered male duets, trios, quartets, sextets, glee clubs, and chorus singers. Singers who continued to perform in blackface in vaudeville and on Broadway, like Al Jolson and Eddie Cantor, softened the dialect in their songs and infused them with modern rhythms and expressions of desire.

Perhaps more than any other vaudeville performers, "boy singers" were increasingly aimed at female audience members and their "feminine" tastes. In the 1890s and 1900s adolescent minstrel stars such as Julius Witmark and John Quigley had made their names singing mother songs like "A Mother's a Mother After All" and "Always Take Mother's Advice." Adolescent boys were increasingly employed to perform romantic numbers in vaudeville at the turn of the century.[70] At the same time that Boy Scout leaders and Teddy Roosevelt were urging all boys to lead "the strenuous life" in the natural world, many urban boys were becoming the primary song pluggers for Tin Pan Alley and frequent popular song performers in vaudeville. Publishers used boys to promote every kind of song, but their particular specialties were emotional ballads that tugged at the heartstrings of patrons, romantic songs like "Because" and "Always."[71] Such boy pluggers were appealing to men as well as women and they were also dispatched to sing at political rallies, at bicycle races, in billiard saloons, and even in lavatories.[72] Publishers plucked adolescent boys with affecting soprano voices out of church choirs and synagogues and planted them in vaudeville and early movie theaters to promote particular songs to the crowd from their place in the audience. After the vaudeville star sang the number, the boy would stand up and sing it again, encouraging others to join him.[73] While the lad's official position was that of a "waterboy" who passed glasses of water to thirsty patrons, this job was "a mere pretext," as Isadore Witmark notes. "These boys were selected for their voices and for the manner in which they could put over a song. . . . A good waterboy could get audiences to sing with him after his first refrain."[74] Many of these early song pluggers were relatively poor Jewish or Irish boys like Jolson, Berlin, and Walter Winchell; these future stars learned early on the value of a heartfelt performance and put it to good use in their later careers.

Song-slide presentations provided another very lucrative venue for song sales, and one where publishers relied heavily, again, on the musical talents

FIG. 1.6. John Quigley, pictured, is billed as "America's Sweetest Boy Tenor." The song is a prodigal daughter story in which Quigley's narrator takes the mother's point of view, begging the father to take the daughter back; he agrees. This is one typical example of the way boy tenors were politically allied in songs with the females of the household and musically associated with the cultural feminine as singers of "beautiful, pathetic ballads." Sheet music, "Don't Send Her Away!," 1896. Words by Raymond A. Browne; music by Monroe H. Rosenfeld. Music Division, New York Public Library for the Performing Arts, Astor, Lenox and Tilden Foundations.

and youthful appeal of children and adolescents. Begun in the mid-1890s, song slides combined a live piano accompaniment with colorful lantern slides that illustrated the song's lyrics, and publishers employed young singers to lead audiences in community sing-alongs that doubled as song promotion. In many ways, song slides prepared audiences for motion pictures by offering them a sentimental narrative paired with a sincerely sung "sob song" to try and wrest tears from the ladies present. Song slides were very popular, and they saw a resurgence in the early years of cinema, which had become the fastest rising entertainment among women by 1908.[75] Song promoters employed young local singers because they could be bought more cheaply than vaudeville acts: the future stars George Jessel and Fanny Brice got their start in show biz singing song slides as children.[76]

Talent was often secondary to the appeal of both song pluggers and song-slide presenters, whose youth, innocence, and beauty were the real keys to their success. Twelve-year-old Walter Winchell had a serviceable alto voice but was a popular song plugger because he was so good looking. Winchell's neighbor Mildred Luber recalled that he cut a "very romantic" figure in his blue serge knickers and "Buster Brown" hairstyle and collar.[77] The use of boys and young men in these roles—which increased between 1908 and 1913, when song-slide use peaked in movie theaters—reflects their enhanced status as fantasy commodities primarily aimed at female audiences, as well as the more general popularity of the adolescent male figure to late Victorians. As Laurence Senelick notes, "The very evanescence and gender ambiguity of the adolescent made him seem both innocent and omnipotential, the perfect sticking place for fantasies."[78] By the late 1910s male singers and chorus boys were routinely evaluated by trade papers like *Variety* on their looks as well as their talent, a practice that only increased as male collegiate acts became the rage in the early 1920s. Given the particular value of sons to their mothers in often single-parent working-class households (which still had relatively high mortality rates), maternal and romantic fantasies often converged in the worship of male adolescents and set the precedent for jazz band crooners' public reception as objects of multiple passions.

Thus women's desiring presence at popular performances from the 1890s through the 1910s fundamentally changed and set the terms for popular music for the next thirty years, culminating in the controversy over radio crooning's youthful, high-pitched, and provocative idols. Women were not simply moved by these early male singers—a first step toward romantic desire for many people; they helped to make many of them mass-media stars who served a variety of emotional and social desires. Women could view them as possible or idealized alternatives to their current relationships, as well as figures of inspiration and identification. By attending multiple performances, buying recordings and sheet music, waiting for their favorite stars at the stage door, donning drag at a party, or, more significant, choosing a mate who respected or reflected their tastes and interests, female audiences significantly reshaped the economic and social dynamics of popular culture.[79]

The jazz band singers, recording artists, and radio crooners who emerged in the 1920s would offer these audiences the opportunity to feel even closer to their favorite male singers. Although the performers discussed in this chapter have much in common with 1920s crooners in the kinds of heartfelt songs they sang and the sort of intimate relationships they conveyed, their crooning sound was still dependent on their energy and force to put over a song. That requirement would abruptly become obsolete in the mid-1920s, as electrification and amplification changed the aesthetics of popular song, replacing muscles with whispers and packed houses with a lonely microphone. These technological changes would give popular singing a cultural prominence and economic impact not seen since the heyday of minstrelsy, even though many of these new sounds would first emerge from media where the body itself was invisible.

(((Two)))

CROONING GOES ELECTRIC

Microphone Crooning and the Invention

of the Intimate Singing Aesthetic,

1921–1928

In February 1925 *Variety*, the popular performance world's leading trade paper, noted the demand for a new kind of male singer in the cabaret speakeasies of Times Square and Greenwich Village. The "confidential tenor," the paper explained, "is one that sings in a muted tempo or practically in a whisper, rotating from table to table and generally picking up change from those being entertained in addition to his house salary."[1] Within two years "confiding" table singers would be ubiquitous in New York nightclubs, with top performers like Chick Endor and Tommy Lyman earning thousands of dollars a week for giving "private table sessions" during public performances and considerably more for entertaining at exclusive society parties. Although Endor was not himself a collegian, he embodied the youthful collegiate ideal of the time and was one of its first celebrity singers, known for his suggestive flirting with individual patrons while serenading them on a guitar or ukulele.[2] The sophisticated Tommy Lyman was best known for his risqué renditions of romantic songs, including his signature tune, "My Melancholy Baby," which he sang into the ears of admiring flappers. Lyman's intense, yearning, erotic delivery style popularized the term *torch singing*.[3]

Confidential singers like Endor and Lyman reflected an important aesthetic and industrial shift in popular entertainment: the gradual move from the muscular, belting, theatrical "popular" style to a conversational, intimate, and personal one that *Variety* began to identify more frequently by the shortened term *pop*.[4] The rise of the intimate singing aesthetic is thus foundational to the rise of pop as a genre, and during these formative years crooning was the primary delivery system of that genre. Although this book focuses on crooning as a style rather than pop as a genre, in this chapter I employ the term *crooning pop*, which was in use at the time, to indicate this historical link.

The development of this new singing aesthetic and sound, soon to be popularly known as modern crooning, did not originate in live performance, however, but in early radio broadcasting. Broadcasting pioneers regularly employed *crooning* as their shorthand for the singular sound produced by the combination of soft voices, microphones, and amplification technology. Unlike stage crooning, which still had to be projected, microphone amplification could replicate the *sound*, not just the words, of an intimate love song, and broadcasting could deliver that intimate sound to thousands of individual listeners simultaneously. While the confidential singer was indeed new to the New York cabaret scene in 1925, the cozy relationship between this kind of singer and his audience was already familiar to radio's "melancholy babies," who had been addressed by soft-voiced warblers since the early 1920s.

The 1920s has been called the "decade of sound" because of the tremendous number of new, often mass-mediated sounds that emerged. Yet historians have tended either to marginalize microphone crooning or situate its rise in relation to the Depression and the collapse of the record industry. In fact the new intimate singing aesthetic dominated the mass media from the mid-1920s onward and began to significantly reshape the world of live performance well before the great stock market crash. Microphone crooning is no less defining of the decade than jazz music and indeed was an integral part of the jazz band's development in the 1920s and beyond. The growing prominence of these microphone crooners and their nascent style impacted every major venue for popular music: radio, records, sound film, jazz band performance, cabarets, nightclubs, vaudeville, and moving picture house presentations.

Microphone amplification overturned established conventions of performance and reception in a remarkably short time. The most immediate and profound impact on popular music resulted from the mighty recording industry's adoption of electroacoustic technology in 1925. Although old and new singing aesthetics would continue to coexist in the diverse public performance world of the late 1920s, the shift in the recording industry was instantaneous: microphones forever changed the requirements for a singing career. Would-be performers no longer needed powerful muscles or years of training to project their voices, since the microphone could now easily pick up the smallest sigh. A new group of young singers emerged, defined by lyrical clarity, narrative phrasing, and a quieter, more conversational delivery style. They were at once broadly accessible and endearingly personal.

The intimate singing aesthetics also brought about changes in the audience for American popular music, in both composition and behavior. The popularity of crooning pop singing among particular audiences—especially youth and women—was central to defining the genre from its inception. The popularity of radio and records in the 1920s meant that crooning singers frequently occupied their audience's private rather than public spaces, serving as comforting companions to their daily routines. By habitually listening to crooning singers, audience members began to feel personally attached to them. Not surprisingly, when sound was added to motion pictures, crooning singers were also among the most prominent voices, since their intimate sound and narrative emphasis mirrored Hollywood film aesthetics.

Radio, record, and motion picture consumers drove the ascendance of microphone singers in public venues. The demands of these consumers changed live performance practices across class lines: confidential singers whispered in the ears of both debutantes and chorus girls in downtown cabarets and speakeasies, jazz band singers wooed collegiate flappers from the bandstands in exclusive nightclubs, and recording stars drew mixed crowds to preshow performances in motion picture houses. Trade papers reported with wonder how audiences reacted to crooning singers with the same anticipation, rapt attention, emotional investment, and, at times, erotic attraction that characterized their reaction to film stars. Crooning singers proved the most popular live attractions in pre- and between-show performances in motion picture houses and quickly made them the most valuable arenas for live song plugging by music publishers.[5] Because of crooners' national mass media exposure, the new crooning pop aesthetic helped to make individual songs and their singers huge hits within weeks, even days. As a result crooning singers began to affect the popularity of unmediated performance more generally, further hastening the demise of vaudeville.

The emergence of intimate singing coincided with and helped define other key shifts in American popular music in the 1920s. As chapter 1 demonstrates, social and commercial factors in the 1900s–1910s had already begun to move songwriting and music publishing away from songs with specific racial, ethnic, or class content and toward more broadly appealing, loving sentiments. The audio intimacy of microphone singers and their ubiquity in recording, radio, and film of the 1920s provided the sonic component to this industrial shift and ensured the dominance of a more generalized romantic sound for years to come. White ethnic accents were assimilated and standardized, and black and rural performers were segregated onto specialty labels like "race" and "hillbilly" records. Instead gender became the primary category of social difference in what came to be called pop music.

The transition to a more intimate, personal singing aesthetic also reinforced the growing ideological shift toward the value of "authenticity" in popular music. In his work on the establishment of the "musical color line" in American popular music of the 1920s, Karl Hagstrom Miller asserts that the racial essentialism the recording industry began promoting in the 1920s (for example, the notion that African American people should be allowed to record only certain genres of music deemed organic to blacks) was buttressed by the "folkloric paradigm," established by leading scholars of the time, that viewed music as "a form of expression, not only of individual feelings or collective culture but also of essential racial characteristics, capacities, and stages of evolution."[6] This paradigm validated certain kinds of performances, genres, and music production as authentic and therefore more culturally valuable than others, and thus greatly reduced the kinds of music that a single performer could record.

Similarly, this period also witnessed a cultural and industrial shift from singing styles prioritizing virtuosity to more intimate styles that privileged the vocalist's genuine feeling. As audiences' tastes changed in this regard, the evaluative criteria in the commercial trade press also changed; *Variety*, for example, began to assess the likely success of recordings based on how "sympathetic" the vocalist seemed to be rather than his or her technical abilities. Simon Frith has argued that the "performance of sincerity" is what defines pop singing in Western culture. This chapter traces this industrial movement toward the first pop singing stars by demonstrating the increasing popularity of intimate crooning singers.

However, as with any broad cultural shifts, these transitions were neither smooth nor total. In many ways, the vocal performance culture of the 1920s was more fluid and diverse than it had ever been before. When microphone crooning began, vocal categories of popular music were remarkably porous; white singers sang blues, black and Asian singers sang in a variety of ethnic accents (Irish, Italian), and everybody crooned, scatted, and yodeled as part of his or her bag of vocal tricks. Additionally, men sang from women's perspectives, lyrically, and women sang from men's. The prevalence of terms like *blues crooning* reflects the overlapping and constantly evolving descriptors for popular styles and genres that characterized the era. The three singers highlighted in this chapter—Vaughn De Leath, Gene Austin, and Al Jolson—are representative transitional figures who mixed older and newer aesthetics in ways their romantic crooning successors largely did not.

This chapter examines how the combination of new sound technologies, industrial changes, commercial interests, performer investments, and audiences' desires created the modern crooning pop sound in the 1920s. Crooning combined the novelty and shock of modern technology's intimate sounds, the accessibility of mass production and distribution, and the familiar comforts of emotional engagement with soft voices and love songs. By the late 1920s crooning dominated popular music and set in motion the aesthetic and cultural transformations that led to the first romantic crooning idol, Rudy Vallée, in 1929.

POP GOES THE RADIO: EARLY BROADCASTING'S CROONING SINGERS

The crooning pop singer was born because early radio needed a steady supply of solo singers adaptable to the requirements of primitive microphones. The early 1920s witnessed the dramatic rise of the broadcasting industry and the public's growing fascination with radio. The year 1922 is remembered as the year of the "Radio Craze," as multiple organizations—from department stores to hotels and universities—applied for radio licenses.[7] Unlike any prior medium, early radio depended on single voices and privileged singers over other kinds of performers. Soloists who could accompany themselves were preferred, since the cramped studios could not accommodate bands. Experienced singers were often not available or adaptable: vaudeville chains had injunctions against their players' broadcasting, and trained singers who were too forceful could potentially overwhelm an amplifier's delicate circuitry (a practice known as "blasting"). Likewise, the vigorous singing required for gramophone recordings or on the vaudeville stage often came across as harsh or shrill on early carbon microphones. Before the era of commercial networks, soft singers with good enunciation quickly became the go-to radio performers. They pleased broadcasters because their easy singing didn't overwhelm the sensitive equipment, they adapted easily to the microphone, and they were young, hungry, and cheap. They also proved to be a surprising hit with domestic listeners who loved their conversational style, personal address, and soothing Tin Pan Alley songs.

Increasingly, the young crooning singer came to represent the new medium itself. For the first time radio's microphones, amplification, and broad reach made possible the intimacy of live person-to-person singing on a mass scale. While performers had embodied crooning mammies and lovers onstage, they could not literally croon when projecting to a large theater audience. A genuine crooning sound was supposed to be so soft and intimate that it could be heard by only one intended listener. Microphone amplification and broadcasting could convey this sense of closeness and familiarity through the *sound* of the voice, not just its words. Moreover, early 1920s radio required the use of headsets, so listening embodied the sensation of having a loved one singing directly into one's ear.

Microphones fundamentally altered popular singing. As I discussed in the introduction, during the first decades of the twentieth century the white middle class constructed singing as masculine, requiring technical mastery and bodily control. Until the microphone era, all popular singing operated to some degree within these requirements, since performers needed strong muscles to forcefully "put over a song." The advent of amplification did not merely undermine these standards; it made them irrelevant. Singers, instrumentalists, and recording artists of all kinds were urged to "take it easy" before the microphone. Muscles were suddenly a liability, and singers were discouraged from projecting from their chests and diaphragms. Skills that singers had taken years to develop for theatrical delivery sounded artificial and histrionic to radio audiences.[8] Conversational singing, more from the head and throat than from the chest, registered to listeners as more intelligible and genuine. Suddenly a new breed of singers had access to massive audiences without having to pay their dues in small-time vaudeville or even break a sweat. As the crooner Al Bowlly attested in 1934, "The microphone brought into being, and sometimes into very prominent being, a whole host of singers who otherwise never would have been heard. There were many performers whose untrained voices, although naturally sweet and pleasing, were not strong enough for the public platform. To these the microphone was more than kind and gave them the power, at the turn of a switch, to drown out the most brazen-lunged, quasi-operatic singer who ever shook the rafters."[9]

Bowlly deferentially referred to his new master as "King Mike," reflecting the new dominance of technology in popular singing and the singer's dependent role. The "requirements of King Mike," as Bowlly termed them, intimidated and unnerved many seasoned vocalists. They not only had to project differently, but they lost the reassuring feedback provided by a live audience. Not surprisingly, therefore, there are many stories of "mic fright" among stage performers.[10] Radio performance shattered the integrity of the publicly performing body, replacing that familiar coherence with a bodiless, boundaryless voice that sang into the dark, reversing decades of tradition in an instant and jeopardizing critical standards of approbation.[11] The world-famous tenor John McCormack, for example, blanched at his first sight of a live radio studio in 1925, and the WEAF announcer held the burly man's hand until he was able to make the adjustment. But what was confounding for many seasoned performers would prove liberating for many younger singers. The absence of a visible audience allowed for more interiority in their performances, which tapped into audiences' imaginations and desires in new ways.

VAUGHN DE LEATH, "THE ORIGINAL RADIO GIRL"

Vaughn De Leath (1894–1943), whose early prominence on New York City radio stations made her an influential figure in the nascent industry, was the first microphone singer to be widely known as a "crooner." She was adept at dialect and character singing, including the crooning mammy character, as well as more contemporary musical genres like jazz and blues. Like other singers of her day, she sang songs that often combined these various influences so that her crooning songs conflated the mother and the lover, comfort with sensuality. She is best known for developing a new style for radio transmissions, delivering her songs in an easy, soft singing voice and with nuanced emotive phrasing that proved to be very popular with listeners. De Leath's combination of old and new crooning song traditions and her contribution to the development of radio singing practices make her both a representative and an innovative figure in 1920s popular music; she was known for many years as "the original radio girl" and "the first lady of radio."

In 1921 radio's first regular announcer, Tommy Cowan, hired De Leath to broadcast into New York from Newark station WJZ. She was a trained contralto singer with great range and excellent enunciation who could perform for hours at a stretch and accompany herself on the banjo, ukulele, piano, and guitar. De Leath was one of the first performers to receive hundreds of

FIG. 2.1. Vaughn De Leath's song "My Dear" is a good example of the gender fluidity of the late 1920s, when more songs incorporated the intimate aesthetic of direct address while still remaining ungendered and thus particularly open to queer readings and reception. There are no gendered pronouns in the lyrics of "My Dear," and the cover image of two women encourages a lesbian reading. DeLeath's work in early radio often combined a vaudeville style of performance, in which speaking "in character" as someone of another gender, race, or sex was considered a skill, with the microphone crooning style of direct address in which singers were assumed to be exposing their own feelings. The possibility for a queer reading exists in part because of the overlap of these styles in the 1920s. Sheet music, "My Dear," 1929. Author's collection.

fan letters after her broadcasts, which was the most common indicator of popular success before the advent of network radio ratings systems. She remained popular throughout the 1920s, spawning hundreds of radio imitators and making several popular recordings.

Radio historians have long described De Leath's persona as a nurturing, asexual, crooning mammy type, but the release of her 1920s recordings in the early 2000s revealed a much more complicated performer. Her soft, low singing held together a mixture of genres and effects that were varied and erotically charged. Her songs combined the tremendous vocal diversity and earthy quality of premicrophone vaudeville singing, including "character" songs performed in different dialects, with the romantic, jazz- and blues-influenced erotic style of delivery that characterized the most successful early microphone singers.[12] She also conflated the crooning mammy and the romantic crooner, singing love songs to men and women of various races and classes across a range of vocal personas. Her vocalizing, which crossed boundaries of race, gender, and sexuality, was characteristic of the cultural normalcy of such vocal nonessentialism in the performing world of the 1920s. Her sexualization of the mammy figure in particular indicates this transitional moment for crooning songs and puts De Leath in dialogue with other crooning female singers of the time, both black and white, who were peppering their mother-and-child routines with rag-and-blues songs containing explicit sexual content.

In her recordings De Leath combined homogenized standard Tin Pan Alley romantic fare with popular jazz and blues delivery techniques that, as sung into a microphone, emphasized her intense emotions. Her renditions of "I Ain't Got Nobody" and "Reaching for Someone," for example, exhibit the plaintiveness of what was notably often called "crooning blues." Her singing employed a variety of vocal effects, again typical of the era, that took full advantage of the new clarity offered by the microphone; she ornamented her interpretation of lyrics with coos, stutters, scats, bird twitters, giggles, street slang, tremolo (trembling, slow vibrato), trills, animal sounds ("meows" and "woofs"), and even choked-up tears.[13]

De Leath's mixture of presentational (stage) and microphone (intimate) performance aesthetics, traditions, and song genres allowed her to take on a number of different personae in her songs that remained disconnected from her personal identity as a singer (in the vaudeville tradition). In her sexually suggestive recordings, some of which were performed in minstrel dialect, De Leath expresses love for particular women and men and talks explicitly about kissing and "making love" to them ("Mah Lindy Lou," "Honey, I'se a Waitin' fo'

You," "Mariana," and "Jeanine, I Dream of Lilac Time"). Her impersonation of a black man romancing a black woman, for example, indicates that having multiple levels of vocal impersonation was normalized at this time. Such choices of material would not have marked De Leath as in any way "queer" in the 1920s; lyrics were generally sung as written without changing pronouns.[14]

Although the radio singers who followed De Leath gradually stopped performing character songs and consolidated their performances into singular vocal personas, De Leath in many ways provided the model for radio success and stardom that would become the norm by the 1930s. She took the vaudeville model of song and talk, lowered the decibel level, and performed it conversationally for the individual listener rather than a large audience. She helped to define the crooning radio singer as a specific personality, a warm friend to her listeners, which distinguished her from being another of the many talented singers that filled the airwaves.[15] As *Variety* observed, "Broadcasting from a studio with nothing but an inanimate 'mic' for transmission purposes, is a pretty trying outlet for a personality. But personality registers all the more because of the abstractness of it and De Leath, the pioneer radio girl, registers with a vengeance." *Variety*'s description of De Leath as "cordially insouciant" and an "intimate comedienne" indicates the companionate warmth and zest that she was able to convey.[16]

The radio historian Paddy Scannell has described broadcasting's personal address as its "sociability" factor: radio personalities had to learn to speak and sing *to* individual listeners rather than *at* them.[17] While this insight seems obvious today, De Leath was the first documented radio performer to make a mark with this approach. Unlike stage performers, De Leath did not rely on applause but rather on her personal enjoyment of making music and her imaginative capacity to connect with invisible domestic listeners. Like the most successful radio singers who followed her, such as Rudy Vallée and Jessica Dragonette, she found long-term emotional satisfaction in the fan mail from her domestic radio listeners, claiming that her "greatest thrill" was the knowledge "that my songs have entertained a sick child or I have helped some tired mother."[18] Likewise, De Leath helped accustom audiences to the crooner's voice in the home; her domestic presence naturalized her "femme-friendly" approach and justified her privileging of female listeners as her audience.

De Leath was not the only singer to discover the efficacy of developing an intimate "song and patter" persona for radio. She remains prominent because she had early access to radio stations in New York City, the center of the entertainment world. But young men such as Art Gillham, Little Jack Little, Jack Smith, and Nick Lucas all built regional reputations at stations in, respectively, Atlanta, Cincinnati, New York, and Chicago. Before broadcasting they were unknown singers, although Lucas had been a successful guitar and banjo player with several major orchestras before he moved to radio. In 1923, during breaks from his work with the Oriole Terrace Orchestra at the Edgewater Beach Hotel in Chicago, Lucas began broadcasting a song-and-chat program from the hotel's radio station, WBEH. His routine was novel because he accompanied himself on the guitar, a new instrument for recording and broadcasting, and the combination of his gentle voice, easy manner, and expert strumming quickly made him a regional star, netting him thousands of fan letters and securing him a recording contract with Brunswick that ensured his national stardom.[19]

Unlike Lucas, most of radio's successful early crooning performers—including Gillham, Little, and Smith—began their careers working as song pluggers for sheet music companies. Art Gillham shilled for Ted Browne's company in Chicago, Jack Smith for Irving Berlin in New York, and Little Jack Little for a variety of midwestern publishers from his base in Cincinnati.[20] The song plugger was a young man or adolescent employed by publishing companies affiliated with Tin Pan Alley to promote their songs, usually by singing them loudly in a public, commercial space. With the advent of the automobile, song pluggers took to the road, traveling to record and department stores across the country to demonstrate their wares; when broadcasting began they added radio stations to their list of stops. Gillham allegedly visited over three hundred stations before becoming a "name" on WSB in Atlanta.[21] Professional musicians and singers had long disdained pluggers for being salesmen first and musicians second. They did not have discernible singing talent according to the standards of the time (wide range, vocal projection, mastery of various vocal skills or character dialects), they did not try to put over a song with the energy and force of a vaudevillian, and they did not offer the kind of individualized interpretation of a song that would invite critical approval. In fact their job required the opposite: a successful plugger appealed to the lowest common denominator, generally characterized as female listeners, who were regarded by professional musicians and song publishers alike as easy targets.

All the characteristics that made pluggers anathema to the performance world made them ideal for early radio. As a song demonstrator, a plugger needed to emphasize clear phrasing, communicating the melody and narrative clearly to the consumer rather than putting any personal stamp on the song. In their radio work pluggers likewise focused on the skills they had perfected as salesmen: expert enunciation of lyrics without a strong accent or adornment and the ability to exploit the song's emotional hook. They were also proficient at accompanying themselves, generally on the piano or on the more portable banjo, guitar, or ukulele. Unsurprisingly, small, spare radio studios did not trouble song pluggers, who were familiar with makeshift performance spaces. They viewed microphone technology as an interesting challenge, taking to "King Mike," in Ian Whitcomb's provocative phrase, "like little boys to a lollipop."[22]

In contrast to the multiple characters De Leath enacted on her radio shows, most song pluggers wholly embraced Tin Pan Alley's generic romanticism, eschewing any kind of minstrel or character dialect that might limit their broad commercial appeal. This brand of "straight" singing was so associated with pluggers that when Jack Smith and Art Gillham made their first recordings in 1925, *Variety* referred to them as "song salesmen"—an unusual descriptor for recording artists that year—to distinguish their baldly commercial, conversational microphone singing from more traditional kinds of popular singing performance, where song selling was not as overt.[23] Radio audiences responded very positively to song pluggers; they were familiar with their brand of salesmanship, and the pluggers had no qualms about directly addressing and wooing the domestic audience. Like De Leath, they created consistent, friendly personae that listeners wanted to invite into their homes and to whom they grew attached. Because of their radio exposure and audience demand, some song pluggers became personalities in their own right and were offered their own radio shows, which started their legitimate singing careers.[24]

These men represented the industrial emergence of pop, which initially referred to any type of performance that was inexpensive, lowbrow, and primarily commercial. Rather than a variety of characters, song pluggers brought a variety of sounds to radio by experimenting with the possibilities of microphone technology. Bowlly was one of this first generation of microphone singers, and he found that soft microphone singing had several advantages; it gave

FIG. 2.2. This piece of sheet music suggests the growing importance of radio performers both as popularizers of new songs and as potential new love interests for the flapper generation several years before the advent of Rudy Vallée. The cover here features the musician and singer Ray Stillwell. Radio is also referenced by the circular waves radiating off the male figure in profile. This radiating male is very much in the mode of the softer, more feminine 1920s dream man: clean-cut, well-dressed, and sporting long eyelashes and lipstick. Sheet music, "A New Kind of Man (with a New Kind of Love for Me)," 1924. Author's collection.

"new timbre" to the voice, enabling singers to "enunciate with far greater clarity than before," as well as an illusion of more depth, "almost a stereoscopic effect."[25] Many singers found that these new qualities allowed them to emphasize the intimate and erotic possibilities of the voice that fit nicely with Tin Pan Alley's romantic focus. Through murmurs, whispered words, nonsense syllables, vibrato, and breathiness they were able to deliver their seductive intentions without going near censorable speech. One writer described Little Jack Little's romancing of King Mike this way: "He tips the mic to his lips and sways with it in a manner that is almost amorous."[26] Radio audiences loved it.

The affinity of song pluggers for radio work did not go unnoticed by disapproving media watchdogs, yet they could not help but admit that these "song sellers" knew how to use the microphone. O. M. Static (likely a pseudonym) in the *Boston Post* provides a typical critical response:

> A voice that in itself is hardly a good voice may be the most popular on the air. No one has yet fathomed the tricks of the microphone. For instance, a song plugger, who was wont to ride around on trucks barking the latest song hits to indifferent audiences . . . is really a pleasing singer when heard over the radio. Somehow the mechanics of radio culls the raucously rough edges from his vocal mannerisms and leaves for the listeners-in only a tender smoothness. . . .

The radio, in other words, has the same effect on his voice as arduous years of voice training. And, sadly enough, by the same token the highly polished voice will on occasion have an indefinite thinness, its beautiful refinement lost out somewhere in the ethereal distance.[27]

In retrospect Static's reaction was an early sign of the class and cultural tensions that would later develop into a full-fledged backlash against crooners, but here his sorrow at the pluggers' rise is mixed with admiration and wonder at radio's ability to spin vocal straw into gold.

Before the commercial network era officially began in 1926, cultural authorities and many of the most prominent broadcasters had perceived radio as a vehicle for uplifting the masses. Although radio content varied locally, informative programs, classical music, opera, light jazz dance orchestras that were remotely broadcast from swanky hotels, and excerpts from Broadway's musical comedies dominated early radio. While many kinds of music were popular during radio's early days, the particular and sustained success of De Leath and young crooning singers on stations across the country indicated that the public was making a choice; they were ahead of the industry in recognizing microphone crooning as a new sound, and they wanted more. Broadcasters were stunned by the volume of letters that poured into stations for early crooning singers and friendly announcers, and they responded by giving the public what it seemed to want.[28] The impressive formal qualities of the electrified modern radio sound—the increased purity and clarity that engineers prided themselves on—proved to be far less important to many domestic listeners than the sense of intimacy, emotion, and personal connection that these improvements offered them through radio's whispering, confiding singers. The emergence of De Leath, Gillham, Lucas, Little, and Smith, along with a variety of other popular "vocal personalities" from 1922 to 1924, precipitated the star-driven commercial populism of the network era.

Radio's song pluggers paved the way for singing's new aesthetic, introducing a number of pop's key elements: homogenized whiteness, singular personae, explicitly commercial emphasis on love songs, conversational tones, excellent enunciation, and intimate microphone delivery. Despite their innovations, most of radio's early crooning singers saw broadcasting as a starting rather than an ending point. Their radio fame and microphone savvy earned these former song pluggers recording opportunities, which gave them the national exposure for live tours. These singers were not yet known as "crooners" but more often as "confiders"; like their cabaret counterparts, they were identified by the intimacy of their *approach* rather than their particular *venues*. The term *crooning* would become more prominent as radio's confiding singers began their conquest of the mighty recording industry in the mid- to late 1920s. Their recording successes would in turn set the stage for the romantic crooner's domination of network airwaves and, for a time, every venue of American popular culture.

ELECTRICAL RECORDING AND ITS WHISPERING SINGERS

Electrical recording nationalized the new singing aesthetic, making soft-voiced warblers the most popular singers in the country and inaugurating the commercial romantic soundtrack of daily life that soon would be commonplace. In the mid-1920s the phonograph industry was far more powerful than radio, with decades of market penetration, a sophisticated promotional apparatus, and a consolidated corporate structure based in New York City.[29] Consequently, the new aesthetics initiated on radio reverberated much more deeply after they were adopted by the recording industry. In 1925 the heads of the biggest three phonograph companies—Victor, Columbia, and Brunswick—decided to shift from acoustic to electrical recording, reinventing the phonograph industry and further entrenching the microphone sound. The unprecedented popularity of electrical recordings resulted in fundamental and enduring changes not only in singing aesthetics but also in personnel, song content, promotion, and critical reception.

The individual popularity of singers such as Gene Austin, Jack Smith, Johnny Marvin, and Nick Lucas ensured that their crooning sounds would become the foundation of pop singing. These singers became leading representatives of the more homogenized commercial sound being promoted by song-publishing and record industries, even as they continued to exhibit other aspects of vocal diversity characteristic of the 1920s. *Variety* provided the initial descriptors of this new sound—"pleasing," "sincere," and "sympathetic"—words that highlighted the social and emotional function that these singers were serving in their listeners' lives and that also quickly became central to critical evaluations of these new aesthetics. These men were thus key transitional figures in the history of popular singing and its largely unacknowledged first pop stars.

Unlike early radio, which in the early 1920s was still heavily regional and largely noncommercial, the phonograph industry was a corporate enterprise dominated by a few very competitive New York–based firms that promoted their records nationally and internationally. The recording industry's response to radio was mixed. Some executives considered radio a minor threat and ridiculed its scratchy sounds and awkward headsets, although others took advantage of radio broadcasting to increase the popularity of some of their artists.[30] After the introduction of the Superheterodyne set in 1924, however, radio's clarity and volume more perceptibly surpassed that of phonographs. Improved signal amplification made headphones unnecessary; they were replaced by a succession of ever-improving loudspeakers that greatly enhanced bass sounds and produced enough volume to fill a room.[31] Radio sales soared.[32] Nevertheless, many recording executives were reluctant or unable to invest the money needed to switch systems, and, as Susan Horning has shown, there was "cultural resistance" as well. Top executives at Victor, while agreeing that the new sound was "more natural" than the acoustic sound, felt that the public wouldn't convert because they were used to the sound of acoustic records. Once their own test audiences eagerly embraced the so-called radio sound, however, Victor's executives saw the need for change.[33]

Electrical recording created a bigger and better sound from much smaller recording instruments than had been possible in the acoustic era. A small condenser microphone replaced the huge recording horn, and an electromagnetic stylus (a needle) and vacuum-tube amplifier replaced the acoustic stylus. The greater sensitivity and strength of this new system produced superior depth, clarity, and complexity and therefore increased the perceived (though engineered) "naturalness" of sound to listeners. J. P. Maxfield, one of the leading engineers of the new system at Western Electric, described it as simultaneously "giving the music 'body and weight' as well as 'definition or detail.' "[34] Electrical recording offered a far greater range and depth of sound, both high and low, than the acoustic system, but it also could reproduce more of the individual notes and more vocal sounds, such as sibilants (the hissing s sounds). Singers now had the ability to convey small, subtle variations in their deliveries. They could record songs with more lyrical and narrative complexity, closer harmonies, and a variety of other vocal effects of which radio listeners were so fond, including whistling and spoken interludes. Variety noted that "for vocal recordings, [the electric recording process] is particularly satisfactory and effective."[35] Likewise, the clarity of many instruments, notably pianos and strings, improved dramatically with the electrical process. The earliest pop recording names—Cliff Edwards ("Ukulele Ike"), Johnny Marvin, and Nick Lucas—helped to widely popularize the ukuleles, banjos, and guitars they employed, ensuring their continued association with the decade.

Many performers embraced the electrical system, which not only produced clearer recordings but was also more efficient and less physically constraining. With the acoustic system, singers had to project into the horn at full volume repeatedly, often for hours, to get a single usable recording. According to one singer, Franklyn Baur, the new electrical recording equipment could produce recordings "in exactly one-third the time it used to take, and no longer is it necessary for us to nearly crack our throats singing into that hated horn."[36] Because the technical needs of the recording horn were privileged over artistic concerns in the acoustic era, technicians needed to be present to guide the performer's singing into the horn and the performers had to crowd around it. In electrical recording, however, the technician could stay in an adjoining booth with the recording device, communicating with performers through an intercom, as in broadcast studios. Singers had the freedom to concentrate on the specific creative aspects of their own performance and to experiment with different styles of delivery and musical accompaniment. While they needed to use a microphone, performers could get different sounds by moving closer to or farther away from it. Multiple microphones could also be used to produce a fuller sound and to better capture the atmosphere of the room, particularly if there were many performers; this setup also allowed singers more movement. While some artists and big bands used this new freedom to reproduce the shape and sound of a live nightclub performance, crooning singers took advantage of the new possibilities for interiority. Instead of having to please a live audience or sing into a demanding recording horn, singers could now ignore the rest of the world and focus on emoting to the mic, redefining the studio as a private space of personal reflection and aligning themselves with their domestic listeners.

Like the radio's carbon mic, however, the recording studio's condenser microphone did not respond well to the aggressive approaches of most trained singers or Broadway showmen. Record producers found that trained Irish and Italian tenor voices, whose "sob ballads" had been audience favorites for decades, came off as too "thick" or "hollow." In the absence of ever-popular tenor solos, phonograph labels hired untrained, conversational young crooners, many of whom were song pluggers from radio, to provide the romantic and sentimental songs that were previously associated with professional singers. While recording adjustments were eventually made for trained tenor voices, they would never be as broadly popular again.[37] With the notable exceptions of Al Jolson and Eddie Cantor, vaudeville belters largely disappeared, along with acoustic recording artists Henry Burr and Billy Murray, whose forceful styles were no longer in vogue.

The gendered implications of this shift in technology were profound. As in radio, electrical recording no longer required the muscular voices associated with normative masculinity. In the acoustic era the sheer vocal force required to make a gramophone recording was often too taxing for even Broadway and vaudeville stars (which is why few made recordings). The phenomenal success of Enrico Caruso's records in the early part of the century was due in part to the perception that he was a "manly singer" who, notes the historian David Suisman, "was praised more over the years for his volume than his tone."[38] Indeed the acoustic historian Tim Gracyk connotes this same masculine virility when he asserts that "stamina was more important than artistry" when making acoustic recordings; he describes the most effective singers as having "latent penetrating power" in their ability to master what becomes, metaphorically, a feminized "receiving" horn (which was in fact shaped like a cone).[39] In comparison the softness and gentleness of electric crooning singers represented a significant change in performance dynamics that at the time was seen to be a more faithful, modern reproduction of the voice, but that in coming years would become increasingly perceived as disturbingly feminine.

The recording industry's choice of a condenser mic over a carbon mic also greatly shaped the particular sound of recordings in the mid- to late 1920s and contributed to crooners' eventual feminine associations. The early radio industry had primarily employed carbon instead of condenser mics in the early to mid-1920s because they could be used outdoors and were easily moved. Although condenser mics had superior sound quality and could reproduce a wider range of sounds, they were temperamental when moved and required a more stable, controlled environment than most early radio stations could provide. The recording industry, however, embraced the condenser mic, and it became standard until the early 1930s, when ribbon mics replaced it. Carbon microphones, developed for use in telephones and early radio broadcasting, reproduced sound within the narrow midrange of the voice to reinforce semantic clarity. Early condenser mics, in contrast, were known for their exceptional reproduction of higher frequencies, which meant that audiences could *hear* more from the higher end of the voice. The perceived *higher* and *lighter* sound of crooning singers from this period—especially when compared to improved low-frequency reproduction dynamic and ribbon mics in the early 1930s—is at least partly due to their use of the condenser mic.[40] The public of the time embraced the lighter, softer, clearer sound of electric voices; they sounded liberated to audiences compared to acoustic singers' voices, which now registered as thick, muddy, mechanical, and artificial.

Although the full cultural implications of these aesthetic and technological changes would take a few years to sink in, the industrial impact was immediately evident in the near-complete turnover of recording talent from 1925 to 1926 and the swift recognition of microphone crooning in trade press reviews.[41] The change to electrical recording also meant the end of studio artists like Burr and Murray generally, who were eclipsed by younger, conversational singers who had made their names on radio and in jazz bands.[42] Critics and promoters initially used the terms *novelty*, *specialty*, or *peculiar* to describe the new aesthetic of soft singing, assuming it would not last, but other descriptors soon emerged. The first, *whispering*, came from broadcasting. When Columbia Records decided to test the new electric process, its executives chose a microphone-savvy Atlanta radio song plugger, the "Whispering Pianist," Art Gillham, to make a series of initial recordings with Western Electric in February of 1925. Gillham's own composition, "You May Be Lonesome," became one of the first electrical recordings Columbia released, and it was an instant hit. Gillham's sound so defined the new era that "whispering" and "confidential singing" became widely imitated.[43] Victor Records hired its own radio confidential singer, song plugger, and pianist, Jack Smith, and very successfully promoted him as "the Whispering Baritone." The two singers engaged in a widely publicized rivalry that lasted for the next several years, making them household names.

In the recording industry the term *crooning* emerged at this same time. Throughout the late 1920s record promoters and critics employed *crooning* almost interchangeably with *torching* to describe this new delivery style for various genres, most frequently as a modifier for jazz and blues subgenres. *Crooning* was not yet a gendered or raced term: women and men crooned across musical color lines. Nick Lucas, whom Brunswick Records promoted to national stardom as "the Crooning Troubadour," was the only singer exclusively billed as a crooner between 1925 and 1928, but he guaranteed the association of the term with the new electrical process. Cliff Edwards, billed as "Ukulele Ike," became one of the biggest stars of 1926, with a string of hits on Perfect (Pathé) Records. His small soprano ukulele playing matched his high-pitched, jazzy love songs, and he was often described as a "crooning jazz" singer because of the scatting interludes in his love songs. Victor Records immediately signed Johnny Marvin to compete with Edwards as the "Ukulele Ace"; Marvin's record sales would be eclipsed only by those of Victor's own Gene Austin, the biggest recording star of the era. Often billed as "the Voice of the Southland," Austin redefined "southern" voices, drawing on southern blues and nascent country, not minstrelsy; he was frequently called a "crooning blues" singer and had an informal style that defined the era and inspired scores of imitators, most famously the pianist and Houston radio personality Seger Ellis. All of these men were adept at microphone performance, experimenting with the new technology's ability to capture every vocal inflection, from Smith's and Gillham's breathy murmurings to the jazz-based effing and scatting of Edwards and Marvin.

This group of recording stars was among the first ethnically assimilated generation of singers, a reflection of the larger cultural assimilation of ethnic groups into "white" America after federal limitations on immigration in 1924. The increased clarity of the electrical sound acted as a technology of assimilation in this political context, in which those singers who spoke in "plain" English with clear diction were rewarded and promoted. As a result, first-generation immigrants and anyone with a pronounced ethnic, regional, urban, or class accent largely disappeared from mainstream recordings.[44] Record companies reinforced artists as commercial rather than culturally specific products by not promoting ethnic, religious, or class affiliations for these singers, despite the fact that some of them, like the Italian Nick Lucas, had "Latin" looks that in previous years would have been a selling point. Moreover, as noted earlier, all the major record companies had already segregated record markets by the mid-1920s, relegating most black and hillbilly singers to particular labels (labeled "race" and "hillbilly" or "old-time" music) aimed at those demographics, a practice that intensified after electrification and encouraged vocal essentialism.[45] Although initially during this transition some singers such as Gene Austin and Aileen Stanley still sang across such classed and racialized markets, by the late 1920s all performers had become segregated along these lines, both industrially and ideologically.

However, differing styles and attitudes among singers that the recording industry tried to brush away remain audible today. For example, the piano man Jack Smith's perfect diction, seductive baritone, dapper dress, lyrical sophistication, and cosmopolitan cool made him a hit on radio and one of the biggest recording names of the era.[46] He kept an emotional distance from his listeners by shifting his address and alternating between points of view, often within the same song. Compared to other early crooners' love songs, Smith's are the least idealistic; they are about romantic and sexual negotiation rather than love, and the women he wants know the game. ("Gimme a Little Kiss, Will Ya, Ha?" was one of his big hits.) His lyrics and conversational presentation reflect the sophisticated atmosphere of an urban cabaret or nightclub, where women's sexual favors are acknowledged as valuable commodities and their price is high: luxury goods or marriage.

Unlike the sly and witty Smith, other crooning singers emphasized their pleasing personalities and relaxed strumming and the comfort of their sweet love songs. Early success for Edwards, Marvin, and Lucas depended less on their worldliness and more on their everyman accessibility, connoted both by lowbrow string instruments and venues such as motion picture houses. While in his recordings Smith negotiated with flappers for sex, the records of Edwards, Marvin, and Lucas focused more on attaining the flapper's love and establishing a traditional home life. Lucas's hits, for example, emphasize romantic love ("My Bundle of Love") over sex and money. Although Lucas's songs are primarily upbeat, his popular hit "Sleepy-Time Gal" focuses on getting his flapper girlfriend to settle down and be a conventional wife:

> Before your dancing is through
> I'll build a cottage for you
> You'll learn to cook and to sew
> What's more you'll love it I know.[47]

The hope that, or threat of, "You'll learn to cook and to sew" (and "love it"!) when "you're a stay at home, play-at-home / 8-o'clock sleepy time gal" reflects some of the larger cultural anxieties over the flapper's potential movement too far away from traditional gender roles and a desire to set limits on women's progress. Ultimately, neither Lucas nor the other early crooners were as consistently devotional in their personae as the Vallée-era romantic crooning idols would be, though Lucas's more traditional sentiments perhaps account for why he (and this particular song) survived the crooning controversy of the early 1930s. By contrast, Smith's sexual sophistication, defenses of the flapper, and subtle critique of gender and economic hierarchies marked him as a queer product of the 1920s, inassimilable in the more gender-normative 1930s.

These men helped create the crooner template; the more one singer's records sold, the more likely his style would be copied, which meant that he had

IF I CAN'T HAVE YOU
WORDS AND MUSIC BY
NICK LUCAS AND SAM H.STEP

NICK LUCAS

FIG. 2.3. This sheet music cover represents the role of many of the earliest radio crooners such as Nick Lucas as catalysts for bringing couples together rather than presenting themselves as an alternative male love interest for desiring listeners. This role was very much in keeping with the social discourses of the 1920s, which encouraged romantic couples to draw on popular culture products to enhance their bonds. Sheet music, "If I Can't Have You," 1925. Author's collection.

more power to choose and craft his next recordings and, ultimately, to have more of an effect on the development of the crooning pop style. Gene Austin, the early crooner who was the most broadly popular singer of the era, therefore had more control over his recordings but faced more industry opposition as a result; a closer examination of his career reveals the particularities of character, background, musical affiliations, and performance aesthetics that helped shape his sound, as well as the industrial tensions over the forced divisions and assimilationist politics of the era that characterized pop's beginnings.

GENE AUSTIN'S BLUES CROONING

The earnest delivery, diverse set of musical influences, and mix of modern and traditional sentiments common among pre-Vallée crooning recording artists were exemplified by Gene Austin (1900–1972). Austin's synthesis of Tin Pan Alley, cowboy, nascent country (then called "old-time" or "hillbilly"), jazz (ragtime), and blues produced a melancholy, wistful sound that stirred millions.[48] Austin's style upended Jolson's belting minstrel style and replaced it with the soft, comforting, intimate sounds on which modern crooning rests. By 1927 Austin had become the leading recording artist in the country, the

Bing Crosby of his generation, defining the sound and attitude of mainstream pop. He sold more songs during the late 1920s (recording and sheet music combined) than any singer had before, and he was responsible for many of the best-selling songs of the decade, such as "My Blue Heaven" (1927), "Girl of My Dreams" (1928), and "Ramona" (1928).[49] While Austin's easy crooning represents the most successful corporate blend of disparate musical influences up to that time, his sound was not easily produced. He embraced the diverse vocal aesthetics of the age, and he fought to incorporate more of what he considered a southern working-class "blues" sound into his recordings against Victor's homogenizing efforts.

Born in 1900 in Texas but raised in the Louisiana Delta, Austin always identified as a southerner. More than any other early crooning singer, he represented the white working class's industrial and cultural break with minstrelsy; he never performed in blackface and, in fact, was most directly inspired by the emotional blues singing of an African American Louisiana sharecropper named Esau. Like others in the new electric generation, Austin became a star behind the microphone, but unlike many others, he had a diverse résumé of performance experience. Professing wanderlust, by the age of twenty-six Austin had performed in urban cabarets, rural honky-tonks, brothels, and taverns, on vaudeville stages and military bases (while in the service), and in Parisian nightclubs, and he had worked on and off as a song plugger. He straddled the electrical and acoustic ages, recording under both systems, although it was the vocal nuances electrical recording made possible that would make him a star. He became the first known singer to travel with a portable electrical megaphone for public appearances.[50]

Austin's impoverished and troubled upbringing in the Delta greatly influenced the kind of singer he became and helps to explain his broad popularity. Although his first singing experiences were as a choirboy in his Baptist church, he was never interested in what the conventional, churchgoing folks around him considered to be "respectable" music. Instead Austin revered the singing cowboys he followed on Texas trails as a child, the singing piano players (known as "professors") he sought out in brothels and taverns, and the black sharecropper who became his lifelong mentor, Uncle Esau. Esau was so inspirational to Austin that he made it his mission in life to try to emulate Esau's soft, low singing.[51] While Austin liked jazz and could rag a melody on the piano with the best of them, he found the rapid tempo of most instrumental hot jazz too aggressive, glumly writing to Esau in a letter, "The Yankees want their Dixie music loud and fast."[52]

Austin's voice was distinctive for the time; his embrace of multiple influences reflected the absence of vocal essentialism for the singers of his generation, in which nearly everyone, regardless of race or gender, played jazz and sang blues. For many performers and producers of the time, the blues designation specifically was more a reflection of class than race; it was most often described in the trade papers as "lowdown" music and was primarily associated with the southern rural poor. This connection was carved in stone by the record industry, which further limited the "blues" genre to black performers (race records) in the mid-1920s while labeling similar styles of southern music by rural whites "old-time" or "hillbilly" music.[53] Its industrial association with the lower classes and, increasingly, with only black performers seems a likely reason why Austin chose to describe his sound to Victor Records' musical director Nat Shilkret as "crooning" rather than "blues," and specifically as "crooning like Al Jolson's mammy."[54]

Thereafter Shilkret and Victor Records referred to Austin's style of singing as "crooning," ensuring the prominence and imitation of the term across the entire recording industry. But record reviewers recognized Austin's blues intentions, and he remained a hybrid performer for a long time in the trade press. *Variety* most frequently described his singing in the mid- to late 1920s as "crooning blues," and that term best describes his style: a conflation of intense blues feeling (characterized by yearning, despairing, lamenting) with standard Tin Pan Alley song form and pop microphone production. Significantly, like Tin Pan Alley's romantic crooning records, Austin's songs jettisoned all trappings of or references to minstrelsy, including the use of dialect, the plantation setting, and the nostalgic longing for the Old South. He incorporated street vernacular and slang but without the twang of "hillbilly" or the rural "rube" accent that was popular in vaudeville and "hillbilly" recordings. Austin's light, plain-spoken tenor combined the "high lonesome" sounds and personal, emotional expressiveness of early country blues, the playful vocal improvisations of jazz, the wistfulness of cowboy songs, and the romanticism and standard song form of Tin Pan Alley.[55]

Like so many early crooning singers, Austin began in the business as a song plugger and songwriter. He started making solo recordings for Victor in 1924, the year before electrical recording took hold. The differences between the two eras of singing are particularly audible on his records and explain why the ascendance of crooners is so clearly a product of the electrical age. The closest any of his acoustic recordings came to a crooning song is "A Yearning (Just for You)," recorded in March 1925.[56] In contrast to ragtime songs, "Yearning" is a personal, private reflection, a song that contains key elements of Austin's future electrical crooning style. The song's primary sentiment and its delivery mark it as a perfect proto-crooning song; as the title indicates, it is about desire (rather than attainment), and it is delivered with a sense of longing for one person ("you"). *Variety* praised Austin's sincere emotional expression ("sympathetic inflections") and his "clear enunciation" of the song's lyrics, both essential characteristics of the successful electrical-era singer.[57] But the unrelieved melancholy of blues feeling is also evident on this record, particularly with his exclamation of the final word of the song, *yearn*. Austin hits this final desiring note very emphatically but does not sustain it, instead immediately fading as if to indicate that he cannot keep up his strength. This particular "attack / fast fade" technique, often on high-pitched, ascending rather than descending final notes, leaves his emotional narrative incomplete, keeping the audience inside his longing and despair rather than allowing them the distance of closure. In order to emphasize their romantic longing, early crooners frequently ended phrases or songs on ascending rather than descending notes, as if to suggest the singer was cut off or overwhelmed by feeling, thereby preventing the restoration of emotional stability. I will refer to these moments as "feminine endings" in the tradition of Susan McClary's famous discussion of how music is created and interpreted as gendered within Anglo-American culture. Austin's songs and those of later romantic crooners are feminine in that they do not produce emotional catharsis or narrative closure, they end from a position of vocal weakness rather than one of strength, and they suggest an excess of emotion that rejects technical precision and spills over and falls between the notes like tears. Such feminine endings became characteristic of his style and greatly influenced subsequent romantic crooners, especially Rudy Vallée.[58]

In the fall of 1925 Victor began to release Austin's electrical recordings, encouraging audiences to play them on the new Orthophonic Victrola, an electroacoustic phonograph that set a new standard for tone quality, volume, and lyrical clarity that exceeded even the radio for many listeners. Electrical recording and the Victrola's superior sound helped to establish Austin's crooning style for the public: his voice is lighter, higher, and clearer, and his recordings are more distinctly *his* particular song interpretations. Electrical recording allowed him to ornament his vocal delivery with personal touches; he frequently riffed on lyrics, repeated words or inserted nonsense syllables or bits of tremolo, and slid between notes, often inserting high notes or half notes into the melody line to accentuate a particular sentiment. Yet Austin's interpretations were also always tied to lyrical intent and emotional realism. Austin's embrace of the electrical medium as a mode for private self-expression, reflection, and confession also fit modern sensibilities; his popularity showed the public's eagerness for sincere self-exposure in a culture that was increasingly focused on the psychological well-being and desires of the individual.

While Austin benefited greatly from Victor's position as the most powerful recording company of the era, Victor continually objected to what it viewed as the low quality and class of his song choices. Austin had just enough of a southern accent and incorporated just enough slang to make him popular without betraying his poor southern roots, especially when his voice was backed by Victor's heavy orchestration. Yet the unmistakable blues and nascent country influence on many of his records demonstrates the universal appeal of the longing for (often lost) love that characterized both genres and that would characterize many crooning songs as well, in part because of Austin. The blues feeling is especially evident, for example, on the popular record "Lonesome Road" (1927), which Austin cowrote; the song is remarkably slow and melancholy, almost a dirge, and Austin incorporates sliding notes to indicate the fatigue of the narrator's mournful but persistent traveler:

> Look down, look down
> That lonesome road
> Before you travel on . . .
> (2nd verse)
> True love, true love
> What have I done
> That you should treat me so?

In mood, sentiment, and narrative, it echoes both the country blues of Austin's fellow southerner Jimmie Rogers and the classic blues songs of black female singers like Ethel Waters.[59]

Austin's success allowed him to win some important battles with Victor over recordings, and some of these songs helped determine the development of pop music in the long term. The most significant example of Austin's own agency within the industry was his desire to record the song "My Blue Heaven," a simple, melodic song that today reads as a cross between pop and country music, with a nod to blues in both the title and Austin's wistful delivery.[60] Victor did not consider the number to be sophisticated enough, especially without heavy orchestration, but Austin ultimately was able

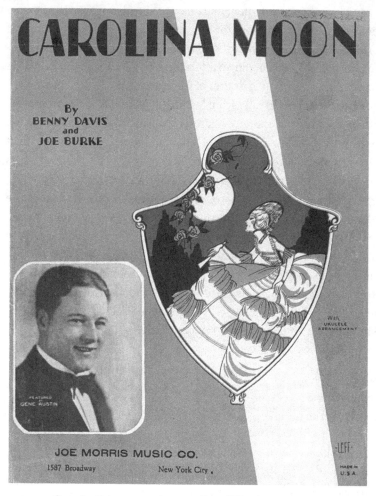

FIG. 2.4. Gene Austin's very popular recording of "Carolina Moon" was released in 1928 and peaked in 1929. The disjunction between Victor Records' heavy orchestrations and Austin's plain-spoken sound is notable in his recordings, and that tension was often represented in sheet music covers. This cover's illustration evokes an Old World aristocracy, connecting Austin's records to the superior sound quality of Victor's new Orthophonic Victrola phonograph, but the song was a standard, unadorned southern-themed romance, which Austin sang simply. At the time, "Carolina Moon" was promoted as a "crooning blues" recording; today Austin's delivery would be described as "country." Sheet music, "Carolina Moon," 1929. Author's collection.

to record the song with only a cello player, a pianist, and a whistler for accompaniment.[61] Completed on 14 September 1927, the recording became a best-seller and a representative crooning song for historians and scholars.[62] While critics have offered various reasons for the song's success, all agree that the combination of a minimal accompaniment; Austin's relaxed, heartfelt, closely mic'd delivery; and a broadly populist narrative of anticipated domestic bliss gave the song an intimacy and emotional pull that was unique in recordings of the time:

When whippoorwills call, and evening is nigh
I hurry to my Blue Heaven . . .
You'll find a smiling face, a fireplace, a cozy room.
Just Molly and me, and baby makes three.

At first listen, the song's simple lyrics expressing the narrator's desire for a home and family may seem dully conventional, especially in comparison to the more urbane songs described earlier; however, there is an openness and inclusiveness to the lyrics that allows for a variety of interpretations. Is "my blue heaven" a real place or a wishful fantasy? The song is neither urban nor rural; instead it constructs an imaginary space that has as much in common with the spiritual world ("I turn to the right / a little white light will lead you to my blue heaven") as it does with the everyday experience of the modern working man. Austin's interpretation further conflates the spiritual with the romantic, as earthly, natural places ("a little nest that's nestled where the roses bloom") are combined with "heaven"-ly ones, reflecting that the American Dream may always remain a fantasy rather than a material reality. Like almost all crooning pop songs, it is about the desire for happiness attained through some kind of love.

The tenderness and sincerity of Austin's voice enhances the emotional impact of the song; he does not sing with the confidence one might expect from a future patriarch, but with a touching wistfulness. His voice is informal but also vulnerable, made even more so by the minimal accompaniment; the song sounds less polished and thereby more intimate than typical recordings of its time. Austin sings the lyrics as written but also murmurs to himself throughout, making the song seem even more deeply private than in other singers' deliveries. As in "Yearning," he ends the song on an ascending rather than a descending note, again employing the "feminine ending" that makes the attainability of domestic bliss an open question. But as personal and individual as Austin's interpretation is, it remains true to its Tin Pan Alley structure so listeners can also sing along. The recording perfects the broadly accessible, democratic pathos that came to conflate pop songs with crooning songs.

Austin's combination of modern technology, accessibility, sincere tone, and broadly appealing simple sentiments (what would later be called "folksy" charm) foreshadows a part of the formula that would prove to be so potent for Bing Crosby and many other musical film stars. In fact crooning singers were key figures from the earliest sound film shorts of 1926–27, and film producers soon began integrating crooning songs into feature film narratives as theme and character songs, most notably in Jolson's 1928 smash hit *The Singing Fool*.

CROONING ON CELLULOID: VITAPHONE AND MOVIETONE SHORTS

Hollywood films would be the biggest popularizer of songs and male singing stars from the 1930s until the advent of rock 'n' roll in the 1950s, but in the mid- to late 1920s sound film was a novelty without established standards for filming singers. Warner Bros.' Vitaphone sound-on-disc and Fox's Movietone sound-on-film systems, the primary short film producers, both made film shorts of musical and spoken performances to demonstrate their synchronized sound systems and to get a sense of which kinds of acts would go over best with audiences. Vitaphone's shorts exposed thousands of Americans to top classical and popular musical acts before the breakthrough sound film *The Jazz Singer* debuted in 1927.[63] While this period of experimentation helped popularize crooning singers and confirmed that crooning could transfer very successfully to film, these early shorts—like early microphone recordings—also demonstrated the diversity of popular singing at the time. Crooning was only one kind of novelty vocal style among many and was not yet exclusively associated with one particular type of singer or genre. When examined in conjunction with Jolson's *The Jazz Singer* and *The Singing Fool* (1928), these shorts provide further evidence that larger aesthetic shifts were taking place that laid the groundwork for crooning to emerge as the dominant male singing style of the 1930s and 1940s.

Vitaphone was by far the most prolific and successful producer of short films, debuting their first group in August 1926; Movietone followed in February 1927. These original "packages" of short films resembled vaudeville or revue bills; they contained four or five acts that were six to ten minutes long and were paired with feature-length films from the same company, sometimes replacing the live performers who usually accompanied a silent feature film. Warner Bros. cleverly targeted midrange theaters that would have enough money to wire their theaters for sound but could not afford the big price tags that came with live star presentations and orchestras. This strategy was very effective, and the shorts were extremely popular with primarily middle-class, urban, white audiences.

Vitaphone's first shorts favored classical over popular singers because film producers initially sought to provide "culture" to the masses, but audiences proved far more responsive to popular performers—so much so that popular acts soon outnumbered classical ones by a ratio of eight to one.[64] Only a fraction of these films still exist, but those available reflect the tremendous diversity of 1920s vocal performance, further confirmed by Vitaphone's program logs.[65] Singing acts (at times in combination with playing an instrument or dancing) typically dominated in musical shorts. Men outnumbered women, which reflected conditions in the performance world and the fact that men's voices initially reproduced better than women's. A typical Vitaphone musical bill offered an opera star like Giovanni Martinelli, a sweet orchestra like Vincent Lopez's band or Fred Waring's Pennsylvanians (both featuring crooning singers), solo "novelty" singers like the early crooners Johnny Marvin or Jack Smith, and singing male and female impersonators like Karyl Norman and Kitty Doner.

Although crooning was becoming increasingly associated with young white men, Vitaphone program logs reaffirm that it was still not considered specific to class, race, gender, or genre. The bandleader Ben Pollack and singers Nick Lucas and Ruth Etting are all identified as "crooning" or "crooners" in these logs as late as 1929. The first appearance of the word *croon* actually refers to the singing-violin duo Wade Watts and Bobby Gilbert in August 1927, where Watts is described as a "blues singer" who "croons the blues." The pair seem to belong to the emerging country blues style since they play "Turkey in the Straw" but are not in minstrel blackface. (They also have a "draped set" rather than the "plantation set" that minstrel acts commonly used.) In these shorts, as in Gene Austin's records, neither *blues* nor *croon* is made to be race- or gender-specific: *blues crooning* and *crooning blues* are used to describe male and female, white and nonwhite singers well into 1929.

In addition to Watts and Gilbert, the logs also associate the male quartet the Croonaders (Cy Kahn, Al Garry, H. R. Cohen, and Marcy Klauber) with the crooning sound; their two shorts performances on a "parlor set" indicate their upscale appeal: "'Crooning Along' describes the lilting songs which these four boys sing and play. They have been featured artists in the New York nightclubs and now headliners on the variety circuits."[66] The Croonaders and similar quartets of handsome young men fit the jazz band singers' profile that would come to define romantic crooners as a group—soft, pop sound and "spiffy," youthful male appearance—but their songs reflected this transitional period in mixing love songs ("I Want Your Love," "What Is It Like to Be Loved?") with syncopated hits in the plantation vein (including the dialect-tinged "Mississippi Mud," the first big hit for Paul Whiteman's Rhythm Boys featuring Bing Crosby, and "The Twelfth Street Rag").

Vitaphone also filmed a number of crooning solo singers, including Tom Waring, Johnny Marvin, and Jack Smith. Released in 1927, Smith's appearance on film was probably the first time many audiences *saw* a crooner perform. *Variety*'s review of Smith suggests how well the intimate singing aesthetic translated onto celluloid: "Jack Smith was the wow of the bill. He oozes personality, and once accustomed to his soft-voiced delivery, there can't be too much." In its review *Variety* compared Smith favorably with Giovanni Martinelli: "The trouble with these opera singers is that they seldom have the figure to go with their characterization, with the movie camera emphasizing this comic note more than in opera itself. Martinelli is of the nice looking banker type, but not as much as the gay cavalier of hot romance."[67] The crooner's ability to sell the song's romantic sentiments was enabled not only by his good looks and lack of training (which made him seem more natural and "in character") but also by the fact that his condenser microphone remained out of view, thus naturalizing the close sound of his voice. *Variety*'s enthusiastic review was also prophetic, as Smith's delivery style would come to dominate the narrative, character-driven Hollywood films of the 1930s and beyond.

Movietone shorts of early crooning singers, which were made between 1927 and 1930 as five different revue packages, also highlight how early crooning singers were better suited to developing sound film aesthetics than were vaudeville-driven popular singers.[68] Although early shorts were filmed to replicate the proscenium stage, on film these sets signify differently than they do for a live public. The shorts are framed and structured so that the vocalist is centered within the frame, often as close to the camera as possible, creating a more personal relationship with the audience.[69] Filmmakers soon began to incorporate editing and multiple cameras that allowed for different angles and, more important, close-ups of performers. Because neither microphones nor cameras could be moved, performers had very limited space in which to work, which favored modern amplified singers over peppy vaudevillians, particularly in making a connection with the audience. This is particularly obvious, for example, in the vaudeville song-and-dance performance of Fuzzy Knight ("Fuzzy Knight and His Little Piano"), who had a hard time keeping his body within the frame because his routine had been developed for a large stage. His personality, meant to carry to the rafters of the theater, seems oversized for the camera.

Johnny Marvin, Jack Pepper, the confidential singer Lee Beers, and Tom Waring all made popular Movietone shorts where they presented songs in the natural-voiced microphone crooning style that was popular in the mid- to late 1920s, yet they were all operating along somewhat different aesthetic lines. Pepper and Marvin use some direct address in their speech and songs, but their vaudeville style distances them from the audience, while Beers and Waring pair intimate performing styles with indirect address. The combination of a soft, intimate performance with consistent direct address, which would be so much a part of Rudy Vallée's radio success, is not yet represented in these shorts. For instance, although Marvin sounds so sincere in his recordings, he comes across as an extroverted vaudeville performer in his short film appearances in *A Movietone Divertissement* (1928; fig. 2.5) and *Metro Movietone Revue II* (1929). He smiles broadly through each number, his strumming unaffected by narrative content, even when he sings a painful love song in direct address: "My heart is breaking—what do you care if it's breaking—if you don't love me?" Similarly, as master of ceremonies of *Metro Movietone Revue I* (1930; fig. 2.6), the youthful Jack Pepper uses direct address to engage the film audience, but, like Marvin, he performs in more of a presentational style. In a remarkable rendition of "St. Louis Blues," Pepper combines crooning with a double-voiced performance (both tenor and falsetto) that replicates and celebrates the style of black female blues performers, specifically Bessie Smith, but he doesn't make the song his own. In contrast, as a confidential singer, Beers offers a more intimate style, playing piano and conspiratorially leaning over to confide his semiscandalous tales of a gold-digging girl to the audience, yet he narrates entirely in the third person. He offers personal address without personal revelation and presents the gold digger as the heroine. The reversed sexual politics here, as in Smith's more sophisticated songs, is what is truly scandalous and needs to be whispered, not Beers's intense feelings.

FIG. 2.5. Johnny Marvin, a popular early crooner, playing the saw, in *A Movietone Divertissement* (MGM, 1928). Marvin's vaudeville style is most obvious in these short films, in which he happily strums, sings, and shows his varied skills by incorporating novelties such as saw playing; one can imagine this particular performance being quite suggestive had Marvin been either more winking or more emotionally expressive, but his image remained culturally unthreatening in part because he never shifted from a genial presentational style. Note his severe black formal wear and slicked-back hair; a dark suit or tuxedo was the common costume for a male vaudevillian or nightclub performer of the era but one that was beginning to give way by this time to the lighter, softer, more collegiate style.

FIG. 2.6. Jack Pepper singing with his ukulele, in *Metro Movietone Revue* (MGM, 1930). Here the playful young performer acts as emcee and performs with his ukulele, the iconic instrument of the 1920s because it was inexpensive and easy to learn. Although his theatrical, quite remarkable double-voice performance (tenor and falsetto) of "St. Louis Blues" in this short marks him as a vaudevillian, Pepper's casual jacket, tie, and striped trousers also reflect aspects of the more informal, collegiate style of dress most popular among young people.

FIG. 2.7. Tom Waring, in *A Movietone Divertissement* (MGM, 1928). This still
from Tom Waring's crooning performance of "My Mother, My Sweetheart,
and I" in the short revue film is reflective of his position as the lead soloist in
his brother Fred's collegiate "entertaining band," the Pennsylvanians. Waring
prefigures the Vallée romantic crooner image and attracted a strong following
of flappers. He is youthful and handsome, sports the soft style of the collegian
(casual, light-colored jacket and wide-legged trousers), and is turned toward
the audience, warmly smiling as he performs his crooning love songs. Courtesy
of the Academy of Motion Picture Arts and Sciences.

Of this lot, Tom Waring comes closest to the romantic crooner style, befit-
ting the key soloist of the popular vocal jazz band Waring's Pennsylvanians.
A young, attractive, soft-voiced piano man with thick dark hair, Waring looks
and sounds the part of a sensitive young man, and it is not hard to see why
flapper fans waited at the stage door for him. Waring clearly courted collegiate youth in his songs. In *A Movietone Divertissement* (1928; fig. 2.7), he
gently sings a song called "My Mother, My Sweetheart, and I," about a man
who lives happily with his wife and his mother. While Waring sets up the
story in an introductory narrative, he sings the rest of the song in first-person
confessional tones, softly expressing the joy of being surrounded by both
women, the two loves of his life. He ends the song with what would become
the signature crooner style: on a very high ascending note, representing both
his vulnerability and his intense feeling.

CROONING IN CHARACTER:
AL JOLSON IN *THE SINGING FOOL* (1928)

Song performances and film narratives most successfully converged at the time in Al Jolson's two feature films: *The Jazz Singer* and the even more phenomenally popular *The Singing Fool*. Film historians have argued that *The Singing Fool* really won the public over to sound film in a way that no previous film had, and indeed it was among the top-grossing Hollywood films of its time.[70] Although viewers today find the film maudlin and almost unbearable, at the time critics and the public alike celebrated its superior sound quality, the greater ratio of sound to silent scenes, and Jolson's improved singing and acting. In *The Singing Fool*, Jolson struggled against his vaudeville performance aesthetic, reining in his ego to play a vulnerable sap who croons love songs to his girlfriend and his son. His intense love for and eventual loss of his child forms the emotional core of the film and is the subject of most of its songs.

Jolson's variation in acting styles reflected the contrasting narrative content of these two films. The core of *The Jazz Singer* is about tortured assimilation and filial love, whereas *The Singing Fool* is a modern story about the war between the sexes. The film begins in a speakeasy instead of the Old World home of *The Jazz Singer*, and the camera lingers on the various staff and clients of this illegal business, underlining the timeliness of the story. Jolson, a singing waiter and songwriter, loves and marries one of the speakeasy's gold-digging performers, Molly, who bears his son but is indifferent to both of them. He turns to the son for love instead and is devastated twice: first when Molly divorces him and takes the child away, and later when the child dies. The film ends with Jolson's public performance of "Sonny Boy," his first and only blackface appearance in the film, where he envisions his dead child and weeps onstage.

The film is an amalgam of old and new performance aesthetics, which are most evident in the shifts in Jolson's performance style. Jolson addresses his first song in the film, the crooning pop hit of the day, "It All Depends on You," to Molly. The song is the opposite of the kind of vaudeville belting number Jolson was previously known for, and the film underlines this by having Jolson's character argue with his piano accompanist, who predicts that he will not be able to sing a "sob song." Here the two aesthetics struggle against each other: Jolson is trying to sing in the new sincere, conversational way, which read as more genuine and "in character" to film audiences of the time, but the showman in Jolson cannot refrain from overplaying the song with big

gestures and mugging. Jolson is much more convincing as a loving and griev-
ing father. He sings two songs to the child while kissing him and cradling
him in his arms. The song "Sonny Boy" became a huge hit, and Jolson's character pours all of his emotion and displaced romantic feeling into his affection
for his child. Moreover, the relative lack of blackface in the film allows Jolson
to really emerge as a *character* more than he did in *The Jazz Singer*, a change
that permitted audiences to identify with his grief more directly. While the
intense physicality of his mourning (numbness, excessive weeping, difficulty
walking) can seem excessive to audiences today, it would have seemed very
appropriate to audiences accustomed to silent film acting.

The Singing Fool offered a model for mitigating the emasculating threat of
crooning's emotional intimacy by pairing it with paternalism, a strategy that
Jolson's great admirer, Bing Crosby, would later employ with great success
in his films. Jolson's vulnerability as a father rather than as a lover permitted
him to embody the new sincere, intimate crooning performance aesthetic
without having to endorse sexual equality or compromise his masculine authority. Patriarchy and paternity rule in *The Singing Fool* as a female caregiver
is replaced with a male caregiver; the mother love that permeated *The Jazz
Singer* is nowhere to be found in this follow-up. Jolson replicates the crooner's intimate aesthetic and loving songs but narcissistically redirects them,
as a minstrel man would, at the white male child with whom he identifies
(and can control).

Despite its success, Jolson's *The Singing Fool* was a singular event fortifying
sound films but had little immediate impact on the crooner's image. The
popularity of crooning's intimate singing style among radio, record, and film
audiences reverberated beyond the mass media in the 1920s and reshaped
New York City's live performance spaces as well—its cabarets, speakeasies,
nightclubs, and live motion picture house presentations. Audience behavior in
these spaces changed in relationship to crooning singers' new aesthetics, altering reception practices on a mass scale. The great demand for crooners in live
public venues proved the growing commercial power of the crooning sound
and its audience and provoked a new set of industrial and social tensions.

"WHISPER-LOW NIGHTLIFE":
THE CABARET CONFIDER

The cabaret scene of the time was a natural home for the new personal singing aesthetic, as *Variety* noted in the emergence of the "confidential tenor"

FIG. 2.8. Al Jolson and his Sonny boy (played by Davey Lee), in *The Singing Fool*, 1928. In the film, Jolson replaces the loving mother of *The Jazz Singer* with his devoted pappy, reflecting the modern turn against the maternal. Davey Lee's brown bob mirrors that of Jolson's brunette flapper love-interest in the film, but Jolson's relationship with his son is far more emotionally intense than his romantic one. Author's collection.

FIG. 2.9. Although Al Jolson sang emotionally excessive, sentimental "mammy" songs, he delivered them in an aggressively theatrical vaudeville style. This 1916 sheet music cover suggests the threat of the feminine to Jolson's hypermasculine style (represented by his cigarette, slicked "hard" hair, swaggering stance, and stern, challenging expression), which was indicative of both Jolson's particular star persona and the vaudeville performer's mandatory thick skin. Jolson's vaudeville star image would provide quite a contrast with that of the sensitive, feminine-friendly male singing stars of the late 1920s. Sheet music, Al Jolson, "You're a Dangerous Girl," 1916. Author's collection.

in early 1925. In his analysis of New York cabarets of the period, Shane Vogel argues that they offered new kinds of performance intimacies: "The shared focus of nightlife performance produces the cabaret as a space not only of physical intimacy—a matter of social availability, spatial arrangements, and bodily proximities—but also of psychic intimacy—produced by and producing a structure of experience and affective connections between those gathered."[71] Because cabaret performers regularly "worked the room," they achieved a greater connection with audience members than did other performers, a connection that was affirmed by tips.

In the cabarets and dance halls of the 1910s, women had paid male dancers to awaken their sensuality through close couples dancing to tangos and jazz; such men—the young Valentino being the most famous—became popularly (and in some circles infamously) known as "tango pirates."[72] A decade later confidential singers offered a vocal counterpart, the erotic thrill of having a handsome young man murmur a love song personally to them. Confidential singers' ability to blur the lines between public and private, the performative and the personal, reflects the greater flexibility of sexual and gender boundaries within the space of the cabaret. Indeed confiders were regularly employed in the queer-friendly cabarets and speakeasies of Times Square, Greenwich Village, and Harlem, where intimate contact and sexual expression were given broad license. Cabaret reviews of 1925 and 1926 are peppered with references to nude dancing, risqué lyrics, open prostitution by both sexes, male objectification (especially of "it" college boys), fairy and pansy performances, cross-dressing, same-sex couples dancing, and same-sex serenading.[73]

The most celebrated confiders were Chick Endor and Tommy Lyman. Endor was the leader of the Yacht Club Boys, a quartet of singer-musicians whose youth and beauty represented a distinct departure from the usual vaudeville quartet or seasoned saloon singer. Endor's approach to performing was also unusually personal and informal for a singer in an elite, uptown club; he sang directly to patrons at their tables, "crooning sentimental and comedy ditties in turn" while engaging in light, flirtatious banter with them. Singing directly to patrons at their tables for tips was more characteristic of lower-class saloon entertainment of the time, so much so that in October 1925 *Variety* identified Endor's intimate style as "new genius of some sort" and his Yacht Club as an example of a trend toward smaller clubs.[74] By the end of December 1926 Endor was the highest-paid nightclub act in town and had begun recording as a soloist; his plaintive, high-pitched recordings resemble those of other crooning singers like Gene Austin, and his youth and attractiveness were much touted by the press.[75]

Likewise, "sweet-singing tenor" Tommy Lyman flirted with the debutantes and flappers who adored him and his self-styled "torch" singing, but Lyman was an older, more seasoned performer than Endor, and, as a Jewish performer originally from Hester Street, he was more culturally associated with downtown rather than uptown audiences. He began as a provocative table singer at Jimmy Kelly's, a black-and-tan saloon on the Lower East Side, and moved up as the demand for confidential singers grew in cabarets that served the middle and upper classes. Lyman's delivery of songs of unrequited love were particularly distinctive, both for his emotional intensity (he could make murderers weep with his soulful "bullet," *Variety* remarked) and because he favored either numbers that already had sexually explicit lyrics, like "Frankie and Johnny," or those he could easily spice up, most often mainstream pop hits like "My Blue Heaven."[76] In 1925 Lyman emerged as a local star, appearing on radio, cutting his first solo recording with Victor, and performing nightly as the major attraction of the trendy Salon Royal in the Acropolis Hotel, a haunt of the famous cabaret personality Texas Guinan. *Variety's* writers attempted to describe Lyman's particular charms in this review from 1927:

> Lyman coos and croons ballads and sentimental ditties in between dance sessions. He handles the average pop song in a manner all his own. He turns and twists lyric phrases to suit his own individual fancy and the treatment more than passively enhances the rendition. The room is just right for the attraction. It is cozy, intimate, atmospheric. Judicious lighting effects further help matters. The SR [Salon Royal] isn't just the place for a stooge. Boisterousness is not countenanced by the others who elect to remain quiet for Lyman's warbling, and they seem to be in the majority. There is something arresting and compelling in Lyman's voice. Somehow or other, no matter one's condition, one really likes to absorb as much of the Lyman technique and lyrics as possible.[77]

In his performances at the Royal, Lyman combined qualities of the new intimate singing aesthetic—a soft crooning voice, close-up sound, and popular love songs—with the artistic license of cabaret culture to create his own confidential style. His audience privileged listening to his vocals over dancing, and their pleasure in him and in each other derived from their mutual absorption of the song's narrative and in its singer. In effect they were reproducing the behavior of rapt 1920s film and radio audiences, where a hushed attention was helpful in establishing shared intimacy, promoting identification, and enabling emotional involvement with the narrative. Cabaret confidential tenors like Lyman and Endor embodied and performed the collapse of psychic distance that was already taking place on a mass scale with the microphone and the film close-up.

Although *Variety's* writers routinely dismissed radio's impact during these early years, many of the new cabaret confiders that emerged in 1925 had already enjoyed lucrative careers as song pluggers over the radio and were adapting what they learned about microphone singing for live venues. In fact many of the early crooning singers discussed in the previous section—including Smith, Gillham, Marvin, and Austin—performed as crooning confiders in the cabarets of the mid-1920s, easily crossing between the live and the mediated performance worlds. Likewise, the cabaret stars Lyman and Endor also made records and appeared on radio; in fact Lyman was one of the first singers in the recording industry to be described as "crooning," in July 1925, and his performances at the Royal were often broadcast by radio hookup on local New York stations.[78]

Industrial and technological changes were not the only factor in the sudden surge in popularity for confidential singers; social conditions also greatly shaped the sudden currency of the intimate aesthetic. There was also a practical component to employing soft singers during Prohibition. As historians have noted, Prohibition resulted in the "criminalization of nightlife" for everyone who wanted to drink liquor, regardless of class, race, or gender. Many middle-class drinkers therefore began to think of themselves as social rebels, and many enjoyed the opportunities these cabarets and speakeasies permitted for crossing gender, ethnic, race, and class lines.[79] Still, one had to be discreet, and confidential tenors provided a type of commercial performance that could be quiet and elude police notice, which was a far cry from the attention-getting antics of vaudeville shouters and jazz bands. Cabarets and speakeasies were particularly at risk for raids because of their location near residences; speakeasies were often furtively located in the basements of brownstone apartment buildings. Indeed the demand for such "soft warblers" was "especially urgent," noted *Variety*, because tenants were complaining about cabaret noise.[80]

In 1926 New York City passed new regulations governing nightlife entertainment, generally known as the "cabaret laws," which intensified the need for low-pitched, discreet entertainment and initiated the era of what *Variety* dubbed "whisper low nightlife."[81] The cabaret laws required that any establishment offering music and dancing with food or drinks must be licensed by the city, subject to inspections, and adhere to a 3 a.m. curfew; these ordinances largely affected the activities of lower-end establishments, since nightclubs attached to bigger hotels were exempt. Although the cabaret laws were irregularly enforced, they still caused more of the smaller cabarets to close and shifted their patrons to "speakeasies or dives" in apartment houses.[82] While the cabaret laws actually increased the public celebrity of some confidentials like Lyman and Endor, who worked in curfew-free nightclubs and hotel salons, the laws meant that most confiders would remain nameless, unreviewed, and lost to history, even as the crooning sound proliferated in both illegitimate and legitimate venues.

While their increasing popularity gave them money and local fame, confidential singers still met with resistance when they ventured into more elite and conservative clubs. Although some high-class patrons enjoyed risqué material and provocative performance styles when they visited cabarets and speakeasies, many objected to these same elements when found in the finer hotels. Lyman's career is a case in point. The trade papers expressed surprise when the daughter of the owner of the elite Hotel Ambassador persuaded her father to hire Lyman: "Booking Tommy Lyman, a frank 'table singer,' into the conservative Hotel Ambassador, NY, was a somewhat radical move, but the high-hat bunches' requests for 'blue song' material surprised even the hardened Lyman." The battle lines were clearly drawn along a gendered and generational divide, as the daughter's favor was not enough to keep Lyman at the Ambassador and he soon decamped back to the Royal.[83] *Variety*'s use of the term *table singer* here indicates continuing suspicion about the cultural status of these workers, men who weren't musicians first and, in the eyes of the upper classes, feminized themselves by relying on women for tips. (The term *lounge lizard* would soon be invented for them.) While Lyman had the good fortune to be able to return to his cabaret life (at least for a while), the cultural prejudices against crooning singers were more deeply felt by jazz band singers who depended on elite nightclubs.

JAZZ BANDS AND THE INVENTION OF THE BAND LEAD SINGER

Nowhere were crooners more integral to the success of a live performance assemblage than in the jazz band, where they originated the role of the band lead singer. While radio broadcasters and recording artists first gave the crooner a voice, jazz band singers were first called "crooners" as a group, and they first associated the crooning microphone sound with young, handsome, visible white male bodies of an increasingly collegiate type. The addition of vocalists represented a fundamental change in the public understanding of the jazz band. Previously, in the 1910s and early 1920s, vocalists had been considered incidental to a jazz band's commercial and critical success, especially in live performances. But the popularity of crooning records made band crooners commercially necessary by the mid- to late 1920s, especially for bands that aspired to mass appeal and national stardom. Crooning band singers quickly became so popular that they supplanted the bands' celebrated musicians as the star attractions and, increasingly, even the bandleaders themselves.

Before the mid-1920s bands developed their names exclusively through their music and star musicians, not through their singers. But some bandleaders, led by Paul Whiteman (whose motto was "Give the public what it wants"), began to include "vocal choruses" on their recordings in the mid-1920s.[84] In the fall of 1925 *Variety* first noted that band records with "vocal interludes" began to noticeably outsell records without them.[85] Not coincidentally, that fall also saw the first major wave of electrical recordings, which gave increased clarity to voices and lyrics. Public demand for what *Variety* termed "a vocal explanation of the number" quickly resulted in vocals becoming commonplace on band recordings, and bands began hiring singers. Many band participants resisted the inclusion of vocalists on recordings, however, and even more in live performance. As a result many of these "vocal interlude" record singers were initially not promoted as names in themselves by the bands or the record labels, often remaining uncredited on the discs.

Vocalists also threatened to undo racialized and classed distinctions between jazz acts. At the time there were two types of bands: "sweet" or "cultured" bands, coded white, whose mellow, symphonic music and professional musicians set them in opposition to "hot" or "instinctive" bands, coded black, that specialized in a more improvisational, informal style of playing.[86] The development and promotion of sweet jazz as a musical and cultural form, led by the aptly named Whiteman, corresponded with the country and the industry's assimilationism. Jazz music's association with African Americans and their perceived sexual licentiousness made the genre controversial for airplay, recording (beyond "race records"), and respectable dance venues, although jazz remained extremely popular with youth. White bandleaders and their promoters tried to distance sweet music from blackness by emphasizing the professionalism of white musicians—their work ethic, technical training, discipline, tidy appearance, and productivity—as opposed to black musicians' "instinctive" playing, disorderly appearance, and lack of affective control.[87] The opinion of Roger Wolfe Kahn, another young white bandleader of the time, is representative of the general view: "There are glaring faults, musically, in most of jazz, and these faults must be eradicated. . . . [White bands] will develop a distant and higher type of music."[88] Although white bands depended, in part, on the mass appeal of crooning singers to ensure their commercial success and national fame, crooners undermined these aspirations of cultural uplift because of their lack of musical training and discipline, song-plugging roots, sex appeal, and blatant catering to lowbrow feminine tastes.

Because of these concerns, bandleaders were initially reluctant to hire singers at all; they tried to sing the vocals themselves or have some of their instrumentalists double as singers, often in trios, a move that saved money and preserved the musical credentials of the singer and the bands.[89] Other bands appear to have employed short-term contract singers, paying them significantly less than full-time band members.[90] Paul Whiteman's celebrity and financial success allowed him to be the first bandleader to take risks, and he began the practice of hiring vocalists, including the vaudeville and picture house singing team of Bing Crosby and Al Rinker in 1926. Even Whiteman was initially cautious in his use of the crooning singer. In his autobiography, *Call Me Lucky*, Crosby notes that he did not get a solo with the band for months, and Whiteman tried to disguise the fact that he and Rinker were only singers by having them hold instruments with rubber strings "so the audience wouldn't wonder why we were doing nothing" (a practice that soon became common).[91]

The mid- to late 1920s thus became the era of "novelty" or "entertaining" jazz bands, which distinguished themselves from so-called "straight" bands not through music (since they generally provided only variations on the same hit songs) but through star bandleader personalities, excessive sartorial and production styles (thematic costumes for band members), celebrity guest players, performance novelty (instrumental sound effects, such as laughing trombones), and attractive young crooning singers. Whiteman was the first bandleader to develop what *Variety* described as a "miniature road show," with himself as the chief impresario, showman, and ringleader of a conglomeration that included "ardent steppers, songsters, comedians, staff production and scenic men, and others."[92] His fellow celebrity bandleaders followed his lead, most notably Ben Bernie, Paul Ash, Roger Wolfe Kahn, George Olsen, Vincent Lopez, Sam Lanin, and Fred Waring, each of whom developed his own distinctive style and attractions.

In 1927 *Variety* identified a "jazz band craze" of which crooners were an integral component, supported in great part by a new and powerful demographic: collegians.[93] Though jazz crossed sex, class, and racial lines in its appeal, its most influential proponents were white, middle-class collegians, the first generation of American youth whose money and tastes came to dominate and dictate the popular culture of their time. Collegians both performed and consumed jazz: hundreds of jazz bands formed on campuses and toured locally and nationally, producing thousands of jazz-influenced instrumentalists. Collegians became a huge and essential market for record producers; young people used their disposable income to snap up new jazz and blues records, and they danced to jazz music on the radio and in public dance halls and nightclubs. Since what many collegians loved most was jazz dancing, it was not surprising that crooning and jazz would combine in order to serve the collegiate market.[94] Band crooners served their collegiate audiences by singing the same songs as Austin, Lucas, and Marvin but punched them up, singing at a faster pace in order to make them suitable for jazz dancing. Popular 1920s band favorites like "You're the Cream in My Coffee" and "Button Up Your Overcoat" were peppier songs than most crooning record solos, although slow performances of ballads became increasingly common for the new crooner-facilitated slow couples dancing.[95]

Collegiate crooners abounded during these years; college crooning groups toured vaudeville and motion picture houses, and collegiate "types" (typically, young male performers wearing sweater vests) were heavily featured in cabaret and vaudeville performances. Collegians were recognizable primarily by their youth, clean-cut appearance, and clothing: the collegiate "casual," boyish look included sweater vests or slim-cut suits (instead of the usual vaudeville suit or tux), tight jackets, patterned clothes or bright colors, baggy trousers with front creases ("Oxford bags"), and two-toned shoes; in winter, it might include a raccoon coat. The most famous singing band of the period, Fred Waring's Pennsylvanians, helped popularize the collegiate look and fueled the demand for collegiate bands that would soon launch Rudy Vallée to fame. By the late 1920s many of the most popular band crooners were themselves college graduates or collegians working part time. These highly educated enunciators were well suited to microphone requirements for vocal clarity, and they took to radio and recording easily.

The electrified "radio sound" that media audiences loved was increasingly replicated throughout public spaces in the 1920s with the installation of public address systems; hotel ballrooms and nightclubs were some of the first public venues to take advantage of radio broadcast technology, combining loudspeakers with transmission technology so that jazz bands could perform simultaneously for radio audiences and those present.[96] Although megaphones were widely used to amplify crooners' voices in some of these venues (and some were electrified), they hid the singer's face. The advent of microphones allowed the men to be seen more easily and proved especially popular because so many boyish vocalists were attractive. Some began presenting themselves directly to young women as objects of desire, often wooing them openly from the bandstands. Critical reviews of these singers regularly remarked on their attractiveness as part of their evaluation of the band's overall success, and sheet music covers began to supplant photos of celebrity bandleaders with these young men to further entice female consumers.[97]

The growing visibility of band crooners also caused them to become targets of hostility, since they were the most visible sign of sweet jazz's lowbrow compromises and perceived feminine pandering. Because all sweet band crooners were white, the objections to them were framed in terms of gender or class rather than race, the primary source of anxiety surrounding jazz music generally. Band crooners, like confidential singers, were popular in middle- and working-class contexts, but such performers often faced ridicule for their perceived emasculation in posh venues. Both Gene Austin and Bing Crosby recount instances when they were ridiculed for effeminacy by elite male audience members during nightclub performances and ended up defending themselves with their fists in back alleys after the shows.[98]

Unfortunately a crooner could not generally rely on fellow band members to come to his defense in such matters, since they were also often antagonistic to his presence. Al Bowlly, England's most popular band crooner and a favorite in the United States as well, was considered a "cissy" by band members in his early career because of his falsetto tenor voice and his "gentle murmurings."[99] His biographers recount that even when Bowlly's crooning became a hit with audiences at the London Savoy Hotel, the members of the backing band were still hostile to him, a pattern the writers assert was typical of the time: "Jazz musicians have always been notoriously indifferent to the singers in their midst. . . . The customers liked him, however, especially the ladies, who responded to his dazzling smile and sweetly romantic crooning."[100]

In retrospect the rise of band crooners inaugurated a particular set of tensions surrounding gender, sex, class, and mass culture that would come to a boil during the early 1930s, but they did nothing to stop crooning singers' ascent in the popular culture of the late 1920s. Crooning singers found a particularly welcoming home in motion picture theaters, whose audiences were happy to adore them on both stage and screen.

THE ASCENDANCE OF THE PICTURE HOUSE CROONER

Before crooners ever sang on movie screens, they were already making a killing performing in movie theaters. The great picture palaces built to attract the middle classes in the 1910s and 1920s, known as "motion picture houses" in the trade papers, were musical meccas. In addition to the organist or orchestra that provided preshow entertainment and musical accompaniment for the feature film, exhibitors offered a variety of other acts before the film, the majority of which were musical, most involving singers. By 1925 the bigger urban theaters were employing regular live performances, known as "presentations" or "prologues," to accompany film showings; among these acts were headliners lured from vaudeville and name acts from radio and records, who would travel west along the theater circuit like vaudevillians.[101]

Picture houses quickly usurped vaudeville in both popularity and cultural impact. In 1926 *Variety* estimated that 97 percent of the country's theaters were picture houses, attracting 60–65 percent of citizens as regular attendees, compared with vaudeville's 10 percent.[102] Picture house audiences loved early crooning, and their demand helped guarantee the shift in live entertainment's aesthetics generally from theatricality to naturalism, from public to personal address, and from visible audience activity to audience absorption. Early crooning singers like Edwards, Lucas, and Smith were presentation headliners who often proved to be a more popular draw than the movies themselves. The grand cinemas, especially those in major metropolitan areas, boasted much better architectural acoustics than were available in vaudeville houses.[103] *Variety* remarked that picture house acoustics were "perfect for lyrics," and singers' soft crooning voices could be clearly heard throughout the theaters.[104] Their instruments—banjos, ukuleles, guitars, and pianos—also sounded rich and full instead of being swallowed by a vaudeville theater, since the picture house space was designed specifically to help amplify musical accompaniment.[105]

But the match between motion picture houses and crooning singers was not just acoustic. Crooning singers' soft, personal, and interior style, fashioned for the microphone, drew on the same kind of audience engagement as film narratives did; both depended in part on an audience's absorption in a

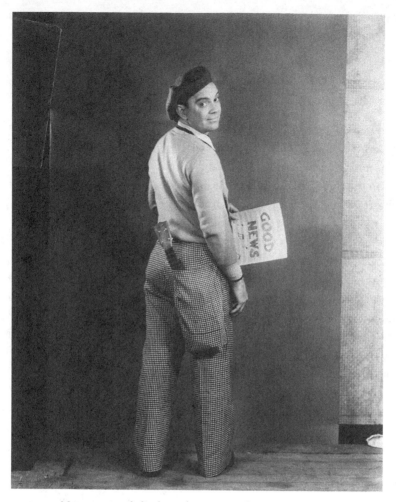

FIG. 2.10. Many crooners helped popularize stringed instruments of the time. Nick Lucas drove guitar sales, and Gibson designed a popular guitar brand in his name. Cliff Edwards, pictured in this still from the collegiate musical *Good News* (1930), became so well known for his ukulele playing that he was considered the primary popularizer of the instrument, which was ubiquitous in the 1920s and early 1930s but would come to be seen as emasculating because of its small size and association with high-pitched crooners. Here Edwards sports a special large back trouser pocket to fit his uke. He is dressed in the collegiate attire of the time and was still a hugely popular performer with the collegiate crowd for his scatting and crooning, although he was thirty-five when he made the film. Courtesy of the Academy of Motion Picture Arts and Sciences.

particular story or an emotional attachment to a personality. The hardworking, high-energy hard sell of the vaudeville veteran was too aggressive for picture house audiences and did not fit their aesthetic or affective expectations. In the mid-1920s *Variety* reported on crooners such as Edwards and Smith who successfully departed from vaudeville performance styles with crooning styles that reflected cinematic aesthetics.[106] Smith in particular was celebrated for his slow emotional build, which offered a better prologue to the pacing and immersive qualities of feature film narratives: "His unassuming and undisturbed method of vocalizing impresses the more he lingers. Smith is not a flash personality. He's got to stay for full results and that they're ready to listen by the end of the second song paves the way for him."[107]

In addition, the largely romantic content of crooning songs echoed (and often was specifically tailored to) the predominantly romantic film narratives, which also suited picture house audiences, especially when attractive young men sang them. The audiences identified with the loving sentiments of crooning singers the same way they identified with the characters on the screen, and they followed the crooning lyrics as they did the film's narrative. For that reason motion picture audiences particularly valued lyrical clarity and good enunciation skills. As *Variety* noted, "The majority of these audiences want to know what a singer is singing about."[108] At times the connection between screen and live performer was made explicit; crooning singers would incorporate songs mentioned or performed in the film and would integrate snippets of its musical score or narrative into their set.

Youthful male crooners were especially warmly received, a fact that was well known in the industry and led *Variety*'s vaudeville reviewers to recommend that all the attractive ("well-groomed," "clean-cut," "best-looking") new young male singers, especially those with good diction, head for the picture houses.[109] The apotheosis of the new performance aesthetic in picture houses was Waring's Pennsylvanians, a novelty collegiate jazz band in the "entertainment" vein that rocketed to stardom mid-decade by strategically targeting motion picture houses.[110] The band's leader, Fred Waring, defied the usual jazz band hierarchies by privileging vocals, pleasing personalities, and showmanship over instrumental prowess; he encouraged his singers to think of their voices as their instruments and specialized in developing the close harmonies, perfect diction, and strong choral arrangements that electrical recording captured with great clarity. He also incorporated a good deal of fun, inventiveness, and good cheer into his shows; band members, for example, used their instruments to mimic the human voice in comic ways,

FIG. 2.11. Waring's Pennsylvanians, in collegiate attire with megaphones. Publicity still from *Syncopation* (RKO, 1929). The Pennsylvanians dress in typical casual, youthful collegiate attire of the 1920s: soft sweaters rather than jackets, light colors, wide-legged trousers with front creases, two-toned shoes, and, of course, megaphones. They invite touch. Reprinted by permission of Fred Waring's America, Penn State University Libraries.

such as laughing trumpets or "trick mutes." Waring looked for attributes other than talent when hiring band members; he wanted energetic, hard-working young men who were attractive and had "personality."[111] The lyrics and sentiment of their songs took center stage, and the Pennsylvanians sang them with the soothing sincerity and easy humor that was familiar to radio and record audiences.

The Pennsylvanians' distinctive playfulness is apparent in a Vitaphone short film they made in 1927. All the men face the audience as they play, smiling and clearly engaged in the material; they seem genuinely to be enjoying what they are doing, a notable contrast with many other filmed jazz bands of the day in which the instrumentalists look down at their instruments in earnest as they play and rarely smile. The appeal to flappers is apparent in the youth and attractiveness of the members, but they also directly solicit female interest and celebrate young women: their first song is "We Love the College Girls," and they perform it with enthusiasm. They play

FIG. 2.12. Waring's Pennsylvanians, in costume for their roles in the motion picture house prologue at the premiere of Harold Lloyd's *The Freshman* (1925) at Grauman's Theater in Los Angeles. The Pennsylvanians here sport an exaggerated collegiate look emphasizing the comedic genre of the film. The thematic pairing of presentation acts with films at major movie theaters became common at this time due to the enormous success of top picture house performers such as the Warings. Their humor, playfulness, personality, and youthful energy helped popularize collegiate styles and performance in motion picture theaters across the country; their appearances were often a bigger draw for movie audiences than the films being shown. Reprinted by permission of Fred Waring's America, Penn State University Libraries.

both slower, smoother love songs and peppy ones using instrumental tricks to make the audience laugh.[112]

In a lengthy dissection of the band's unexpected ("freak") success, *Variety* remarks that the Pennsylvanians were doing something new, "entertaining in an entirely different way, essaying the hokum and progressing their own smooth way, depending on the vocal and ensembles and ultra arrangements with which to 'register.'" *Variety* further notes that the Pennsylvanians did not try to force anything, working "politely, smoothly and modestly" to make "many beautiful musical effects." Picture house audiences reacted to the band as if they were listening to their records or watching a narrative film: "the audience being content to sit back and be entertained, coming out of the apparent state of ease only for the conclusion of each number, when the hand-to-hand music leaves little doubt as to the strength of their impression."[113]

Although the Pennsylvanians' audiences exhibited the same rapt attention as Broadway theater or film audiences, they were hardly passive. There was an active romantic and erotic component to many audience members' appreciation, especially for the crooning soloist Tom Waring, that was as yet unrecognized for crooning singers but would soon become an integral part of their personae and their reception. Much like the "matinee girls" who repeatedly swooned over John Barrymore on the stage or the record buyers whose attachment to singers intensified in repeated listenings, the Pennsylvanians' fans also developed long-term libidinal and emotional attachments to individual members. The Pennsylvanians became favorites of debutantes and flappers early in their careers, and they regularly attracted flapper groupies ("stage door janes"), who followed them to different venues and constantly sought signed photos.[114] *Variety* dubbed them the "jazzical sheiks of the movie theaters" for their Valentino-like matinee idol appeal. Knowing where their bread was buttered, the Pennsylvanians accommodated an average of 250 picture requests per week.[115] Although singers such as Gene Austin were sometimes targeted by individual women, early crooners largely functioned as catalysts for others' romances rather than as romantic figures themselves. The success of the Pennsylvanians offered a performance model that individual crooners, most notably Rudy Vallée, would go on to further exploit and develop: romantic songs sincerely and smoothly sung, well-groomed collegiate appearance, a desire to please, and a relaxed style that encouraged the development of an emotional and erotic investment on the part of the audience.

By the mid-1920s it was clear that the new crooning style represented a significant departure from previous modes of musical appreciation and engagement. The crooning singer was more akin to a film actor than a vaudevillian; his success was not based on training, vocal projection, or local appeal but on his effective establishment of intimacy and convincing personal emotional involvement. Although a popular singer's ability to sincerely perform love songs had always been important, the amplified close-up sound of the microphone gave crooning singers' narratives more power and resonance with audiences. Indeed, the new singing aesthetic was even more potentially involving for an audience than the cinema was because the crooning singer often seemed to break through the fourth wall to address his love objects (and seemingly the listeners) directly—and, via radio broadcasts and recordings, he entered listeners' private homes and lives.

More than any other popular singers before them, crooning singers reflected 1920s commercial culture's focus on romantic and sexual fulfillment as the keys to personal happiness and social stability. Since an audience's feelings of attachment to singers intensified in direct proportion to their romantic and erotic appeal, having the youth and good looks of a matinee idol became an increasingly important component of the crooner persona and would come to divide early crooning stars like Austin, Smith, and Marvin from the romantic crooning idols that immediately followed. The breakthrough crooner to actively engage his audience's romantic fantasies on a grand scale would become the first pop idol, Rudy Vallée, who rose to fame in 1928–29. The attractive young bandleader exemplified singing's new era, wooing his audience as the kind of devoted friend and ideal lover-companion they were now ready to embrace.

(((Three)))

FALLING IN LOVE WITH A VOICE

Rudy Vallée and His First Radio Fans, 1928

Above all, I love to hear you sing, it seems to *thrill* me *through* and
through. I have heard many singers, but none other has made me feel
that way, cannot explain, can you? . . . You sang "Lovely Lady" the
other night—*that* is *me*, that is the way I feel.
—Miss Lillian L., New York City, 12 March 1928

The sexual impulse is far more often powerfully stirred by the
intensely personal medium of the human voice; of a special voice. The
tone-colour of a voice, and the intonation of a single word—and it
may be a word with no special meanings or associations in itself—may
excite incredible intensity of desire. . . . Vision is not *necessary*;
the sense of hearing *alone* can also convey the highest bliss.
—Th. H. Van de Velde, *Ideal Marriage*, 1928

In spring 1928 WABC radio listeners in New York City became increasingly
attached to a single band and its soft-spoken singer-director. Aside from the
young man's trendy moniker (reminiscent of that of the recently deceased
Rudolph Valentino), there was seemingly nothing noteworthy about twenty-
six-year-old Rudy Vallée. His sweet jazz band, the Yale Collegians, couldn't
even afford brass instruments, and his singing lacked technical skill, volume, and range when compared to vaudeville or nightclub performers or
even the practiced standards of the typical radio or record crooning song
plugger.

Love Letters of a
RADIO ROMEO

How Women Long for Romance Revealed by
Rudy Vallee, Popular "Mike" Musician,
as He Tells of the Many Amatory
Messages Addressed to Him

Hungry for Love

WOMEN long for anything that will
help them forget the cruel realities
of life and make them believe they are
as loving or as beloved as they have
always dreamed of being, says Rudy
Vallee.
    Romance is the dominant theme of
woman's life; if she does not have it,
then all beauty of life is lost to her.
American women are starved for it.
The American man, inarticulate in love,
especially after marriage, lets the
woman he loves take it for granted.
    Marriage is only beautiful and
sacred when both man and woman are
devoted to each other. No marriage
should continue
after affection
has died.

FIG. 3.1. This is typical of the tabloid media's promotion of a female-only audience for Rudy
Vallée, even as the paper's own photos, letters to the editor, and radio polls showed otherwise (see, for example, fig. 1.2). Women were often portrayed as obsessive and desperate; this
subheading says they're "hungry for love." "Love Letters of a Radio Romeo," *New York Mirror*,
15 September 1929. Courtesy of Rudy Vallée Collection, American Radio Archives.

Yet audience responses to Vallée were immediate and unusually intense,
both in the volume of fan letters and in their writers' struggles to articulate the depth of their feelings for Vallée's voice. Finding no other words
to express the emotion they felt, several listeners described it as "falling in
love." Hundreds more listeners felt compelled to write over the next several months, and their personal correspondence to Vallée, which he carefully preserved, reflects how they felt that he had moved them personally.[1]
Such responses were unusual among radio listeners in 1928; although radio
performer popularity was often measured by fan mail, especially before the
network era, most letters were not so intimate, nor did they contain the same
emotional and sensual intensity that marked Vallée's reception.

This collection of letters reveals that Vallée's version of crooning—what
would soon be widely known as romantic crooning—was in fact a new, distinctive sound to most radio audiences, even those in cosmopolitan New York
City. Despite the popularity of early crooning on radio and records, *crooning*
and especially *crooners* were not yet household words. Vallée redefined crooning as exclusively romantic and devotional, exploiting radio's possibilities for
intimate address more fully than previous performers had been willing or

able to do. His fan letters give us the opportunity to know what it was like for radio listeners to experience the aural sensation of a close-up broadcast addressed specifically to them, to be befriended and romanced by a radio performer. The sense of familiarity and intimacy that listeners felt toward Vallée was at once comforting and bewildering to them ("I can't understand why I am so attracted to you").

These listeners also shed new light on the particular significance of Vallée as a star personality and as a radio and popular music innovator. In many ways Vallée is the endpoint of the industrial journey from song plugger to microphone idol; as I demonstrate in this chapter, Vallée brought together the characteristics that still define the pop star and have long since become conventional. The music historian Simon Frith has defined "pop's dominant vocal convention" in the period before rock 'n' roll as "crooning intimacy: Songs were written so that singers seemed to talk straight to their listeners. . . . Listeners could now pretend that they knew the singer, that the singer understood or at least articulated their own feelings. This brought a new kind of emotionalism and eroticism into pop."[2] While previous radio performers gave people access to urban entertainment in their homes and many crooned love songs, Vallée deliberately personalized his romantic songs with consistent direct address ("I love you"), emotional generosity and transparency, personal revelation, and responsiveness to fans.

Although the public memory of Vallée's intense early appeal has been obscured by the comic persona he developed later, the fan letters from his first listeners take us back to those moments before he and romantic crooners as a group became national objects of public adoration and scrutiny. Audiences speak for themselves in such letters and struggle to describe precisely what they feel is original and attractive about Vallée's performance style and personality. As a result their letters reveal a rich, complex narrative of romantic crooning's initial reception. They suggest the profound industrial and cultural implications of Vallée's initial success, particularly his and his fans' impact on the development, content, and social uses of radio broadcasting and popular music.[3]

Vallée and his earliest fans *together* developed the conventions of the romantic crooner sound that in turn became the foundation of pop singing: intimacy, sincerity, accessibility, affective engagement, and self-exposure. Vallée's fan letters attest to a significant degree of reciprocity in the relationship between fans and star, since Vallée was both willing and able to respond to listener letters. Because he was still a struggling musician, he treasured fan feedback and eagerly incorporated it into his broadcasts in order to please listeners and ensure his commercial success. Just as significant, he was also able to control his program's content because he was broadcasting from a regional, non-network station. With no promotion, no reviews or news coverage, no administrative interference, no secretarial assistance, and no announcer, the communication between performer and audience was, ironically, one of the least mediated in the history of popular performance. Vallée encouraged this intimacy by being unusually responsive to his listeners, proving his devotion to them by answering their letters, fulfilling photo requests, and playing the songs they asked him to play. He even requested photos back from them, encouraging a two-way relationship.

Listeners' letters also reveal the larger cultural significance of Vallée's voice, its many applications and meanings for working- and middle-class audiences in the late 1920s. In the preceding chapters I outlined the historical, industrial, and technological developments that made modern microphone crooning possible. But these changes would not have evolved or mattered the way they did had the audience not responded so intensely to them. Romantic crooning became such a nexus for powerful emotions during this era because gender and sex had become the primary discursive frames for understanding American life and identity. Immigration restrictions and the assimilation of various immigrant groups into a "white" American identity by the mid-1920s had shifted the primary topic of social concern from overt racial exclusion to tacitly racialized reproduction; likewise, America's youthful collegiate and second immigrant generations were pushing at the boundaries of sexual conventions and using their consumer power to enjoy the titillation provided by Hollywood films, jazz music, and speakeasies.[4] As a result of these shifts, gender behavior, sexual identity, and erotic satisfaction became newly central to social life. Cultural authorities marginalized, subsumed, or erased other kinds of identities and behaviors—racial, political, religious, regional, and economic—and instead emphasized heterosexual marriage and the foundation of the nuclear family as life's most vital pursuits, central to health and happiness.

This agenda was disseminated to the public in two primary and related ways: through marriage and sex advice manuals and through the mass media, which offered up romantic narratives and imagery to an unprecedented degree. These discourses overlapped considerably, as modern marriage counselors encouraged newly married couples to rely exclusively on one another for emotional intimacy and to look to consumer culture to serve any remaining unmet desires. Marriage and divorce rates rose markedly in the 1920s, as people struggled to connect with each other within a new set of cultural permissions, expectations, and constraints.

Vallée resonated for those in the grip of these changes in gender and sexual norms, an audience that was broader than history has acknowledged. Vallée's combination of soothing music, romantic longing, and personal vulnerability ingratiated him to *both* sexes at the time. For some his comforting, melodious voice and personal address fostered family togetherness and soothed children; for others his romantic singing facilitated lovemaking between couples. He opened up the domestic listener to urban and consumer culture in new ways. As the epigraphs to this chapter suggest, marriage advice manuals encouraged both members of couples to recognize the power of the voice as a romantic aid. The broad social appeal of romantic crooning music was confirmed by the number of letters Vallée received from men attesting to the camaraderie and emotional solace they felt listening to him, as well as their amorous uses of his voice. Single people were especially encouraged to look to consumer culture for companionship, and Vallée acted as a source of identification for those who were lonely and alienated, either outside of the heteronormative happy-marriage scenario or socially excluded by class, ability, ethnicity, geography, or age.

While the letters affirm that Vallée's 1928 audience clearly consisted of both male and female fans, he offered women in particular a new model of masculine attention and sensitivity, a powerful figure of identification that crossed gender lines, and a vehicle for erotic pleasure beyond the marriage bed. As the intense sensual pitch of some of Vallée's letters from women indicates, his voice stimulated desires that subverted as well as reinforced new sexual norms. Vallée and the crooners who followed him recognized the new options women had in choosing their lovers, and he privileged them. He portrayed himself as submissive in relation to women and offered them a new model of sensitive, vulnerable masculinity and erotic desire that women found intensely appealing and that encouraged them to be active regarding their own desires—whether with partners or without them. Most important, Vallée's fan letters suggest that women fell in love with his voice and personality because he provided *them* with a voice by encouraging their public fan behavior and by giving them permission to act on their private desires. By acceding to their wishes regarding his own "performance"—something many could only wish of their lovers—and actively wooing them over the air, Vallée became the cherished voice of and for many female listeners. Together Vallée and his fans would alter the shape and direction of popular entertainment.

HUBERT PRIOR (RUDY) VALLÉE
AND COLLEGIATE CULTURE

Rudy Vallée was a member of one of the most culturally influential groups of the 1920s: college students. His early fans always pointed to his voice and his youth as his most attractive qualities. Like many of his student contemporaries, Vallée was born on the cusp of the new century and showed the influence of both the Victorian, middle-class culture of his New England childhood and youth, and the modern, sophisticated values of 1920s New York City, in which he came of age. He was born Hubert Prior Vallée on 28 July 1901—the year Queen Victoria died—in Island Pond, Vermont, to middle-class Catholic parents with French and Irish roots.[5] His family moved to Westbrook, Maine, when he was very young, and he always regarded Maine as his home state and prided himself on his New England heritage. His father expected that Vallée would follow in his footsteps by becoming a pharmacist. Instead young Vallée developed an early interest in music, which he attributed to his Irish mother, to whom he was devoted. In high school he participated as a singer and drummer in amateur bands. After graduation he became passionately attached to the saxophone, a relatively unknown but increasingly popular instrument. Vallée was himself a devotee of the fan practices he would soon solicit from others, and he initiated an admiring correspondence with Rudy Wiedoeft, the most prominent saxophonist of the time. Wiedoeft's talent, specifically his "fast tonguing," so impressed young Vallée that he earned the nickname "Rudy" in college and kept the moniker in Wiedoeft's honor. The change in his name from Hubert to Rudy typified the way his interest in the saxophone modernized him, putting him in the company of other would-be musical innovators and inevitably drawing him to New York City.

America's youth, especially collegians, had a stronger role than ever before in propelling mainstream culture forward in the 1920s. Although the population of this age group, between fifteen and twenty-four years, was smaller than preceding generations had been, these youth exerted far more influence because smaller families, increased income, and technological advances kept them from having to enter the workforce immediately. For the first time youth could enjoy a "more leisured pace of development" that for many in the middle class included more education, social activities, and consumer goods targeted to them.[6] The number of young people finishing high school rose dramatically, and college enrollment tripled from what it had been in 1890. Although college students represented only 12 percent of the population for their age group, these privileged youth formed a "distinctive subculture" that had a pronounced influence on national culture, especially regarding leisure activities, fashion trends, and sexual norms.[7] As enrollments skyrocketed, college education and social activity broadened. Participation in fraternities and sororities increased considerably, dances became important events on campus, and college athletic teams took on national prominence. Dating was very important in the new college culture, and sexual activity, especially "petting" (kissing, caressing), became an expected part of dating life. Intercourse was also more commonplace in a culture where birth control, although technically still illegal in most places, was more widely available and accepted than it had ever been.[8] Flappers and jazz babies abounded in this more sexually expressive culture, but there was no corresponding feminist critique from these young women, unlike the previous generation. Although women's college enrollment reached new heights (40 percent), female college students were encouraged to focus on pursuing husbands. Some worried that students seemed to be guided more by their hedonistic peers than their disciplined elders, as these youth relished the new opportunities for leisure and the mass media.[9]

Chief among these new pleasures was music, and Rudy Vallée was at the center of college music culture. However, as an entertainer who performed to pay for college, Vallée worked more than he played during his college years. Jazz music and white "sweet" jazz bands (in contrast to the more improvisational black "hot" jazz bands) were extraordinarily popular on college campuses in the 1920s; many students formed their own bands, most famously Waring's Pennsylvanians. *Variety* credited college students with starting the "jazz band craze" of the period, and non-college bands adopted the "collegiate" style of dress (sweater vests, bow ties, baggier pants, slimmer cut jackets, pinstripes, light pastel colors) to appeal to them.[10] Vallée was one of the best-known college musicians on the East Coast, first at the University of Maine and then at Yale, where he transferred in 1922. He worked his way through Yale as a bandleader and saxophonist, often traveling to out-of-town jobs (including the occasional New York nightclub) as well as becoming a fixture at Yale dances and football games, sporting his 1920s trademark raccoon coat. In 1924 he took a leave from Yale to earn money playing saxophone at the swanky Savoy Hotel in London. While there he made his first phonograph recordings (as a saxophonist) and was first heard on radio when his band was broadcast from the hotel.

Vallée loved England, particularly London haberdashers, and he returned to Yale with renewed confidence and considerably better dressed; like many urban professionals of his day, he valued well-tailored clothes. He finished his remaining two years at Yale and graduated with a degree in psychology, which he would later draw on to help him anticipate his audience's desires. Upon his graduation in 1927 his Yale pedigree and contacts, as well as his talent and experience as a saxophonist, made him a popular performer in New York nightclubs. After working with several bands in the New York and Boston areas, most prominently the Vincent Lopez orchestra, Vallée formed his own band when the house band for the Heigh-Ho nightclub in New York had to be quickly replaced. He named his band the Yale Collegians (although he was the sole member to have attended Yale, not uncommon for "collegiate" bands of the time), and they auditioned for the Heigh-Ho's manager, Don Dickerman, in January 1928.[11] Vallée had hired a "trained voice" singer for the band, but in one of those twists of fate so essential to a star's biography, Dickerman disliked the man's voice. Worried that his new band might lose the gig, Vallée took on the singing himself, using a megaphone to amplify his soft voice. In less than a year radio listeners would make both the Heigh-Ho and Rudy Vallée famous.

DOMESTICATING RADIO:
REGENDERING EARLY RADIO

Before radio superstars could be born, however, radio had to change. Radio had originally been considered a masculine, individualist's hobby. Prior to World War I, wireless radio sets had been conceived of as an active sport for men and boys, who would build their own sets and then spend hours scanning the skies for signals. Although girls also enjoyed being amateur radio operators, their participation received much less attention and public encouragement.[12] Early radio sets looked like masses of wires, were battery-powered and dripped acid, were very noisy, and required constant attention and adjustment; as a result, radio use was generally confined to the work-shop or garage.[13] Improvements in loudspeakers, tuners, and batteries by the middle of the decade, however, transformed the radio from an amateur pastime into a permanent fixture in the family parlor.

Radio's domestic presence as well as the growing commercialization of broadcasting definitively shifted the gender association of radio from masculine to feminine. The advent of the Superheterodyne radio set in the mid-1920s, with its improved clarity and amplification, meant that listeners were now freed from headsets and didn't have to strain to hear, though many people still chose to sit as close to the speakers as possible, intensifying the singular importance and intimacy between themselves and radio's voices.[14] The question surrounding radio was no longer "How far can you hear?" but "How close can radio make us feel to its voices?" Radio's importance as a daily companion in people's lives was underlined when sales of sets and speakers soared in 1925.[15]

With radio's move into the parlor (and, for many, the kitchen) came the wooing of the female consumer, whom radio manufacturers, broadcasters, and advertisers considered to be their target audience. Popular images of telephones had long portrayed women as listeners while men produced the sound, and radio commercial advertising reproduced these gendered practices.[16] With radio, male advertisers' voices now came directly into the home, speaking softly, politely, and persuasively in order to appeal to what advertisers conceived of as "feminine tastes."[17] The radio's sociability and intimacy were exploited in courting female consumers.[18] Broadcasters unified in their promotion of radio announcers as "friends" within the home, and their advertising was suffused with middle-class ideals of home and family.[19] "Radio is the most intimate form of entertainment to which the public has ever been subscribed," declared the *Journal of Home Economics* in 1932, and its writers urged radio speakers to remember, "After all, [you] are not speaking to the Public. You are speaking to a family. . . . Radio speakers must be entertaining, natural and friendly, precisely the qualities that make a great guest around the house."[20] This feminization of radio meant naturalizing its voices, making them friendly and familiar, and masking the technology in wood cabinets that emulated furniture. This sense of transparency and closeness in early commercial radio would become unsettling once romantic crooners began dominating the airwaves, as would women's consuming power; initially, however, such rhetoric served—at least in broadcasters' minds—to smooth radio's appropriate transition from masculine to feminine space.

One of the chief ways that broadcasters sought to appeal to women was through music. Music within the home had long been considered women's province, but women also made up the majority of audiences at public concerts and 85 percent of music students, even as men still dominated professional music teaching and performance.[21] Women had been the primary targets of music periodicals and sheet music since the late eighteenth century, and the piano had been central to the middle-class home since the mid-nineteenth century, with women as the designated family pianists (piano playing indicated a woman's gentility). Like radio advertisers, music sellers and music magazines suggested that women could use their products to enhance domestic life for all concerned. The equation of women with music did not guarantee them a higher cultural status, however, but rather positioned them to be commercially exploited.[22] Music on radio was conceived of in a similar way, and with similar cultural tensions. While music needed to please female audiences in order to be profitable, broadcasters were also continually wary of women's judgment and influence because of the female audience's perceived susceptibility to the vulgarities of mass culture.[23]

Of course radio was not the first music technology in the home. The acoustic phonograph had been a staple of middle-class homes since the early 1900s, and women the chief consumers of phonographs and records. Women did not have to spend time learning musical instruments if they could buy records, and buying their own records offered them "a psychological space outside the domestic sphere."[24] In many ways women's use of phonograph records anticipates their later mass response to radio. Phonographs naturalized the idea that mass-produced music could be emotionally and personally affecting, and in fact that repeated listening to the same singer or recording could enhance rather than diminish listener pleasure.[25] Women were the primary purchasers of recordings by Enrico Caruso and John McCormack and made male tenors the favorite operatic voices on record.

Still, radio represented a significant change in domestic listening. The historian Susan Douglas identifies radio music as the cause of a "musical awakening in America" in the 1920s, making it "one of the most significant, meaningful, sought after, and defining elements of day-to-day life, of generational identity, and of personal and public memory."[26] Radio allowed audiences to listen to music for long periods and offered a larger variety of music and greater opportunities to identify new, specific sounds that pleased them. By 1924–25 most radio sounded as good as or better than records, forcing the record industry to electrify and reproduce "radio sound." Radio music was also often performed live. Local bands like Vallée's regularly performed live from radio hookups in hotels and nightclubs, giving listeners the sensation of being in the same space as the performer, a part of the extended audience at a shared event.[27] Radio made mass communal listening of both live and reproduced music possible for the first time, creating communities of consumer advocates around particular voices. With the growth of regional and national network broadcasting in the 1920s, radio listeners could create vocal stars and hit songs literally overnight.

UP CLOSE AND PERSONAL:
THE VALLÉE RADIO SOUND

Vallée's ascendance to radio's first idol was the result of a combination of factors, both personal and professional. The club manager Don Dickerman's preference for natural-sounding, conversational singers echoed a larger shift in popular taste, and Vallée's own musical preferences reflected those of the public. But radio broadcasting really cinched Vallée's success. Vallée was particularly fortunate to debut on the powerful local New York station WABC. Within a year of his first broadcast, it would become the anchor station of the newly formed CBS network.[28] Before the network era took definitive hold, however, broadcast schedules were much less fixed, allowing for more variation in scheduling and little content regulation. It was common practice for radio stations to call on local hotel and nightclub bands to fill time. Although the bands were unpaid, they were usually eager to get the free publicity.[29] Vallée was thus able to enjoy the benefits of WABC's clarity and reach without having to bend to network oversight.

The Collegians' first broadcast in February 1928 proved surprisingly popular, and WABC quickly signed the band to fill in as many gaps in the station's schedule as they could play. Other stations followed suit, and during that year Vallée could be heard on three New York stations, often within the same week: WABC; WOR, a New York station with an even larger range; and WMCA, where Vallée secured a weekly sponsored (paid) program for Herbert's Jewelry in Harlem. On this schedule the industrious Vallée was able to broadcast seven or eight times a week during the spring and fall of 1928, saturating the regional airwaves and attracting an increasingly large and loyal group of fans in the New York–New Jersey area, as well as listeners as far away as New Hampshire and Philadelphia.

In his autobiography, *Vagabond Dreams Come True*, published at the height of his fame in 1930, an enthusiastic young Vallée describes at length how he developed his band's sound and what he hoped to accomplish with it. His approach to music was very much a reflection of his own tastes and happily overlapped with his commercial desires. Where other sweet bandleaders focused on musical complexity, artistic achievement, and critical recognition, Vallée was an internalized, emotive performer who wanted to elicit an affective, personal response from his listeners.[30] As a former movie projectionist and theater usher, he loved movies and movie music and was inspired to try to replicate the way film music encouraged specific emotional responses.[31] Es-

FIG. 3.2. Rudy Vallée and his Connecticut Yankees (née Yale Collegians) broadcasting over a WOR station hookup (note the hanging microphone) in 1928. Vallée himself is typically posed very casually, his body curving rather than stiff. Rudy Vallée and the Yale Collegians, 1928. Reprinted by permission of Eleanor Vallée. Courtesy of Rudy Vallée Collection, American Radio Archives.

sentially, Vallée *scripted* sweet jazz, foregrounding the main melody, lyrics, and vocals of a number rather than its instrumental jazz accompaniment so that listeners would feel a sense of emotional involvement with the song's narrative and identify with the feelings of the singer. In doing so he combined sweet jazz music with the narrative principles and commercial qualities of Hollywood films, Tin Pan Alley songs, and crooning recordings.

Vallée was not the first to promote the new intimate, crooning singing style; every performance forum, whether mediated or live, in some way incorporated the new aesthetic as a commercial imperative. Crooning singers such as Nick Lucas, Cliff Edwards, Jack Smith, and Gene Austin were already ubiquitous on radio and records and in motion picture houses. The public demand for the close-up microphone sound forced jazz bands to employ vocal interludes and choruses on their recordings and to include more vocals in their live performances. Many celebrated bandleaders of the day—including Ben Pollack, Ben Bernie, and Ben Selvin—performed their own vocal accompaniment through megaphones and microphones. Waring's Pennsylvanians built their spectacular success in the 1920s by reversing the emphasis on instrumental prowess in order to focus on intricate vocal harmonies and a playful, charming performance style that targeted young women.

Vallée differed from his bandleader peers by privileging the radio listening audience over the nightclub audience. By all accounts an average jazz bandleader on site, Vallée was a phenomenal bandleader over the air. Although the Yale Collegians had been hired as a dance band, Vallée was actually more interested in moving people emotionally than physically. Despite years of performing for country club and nightclub audiences, he identified instead with the middle and working classes, the New York movie audience. Thus he strove to make his jazz music more accessible by foregrounding song melodies so "the average person would be able to carry the melody along."[32] He also slowed the tempos for his numbers; although most of his numbers were described as dance fox trots on the sheet music, Vallée was given credit (and later blame) for pioneering as a bandleader the "very slow fox trot," which would become one of the hallmarks of the romantic crooning era.[33] His risky approach did not endear him to those New Yorkers eager to dance to hot tempos, but it charmed collegiate clubbers and radio audiences. The bewildered but enthusiastic response of listeners suggests that Vallée had indeed concocted something potent and unfamiliar to many radio listeners ("your most unusual music," "so different from the others").

The dominance of reeds and strings in Vallée's band turned out to be an attraction for radio listeners, who valued the music's melodic consistency and smoothness, anchored by his sincere crooning singing. Vallée's listeners pointed to such characteristics as they struggled to differentiate his sound from that of other bands of the time. A New York woman wrote, "You have toned your collegians down so that even the jazziest compositions sound melodious." Another "admirer from Brooklyn" wrote in March 1928, "You have a type of music which is both full of pep and as sweet and mellow as the most dreamy lullaby. . . . You must have some very soothing qualities to your music because all I need to do when my baby is restless is turn on your program and she is soon asleep."

Vallée's relaxed, soft instrumentals enabled him to focus on other aspects of his radio performance, fostering listener familiarity and easy emotional investment. Unlike earlier crooning singers, he continually used direct address in his songs ("I love you") and his speech, which personalized the experience of listening to him. Most bands were introduced by station announcers, but WABC couldn't afford one. By acting as his own announcer, Vallée successfully shaped his entire program, including his persona. His personal anecdotes about each number endeared him to his listeners and helped create an identity for him that transcended the medium. Further, unlike most announcers of the time, Vallée insisted on having a continuous musical background to avoid interrupting the mood of the music when he spoke. This practice of scoring an entire radio program, which was characteristic of film music, gave Vallée's programs a sense of continuity that most radio programs of the time lacked but would adopt during the network era.

Fans wrote repeatedly in appreciation of Vallée's friendly announcing style, in which he addressed his listeners as individual friends rather than a mass audience, celebrating his ability to "bring a personal touch of individuality" to the cold technology of radio. "It is a real treat for me to hear the voice of an old friend each night," wrote a Brooklyn woman. "I had begun to lose interest in radio," wrote another listener, "until quite by chance tuned in on the Heigh-Ho hour and since then have been faithfully one of your audience." Vallée's ability to solicit loyalty from radio listeners further attests to the way they perceived themselves as having a personal relationship with him.

Although individual radio performers such as Vaughn De Leath, Wendell Hall, Art Gillham, and Samuel "Roxy" Rothafel had also been able to breathe human warmth into the ether, Vallée cultivated his listeners' emotional attachment to his singing and song choices beyond what anyone had done before him. Vallée's songs were easy to learn, almost entirely romantic, and, like crooning recordings, grew on listeners through repetition. He was happy to accede to his listeners' wishes in terms of song performance and content. When his fans wrote that they liked vocal solos as much as if not more than instrumental solos, Vallée immediately privileged the vocals rather than the instrumental accompaniments to his songs.[34] He also emphasized the choruses of songs, repeating them often to help listeners memorize the lyrics and regularly replaying fan favorites like "Sweet Lorraine," "Georgie Porgie," and "If You Were the Only Girl in the World." Wrote one Brooklyn man, "May I state right here that 'Sweet Lorraine' never tires me no matter how often I hear it, but just the opposite. I like it more." Lyrics were especially important to these listeners, who often commented on Vallée's perfect diction and appreciated the fact that his pronunciation made it easier for them to learn the words to particular songs. A song's popularity in 1928 was still judged in part by the copies of sheet music sold, and these fans indicate Vallée's growing importance for this market through their frustration with stores that were running out of copies of their favorite Vallée songs.

By far the most popular feature of Vallée's sound, however, was his singing voice. "I have never heard any singer put the expression and feeling in [their songs] that you have," wrote a woman from Bogota, New Jersey. Although by today's standards Vallée's voice is nasal and marked by a New England accent, it registered as clear, unaffected, and unforced to his listeners, especially an audience accustomed to classically trained radio voices and the vaudevillian's projection and variety of heavier accents. Most important, radio amplification intensified the sense of Vallée's emotional yearning, permitting the kind of confidential tone that took listeners by surprise and made them feel as if he were indeed physically, and certainly psychically, close to them. These fans identified qualities about his voice that would come to be associated specifically with the romantic crooner persona: emotional transparency, vulnerability, and devotion to and privileging of fans, especially women.

While only one of these early letters identified Vallée as a crooner, it is clear even this early on that his crooning defined his particular sound for many fans. Unlike his crooner contemporaries Edwards and Marvin, crooning wasn't simply one of the skills in his bag of tricks—crooning was what made Vallée *Vallée* for his listeners. Some fans, for example, protested when he sang "St. Louis Blues," which everyone else was also singing at the time: "Your voice is too sweet for those 'St. Louis Blues.' So sing the sweet romantic [songs]." Vallée adapted his repertoire and style in response to fans' suggestions, eschewing other popular vocal styles, such as blues, scatting, and yodeling. In this way his fans helped develop the crooner persona and pop delivery style.

One aspect of Vallée's singing that his fans especially appreciated and which he described as giving his radio voice that "personal touch" was his selective employment of what was then called tremolo or vibrato. *Vibrato*, from the Latin, meaning "to shake," is a controlled, rapid fluctuation of the pitch and intensity of a note. Although trained singers regularly employed vibrato in their singing to convey emotion—and many popular singers of the 1920s were trained this way—it was less common for a popular singer to employ it sporadically, for directed emotional effect. Indeed Vallée's use of vibrato was adapted from his experiences "fast tonguing" on the saxophone and the clarinet, a common expressive effect for jazz wind instruments. Vallée took what he learned playing jazz and applied it to vocal delivery.[35] For the radio listener, Vallée's use of vibrato evoked the classical tenor voices many listeners loved, yet his lack of training marked his delivery as more sincere, intimate, and modern. Because of the unexpected quality of his vibrato, his vocal quivers foregrounded the presence of his live body and made hearing him a sensual experience that helped define what was romantic about the romantic crooner. Among home audiences in the 1920s who were increasingly turning to consumer culture to provide them with companionship, comfort, and romance, Vallée's radio voice could indeed touch them in a multitude of new and exciting ways.

PRIVATE AUDIENCES:
RUDY VALLÉE'S RADIO FANS

Although Vallée's fame has been widely credited to his young female devotees, his collected fan letters from 1928 portray a much more diverse audience. Most of the letters came from New York City and its environs, and their generally clear, readable prose indicates some (although varying levels of) education. Appreciation of Vallée's crooning crossed gender, generational, ethnic, race, and class boundaries; his fans included working-class people and professionals, married and dating couples, mothers and daughters, extended family groups, girlfriends, friendship circles, and entire sports teams, as well as those even more neglected in surveys of music audiences: the infirm, the blind, and the elderly.

These letters tend to emphasize aspects of Vallée's music that both women and men associated with their private lives and interior selves: family and friendship, emotional expression and connection, comfort and support, romance and eroticism. I refer to this audience as "private listeners" not because they are necessarily linked to private domestic spaces but because they commonly listened and responded to Vallée from a private—that is, personal—perspective. Like Vallée, these listeners embraced the new intimate singing aesthetic and were not interested in technical proficiency, vocal training, voice projection, or musical complexity and variation. Rather they appreciated Vallée's comforting, conversational tones—what *Variety* called a "sympathetic" voice—and the seeming sincerity of his own affective engagement. Listeners responded to him in kind, with friendship, gratitude, passion, and self-disclosures.

Because these listeners were so open with Vallée, their letters offer glimpses into their social world, suggesting how his sound was woven into the texture of their daily lives in a number of meaningful ways. Many scheduled shared family time around Vallée's program; he became "appointment radio" for them, still a rare experience before network saturation. Family members wrote Vallée letters expressing their gratitude toward him for providing music they could all listen to together. His refusal to use slang expressions or sexually explicit lyrics was especially reassuring for some parents. A physician at City Hospital noted how "the complete absence of any vulgarity from your program" was key to making Vallée "an All American star with my family and myself." For other families Vallée was an activating force, encouraging members to participate by singing together: "When you sing we all hug the radio and [listen] with extended ears and show our tonsils to the cock-eyed world." Vallée was a particular favorite with women, both flappers and their mothers, whose responses often indicate shared erotic stimulation: "Mother and I listen religiously for every one of your 'Heigh-Ho' hours on the air. . . . The positive little thrill of pleasure that came when we heard 'Your Way is My Way'—in your familiar voice, was one that would greet only one's best friend's appearances."

While the nuclear family was the social ideal among the middle classes of the 1920s, these letters also make clear that the public's definition of *family* still varied considerably and that Vallée's music often facilitated a broader community with extended family, friends, and neighbors. Some listeners did not own radios and wrote of going over to friends' houses to hear Vallée sing. Having public entertainment in private space also allowed listeners to entertain guests cheaply within their home; one writer, for example, pointed out that the smoothness of Vallée's music made an excellent accompaniment for his weekly card games with friends.

The cross-class applications of Vallée's music are also evident from the letters. While middle- and upper-class listeners would write of hoping to see Vallée live at the Heigh-Ho Club, others wrote of their disappointment that they could not afford such outings. His listeners were very aware of social hierarchies, and, as Vallée noted regretfully in his memoirs, the Heigh-Ho did not admit Jewish or nonwhite patrons nor those who could not afford black-tie evening wear. This socially marginalized home audience was who Vallée hoped to reach with his music, although his success also encouraged people to idealize and identify with an exclusive urban entertainment culture that might not otherwise include or accept them. This tension is one that Vallée attempted to negotiate by paying more attention to the requests of his at-home audience than to the nightclub crowd, such as playing music that was initially deemed too slow for dancing. For most of his audience in 1928, Vallée remained a domestic companion, and the 1920s home was especially fertile ground for his voice.

Family and sexual roles had undergone significant changes since the turn of the century, which radio's new intimacy both addressed and ultimately would help define. Economically the family as codependent producing unit was no longer as relevant in an industrialized, urban environment structured around individual wage earners.[36] Progressive Era changes had further de-emphasized the cultural priority of the family, as the concerns of larger social groups (laborers, women, the poor) dominated much of public discourse. The changes for women were especially significant. The suffragist movement, increased educational opportunities, and more participation in public spaces of work and leisure enabled the emergence in the 1900s of the "New Woman," one who was well educated, financially independent, and socially engaged, who placed marriage and children low on her list of priorities, and whose primary affective and social relationships were as likely to be with women as with men. The growing independence of white, middle-class women, especially, concerned economists, sociologists, and other cultural authorities who feared social instability as a result of feminism and who bemoaned the declining birth rate among their class and race. In order to make marriage more attractive to this group, social mores defining marriage and courtship changed. Marriage was reconceived in the 1920s as a sexually egalitarian, "companionate" institution. The "modern family" promised emotional fulfillment through heterosexual union, consumer products, and the raising of children, and its promoters discouraged involvement in political or community activities and emotional relationships beyond the immediate family. In return, constraints on heterosexual erotic courtship were loosened; unchaperoned dating became more common, petting became permissible, and sexual acts and positions became more varied.

Reflecting a shift toward understanding sexuality through scientific rather than moral frameworks, social scientists advocated for the sexual liberalization of the American middle class as a key component of the 1920s marriage. Popular marriage and sex advice manuals of the time promoted the ideal of the "companionate marriage," which emphasized the importance of emotional intimacy, sensitivity, romantic feeling, and sexual satisfaction within marriage for both partners.[37] Indeed its proponents viewed sexual desire and activity for both men and women as a public good and advised men to drop domineering attitudes and to instead focus on helping their wives achieve sexual pleasure. Husbands were encouraged to be more sensitive to their wives' desires, to be gentler and more romantic, and to actively please them in the bedroom.[38] Instead of dominating women, men were encouraged to try

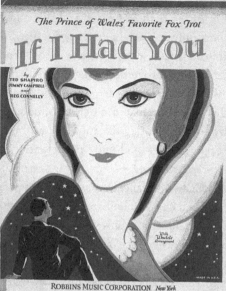

FIG. 3.3. The increasing centrality of women in men's lives and fates is obvious in many of the sheet music covers of the late 1920s, such as this one from 1928, in which the woman's image is much larger than the man's, dominating him. In contrast to Jolson's cover (fig. 2.9), the young male narrator of this song has clearly succumbed to his romantic longing for his dream girl, and she is all he thinks about. The cover reflects both the increasing cultural focus on heterosexual coupling and reproduction, and the more vulnerable, romance-minded male ideal of the era. Sheet music, "If I Had You," 1928. Author's collection.

to understand women's points of view. These writers regarded sex education for married couples as essential. Their books contained anatomical diagrams that encouraged husbands to engage in foreplay, employ contraception, and help their wives to achieve orgasm through "clitoral stimulation," which included oral sex ("genital kissing"). Remarkably, the concept of a vaginal orgasm was either not mentioned or marginalized in importance, showing the initial resistance of many sex experts and marriage advocates to aspects of Freudian psychology that made vaginal orgasm central to female sexuality. The historian Christina Simmons observes that these manuals "clearly promoted sexual relations that were as intense and pleasurable for women as they were for men" and suggested a largely unacknowledged bounty of public information regarding sexual practices during the late 1920s and early 1930s that resonated in the popular culture of the time.[39]

For couples who needed additional help in meeting the new companionate goals for romance, Vallée's voice proved a new, and vital, third party within the marriage. A large number of fan letters came from couples who utilized Vallée's live romantic voice as an aphrodisiac, making marriage a threesome: "I am a bride of a week and [Vallée's] songs make our little love nest so rapturous. . . . Hubby and I just sit and hold each other tight while he is on the air. We just look into each others eyes while he is singing." Other couples

Ivor Wooes in Rudy Vallee Manner

Ivor Fuhrman, who croons like Rudy Vallee, is shown with his bride, Helen Fuhrman, as he used to croon to her before her mamma and papa tried to stop their marriage. But they wedded in Baltimore yesterday after winning parental consent.

FIG. 3.4. This newspaper photo of a newly married couple attests to Vallée's importance in promoting companionate marriages by helping men to woo women more successfully. Ivor Fuhrman courted his bride, notes the caption, by crooning to her "like Rudy Vallée." *New York Mirror*, 31 December 1930. Courtesy of Rudy Vallée Collection, American Radio Archives.

wrote of dancing together in their home to his music. And not all couples benefiting from Vallée were newlyweds; others thanked him for "keeping the romance alive" in their marriages. A couple from Mt. Vernon, New York, wrote, "We are not young people. . . . Now don't take this as flapper talk, as I may be old enough to be your mother . . . but you do really send over the air great pleasure for both of us." For couples who were apart, Vallée provided a worthy substitute, as this woman wrote: "[My] sweetie is a travelin' man, I get real lonesome. You sing with such expression."

Vallée's model of devoted attention, self-revelation, and sensitivity made an especially profound impression on a generation looking for love. Vallée fit the qualifications of an ideal mate according to the companionate marriage rhetoric and the youth surveys of the time, which, as Paula Fass has shown, favored "personal compatibility, including disposition, personality, and intelligence," over "economic position, religion or sexual purity, qualities their parents considered essential."[40] While the 1920s emphasis on emotional and sexual fulfillment through marriage had marked benefits for some young people, its narrow heterosexual focus privileged the straight couple over other kinds of social and community connections and isolated both couples and single people in ways that disproportionately affected women.[41] Cultural authorities encouraged people to depend on commercial consumption rather than other kinds of community connections to fulfill unmet emotional needs. Many turned to Vallée's voice to ease their loneliness, a common theme among these writers, who found relief and understanding in his voice. "No matter how blue I feel and I often feel blue," wrote a New York woman, "I forget all my troubles when I hear you sing."

For others, especially the ill and elderly, Vallée was an especially valued presence, often a primary companion. Throughout his career he had a huge following among the blind, and many of these early letters mention physical infirmities that confined listeners to their home or to hospitals.[42] The importance of popular music to these groups has perhaps been the least documented by historians who have focused, by and large, on 1920s public dance culture. Because the infirm could not participate in that culture, radio access and Vallée's intimate address were especially vital. "I want you to know how much your music and singing has meant to one who would love to dance but has been in bed for the last eight months," wrote Barbara P. Another woman "confined to a hospital bed for the past five months" wrote that she'd been staying up "against doctor's orders" to listen to Vallée's program from eleven to midnight.

When listeners connected Vallée's voice with their most vulnerable selves, his music took on more emotional weight for them than the simple songs themselves might seem to warrant. Cultural critics have often written about this phenomenon, arguing that what distinguishes pop music from high art is its generality, the use of "everyday language" and "commonplace feelings" that allows people to more easily personalize the music. Frith has argued that pop songs "are soon encrusted with uses and memories and references. . . . It is pop—more than any other form of music—that changes if not our lives then certainly the ways in which we feel about them."[43] Direct address would later become recognized as a key component in a successful pop performance; Frith notes that pop must speak to us "in sufficiently individualized ways to appeal to us as individualized listeners. And the secret here lies in the pop singers' ability to appeal to us directly, to lay their personality on a song such that we can make it our song too."[44] While this point may seem obvious today, such practices were new for Vallée's early radio listeners. Vallée didn't just sing a love song; he sang *your* song, as his fans testified: "You sing your songs as if there were one particular person listening in and you were singing to them and I hope you will always sing this way." Even though commercial culture had for many years encouraged consumers to attach personal meanings to movie images, stars, songs, and pulp fiction, these fan letters suggest that many consumers had never before personalized a radio voice in this way or experienced this type and degree of daily, domestic media companionship.

One widow's unease regarding her devotion to Vallée's radio transmissions provides a moving case in point. In her letter, she sent Vallée her husband's obituary and attested to the way Vallée's music had become inextricably linked with her final memories of him. As a result she felt very attached to Vallée but worried it would be disrespectful to turn on the radio, a vehicle of the supposedly impersonal "mass media," during her mourning: "I have not been able to 'hear' or listen since last Friday afternoon as Mr. N passed away on Saturday so I surely miss your music and beautiful voice so soulful in tone—I wonder, would it be proper for me to tune in on the Radio? The time seems so long for just my Pekinese dog and self. [The dog] knew your music and voice as soon as we would tune it and often sits watching the radio and I suppose wonders why I don't tune in." By becoming her and her husband's companion during his final days, Vallée became inseparable from a personal and tragic event in this woman's life, redefining her previous view of radio as simply an "entertainment" machine.

At times Vallée deliberately sought to evoke shared memories of his listeners' pasts, both pleasant and painful. His Armistice Day program in November 1928 drew many letters praising his selection of music that brought back "memorys [sic] we cannot quite forget" of the war. During the broadcast Vallée did not trumpet the glories of war in a masculinist, nationalistic manner; audience reactions suggest that his sensitivity and expressiveness functioned as a kind of radio therapy for listeners. One remarkable letter from a Long Island woman suggested the depth and variety of emotion Vallée's program stirred in her:

> From all the stations with their evident effort and preparation to do honor to the day no one reached me as did you, Rudy—you bridged the gap from those sad moments to today with its sweet promise and beauty. Oh how you understand BEAUTY! There is a haunting tenderness of touch in your voice so like your music—it is astounding how closely allied your voice is to your music—it thrills and soothes. You will receive many, many letters of appreciation for tonight's beautiful tribute to Armistice Day—so I shall be brief—but like your adorable song, a bouquet with forget me nots, so shall your tenderness, sympathy and understanding live on—never to be forgotten. . . . I love all that you give us.

This writer's use of *beauty* and *sweet*—common descriptive terms in these letters—evokes the idealist aesthetics of the Victorian critic Matthew Arnold, which called for art to be beautiful, sincere, and uplifting.[45] The writer suggests how Vallée was able to intensify the affective impact of these sentiments through his use of the modern microphone; radio's live intimacy ("a tenderness of touch") heightened the emotional connection between Vallée and his listeners, and he fully utilized radio's potential to move them through personally addressing them in words and soft sounds that they perceived as unusually sensitive and emotionally generous. His approach distinguished his voice among many for his listeners, and they in turn made him a reliable, cherished companion in their daily lives.

REAL MEN *LIKE* CROONERS

Women were not the only listeners to become emotionally invested in Vallée's music. While about three-quarters of these early letters came from women (often writing on behalf of "the family"), men represented a sizable portion of his listening audience. Men's letters were similar in content to many of the women's (except the most explicitly romantic ones), but they were also much more likely to address Vallée formally as "Dear Sir" and to give "kudos" or make specific requests than to discuss personal meanings of his music. Nonetheless, it is clear that men were as touched by Vallée's delivery and sentiments as women were and affirmed several different categories of appreciation for music that would soon be considered as appealing only to the female sex.

Many letters from wives, for example, mention that husbands too enjoy listening to Vallée's music on the air—and indeed one can imagine the relief of some novice husbands, knowing that Vallée's music was one surefire way to set a romantic mood. Letters from men themselves, however, often came from their workplace rather than their home and revealed a range of classes and occupations. Physicians and businessmen wrote from their offices, football coaches wrote on behalf of "the team," and policemen wrote from their precincts; one police lieutenant noted how much he enjoyed "the predominance of violins and your vocal solos, to such an extent, that I am moved to let you know your work is being appreciated." Often these letters indicated strong emotional responses to Vallée's music; men were particularly enamored with the song "If You Were the Only Girl in the World" and often requested it. (Wives reported that their husbands were "wild about it.") A Long

Island man wrote, "The way you sang 'If You Were the Only Girl' was almost heartbreaking and brought tears to my eyes, often. I could listen to the music and singing for hours."

These men did not devalue Vallée in any way for his sensitive persona and romantic songs—indeed they championed him. There is no sense that for these writers liking football and liking Vallée were at all antithetical, as they would become in public discourse within the next few years. For instance, a Harvard man, depressed over Harvard's loss in the Harvard-Army game, wrote to beg Vallée to sing "Deep Night" to cheer him. One man canceled his weekly poker game so he could tune in to Vallée's program: "My friends and myself, all from the fair state of New Jersey, think that your music is the best in the world." In one sense these men were able to enjoy Vallée because homosocial male camaraderie was still widely acceptable, made more so for some fans by his position as a fellow collegian. But even more significant, the admiration these men had for Vallée is a testament to a world where middle- and working-class men could still revel, laugh, or weep at the performances of crooners, female impersonators, falsetto singers, jazz musicians, and a variety of other kinds of musical performers without fearing emasculation.

Standards of normative masculine behavior also varied considerably in the 1920s, particularly along the lines of ethnicity and class, and such distinctions were evident in the different approaches taken by some of Vallée's fans.[46] In general the higher the class position, the more inhibited the writer. While none of these men appear uncomfortable about admitting that they were emotionally moved by popular music, the act of writing a fan letter made some men self-conscious, likely because celebrity fandom was increasingly considered a feminized activity. Some men expressed concerns about the propriety of writing to another man, but such a reaction was by no means dominant; many male writers bared their emotions with no self-consciousness at all, suggesting the lack of a consistent social standard. Several men acknowledged being conflicted about writing but felt compelled to do so ("I have never before, and probably never will again feel the urge to write in appreciation") and to apologize for that compulsion, especially the attraction it seemed to suggest ("I hope I am not too familiar in my remarks"). A few men took pains to explicitly disavow any possible erotic component to their appreciation, even as they sent him "verbal bouquets." "Mr. Vallée," writes one, "This is the first time I've ever written a radio performer. But I felt I must write and tell you how much I enjoy you and your Yale Men. I presume you get many verbal bouquets from your radio fans, but I honestly think yours is

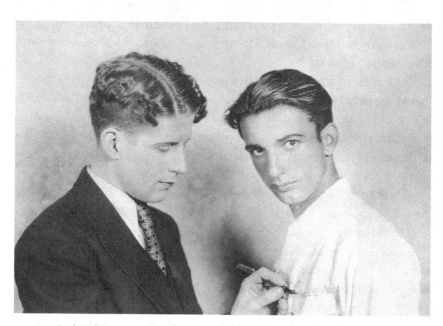

FIG. 3.5. Rudy Vallée autographs a fan's shirt. Vallée took as many photos with male as with female autograph seekers, which were also published widely in his early years of stardom. Unidentified news clipping titled "Getting Inspiration from Rudy," August 1929. Reprinted by permission of Eleanor Vallée. Courtesy of Rudy Vallée Collection, American Radio Archives.

the nicest and most adapted to broadcasting of any male voice heard over the air today. Incidentally, I'm no love-sick sheik, having been married several years, as a wife and two kids will prove, but when you sing 'If You Were the Only Girl in the World' I'm certainly glad I bought a radio."

For other men, it was most important that Vallée not think them effeminate, though they were comfortable using the language of a lover. One man wrote, "I love you for the pleasure you have given me over the radio. Your voice has brought untold happiness to me," and signed his letter "A He-Man." A few writers, however, indicated a more openly romantic attachment to Vallée by requesting, for example, that he sing more songs directly to men, especially "The Man I Love" and "My Man" (which Vallée seems to have done). As with female fans, such requests for particular songs were accompanied by requests for signed photos for the men to treasure and display. These fans suggest Vallée's appeal for some gay men and the employment of his songs in same-sex as well as heterosexual courtships. Indeed, a common subgenre of crooning sheet music at this time featured "lonely men" with no women in sight, staring out across the water or out a window (fig. 3.6); their gender neutral lyrics further encouraged queer uses.

Vallée's letters from men are perhaps most revealing, however, in what they *don't* say. There are almost no indications in these letters of the divide between husbands and wives over Vallée that would begin driving press reports within the year (quite the opposite). The one male complaint registered here was reported by a young woman married to an older man; her husband objected to the provocative lyrics of Cole Porter's song "Let's Do It," a Vallée staple: "He said last week that it should not be broadcasted. But he is one of those old fashioned bubs. He is nearly 15 years older than I and Oh what a time I have Believe me. I certainly do like the number." Clearly this husband was not so keen on the sexually frank 1920s public culture; Vallée, however, was firmly allied with both modern sexual mores and the female of the household, alliances that would eventually cause him a great deal of trouble.

STRANGE INTERLUDES: ROMANCE BY RADIO

Although male as well as female writers appreciated Vallée's voice, women were generally less reticent about expressing their strongest passions. Women in the 1920s were more socially prepared to be wooed by a voice emanating from a piece of living-room furniture. As feminist historians have shown, this was the first generation of middle-class women whose definition of modernity included at least some hope of being able to have both career and family, although generally such hopes were disappointed.[47] Consequently, even as women worked more, they were also marrying more; only 5 percent of women were unmarried. Although the flapper era gave women more possibilities and expectations regarding individual expression, romantic partnership, erotic fulfillment, and consumer choices, the married woman was still expected to conform to the social ideal of the nuclear family and to channel her self-expression into a primarily domestic, maternal role.[48] Modern marriage advocates acknowledged the existence of wives' sexual pleasure apart from maternity—a significant break from previous cultural definitions of American womanhood—yet these discourses nevertheless sought to preserve gender hierarchies, heterosexual ideation, and reproductive focus for middle-class whites, in part by more actively discouraging other sources of erotic satisfaction such as masturbation and same-sex affections.[49] Thus women were encouraged to feel sexual desire, given detailed anatomical information about how to achieve sexual pleasure, and told to be demonstrative

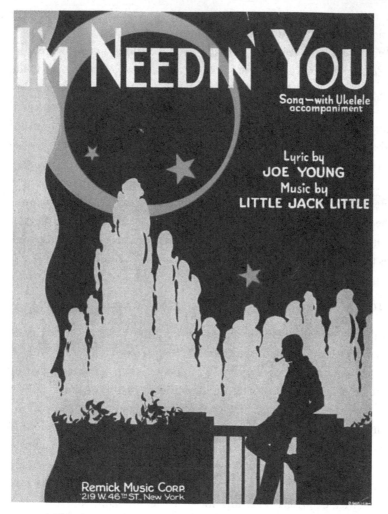

FIG. 3.6. This sheet music is representative of a particular subgenre of sheet music illustrations from the late 1920s and early 1930s in which a solitary male pines for a gender-neutral "you," typically while staring at the moon or across the water or through a window. Like the female-dominated sheet music covers of the time (fig. 3.3), the male figure is feminized in his romantic longing, but in this subgenre the object of his longing is notably absent. The phallic shapes on this particular cover would seem to suggest that the ungendered "you" of the song is likely *not* a woman. Like fig. 2.1, this cover is reflective of a transitional period in popular song in which direct address made straight and queer reception equally possible. Sheet music, "I'm Needin' You," 1930. Author's collection.

in their enjoyment of sex, but they were simultaneously counseled not to act on their desires directly except with their husbands or boyfriends and never to initiate even with them.[50] Such contradictory and frustrating advice left women in a perpetual state of anticipation with little direct release. The only ways women *were* encouraged to be active was as consumers.

The combination of an intensified sexual culture and women's need for self-expression helps contextualize the heightened erotic response Vallée inspired in many of his fans and the enhanced female fandom that produced America's first pop idol. As women's public roles narrowed, their consumer roles expanded. They were explicitly encouraged to view consumption as a substitute for civic participation and as a solution to their personal problems through their identification with Hollywood stars and their purchase of beauty products.[51] Women had become primary consumer targets by the 1920s, and the narratives of movies, magazines, novels, tabloid newspapers, and unprecedented levels of advertising encouraged them to focus on romantic love and erotic pleasure above all else. Newly affirmed as sexual beings, women looked to the mass media as a useful testing ground, a way to identify and differentiate their desires. Popular idols such as John Barrymore, Rudolph Valentino, and Charles Lindbergh quickly replaced political, ethnic, or religious idols in the psyches of this generation.[52] Women were also the primary consumers of popular songs through radio, recordings, and sheet music, and they prompted the transformation of radio's friendly, domestic airwaves into emotionally charged, erotic ones. For many women, Vallée's voice offered not only a catalyst for heterosexual lovemaking but also an alternative object of desire and pleasure.

No matter how much the 1920s sexualized culture and the radio industry itself had seemingly laid the groundwork for the rise of a radio Romeo, many women were still shocked by their own arousal when they first heard Vallée's voice. Like some of the men, many women denied any erotic impropriety in their feelings, prefacing their fan letters with disclaimers that they were not writing "mash notes," that they were "happily married but . . ." Nevertheless, a typical letter of this type inevitably included language that suggests orgasmic release: "I am married and happily so, but really I enjoy your programs so frightfully much that I just have to speak of it or I will burst with admiration of your talents." This need to have an outlet for the release of explosive feeling is common to all Vallée's fan letters, but especially this group: "I feel compelled to write"; "I really cannot contain my appreciation"; "I feel unable to remain silent."

When women *did* try to describe their reaction to Vallée's voice, they most commonly identified it as "falling in love," but "love" was often tellingly spoken of in terms of bodily activation and physical pleasure; one woman reports "jumping three feet in the air" when she hears his voice. Some women were more blunt about the specific erotic appeal of Vallée's voice. "I'm burning up," wrote a young woman in Maspeth, New Jersey. A fan from Brooklyn confessed, "A long time ago, I listened to you sing 'Rain' and all sorts of shivery thrills ran up and down my spinal column. Is it possible I've fallen in love with a voice?" Another early letter acknowledged the erotic power of Vallée's voice by borrowing a term from Hollywood that would later become common in press descriptions of Vallée: "I think you are endowed with 'It' that's why I sit up night after night losing my beauty sleep to hear you." In Vallée the radio voice had become a sexually potent object and an unanticipated source of consumer satisfaction.

Women's willingness to emotionally invest in Vallée's radio voice to such an extraordinary degree represented a boon for the industry and for consumer culture, but it also indicated women's keen ability to choose the voice that best served their desires. Although their professional choices were narrow, women of this generation were encouraged to be particular in choosing their lovers. The women who fell in love with Vallée in 1928 did so because they believed he shared many of their feelings, both speaking for them and arousing them. There were four qualities of Vallée's performance that were essential to these listeners' attraction: the perceived sincerity of his feeling (expressed in his willingness to self-reveal), his direct address and responsiveness to them, his frequent identification with a culturally coded "feminine" point of view, and the alternative pleasures and fantasies he stimulated.

Writers used the word *sincere* again and again to identify the quality that they felt set Vallée apart from other performers. This was not a new criterion to apply to popular song, since minstrel tenors and vaudeville's sentimental singers had been making audiences cry for decades, but it became more important to private listeners because of changing technology and changing times. While sincerity was sometimes present (but not essential) in public performers, it became an integral component of successful radio crooning. Radio broadcasting directly addressed people personally in their homes, as individuals rather than members of a mass audience, so that with radio, for the first time, "public singing [was] used as a vehicle for intimacy."[53] Moreover, because family relationships and modern marriages had come to be based more on personal affection than ritual, sincerity had become an essential component of familial and romantic life. "Young America," noted *Harper's*, "exalts sincerity, truth, naturalness." A sincere, trustworthy lover was especially important for women, who would likely have to depend economically as well as emotionally and erotically on their spousal choice. In order for Vallée to have the effect he did, audiences had to believe he meant his love for them, and because of his yearning, passionate delivery, they did believe it. Richard Dyer has described this kind of star power as appearing to "experience emotion directly, unambiguously, 'authentically,' without holding back," and asserts that this kind of "transparency" is essential to an audience's perception of the performer's sincerity.[54] For example, Vallée's sincerity was confirmed for some listeners because of the physical toll his emotionally intense performances seemed to take on him, and they applauded his efforts on their behalf. His use of vibrato verified his physical exertion for listeners, as did his inability to sometimes reach the highest notes; they simply exhausted him. But it was Vallée's emotional exposure and vulnerability, his willingness to open up and express painful feelings that most impressed his listeners, who interpreted it as testimony of the genuine emotional energy he was putting into his performance. "What is it that makes your singing feel as if it was an effort for you? Why are you so sad and your voice so heavy as if crying? You can't possibly say nothing happened."

Vallée's unusual intimations were even more stimulating to his listeners given the heavy romantic content of his songs, his consistent use of direct address, and his receptiveness to requests. He answered every piece of mail himself during his first year and always fulfilled photo requests; many of these fans wrote second and third letters thanking him for his replies: "I never in my wildest dreams expected such a nice letter from you and a picture, too, really I don't know how to thank you." When he realized that his audiences responded most to love songs, he sang more love songs and regularly met individual requests; in fact romantic and more sexually provocative songs (for example, "99 Out of 100 Want to Be Kissed—Why Not You?") dominated his earliest broadcasts. Scripts from Vallée's 1929 broadcast schedule reveal a predominance of love songs, many of which contain the words *love* and *you* as well as first-person pronouns:

16 MARCH 1929

"My Time Is Your Time"
"You're Wonderful"

"You Can't Blame Me for Loving You"

"I'm Still Caring"

"My Kind of Love"

"Kansas City Kitty"

"The One I Love Loves Me"

"Just You Alone"

"The Song of Songs"

19 JUNE 1929

"Love Lit Hollow"

"I'm Doing What I'm Doing for Love"

"I'll Be Reminded of You"

"You Came, I Saw, You Conquered"

"Moon Love"

"Pagan Love Song"

"Just Another Kiss"

"Pretending (I Just Pretend)"

"Vagabond Lover"

"That's My Idea of Heaven"

"Baby"

"I Kiss Your Hand, Madame"

"Lonely One"

"In the Hush of the Night"

"I Fell in Love with You"

The titles and lyrics of love songs took on a new significance in the age of the crooner and helped define his alliance with the cultural feminine.

Some of Vallée's early songs actually position the singer in the female role in lyrical terms, not an uncommon practice in the 1920s but one that had greater resonance when combined with Vallée's intimate delivery style. According to his playlists, Vallée frequently sang "The Man I Love," for example, and his early hit "Georgie Porgie" was sung from the point of view of someone erotically attracted to a man: "I only wish that he would just kiss me."[55] Even in this song the crooner plays the yearning girl rather than the flapper, identifying with the more traditionally feminine position. Vallée's lyrics frequently refer to his own tears and depict him as excessively emotional: "For all these years, I'll go on shedding tears / For the girl who belongs to somebody else."

The lyrics are romantic in standard clichéd ways of first-generation Tin Pan Alley songs, with frequent references to "dreams," "gardens," and "flowers," again references more associated with women than men: "I'll spend all my hours among fragrant flowers—then I'll be reminded of you."

In many ways the crooner is the gender flipside of the flapper, a Fitzgerald hero yearning and pleading for his dream girl, who is always portrayed as more powerful than he. If the flapper transgresses her sex role by being aggressive, confident, independent, and optimistic, the crooner is most often sexually desiring but submissive, longing, and dependent ("You Came, I Saw, You Conquered"). His song choices also recognized that women in the 1920s now had more choices in the field of romance ("When You Fall in Love, Fall in Love with Me"). In Vallée's songs the man waits and pines for the woman, pinning all his hopes and dreams on her ("My Life Begins and Ends with You," "Nothing to Do All Day but Think of You"). He has no other desire but to be with her, and when she leaves him, he is devastated ("Lonely Vagabond").

By passively positioning himself in relation to his lady love, Vallée bridged the gap between the traditional romantic and the modern sensualist. He helped women to negotiate these cultural shifts by offering them the opportunity to interpret his vocals in a variety of ways that provided some with much-needed relief from the limitations of companionate marriage. Under the new norms, women felt pressured to show levels of sexual enjoyment and desire with which they were often uncomfortable. Women who did not always enjoy sexual contact with their husbands were frequently accused of being frigid, prudes, or lesbians; the shyness and pain Vallée expresses mirrored such women's discomfort and disillusionment with modern expectations, reasserting their desire for romance and emotional connection.[56]

Conversely, women who were *too* assertive in their sexual desires within marriage were also seen as problematic and unnatural. Many listeners therefore enjoyed the way Vallée's surrender reversed gendered social roles, allowing women to occupy a position of aggressor in their relationship with him. Women wrote about wanting to touch Vallée, pick him up, or devour him. "When you sing 'Rain,'" wrote one Brooklyn woman, "I could eat you up—literally." Another wrote, "If I could pick you up out of the cone speaker I would do so." Sex was definitely on the mind of many of these writers, who expressed their appreciation for the "suggestive" content of songs such as "You'll Do It Someday, Why Not Now?" In these early letters a couple of women even directly propositioned Vallée, sending their pictures and phone numbers, which would become common practice for his female fans by 1929. Much more typically Vallée empowered women to assert themselves with the men in their lives; women wrote that in addition to forcing their boyfriends to listen to Vallée, they were going to persuade them to take them to Vallée's Heigh-Ho Club.

Vallée's voice and persona also provided a vital space for women in which identification and desire could still overlap, permitting them to refuse the divisions of gender and sexuality that cultural authorities were attempting to cement. One of Vallée's earliest letters, from Miss Lillian L. in New York City in 1928, quoted in the epigraph to this chapter, exemplifies this intersection: "You sang 'Lovely Lady' the other night—*that* is *me*, that is the way I feel." This receptive position—which was common in the gender-fluid entertainment world of the 1920s but would become increasingly rare as modern psychology took hold—allowed listeners to occupy multiple social roles simultaneously; Vallée fandom permitted feminist and proto-queer fans, for example, to "love a boy and to be a boy" at the same time.[57] Just as female divas and blues singers have historically provided gay men with a public voice in which to sing to their same-sex lovers, romantic crooners gave women this same mode of transgressive public identification and expression, even as same-sex affections—widely prevalent—were being actively discouraged.[58] Vallée also represented the desire among women to identify with the power and privileges that men had; many of his female fans wrote that he provided a professional model and inspiration for them.

Finally, women's responses to Vallée suggested that his voice enabled them to find alternative ways to achieve their desires, including rejecting unsatisfying lovers and pleasuring themselves. Although marriage manuals advised men, in detail, about how to please women, the manuals also suggested that many men were not up to the task and did not provide the level of communication and foreplay that their wives wanted.[59] Although Vallée's songs highlight male-female pairing, they also enact fantasies of women leaving men, of escape (however temporarily) from unions that are unfulfilling. His voice provided a substitute lover for such women, one who promoted their interests and privileged their desires. Listeners wrote of forgoing dates to "stay home, slip into a negligee, curl up to my Lawson [radio] and listen to you!" More provocatively, these letters suggest a variety of autoerotic practices among some of Vallée's listeners (the orgasmic "explosions" referenced earlier), which mirrored those indicated in sex surveys of the time. Katherine Bement Davis's 1929 survey notes that in addition to genital masturbation, which was widely practiced, women participated in "sex reveries or day dreaming . . .

the effects [of which] may range from mild sex excitement to the actual inducing of the orgasm, the latter without any manipulation of the organs."[60]

The practice of masturbation was discouraged by advocates of modern marriage. A successful companionate marriage was judged on its ability to "supply a satisfactory adjustment to the sex-impulse" of women; proof of that adjustment would be in women's refraining from masturbation, which was considered "devastating and pernicious" to sexual health.[61] Men who were lonely or unsatisfied with their marital lives could find sexual relief as independent men out on the town, but women had fewer options. Vallée's voice helped give some of them comfort and release. By fostering the potential for self-pleasure with his romantic vibrating voice and fast-tonguing on his saxophone, Vallée represented a way for modern women to retain sexual agency; their responses to him indicated that they did not need a man's actual touch to be erotically stimulated or satisfied, and that their sexuality was not containable or controllable within marriage. This assumption was soon to be dramatically verified by the swooning reaction to Vallée's public appearances.

Vallée's success is a testament to the power and unpredictability of consumer culture. Despite or perhaps because of consumer efforts to channel the public in the direction of ideal romance, comfort, and sex, audiences responded by creating a celebrity who most exemplified the qualities they wanted in a companion or lover and who activated their own desiring impulses. Vallée was an aspirational figure for women because he represented a less restrictive, less gendered, more genuinely egalitarian social relation than marriage advocates could offer them.

Vallée did more than bring urban culture into the privacy of the home; he also allowed his listeners' voices to be heard through him, giving public expression to their private desires. Through their appreciation and encouragement in 1928, these listeners—both men and women—enabled, anticipated, and participated in crooning's enormous cultural impact. In doing just what the culture around them had instructed them to do—to be appreciative, active, desiring consumers—these listeners would soon discover the power they had to unsettle that culture.

(((Four)))

"THE MOUTH OF THE MACHINE"

The Creation of the Crooning Idol, 1929

Suddenly, Rudy picks up a megaphone, stands quietly at the corner
of the stage, and begins to sing. The audience holds its breath in joy,
in adoration. The orchestra plays softly, slowly. He has chosen "I Kiss
Your Hand, Madame." It was a wise choice. His voice is low, pleasant,
natural. . . . The words drift from the megaphone like a caress, a billet
doux for each gasping female in the vast theatre. . . . When he stops, the
audience's breath, held in an exquisite agony of waiting, is unleashed.
And with it comes pounding applause. [The audience] is enraptured,
fanatical. It has been carried up Parnassus on this insinuating, wooing
voice. He is their darling, their Song Lover. He's the best yet. Rudy
Valentino wasn't it. . . . Give us Rudy Vallée. Give us this tall, slender,
simple boy, with his blond, wavy hair, his tanned face, his blue eyes, and
his gentle voice that makes love so democratically to everyone.
—Martha Gellhorn, "Rudy Vallée: God's Gift to Us Girls," 1929

In response to radio fans' requests that he "show himself," Rudy Vallée arranged for a four-day weekend appearance at a New York City vaudeville
house. Vallée promoted the event himself on local radio, but otherwise there
was almost no buildup; the Keith Theater's booking agent was dubious about
Vallée's drawing power and offered him little pay for the spot.[1] Theatrical
producers still considered "radio acts," as *Variety* called them, short-term
novelties, and industry critics derisively referred to radio's audiences as dim,
undependable "deadheads."[2] Although the few radio-focused magazines of

the time had begun to shift their coverage from radio technology to radio content and personalities, the private lives of radio performers still remained largely unknown and unexploited, in contrast to film stars elevated to the status of cultural icons.[3]

This situation changed after Vallée's appearance at RKO Keith's "neighborhood" vaudeville theater at Eighty-First and Broadway on the Upper West Side, in February 1929. The event was "an explosion in the theatrical world," in the words of one daily.[4] Police were called to oversee the tremendous crowd outside the theater. Vallée broke all house records for attendance and was held over for several days. No one was more surprised than Vallée himself, who describes the opening in his 1929 autobiography, *Vagabond Dreams Come True*: "On the opening strains of 'Down the Field' [his signature tune], the house went mad, and after our opening number, as I stepped forward to say 'Heigh-Ho Everybody,' my greeting was received with deafening applause, and at the beginning of every number there was a tremendous outburst of handclapping. I was astounded by the power of radio."[5] Vallée's audience members were themselves live wires, sitting at the edge of their seats, frequently jumping up to applaud or toss him bouquets of orchids. Although the popularity of the intimate microphone aesthetic was well established in live and mediated venues by 1928, Vallée's insistently romantic affect and song choice, use of direct address, and emotional intensity activated many of his listeners in new ways for the live entertainment world. Most music and theatrical promoters had not followed the popularity of local radio personalities and were unprepared for such an intense reaction; when Vallée appeared, it was as if someone had suddenly turned on a spotlight, and the first American pop idol was just suddenly, inevitably *there*.

Vaudeville promoters assumed Vallée was just another novelty sensation and accordingly sought to take quick advantage of his appeal. Keith producers offered him a ten-week tour of their top New York vaudeville and motion picture houses, and at every venue he was a huge success. By April he was playing the legendary New York Palace, where again he was a smash, though the Palace staff did not know what to make of him: "there was a certain air of disbelief and incredulity on the part of the doorman and the stagehands," who had never heard of him.[6] Most vaudeville acts worked for years before headlining the Palace; "playing the Palace" was a benchmark in any vaudevillian's career. Vallée's radio following had propelled him there less than a year after his first local WABC broadcast.

After these gigs 1929 belonged to Rudy Vallée. Early press notices speak of Vallée's "overnight fame," and for once they were not being hyperbolic. His

FIG. 4.1. Rudy Vallée lights a fire under the popular vaudeville singer and actress Belle Baker at the Brooklyn Paramount, December 1929. The giant phallic symbol makes comedy out of Vallée's appeal to women. Reprinted by permission of Eleanor Vallée. Courtesy of Rudy Vallée Collection, American Radio Archives.

meteoric rise to stardom was confirmed with his first headlining vaudeville and motion picture house tour, during which NBC signed him to an exclusive broadcasting deal. The rapidity of his ascent was largely due to the fact that he became a star at a unique moment of institutional and corporate convergence, which permitted him to work across several different performance venues. By year's end he had secured his own NBC network radio program, an exclusive Victor record contract, and the starring role in a Hollywood feature film, in addition to earning impressive sheet music sales, leading successful band tours, and having his new nightclub, the Versailles, change its name to Villa Vallée. He quickly became not only the "talk of the town," according to *Vanity Fair*, but the talk of the nation. Throughout that year entertainment industry veterans, newspaper columnists, and cultural critics puzzled over the Vallée "phenomenon," seeking to define (and, of course, capitalize on) what made Vallée so popular. Headlines read not only "Who Is Rudy Vallée?" but more significantly "*Why* Is Rudy Vallée?"[7]

FIG. 4.2. Movie ad for *The Letter* at the New York Paramount, April 1929.
Vallée performed prologues at both the New York and Brooklyn Paramount
theaters throughout 1929, often on the same day. He was usually paired with
popular "women's films" such as *The Letter*. Like many pre-Code films, *The
Letter* was far more sympathetic to its heroine, an adulterer and murderer
played by Jeanne Eagels, than Code films would be. Courtesy of Rudy Vallée
Collection, American Radio Archives.

Vallée's popularity was portrayed as a paradox by the press because he combined elements of both genteel Victorian New England and sensual, modern urban culture: he was a modest, hardworking, devoted son with a quiet, melodious jazz band, but he was also a modern "vamp of the machine" who made women swoon. He was the favorite of both "hard-boiled" flappers and their "sentimental" mothers, according to the *Brooklyn Eagle*: "[Vallée is] the Sweetheart preferred of Miss America, to say nothing of her mother and her maiden aunts."[8] His early coverage underlines his status as a contradictory cultural freak, a crooning novelty act whose combination of sensitivity and erotic power was the subject of much purported "surprise" and amusement among journalists. However, the press's "shock" was overstated for dramatic purposes, given that many male performers of the 1920s combined qualities of femininity and sensuality. What was new and baffling about Vallée's appeal was the fact that his *voice* was key to his popularity even more than his boyish looks, Yale pedigree, or musical simplicity. Further confounding those in the industry, his was a voice that registered as unremarkable when heard live, and critics were unsure whether he was even a tenor or a baritone. His fellow sweet jazz bandleaders were equally flummoxed; putting aside his lack of training, range, and projection abilities, Vallée's voice did not seem to them all that different from the smooth, well-enunciated, megaphone or microphone crooners in their own bands. Vallée's band even lacked the polished vocal harmonies that distinguished Waring's Pennsylvanians and others.

Vallée's sound was born of the new intimate microphone aesthetic, and his success would permanently redefine it. Commentators first looked to Vallée's audience to help explain the popularity of his sound. After observing his audience's intense reactions at his vaudeville performances, critics concluded that his particular affect was the attraction: "Mr. Vallée's popularity transcends all matters of musical skill, technical prowess, looks, or orchestral effectiveness," wrote the columnist Richard Watts Jr. "It is entirely a matter of emotion." Opined the *Evening World*, "Nothing of the romantic in his voice until he starts to sing." Other critics identified this elusive quality as "it," that is, "the voice with sex appeal."[9]

The term *sex appeal* had not generally been used before to describe a voice. Vallée's vocal popularity preceded his physical appeal and bewildered critics like those at *Variety*, who found that "the abstractness of microphone transmission makes this [effect] almost a paradox." But critics also noted that Vallée's microphone voice, so different from externalized performance styles, had a new, different kind of erotic appeal: "yearning rather than seductive, and hardly in a world with the Broadway conception of voice appeal."[10] *New York World's* smitten columnist Gladys Oak referred to him as the "soothing, bewitching, inflaming mouth of the machine."[11] Having no vocal equivalent with which to compare Vallée's appeal, the press likened his effects to those of previous sex idols such as the actors Rudolph Valentino and John Barrymore and dubbed him a "matinee idol" based on the besotted behavior of fans. *Variety* noted that "many believe him . . . to be the champ femme freak attraction to date, in any line of theatricals."[12]

Women *were* extremely demonstrative in their appreciation of Vallée, but what's notable about such coverage is that women were repeatedly cited as his *only* fans, constructing women's behavior and taste as freakish in opposition to male restraint and discerning taste. Even though audience reports, photographs from Vallée's public appearances, fan letters to him as well as to newspapers, and an array of concert requests demonstrate that Vallée appealed to both sexes, male fans were largely erased from his press coverage.[13] Instead highly influential New York tabloid columnists—overwhelmingly male—gleefully and repeatedly affirmed Vallée's woman-made persona, portraying him as a potential home wrecker and creating a dramatic narrative of marital strife surrounding him—all with tongue in cheek. Such a designation served the immediate purpose of Vallée's vaudeville producers, who wanted to narrowly define and exploit him as a female-only novelty act, although this designation would ultimately serve larger ideological purposes and be used to degrade Vallée and his audiences as gender norms narrowed.

In 1929, however, Vallée was hardly a disturbing figure in an urban landscape, where white middle-class standards of masculine behavior still remained largely irrelevant in popular performance. The New York performance scene of this time encompassed an unusually broad spectrum of gender behaviors, especially among men, who still far outnumbered women as performers. Manhattan cabarets, speakeasies, nightclubs, restaurants, dance halls, and theaters in the 1920s brimmed with male "double-voiced" falsetto singers, chorus boys, female impersonators, collegiate acts, drag ball performers, singing waiters, "sissy" quartet and burlesque singers, confidential cabaret tenors, tango pirates, and queeny masters of ceremonies. Frequently these personalities found their way into the mass media, such as Vitaphone short films, suggesting their appeal beyond urban venues. Indeed Vallée became popular simultaneously with the celebrated "pansy craze," a phenomenon wherein male performers brazenly celebrated camp gestures, language, and affect, drawing crowds of curious social elites. Although some acts ridiculed gender-bending effeminacy for comic effect, many others did not, suggesting a degree of inclusivity and indeed naturalization of what we would today call gender-queer behavior. It was, in a word, the twenties.

Thus when *Variety* labeled Vallée a "femme freak" because of his large crowds of passionate female followers, those writers were not yet insinuating that Vallée himself was effeminate. At the time Vallée's act was novel for the ways his intimate vocal performances seemed to spark *heterosexual* desire by speaking directly and specifically to female audiences. Within a few years his association with female fans would mark him as insufficiently masculine, but when he first took the scene by storm, gender and sexual norms were simply less codified for many popular performers and their audiences than they would be a few years later—and for decades thereafter. Vallée's rise to fame must be situated within the popular culture of the period, which challenged later notions of normative gender behavior.

What the entertainment industry did begin to regard as significant was that Vallée's stardom suggested crooning's potential as a popular entertainment and inspired successful imitators. Vallée was the first singer who did not simply croon, but for whom crooning became an identity; he was designated a crooner in both his public and his private life. Audiences in 1929 craved photographs, autographs, and details of Vallée's personal life, resulting in enormous national publicity and inaugurating a radio star culture on a mass scale. His nationwide celebrity also supported and validated the emerging commercial radio network system, which would rely on new star voices to help promote its nationalist, unifying rhetoric. But Vallée's stardom extended beyond radio. As the first pop idol, he reshaped public understanding of crooning around the act of democratic direct address, of "making love to everyone" by consistently framing his singing as the loving, intimate communication between a performer and his listener, even as legions of fan communities took shape around him. His romantic crooning and the devotion it inspired would become defining characteristics of American pop music and an intrinsic part of the new commercial sound culture that would transform American daily life.

A MAMA'S BOY AND "THE SHEIK OF THE ETHER": THE STAR CROONER PERSONA

Stars become stars, as Richard Dyer has argued, because they speak to and about the society in which they live, frequently embodying seemingly contradictory qualities in ways that resonate with a significant number of people.[14] As much as the 1920s are remembered as the decade of modernity, Vallée's appeal suggests a more complex picture, one in which modern and Victorian-era mores often overlapped and had to be negotiated across lines of class, race, ethnicity, and gender. Vallée rose from being a regional radio star to a national idol in part because of the way his radio crooning brought together seemingly antithetical elements of his era. On an individual level, his persona combined aspects of both Victorian and modern urban cultures: New England and New York City, simple melodies and jazz music, technology and sensuality, gentlemanly romantic idealism and contemporary erotic desire, femininity and masculinity, public and private. Vallée's singing bridged class, ethnic, and racial divides, proving equally pleasing to suburban, middle-class whites and urban, working-class immigrants and blacks. He especially pleased females of all ages; he was every mother's loving son and every flapper's collegiate dream man. In the discourse surrounding Vallée, these generational divides were presented as a contrast between his collegiate, youthful appearance and good behavior and his seductive voice.

When Vallée first appeared on the scene, both his fans and the press characterized him as the "all-American boy." While this designation ironically became virtual heresy within a few years, in 1929 it reflected a type of nationalist rhetoric connected to the growing nativism of the period and the homogenizing aims of the corporate mass media. The French Irish Catholic Vallée represented the racially assimilated white ethnic male performer, a college graduate with decidedly middle-class manners. Even though he was an urban jazz bandleader, Vallée was frequently contrasted with other bandleaders of his day as representing a more refined (middle-class, white) New Englander rather than a dissolute (working-class, ethnic) New Yorker. In April 1929 the *New York American* reported that people they interviewed felt that Vallée was "a relief after the wisecracking, smart aleck orchestra leaders." Many press reports mentioned his modesty and sincerity, noting that he never dominated his orchestra with "that wiggling of shoulders and bending of knees" common to other orchestra leaders nor employed "tricks" to draw attention, such as wearing a "freak hat" or "twirling a cane."[15] Instead, they pointed out, Vallée stood "still," "quiet" and "dignified," barely moving the baton, and he frequently stood off to the side when not singing in order to direct the audience's focus toward his orchestra rather than himself. Reporters also described how hardworking and responsive he was, citing his attention to fans and the time he took to be gracious in interviews.

MRS. MARGUERITE CAPRON.
Skeptical and inclined to belittle the halo of romance and heart throbs wound around Rudy Vallee as a menace to feminine hearts of all classes and degrees, Mrs. Marguerite Capron went to see for herself in a visit to Villa

RUDY HERE, THERE, EVERYWHERE.
Vallee. And it wasn't long before this daughter of a military man and bride of a West Point cadet discovered why for herself as Rudy's insidious charm gradually brought her down from her critical vantage point. Her

IN PENSIVE MOOD.
Impressions of the visit are shown in the center photo, giving a panoramic view of the Villa Vallee, with tireless yet weary Rudy dominating the place with his personality. At right is one of the "Great Lover's" latest pictures.

FIG. 4.3. Vallée's most enthusiastic press coverage was often written by the many female journalists working in New York City in the late 1920s. Here Marguerite Capron (pictured left) admits being charmed by him, and her paper endorses her opinion, noting that she is particularly credible because "she is the daughter of a military man and the bride of a West Point cadet." The center illustration identifies the factors she attributes to Vallée's appeal: "Half-closed eyes, tired look appeal to ladies"; "Doesn't flirt with ladies on dance floor"; "Looks directly at you and talks seriously"; and "His rumpled hair—and that grin!" "Found Romeo Despite Skepticism, A Big, Lovable Boy," *New York Evening Journal*, 7 December 1929. Courtesy of Rudy Vallée Collection, American Radio Archives.

"Sitting in his dressing room," wrote one interviewer, Marguerite Tazelaar, in March 1929, "the spirit of New England seemed to be speaking through the slender young man, accounting for the character, the rigorous determination that have brought him to a coveted place along Broadway's Tin Pan Alley."[16]

As a Yale graduate Vallée also represented the new cultural vogue of the collegiate performer. In a popular performance world that, until the 1920s, had been dominated by the working classes and remained disreputable, Vallée's decidedly middle-class status made him broadly acceptable. Simon Frith has defined pop music in part as "family music" suitable for all ages, and Vallée embodied that definition as no one else had before him.[17] Letters from male heads of families in 1928, for example, indicate how well he suited standards of middle-class decorum. One such "family" letter came from the previously cited doctor in New York City, who praised Vallée's lack of vulgarity. Vallée's refusal to use slang made him more respectable and also separated him from other crooning singers of the time, like the 1920s recording king Gene Austin, who did employ slang (for example, "shinin'" for "shining"). While the two men's songs are often conflated today, Vallée's lack of vernacular language made him emphatically middle class in contrast to Austin's southern, working-class style, and Vallée deliberately cultivated this distinction.[18] Jazz and blues delivery tracings were much less evident in Vallée's solos than in Austin's singing; fans and the press frequently noted Vallée's emphasis on "pure melody" over "fancy interpretations." His style represented and defined the assimilated sound of pop singing. Finally, the fact that Vallée sang songs in French, Italian, and Spanish reflected his cosmopolitan education and urban sophistication and made him immune, for a time, to the broader xenophobia and nationalism that characterized 1920s politics and would begin to more strongly impact popular culture in the early 1930s.

In fact some writers identified Vallée approvingly as a direct descendent of European troubadours. A noteworthy August 1929 article in the *Cleveland Plain Dealer* entitled "New Minstrel Sings and the Ladies Sigh" identifies Vallée not with the blackface minstrels from whom crooning developed but with the troubadour minstrels from Sir Walter Scott's poem "The Lay of the Last Minstrel": "While the rest of the world's entertainment midway[s] are busy singing lightly vulgar, obvious and maudlin sentimental ballads, Rudy Vallée has the good sense to stick to songs about the desire of a man for a maid, about lips that long to be kissed, about canoes and moonlit nights, and principally about the age-old universal quest for a dream girl."[19] The author describes Vallée's life as unglamorous, just that of "the average well-brought up boy." In this scenario she connects Vallée's music with the first popular songs in America, English imports from the late eighteenth and early nineteenth centuries about the love of a knight for his lady fair.[20] Less benignly, however, some commentators embraced Vallée in part because of his perceived racial purity. The ubiquity of eugenics rhetoric in the 1920s is startling, and once Vallée became a visible presence, his "Nordic" attributes were singled out for praise (and his Irish Catholicism erased, which his French name made easy to do). Eleanor Clarage of *College Humor* noted, perhaps satirically, that Vallée's "fine features . . . indicate good ancestry."[21] Indeed previous historians of the New York entertainment world have viewed the advent of crooners entirely through this lens, as culturally reactionary commercial forces.[22]

But such accounts fail to appreciate the complexity of Vallée's reception and the wide range of his—and romantic crooning's—appeal. His popularity was just as much a product of (and dependent on) New York's ethnically and

They Could Be Doubles

Though only five years old, little Jimmie Bingham has achieved more than the usual share of recognition. First of all Rudy Vallee has picked him as his very own protege, not as you may suppose, because of the physical resemblance, but because Jimmie is an embryonic saxophone player all on his own account. Second, Jimmie seems to be possessed of considerable pulchritude, for he carried off two beauty prizes in the Asbury Park Baby Parade, receiving not only the first prize, but also the Governor's cup.

FIG. 4.4. Vallée's appeal to the family audience meant that he received a great deal of mail and photos from children (and parents writing on behalf of their children) who loved him and were inspired to play the saxophone because of him. This particular photo suggests the continued cultural resonance of the child as romantic figure (more derisively referred to as the "mollycoddled boy"); the caption notes that Vallée himself is encouraging the young sax player, five-year-old Jimmie, who was also a recent child beauty contest winner. Within three years star crooners' influence on American youth would be widely decried as feminizing and immoral. "They Could Be Doubles," *Tattler and American Sketch*, October 1930. Courtesy of Rudy Vallée Collection, American Radio Archives.

racially varied urban culture as it was of New England's Puritan culture, and he strongly identified with and privileged his middle- and working-class audiences. His homogenized sound was rooted in Tin Pan Alley songs that had been broadly popular among diverse audiences for decades; likewise, by the time Vallée became a star, crooning was well entrenched in 1920s popular performance to the same degree, in the same venues, and among the same audiences as jazz music. The attraction of Vallée's romantic approach and youthful persona crossed class, age, racial, religious, and ethnic lines. When he made his initial public tour of New York City in 1929, he received his most enthusiastic crowds in immigrant neighborhoods with heavily Jewish, Irish, and Italian populations, but he was also popular in Harlem's black commu-

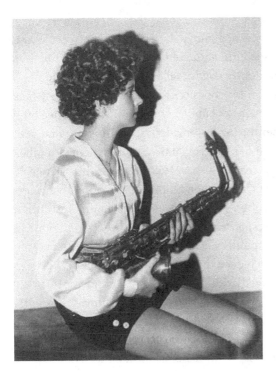

FIG. 4.5. Fan photo sent to Rudy Vallée from Virginia S., 1930. This is one of many photos from young female saxophonists who viewed Vallée as an ally in their achieving professional careers. Reprinted by permission of Eleanor Vallée. Courtesy of Rudy Vallée Collection, American Radio Archives.

nity, in the boroughs, and in white suburbia.[23] Vallée was certainly a step removed from urban ethnic performers like Al Jolson, but not in a simplistic, regressive way; rather, Vallée's success indicated the way gender had displaced ethnicity and class as the primary identity category in popular songs. Moreover, although Vallée's romantic love songs did not emphasize ethnic or class distinctions, as had prior minstrel and vaudeville stars' songs, this did not preclude ethnic and class identifications in his reception and popularity. Vallée's fans were multiply identified, and they chose him because he spoke to them in a variety of ways.

A key factor in Vallée's particular cross-cultural appeal for both the white middle class and the immigrant working class was his well-publicized devotion to his mother. This crucial aspect of his persona clearly allied him with the New England matriarch and the Victorian "feminine," sentimental culture being rejected by many of his 1920s contemporaries as old-fashioned and repressed, but it also made him a favorite of social groups outside the white middle class for whom matriarchal households and mother love were still culturally central.[24] Although histories of this transition have tended to focus on the modern rebels, Vallée's popularity represented the matron's revenge. As I discussed in chapter 1, "mother songs" had been a Tin Pan Alley staple, but the lyrics of popular songs shifted decisively from *mother* to *lover* in the late 1910s and 1920s; modern culture emphasized youthful romantic couples over familial or community bonds. Vallée's use of direct address in love songs, however, meant that his songs could satisfy all ages, since most could be interpreted as expressions of familial *or* romantic love. Vallée often explicitly spoke of his mother during his broadcasts, praising her and dedicating numerous love songs to her. His romantic crooning helped mothers regain some cultural footing, creating a space within which they were celebrated and publicly beloved at a time when mother songs—and the trained tenors and boy sopranos who often sang them—were becoming institutionally obsolete. The approving response of Vallée's audiences and the press indicates that the matricidal impulse of many cultural leaders was far from universal or unchallenged, and indeed the tremendous amount of approving coverage Vallée's mother received by the New York press confirms this.

Vallée's mother, Catherine, was lovingly covered by the press during the first years of his fame; she was repeatedly interviewed at her home in Maine, where Vallée spent his vacations. Vallée was a textbook product of what many moderns sneeringly referred to as "mollycoddling" (pampering) but that was still widely championed as good parenting by many in the 1920s. One of the qualities most often cited by commentators is Vallée's good behavior, which they invariably attribute to his mother's fine upbringing. In fact writers saw Vallée's love for his mother as evidence of his sincere privileging of women and their interests. Vallée himself repeatedly credited his mother for his musical talent and for those aspects of his character people found worthy, such as his work ethic, good manners, and temperance. His mother was the woman fans most associated with him at the height of his fame, until her death and his marriage in 1931. Front-page photos of Vallée kissing his mother accompanied many reports. Press coverage noted that when his mother visited him in New York, Vallée would devote himself to her; Catherine proudly told the *Boston Globe*, "Rudy would stay home regardless of all the invitations he had and the other things he ought to do just so he could sit on the side of the bed with me and hold my hand."[25] It is not surprising that matrons loved Vallée, given his devotion to his own mother, especially at a time when they were being unappreciated and increasingly marginalized.

Vallée's mother love gave him a cross-class and cross-ethnic appeal that was important to him and integral to his urban stardom. Catholic and Jewish households, in particular, had long cultural traditions of popular and reli-

FIG. 4.6. Vallée embracing his mother, Catherine, 1929. Her close, affectionate relationship with her son was widely publicized by the press, and she was the woman most associated with him by fans. When she died in 1931, Vallée at her side, one tabloid headline announced, "The Best Mother in the World Is Dead." Vallée epitomized the cultural tensions between the popular championing of mother love among Victorians and ethnic immigrant groups and the increasing disdain for the maternal by masculine modernists. Reprinted by permission of Eleanor Vallée. Courtesy of Rudy Vallée Collection, American Radio Archives.

gious male singing, and mother love was central to the cultural identity of each. Such households were also frequently matriarchal by default or necessity, and many of the young men there did not leave home because they couldn't afford to be married. Their mothers were often their primary emotional attachments and support in both their pre- and postadolescent lives, as Vallée's mother was for him.[26] Jewish and Catholic immigrant families would remain crucial supports to popular crooners for decades, as well as being (with African Americans) the primary social groups from which future crooning stars would emerge.

If Vallée gave the appearance to the press of a lovable son, his voice marked him as a seductive lover. Overwhelmingly the popular press and trade papers identified his voice and the reaction it elicited as characteristic of a modern, sexualized urban culture. *Variety* credited Vallée with liberalizing radio, noting that even the "conservative National Broadcasting Company" was advertising him as "the voice with sex appeal."[27] Vallée's brand of sex appeal was indeed new because it was primarily vocal and therefore hidden until he began to sing. As the *Evening World* noted in April, "No matter how still and straight and unaffected [Vallée] may look as he stands among his men and sings through his little megaphone, his eyes closed and his saxophone slung behind his shoulder, that voice is telling the world something that calls forth those agreeable little shivers so eagerly sought after by young America."[28]

In speech as well as song Vallée championed many of the urban values of his contemporaries, especially their sexual freedom and passion; he was frequently described by the press as "pash" or "pashy," popular slang for "passionate." In interviews he emphasized his alignment with women and romance. He admired the modern girl and gave interview after interview describing his "dreamgirl" as the prototypical flapper: slim, brunette, and an energetic dancer.[29] He supported the choice to divorce, did not believe he was "fitted for marriage," and admired the French for what he saw as "their honesty in acknowledging the importance of romance." Love was more important to him than anything else, Vallée confessed time and again: "My audience is a girl, or many girls—sometimes I am thinking of a real girl, sometimes a dreamgirl—but when I sing I am always a lover."[30] Just as the companionate marriage manuals of the 1920s advised husbands to be more sensitive to their wives' desires, Vallée was very open about his desire to "please the ladies," but he went even further by asserting that "a woman's likes and dislikes are always to be considered first." He admitted that he was not a "man's man" and that he would rather spend time with women than men because he had more in common with them. "I have never been able to understand men going off together on little sprees, neglecting their wives," he told *Outlook*.[31] Vallée catered to the desires of female consumers and projected himself as an object of desire for them, as Tin Pan Alley song pluggers, high-pitched minstrels, dance hall sheiks, and cabaret tango pirates had done before him.

But his performances differed from previous female-attentive performers in that radio helped him to develop a vocal appeal that both preceded and guaranteed his physical appeal; he didn't need to look like Valentino to make women swoon. While electrical recording and singers like Gene Austin and Jack Smith cultivated the new crooner aesthetic, Vallée heightened its emotional impact, making intimate singing more intensely personal with his use of first person and direct address. His singing privileged the strong feelings of the narrator more than any other aspect of performance; a particularly good example of this innovation (or deviation) is that Vallée frequently could not quite reach the higher notes of a song. To audiences he seemed constantly on the verge of expiring, always on the edge of attainment. Austin had occasionally used a similar effect by frequently ending songs on an ascending note, a "feminine ending" that refused a return to narrative stability or closure. Such endings allowed audiences to keep feeling the song, to stay inside of it in a more obviously constitutive way.[32] Vallée used this concluding effect as well, but he combined it with the strain of achieving higher notes throughout the song; he also made constant key changes during the course of concerts, going steadily higher and higher for increased dynamic and emotional effect.[33] As Martha Gellhorn's review in the epigraph to this chapter suggests, this delivery style was incredibly provocative and sexually stimulating to his audiences. For them the pleasure was in the "feminine" narrative of continual desire his crooning offered, the struggle and strain for attainment of the note, rather than the masterful achievement of it. As Vallée reported cheerfully to the *Evening World* in April 1929, "My audiences never know whether I'm going to reach the top note, and neither do I."[34] This style was in opposition to the established masculine standards of classical vocalists and most popular stars, whose reputations were made by their ability to project their voice and reach their high notes with seeming ease. Vallée took his audiences on a journey with him in each performance; he gave them an alternative erotic narrative to identify with, one that emphasized emotional investment and community feeling.

The sexual frankness of the jazz age separated Vallée in reviewers' minds from previous Tin Pan Alley songsters, as did his eschewing of songs about the virtues of home and family despite his vaunted love for his mother. Physical love ("kiss you, hold you") was of paramount importance in his songs, so much so that his singing was the equivalent of vocal petting. Yet such expressions of desire needed to be convincing as sincere love, not mere "sport" for audiences, and listeners believed him. The *Cleveland Press* columnist George Davis pointed to this aspect of Vallée's delivery as his innovation in popular singing: "Vallée sings a love song in a more confident, wooing way. . . . The way he sings a song expresses devotion rather than wailing appeal. . . . The mood he expresses is more characteristic of this America. The secret of this singer's success is entirely emotional and emotion is something love songs are about. . . . We think he has set a style which will be adopted by many other singers of popular songs of the more romantic sort."[35] Here Davis identifies as modern Vallée's intense, intimate pop performance as opposed to the more obviously *performed* style characteristic of the era before pop, when Irish tenors and vaudeville performers attempted to "put over" their sentiments through vocal technique and force. In contrast to those who characterized Vallée as an "all-American boy," Davis was among the reviewers who believed that Vallée represented something new with his emotional vulnerability and directness. Indeed the division Vallée would come to represent would not be between the modern and traditional but between masculine and feminine. However, that was a few years away. In 1929 he had the good fortune to become a star in a New York performance world in which gender "in-betweens" were not only accepted; they were all the rage.

RUDY VALLÉE IN CONTEXT: MASCULINITY AND PERFORMANCE IN THE 1920S

In the 1920s the promotion of companionate romantic relationships, commercialized leisure opportunities, and the rise of youth culture intersected to make cultural space for more flexible ("softer") gender roles for men, particularly in urban areas. Theodore Roosevelt's model of a "strenuous life" of muscularity and aggression for American men, although still an ideal for many, was less influential after the mass slaughter of World War I. War had disillusioned and dislocated many men, who subsequently converged in the cities; likewise, many black men sought to escape their own battlefields in the South by moving to northern cities in what became known as the Great Migration, and men who self-identified as "fairies" or "queers" moved from small towns to cities and formed their own communities.[36] The public presence of the fairy who defined himself by his feminine presentation also helped create a broader spectrum of acceptable gender behavior for all men. Working-class migrants, immigrants, and middle-class professionals like Vallée, instead of identifying with hypermasculine military or political figures, defined their modern masculinity through consumption and leisure activities. The live performance world and, in turn, the mass media magnified this male variety for a national audience, promoting romantic idols and gender in-betweens with great success, culminating with the craze for pansy performers in major cities across the country by the decade's end.

In the 1920s men were encouraged to see themselves as women saw them: as romantic, even sexual objects. Ironically the social discourses of the time that were so intent on promoting marriage also encouraged men to make themselves more attractive to women by developing more feminine-connotative behaviors such as paying attention to their physical appearance, learning to dance well, and being sensitive and romantic in lovemaking. In this era both women and men were described blatantly in terms of their sex appeal. For a man, this meant being clean-cut, shaving every day, grooming his hair with cream and pomade, wearing face cream and powder (talc), getting regular manicures, and, most of all, keeping up with the latest fashionable clothing styles. Behaviors that would soon be considered emasculating or effeminate were promoted by advertisers as necessary to maintain a youthful, attractive appearance to women, and embraced by a wide spectrum of men.[37] Movie actors regularly and visibly wore makeup (powder, blush, lipstick). Profiles of Jimmy Walker, the fashionable mayor of New York in the 1920s, claimed that he changed his clothes three times a day. The hard-boiled writer Damon Runyon was also obsessed with his clothes and took great care in his personal appearance, and both the FBI and their most wanted men, like John Dillinger, shared a love of good tailoring.[38] Such men also enjoyed cabaret performances, motion pictures, sentimental tunes, motoring, tanning, and jazz dancing, all of which provided the romantic settings for intimate courtship behavior.

The prototype of this urban sophisticate was the so-called male flapper, a popular figure in the novels of the era, most prominently those of F. Scott Fitzgerald. The male flapper, explains the historian Kevin White, was "coy, sensitive, gentle, but capable of being sexual."[39] Amory Blaine, the mollycoddled boy and collegiate hero of Fitzgerald's tremendously successful 1920 debut novel, *This Side of Paradise*, provided a nationwide popular model for this new kind of male, who was more feminine in looks, tastes, and culture than men in previous generations and for whom romance was king. In his review of the book in the *New York Tribune*, the journalist Heywood Broun expressed incredulity and dismay at the feminization of the American male, finding it "inconceivable" that "the attitude toward life of a Princeton undergraduate, even a freshman, should be so curiously similar to that of a sophomore at Miss Spence's."[40] By the mid-1920s, however, Fitzgerald's hero and Fitzgerald himself had come to define the age. Much like Rudy Vallée, the Fitzgerald hero loved popular culture and romantic songs, dressed divinely, and worshipped flappers.

While the romantic young man was a popular mainstream figure, he was far from the only gender-queer one by current standards, especially in the New York performance world. The center of the live performance world, as well as the radio and music industries, New York City was exceptionally diverse regarding gender performance, offering no single standard of femininity or masculinity and varying a great deal along class, ethnic, and racial lines. Because the city was the center of vaudeville, radio, and popular music in the 1920s, New York urban culture enabled or at the very least inspired much of what we think of today as 1920s popular culture, in which men and women appropriated each other's styles with much more frequency than they ever had before (or perhaps since).[41] Young female flappers wore their hair short and enjoyed petting parties, just as many young men dressed in colorful silk dressing gowns and mooned over their romantic prospects.

While the romantic popular songs youth like Amory Blaine hummed to themselves—songs by Rodgers and Hart, Cole Porter, Jerome Kern, and the Gershwins—have since become standards, the remarkable variety in the ways they were performed and interpreted at the time has been largely forgotten.[42] The vaudeville traditions of character (dialect) and parody singing converged and overlapped with the new intimate vocals of microphone crooning, producing a range of vocal possibilities that were not yet divided by race, class, ethnicity, or gender. Venues for popular singers also proliferated to include live venues such as Broadway operettas and musical comedies, vaudeville, picture houses, restaurants, cabaret, nightclubs, and revues, as well as mass-mediated formats such as records, radio, and film.[43] In the vaudeville tradition, which remained popular through the 1920s, the ability to convincingly perform in vocal masquerade as a person of a different social group (defined by race, ethnicity, gender, age, class, region, sexuality) was still widely considered a mark of virtuosic range rather than reflecting or revealing the performer's own identity or sexual preference. Although bodily markers of race and, especially, sex often severely limited performing opportunities, vocal essentialism had not yet been codified.

In the absence of an institutional regulation according to gender, men and women sang the same songs, in whatever genre, at whatever pitch, and with whatever content they and their audiences desired. Both men and women of every color were regularly described by reviewers throughout the decade as blues-singing, "torching," falsetto-singing, crooning, scatting, effing, yodeling, warbling, and impersonating other popular singers across sex and racial lines. In *Variety* reviews throughout 1925–26, female singers were often identified as singing baritone and male singers as producing soprano or falsetto with no comment beyond the quality of the sound produced.[44] Tenors and countertenors (male altos and sopranos) remained mass audience favorites; indeed the higher a male could sing, the better he was liked, and such talent was often a point of Irish and Italian ethnic pride. The softer, more intimate singing styles required by early microphones were widely embraced by the general public, who loved the soft, light male singing sound produced by condenser microphones. In addition men and women routinely sang love songs addressed to members of the same sex through the early 1930s. Even Vallée sang songs like "The Man I Love" over the radio. Although his use of direct address often suggested internalization of his song's lyrics, his was just one approach among many.

Vallée's rise coincided almost exactly with that of the pansy performer, another new kind of male vocalist. In 1927 New York City instituted new rules preventing explicit presentation or discussion of "sexual degeneracy or sexual perversion" on the legitimate stage, a ruling specifically aimed at the lesbian theme of the popular play *The Captive* as well as Mae West's two satires, *The Drag* and *Sex*.[45] But this censorship did not yet touch the presentation of sexual innuendo, pansy performance, and drag in popular entertainment, nor did it affect cross-gendered vocalizing, which was commonplace and more difficult to regulate. In fact censorship of queer content on the legitimate stage served only to increase public fascination with homosexuality among the middle and upper classes, climaxing in what historians refer to as the pansy craze of the late 1920s and early 1930s. Queer cabaret performers, especially male pansy acts, became huge draws in the mainstream, Waspy nightclubs where they had previously been unwelcome.[46] These pansies went beyond the "sissy" character that performers had been doing for decades in vaudeville and burlesque to confidently embody and celebrate sexual nonnormativity in camp references and sexual innuendo, reflecting the more sophisticated attitude of the cabaret. While queer and sexually provocative

FIG. 4.7. Harry Rose and Grace, *Metro Movietone Revue*, 1929. Harry Rose was one of the best-known pansy performers (or "lavender emcees") during this period. This still is of his role as master of ceremonies in MGM's *Metro Movietone Revue* (I and II, 1929), here with the child performer Grace Rogers. Rose's swish gestures, vocal inflections, and innuendo-laden asides mark him as a pansy, but his assertiveness and edginess, even arrogance, reflect his status as an unflappable vaudevillian, more akin to Al Jolson in attitude than Rudy Vallée.

singers and "lavender" masters of ceremonies had been part of the texture of life in 1920s cabarets and speakeasies, they were new for many of the audiences at more exclusive establishments, whose managers had largely resisted hiring them because of their low-class, low-culture, often sexually provocative or racially transgressive associations.[47] Increased if inconsistent regulation of cabarets and the impact of the Depression shifted these titillating acts to more elite cabarets and hotel nightclubs, which were not subject to curfews and whose owners began hiring pansy performers to stimulate business.

The presence of pansies in the most elite Broadway institutions brought more public attention to the presence of a gay male subculture and, initially, provided the ideal foil for crooning singers like Vallée. Next to the sexual openness of pansies, crooners were hardly a subject of concern for cultural authorities, even though their high, soft voices, sensitivity, and fancy dress marked them as in some ways feminine. In 1929 even press acknowledgments of an explicitly homoerotic following for Vallée were reported with amusement rather than condemnation: "A male beauty contest was held at the Washington Baths, Coney Island, last week. . . . Rudy Vallée was billed as the judge of honor, as it were, but Rudy wisely stayed away."[48] Ultimately, however, the pansy represented a double-edged sword for queer performers. Pansy acts helped to create a "vogue for effeminacy" in the 1920s that allowed greater flexibility within middle-class urban values. But the pansy craze also helped to codify the homosexual/heterosexual binary for the general public by linking sexual identity and gender behavior to vocal performance for the first time; this connection between voice and fixed sexual identity would ultimately be used to undercut all queer vocal culture, including soft or "unmasculine" singers like Vallée. In 1929–30 Vallée was not considered a pansy, but by 1932 he would be attacked as one.

SOFT POSES AND SERVICE POSITIONS: THE ICONIC CROONER

In 1929 Vallée was not yet attacked for his "feminine" attributes or his female audience, although both subjects remained topics of intrigue and discussion in the press. Instead the press focused specifically on Vallée's unusual passivity and vulnerability in relation to his female audience's activity—their public, vigorous adulation, including their desire to touch him. Indeed the uniqueness of his gender reorientation was not primarily about his taking on a more feminine or androgynous appearance but rather about his inverting traditional sex roles of dominance and submission. Far from being the sexual aggressor, Vallée's public persona mirrored his singing persona; he continually emphasized his own shyness with "modern girls," whom he worried he would disappoint. His press coverage explained his sensitivity by constructing him as a perpetual adolescent who had not yet achieved "mature" (phallic) sexuality, his cracking voice contributing to this characterization of him as pubescent. In the press he was always a "boy," alternately a Peter Pan figure, a college boy, or a playboy with soft, thick, blond wavy hair that his fans longed to stroke—a notable contrast with the "hard-haired," slicked down, "Broadway showman type." He was the antithesis of muscular, thick-skinned masculinity, and his softness, gentleness, and vulnerability, which prompted his fans' adoration, were a big source of amusement in the press, which referred to him as "the prince of frails." "Maybe we like 'em sappy instead of tough," mused the columnist Herbert Corey.[49]

The first published photographs of Vallée in 1929, which established his crooner image, foregrounded his boyish appeal, but, precisely because he was not a child, they also suggested a queer sensuality in service to the female sex. Many of these pictures seemed randomly posed by newspaper photographers; although film studios attempted to both shape and control the images of Hollywood stars (with admittedly mixed success in the 1920s), the idea of needing to control a radio star's image was new. The intensity of Vallée's coverage—particularly in relation to his private life—was not only unusual for a radio performer; it was equaled only by that of Valentino in the 1920s. In part this was because Vallée was a New York star who emerged during the zenith of the city's tabloids and their celebrity columnist culture; the New York press built up Vallée in response to audience demand, covering and photograph-ing him on a daily basis and widely syndicating his image across the country. When NBC began to organize some publicity for Vallée after he signed a contract with them in March 1929, the network didn't need to do much to promote him. As the press remarked, Vallée did not have a press agent—and didn't need one. "Rudy Vallée is one of those rare beings who happens to be natural news," wrote Nanette Kutner in *Dance Magazine*. "The public itself is his press agent."[50]

Images of Vallée did not yet conform to the conventions for publicizing male stars that would be developed by Hollywood within the next few years and that perpetuated more narrow, normative gender roles. The film histo-rian Richard Dyer has demonstrated how these classical Hollywood conven-tions for masculine photography mandated that images of men designed for women must "disavow passivity if they are to be kept in line with dominant ideas of masculinity-as-activity."[51] As a result, male stars were most often posed engaged in activity or, if at rest, revealing taut and controlled muscles, "poses that emphasize hard lines and angular shapes [rather than] the soft roundness of the feminine aesthetic."[52] In contrast Vallée's photos from 1929 usually showed his body in relaxed, submissive, or soft positions. Whether depicting him at home or at work, photos of Vallée invariably gave him a curving, yielding, feminine look.

Literary Digest reported that women preferred to see Vallée relaxed, for "in repose, he's more enchanting than ever," and *Outlook* equated his effect with the "joys of a plate of fudge."[53] Early photos of his face emphasized his masses of soft blond curls, making him appear younger and girlish, charac-teristic of the androgynous, often eroticized images of adolescent boys in the late Victorian era. (Photo-essays of Vallée's life, which were legion, included childhood images of him with shoulder-length, wavy blond hair.)[54] His facial

NRA

THE
MICRO PHONE
NEW ENGLAND'S
RADIO
NEWSPAPER

3ᶜ Week Beginning November 25th   Published Weekly

Radio Weekly

Rudy Vallee, caricatured by Xavier Cugat

FIG. 4.8. Xavier Cugat cartoon of Rudy Vallée, *Microphone*, 1933.
This caricature of Vallée by his fellow bandleader exaggerates his
curvy posture and wavy hair; it is typical of the many similarly "wavy"
body poses of Vallée that characterized his coverage beginning in
1929. Courtesy of Rudy Vallée Collection, American Radio Archives.

expressions were often hurt or wounded, suggesting a vulnerable young man
rather than the confident masculinity of other jazz bandleaders of the day or,
for that matter, of pansy performers.

Full-body photos of Vallée for interviews "at home" or in his dressing room
reflected an urban sophistication that was both soft and sensual; in pictures
of Vallée at rest, curling up on a couch or in bed, he often wore his striped silk
dressing gown or pajamas and slippers (fig. 4.10). Although this was standard
evening wear for well-to-do moderns in the 1920s and early 1930s, photographs
of Vallée in this state of domestic undress were particularly prominent in coverage of him, so much so that fan clubs sent him pajamas as gifts. Appearing

RUDY VALLEE—Yale's gift to girls. Ladies cry for him and strong men curse his name. With no other weapons than a saxophone and a come-hither voice, Rudy stepped from the cloistered halls of his alma mater and broke more hearts than the income tax. Now, the Great Vallee is to be heard in the talkies

FIG. 4.9. This widely reproduced image features Vallée's wounded look, indicating a vulnerability that was very appealing to his fans. Like many publications, *Photoplay* references Martha Gellhorn's famous review of Vallée, "God's Gift to Us Girls." The magazine also promotes a female-only appeal for him, reinforcing the "home wrecker" narrative popularized by newspaper columnists; the caption notes, "Ladies cry for him and strong men curse his name." Rudy Vallée, "Yale's gift to girls," *Photoplay*, October 1929. Courtesy of Rudy Vallée Collection, American Radio Archives.

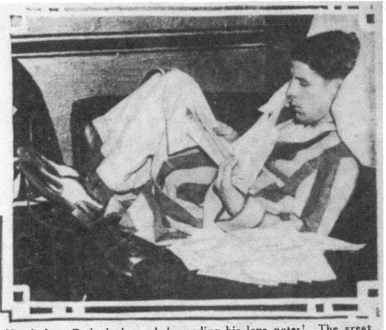

Here's how Rudy looks as he's reading his love notes! The great
Vallee reclining in his dressing room.

FIG. 4.10. Rudy Vallée in his striped silk robe, his common uniform for interviews.
The caption reads: "This is how Rudy looks as he's reading his love notes! The great
Vallee reclining in his dressing room." *New York Daily Mirror*, 27 June 1929. Courtesy
of Rudy Vallée Collection, American Radio Archives.

in robes and pajamas suggested that he was so hardworking he had to squeeze
in interviews in his dressing room between shows or late at night, but such
images also attested to the public's desire to see the private life of their star and
his willingness to expose himself in this way. Vallée in robes and pajamas reinforced his association with the feminine comforts of domesticity, as well as the
erotic possibilities of the boudoir—that just-rolled-out-of-bed easy sensuality
that reflected loosened attitudes toward both gender and sex.

In contrast, again, to classical photos of male Hollywood stars that often
surround them with phallic iconography to reinforce their manliness, Vallée's
two trademark props in photos, his saxophone and his megaphone, do not
function in that way. They reinforced his image as a lover but not necessarily a conventionally *masculine* or assertive one. Despite their phallic shapes,
both instruments connected to his mouth on one end and flared out into
ambiguous orifices at the other. The saxophone's positioning in Vallée photos

FIG. 4.11. The suggestive shadowing of this sheet music cover
for this typically yearning Vallée number was actually very common for the period, although a few years later such photos would
be suppressed because of their implications of fellatio. Sheet
music, "Lonely Troubadour," 1929. Author's collection.

clearly suggested a kind of phallic extension, underlining his status as a lover,
but the way he frequently cradled it and gazed fondly at it also suggested
an autoerotic or oral attachment rather than a penetrative one (fig. 4.11).
Moreover, some photos positioned Vallée playing *underneath* women's legs, a
common iconographic male-female pose of the time, underlining his appeal
as someone who was dominated by and serviced women (fig. 4.12). Vallée's
oft-repeated description of his own "fast-tonguing" on his saxophone makes
the allusion to cunnilingus even stronger.

Vallée's iconic megaphone photos functioned in a similarly complex way.
Vallée often sought to reproduce for fans the intimacy of his radio performances

FIG. 4.12. This publicity photograph of Rudy Vallée with his saxophone mentor Rudy Wiedoeft and the dancer Alice Weaver is an example of one of the most iconic and popular poses of the 1920s, in which men play instruments or sing beneath a woman's uplifted leg (a move from the Charleston dance). The position of the men is provocative in part because of its suggestion of oral sex; marriage and sex advice manuals of the time encouraged men to perform cunnilingus ("genital kissing") to sexually stimulate their wives. Vallée's self-described "fast-tonguing" on his saxophone supports the larger cultural turn toward women's sexual satisfaction and reinforced his image as the man more than willing to service them. From "Personalities of Stage and Screen." Courtesy of Rudy Vallée Collection, American Radio Archives.

FIG. 4.13. Rudy Vallée playing leapfrog with his band mates on the beach, 1930. It was very common for jazz bands to perform at beach resorts, often right on the sand in their bathing suits. Newspaper photos of band members engaged in homosocial play, while very common for the time, would become much less so as the 1930s progressed. Reprinted by permission of Eleanor Vallée. Courtesy of Rudy Vallée Collection, American Radio Archives.

by electrically amplifying his trademark megaphone in concerts. Photos and promotional ads of him with the megaphone, like those in *Variety* or the famous *Vanity Fair* photo on the cover of this book, connected the megaphone to his thrilling, romantic voice and thus his swooning female audience. In the *Vanity Fair* photo he assumes a submissive posture; the megaphone is tilted up and he is singing underneath it, giving himself to the needs of the song and the pleasure of his audience. This is the romantic crooner pose that would become iconic: open mouth, closed or half-closed eyes, head tilted slightly back, suggesting both intense feeling and the orgasmic bliss of surrender. The saxophone lies ignored in his lap, the hint of sex in its curve mirroring that of the curl over

FIG. 4.14. Rudy Vallée sparring with his friend, the Argentine boxer Vittorio Campolo, August 1929. This publicity photo worried Vallée fans, who were concerned he might hurt himself. Reprinted by permission of Eleanor Vallée. Courtesy of Rudy Vallée Collection, American Radio Archives.

his brow. His long manicured fingers lovingly caress the megaphone. This closed-eyes pose makes the crooner the unquestioned object of the viewer's gaze, emphasizing his youth, vulnerability, softness (fluffy curls), and openness to touch or penetration. This iconic posture reflected and reinforced the supplicating position Vallée often assumed in his song lyrics.[55]

Even when Vallée was portrayed in outdoor sporting scenes, the photographs did little to reinforce a "natural" masculine image. Vallée, who loved tanning on the beach, was often photographed in a bathing suit lounging or cavorting with members of his all-male band (fig. 4.13). He generally wore the latest in fashionable swimwear for men—a fitted tank top that showed off his shoulders, arms, and small waist—but he usually assumed slack body poses that did not emphasize his muscles. Vallée's unposed, "at rest" photos and playful carousing inscribed an image of youthful charm and leisure rather than a display of active masculinity. Indeed, when he did show his bare chest, any pretense at manly strength was only further undermined. In one widely reproduced set of photos, arranged by a friend to promote a young boxer, Vallée is dwarfed by his opponent, the boxer Vittorio Campolo (figs. 4.14–4.15). If such photos were meant to assure fans of Vallée's physical

FIG. 4.15. Rudy Vallée playing the sax with boxers, August 1929. After the "boxing match" with Vittorio Campolo, Vallée sat down to play and sing with him and another well-known boxer of the era, Frankie O'Brien. Both boxers' enthusiastic participation in this music session suggests that there was nothing antithetical about a boxer who also loved to sing and play popular music or who appreciated Vallée. Reprinted by permission of Eleanor Vallée. Courtesy of Rudy Vallée Collection, American Radio Archives.

fitness, they did just the opposite; fans wrote to the newspapers begging him not to fight because he might injure himself. Such publicity visually reinforced Vallée's persona as physically weak, gentle, playful, and vulnerable, a star image that definitely solicited protective feelings but made the seductive power of his voice and persona seem all the more inexplicable to pressmen.

In fact, because Vallée's voice appealed to a more diverse audience than most popular vocalists, even he was sometimes unsure of how to present himself visually to please everyone. His appearance at the Brooklyn Paramount in the spring of 1929 offered one example of the presentational challenges posed by the Vallée body. Producers decided to emphasize his physical fitness, a popular trend in the 1920s, by having a famous Russian acrobatic team of four men juggle him. While Vallée agreed that this would show he was a "regular" guy to some "Brooklyn boys," he was concerned that his more traditional fans would think it improper of him to take off his coat.[56] As a result, the photos satisfied neither the traditional nor the modern eye, but they do underline the

FIG. 4.16. Rudy Vallée with an acrobat identified as Max Ello at his Brooklyn
Paramount show, 1929. Vallée attempted to demonstrate his athleticism to some in
his Brooklyn audience through a routine with the Ello acrobats; publicity photos
like this one suggest the awkwardness of this combo. Reprinted by permission of
Eleanor Vallée. Courtesy of Rudy Vallée Collection, American Radio Archives.

convergence of these agendas in the gender queer 1920s. The male acrobats are
simply clothed, while Vallée is dressed for dinner. The acrobats do the work,
and their muscles appear tense, whereas Vallée merely flops on top of them or
between their legs (fig. 4.16). The photos do little to convey Vallée's athleticism
or show off his muscularity since they position him as an accommodating object thrown about by more active men, but the awkwardness of the poses and

their lack of sensual appeal also undercut either a male bonding or a playfully homoerotic reading. Instead they portray Vallée as a docile player, performing what would soon be considered an emasculating cultural role.

However paradoxical his submissive-seductive persona may have been, Vallée's soft and relaxed poses, his silk robes, and his youthful blond curls did not cause him real problems in New York or nationally for a few years; most of Brooklyn's boys still loved him, even if some found him "a bit effeminate." Because pansy acts, female impersonators, and street fairies were still so visible and fascinating, there was more room for early crooners like Vallée to exhibit more feminine qualities with relatively little censure (beyond the sneers of other sweet jazz bandleaders). Indeed the press often referred with curiosity but without criticism to Vallée's singing and his persona in terms of androgyny or femininity. The newspapers dubbed him the "it" boy. In his column Walter Winchell referred to him as "the male Clara Bow" and noted the sexual ambiguity of the term: "'It' means neither masculine or feminine."[57] Yet neither Winchell nor any of the other writers who employed the term in 1929 couched it as necessarily derogatory. Vallée's unimpeded rise to fame attests to urban culture's acceptance of "in betweens" as objects of consumption in the 1920s. It was Vallée's erotic effect on women that most fascinated New York newspapermen and on which they focused most of their coverage. These columnists portrayed Vallée, at first facetiously, as a home wrecker, an image that would come to form the core of his public image for years.

TABLOID COLUMNISTS AND THE HOME WRECKER NARRATIVE

> Even the adolescent frenzy [caused by Frank Sinatra] failed to approach the fervor of the Rudy Vallée maniacs. During the span between 1928 and 1933, the "king of crooners" won a degree of adulation surpassed only by that given to that other Rudy, the movie star Valentino. The Vallée fans were the original fanatics of radio. As someone has said, they had love in their eyes and murder in their hearts, with the homicide reserved for unappreciative radio critics.
> —Columnist Ben Gross, recalling Vallée's rise, 1954

Before his first vaudeville run was even complete, New York columnists had established Vallée as not only a woman-made star but a source of division between the sexes, a potential home wrecker whom wives adored and husbands despised. Columnists such as Walter Winchell, Mark Hellinger, Ed Sullivan, Ben Gross, and Nick Kenny regularly covered Vallée in the major tabloids, the *New York Daily News*, the *New York Graphic*, and Hearst's *Daily Mirror*; beyond the tabloids, the comparatively respectable Heywood Broun also wrote extensively on Vallée for the *New York Telegram*, as did Rian James and Arthur Pollack for the *Brooklyn Daily Eagle*.[58] They were not interested in the nuances of sexuality in New York, nor did they spend time investigating the actual demographics of Vallée's radio audience. Vallée's male fans largely remained invisible as a result, but his female fans would never again be able to hide; instead they became figures of public amusement. Columnists regularly derided women's adoration of Vallée and issued mock warnings to husbands about the new "Vallée peril" with rhetoric as pervasive and influential as it was hyperbolic. The local tabloids far outsold the more respectable New York papers, and many of their columnists were syndicated nationwide, giving this relatively small group of men a defining role in shaping the public's image of Vallée and of crooning.

Close examination suggests that these columnists had little personal investment in the narrative they were constructing around Vallée; rather they were populists and mercenaries who were primarily interested in amusing the masses, flouting the elite, and advancing their own careers.[59] New York columnists were extraordinarily plentiful, powerful, and competitive in the entertainment world of 1929. They wrote without fact-checkers and were always scouting for a dramatic angle to sell papers and create controversy. The home wrecker narrative offered the greatest source of both dramatic conflict and amusing anecdotes in relation to the crooner. But the columnists themselves—as men, husbands, and members of the urban working class, most of them near Vallée's age or younger—were not especially troubled by him. Indeed Vallée's unprecedented popularity represented a great opportunity for them because he opened a new venue for star reporting: radio. Many of these men used their acquaintance with Vallée to help them carve out careers as radio specialists and commentators, while others used their analyses of his early career as the foundation of novels and screenplays about the crooning phenomenon.

Fanciful or not, the home wrecker narrative had long legs, repeated so often it became widely accepted as common knowledge (and remains so). The typical columnist's pattern was to write something unflattering about Vallée, receive a lot of letters in protest, quote the letters for the next several days, and conclude by suggesting that women were crazy and that their husbands should be wary of Vallée's influence. For example, on 19 May 1929 the

New York Daily News columnist Mark Hellinger "confessed," "Rudy Vallée is getting on our nerves. . . . In all our experience, we have never seen a man raise such particular havoc among the damsels. He has women of 50 bouncing around as though they were 15. Wherever you go, women are talking of Vallée. Yet at the risk of receiving thousands of letters telling us we're crazy, we hereby go on record as asserting that both Mr. Vallée and his orchestra give us a slight pain."[60] In response fans deluged Hellinger with mail, four thousand letters defending Vallée and telling Hellinger to "go hang himself." Hellinger delighted in reprinting the most incensed rants (especially those that threatened him with physical violence): "You are jealous. You are stupid. You must be insane. That sweet boy is the genius of the age." Hellinger responded to these letters as if they were characteristic of women's hysterical behavior in general, wondering in feigned bewilderment how "people can get so worked up over a stage figure."[61]

Others copied Hellinger's publicity gambit, often citing another's column in a kind of continuing conversation (a common practice among this tight circle). Ben Gross's "Radio Review" column in the *Sunday News* used this strategy of Vallée fan-baiting, as did Kenny (also of the *News*, then the *Daily Mirror*) and Broun. Fans became so used to these slights that one noticed when Gross suspended them for a few weeks: "I see you don't knock Rudy Vallée any longer. I guess you're just plain afraid having found out how popular Rudy is. The sweetest music to my ears would be to hear Rudy play a march at your and Hellinger's funeral." Unlike the attacks that would be made on him two years later, the exposure these columnists gave him helped Vallée's career, and he was in fact good friends with a number of them, particularly the rising star Winchell. Columnists even forwarded to Vallée the mail they received about him, with notes attached, such as Winchell's note from February 1930: "Rudy: This gives you a rough idea what 'exploitation' means. Here's a guy from Clearfield, Pa defending you. And I get oceans of this type of mail."[62]

These columnists did at times reprint letters from men defending Vallée, although usually without comment. Male listeners applauded Vallée's music and spoke of employing his singing to enhance their intimate relationships. "I don't begrudge Rudy his fame one bit," wrote John C. to Hellinger. "He has taught me how to love. When his crooning voice is on the air, my girl turns down the lights and nestles deep into my loving arms. Mark should learn about love making from Rudy instead of panning him all the time."[63]

Such letters directly contradicted the home wrecker narrative, but they did little to undercut it. Although the narrative misrepresented Vallée's audience, its popularity suggested that it did resonate with some of the public. Indeed part of the cultural significance of tabloid columnists is the way they troubled social ideals, seeking to expose the problems beneath the surface of the "respectable" middle and upper classes. The home wrecker narrative really drew power from implying women's dissatisfaction with the modern home and the marriage bed. By suggesting that Vallée's voice had disrupted the domestic cohesion and sanctity of the home, the home wrecker narrative implied that the home was ripe for disruption and that perhaps consumer culture and egalitarian companionate marriages—the very vehicles that were supposed to help bind the modern family together—were at best unpredictable and unstable social balms.

The most revealing columns suggested that men's dislike for Vallée stemmed from the way he threatened their control over women at home. "What have we come to in this dreadful mechanical age," asked the *Brooklyn Eagle* columnist Arthur Pollack, "when a young man with a new-fangled mouthpiece and far away from his victims can break hearts with ease. No whispering of soft-nothings in shell-like ears, no pressing of the little hand, no strong protecting arm finding its way about the slender waist. Rudy merely takes his mouth-machine and sings into it and women drop East, West, North, South, all over our brave broad land as if from great blight."[64] Radio offered women a vibrating voice as an alternative lover, one that could just as easily be a competitor for as a conspirator with their husbands or boyfriends. Acknowledging Vallée's power as a romantic catalyst would confirm that a man *needed* one, that a mere "strong protecting arm" would no longer do for the modern girl. She wanted *her* desires met.

Vallée's designation as an exclusively female attraction would ultimately prove to be the first step toward his demise in an increasingly masculinist modern culture. By drawing attention to and exaggerating the differences between male and female appreciations of Vallée, New York columnists unwittingly helped lay the foundation for gender norms in popular music as they exist today. But such connections are much clearer in hindsight. In 1929 columnist publicity benefited Vallée, helping to make him the biggest star of the year.

AN AMERICAN CROONING STAR: NETWORK RADIO AND THE NETWORK AUDIENCE

Vallée was the first and perhaps the only star to become famous in radio, records, vaudeville, motion picture house presentations, nightclubs, and films within a single year. Just as he bridged modern and Victorian social mores, he also emerged at a point of major transition in the entertainment industry. The film industry had reached new heights of popularity just when it had to cope with its silent-to-sound transition. Radio was beginning its nationwide network dominance, while vaudeville and the music industry were on the verge of a depression that would devastate both. By the time Bing Crosby first became a national celebrity, only two years later, vaudeville's famous Palace Theatre had closed down and its big stars had begun their exodus to radio and Hollywood. Vallée experienced a kind of stardom unique among the romantic crooners who followed him because he continued to perform in both live and mediated venues after becoming a star and had been the focus of intense gossip and discussion by the New York press without Hollywood studios regulating publicity as they quickly would for subsequent crooning stars like Crosby. Vallée's New York associations would always remain with him, at first benefiting him and then limiting him as entertainment industries and personnel increasingly moved west to Hollywood. In 1929 New York still held sway as the home of vaudeville, Broadway, the music industry, the important nightclubs and cabarets, the most influential press, and—most important for Vallée—the National Broadcasting Company.

Vallée was not the first national network star on radio, but he was the biggest star radio had created, both because of the degree of press attention he received and because he joined NBC when the network was at the height of its powers.[65] The mighty Radio Corporation of America (RCA) formed NBC in 1926, and federal regulations favoring commercial stations helped facilitate network building by allocating the clearest and most powerful stations to NBC's network affiliates, which doubled between 1927 and 1930. By 1929 NBC's monopoly on broadcasting included two network chains, the "Red" and the "Blue," with affiliates in major urban centers throughout the United States, and the network was as yet unthreatened by its upstart rival, the Columbia Broadcasting System (CBS). Thus when NBC signed Vallée in the spring of 1929, the network was able to offer him unprecedented media saturation and audience access.

Vallée's relationship with NBC began several months before the network signed him to an exclusive contract in March 1929. His nightclub performances at his new club, the Villa Vallée, had been broadcast over NBC's New York Red network station WEAF since fall 1928, and Vallée was so popular that NBC did not require him or the club to pay for the publicity (counter to NBC's practice at the time). Vallée also briefly fronted a commercial program for NBC touting cod-liver oil capsules; although the capsules proved faulty and the show was pulled, Vallée was a success, and, after listener protest, NBC allowed him to announce his own show, another break from network policy.[66] After Vallée's stunning vaudeville premiere in February 1929, NBC finally signed him to an exclusive contract and its Artists Bureau began negotiating all other contracts for him, securing him much higher fees for subsequent appearances. NBC's signing of Vallée was a media event. While bands had often paid to be broadcast by NBC, columnists declared that this was the first time the powerful network had begun regularly paying a band for exclusive broadcast rights.

In many ways Vallée was a good fit for NBC, which prided itself on providing quality entertainment to its listeners. The format of his daily broadcast was similar to that of his local radio appearances: he sang a number of his standard crooning ballads and novelty songs, often highlighting songs that were current Broadway hits. His pedigree and sophistication fit in well with the highbrow image the network promoted, and Vallée saw the move as increasing not only his bookings but also his prestige.[67] NBC preferred to discover its own talent and groom it for national exposure rather than hire established stars; although Vallée had achieved regional stardom, NBC made and sustained his name nationally. In turn, he would primarily be affiliated with NBC radio for the next decade, despite working in other media. He became the signature musical sound of the network and of radio generally for years to come, and NBC gladly took credit for his success.[68]

And his success was immense. National exposure made Vallée hugely influential throughout the entertainment industry. His romantic singing brought in thousands of fan letters each day, and NBC as well as other radio stations scrambled to develop more romantic crooning singers to try to replicate his successful sound.[69] NBC publicists feverishly promoted radio's first big star. Hearst's tabloid the *New York Daily Mirror* ran a twelve-part story of Vallée's relatively short life in June 1929, receiving grateful letters from fans who would much rather read about Vallée than "[President] Hoover or [Governor] Al Smith"—further proof of how consumer icons were replacing political figures in public importance. He dominated music and radio publications in 1929, and many radio fan magazines were founded and began publishing because of Vallée's success, the most famous being *Radio Guide*, which launched in October 1931 with an issue devoted primarily to Vallée.[70] Hundreds of national fan clubs formed around Vallée. Music publishers, songwriters (for example, Irving Berlin), and song pluggers intensively courted him, and he signed the first radio-records-vaudeville contract, securing his services for NBC, Victor Records, and the Keith-Orpheum vaudeville circuit exclusively.[71]

Because of his prominence on a national network, Vallée could make a song a hit by performing it only a couple of times. Radio's effectiveness as a song plugger was first demonstrated by Wendall Hall in 1923; his song "Ain't Gonna Rain No Mo" is considered to be radio's first national hit song. But poor Hall had to journey across the country and plug the song repeatedly on local stations, a process that took many months.[72] Network play could now instantaneously make a song a hit nationwide and began to reorient the industry toward a "top ten" rankings model that would boost both public recognition and national unity for popular music. Network song plugging changed the music business forever, making radio the primary outlet for song publishers and record producers, especially when the record industry began to crash at the onset of the Depression. Vallée's songs hit the top in national sales for records and sheet music when his program went national; he had several best-selling songs in spring 1929, and sales of songs he popularized through radio, either his versions or others', increased throughout the year.[73] Even Al Jolson and Gene Austin rarely had more than five or six hit songs in a single year. If anyone still doubted that Vallée's radio popularity was the key to his success, such doubts were dispelled when two of his best-selling songs that year were his radio show theme song and his radio show greeting. Established crooners benefited immediately from Vallée's success, although the press now reported that their audiences too were suddenly exclusively female. The *New Yorker* noted that record sales of previous crooning singers had gone up tremendously since Vallée started broadcasting and recording: "Women are the predominant buyers and they like to bring Rudy Vallée, Gene Austin, Nick Lucas and James Melton home."[74]

Even as the New York press continued to deny it, Vallée's popularity as a vocal personality was wide-ranging and unprecedented throughout 1929 and 1930, transcending class, sex, ethnicity, political affiliation, and race. He gave one-time-only concerts for a variety of organizations that speaks to the tremendous breadth of his appeal at the time, although it is worth noting that many represented the ethnic white working- and lower-middle-class people who most championed him. He performed for the Brooklyn Navy, the socialist *Jewish Daily Forward*, the Women's Campaign Committee of King's County, the Newspaper Guild, the Police Association, several Elks lodges, and the Post Office Clerks, as well as headlining innumerable benefits for children's hospitals, zoos, and playgrounds. Vallée also performed at least two benefits for black audiences in Harlem; John Moses, the editor of the short-lived *American and West Indian News*, asked him to perform because "you owe your colored admirers this favor." Indeed Vallée seems to have performed for most groups that invited him, frequently clocking in eighteen-hour workdays (to the chagrin of his Connecticut Yankees, who liked their sleep). His prominence as a star musician also earned him a greater role in the musicians' union, where he intervened in labor disputes and, predictably, headlined benefits to help his unemployed colleagues.[75] His status as a new American icon was underscored by the number of requests he had from the American Legion, war veterans, police and firemen's groups, military branches, and even the U.S. Congress, where he performed at a congressional breakfast. On that same visit to Washington, he met with President Hoover, to whom he famously remarked, "I've heard of you, too, sir."[76] Such appearances reinforced the national power and influence of network radio, and Vallée worked hard to ensure that his music would resound throughout the New York entertainment world and beyond.

Vallée's popularity encouraged advertisers and the networks to invest more in promoting radio stars and developing regular programming. NBC had its second astounding success when it began airing the popular syndicated minstrel show *Amos 'n' Andy* in August 1929, which immediately became a nationwide obsession. John Reber of the J. Walter Thompson agency, one of the most powerful advertising agencies of the time, was at the forefront of such program innovation. Reber believed that JWT should not only sponsor but even directly develop radio programs that reflected broad popular tastes, and he favored big stars in variety formats.[77] Reber recognized that Vallée fit NBC's desire for "quality" entertainment and his stardom and intense audience appeal also made him an attractive candidate for commercial sponsorship. Together they took the unprecedented step of developing a national radio variety program around a single star, and the hour-long program debuted in the midst of the stock market crash, on Thursday, 24 October 1929. *The Fleischmann Hour*, sponsored by Fleischmann's Yeast ("stimulating action on the digestive tract"), was an enormous critical and popular success and would eventually be considered the most influential variety show in the history of the medium.[78] For the first couple of years, *The Fleischmann Hour*'s format was much more Vallée than variety, since he was at the height of his popularity.

Although NBC helped make Vallée a national icon, the network put new constraints on his freedom as a performer and also misrepresented the breadth

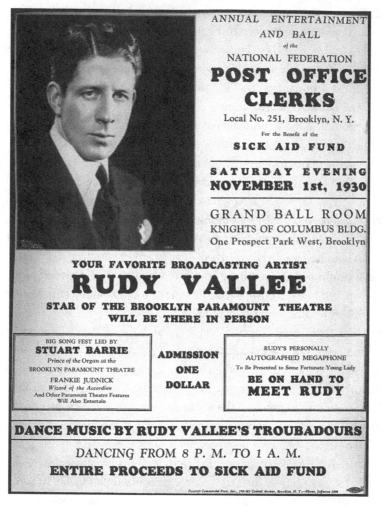

FIG. 4.17. Benefit for the Post Office Clerks' Sick Aid Fund, 1 November 1930. Vallée performed numerous benefits for a variety of groups across New York City. This ad notes that Vallée will personally autograph a megaphone for "some fortunate young lady." Reprinted by permission of Eleanor Vallée. Courtesy of Rudy Vallée Collection, American Radio Archives.

and diversity of his audience to serve its own commercial and nationalist aims. For example, NBC prevented him from entertaining at a benefit for the Brotherhood of Sleeping Car Porters, a black labor organization led by A. Philip Randolph. Despite this, Randolph sent Vallée a remarkably kind letter: "I am sure that the boys will be greatly pleased to know that it was

FIG. 4.18. Vallée with the Naval Coast Guard, June 1930. Vallée was a former sailor and briefly served in the navy during World War I. He was a very popular figure with military groups, who frequently asked him to perform and sent him numerous fan letters. Reprinted by permission of Eleanor Vallée. Courtesy of Rudy Vallée Collection, American Radio Archives.

your desire to come and will not be there because of the refusal of the National Broadcasting Company to permit you."[79] It seems likely that NBC's objection was based on the fact that the Brotherhood was a controversial new labor organization and the network was antiunion rather than the fact that it was a black organization, for Vallée performed for other all-black charities and unions without network objection. His affiliation with the conservative, elitist network thus cut him off from some of his more radical fans, distanced him from his working-class audience, and would ultimately help buttress later attacks labeling him as a snob who could not comprehend the plight of the common man. In addition, NBC promoted Vallée as an entirely female-made star in order to target the audience most likely to buy Fleischmann's Yeast. Although Vallée remained widely popular with both sexes according to radio ratings, his program was advertised specifically to women: "Remember girls, Rudy's on tonight!"[80] Ironically, the network's association of Vallée with the homemaker would ultimately help support the more insidious version of him as a genuinely threatening home wrecker in the coming years.

The network's intent to portray Vallée as both high-class and female-friendly is clear in the broadcast script of the first program, but the script also incorporates the companionability that Vallée's audiences had come to expect from him.[81] Graham McNamee, NBC's announcer, introduced the first program by trying to evoke the nightclub atmosphere of a Vallée band performance, including the admiring girls:

> Tonight, we want you to picture a quiet, luxurious supper club, where soft, mellow blue lights cast their shadows over white linen and sparkling glass and silver. Waiters hurrying to and fro, palms all around. Clear-eyed, clean-cut men dancing with beautiful girls in lovely gowns. And up here on the stage at one end of the room Rudy Vallée and his Connecticut Yankees providing that wonderful music of theirs. Everybody is looking and feeling his best tonight. All the girls seem to have smiling lips and sparkling eyes and lovely complexions. And of course, we're all having a great time, and we hope you'll enjoy it, too.

Here NBC capitalized on the Vallée nightclub persona to validate its own quality brand. But McNamee's introduction also served the desires of Vallée's audience by allowing them access to cosmopolitan New York life and promising to showcase Vallée and his lover-like attentions specifically for them. Like Vallée, McNamee also employed direct address ("we" and "you") to emphasize the communal feeling of the broadcast, a practice that would become a convention of all radio programs, even though the environment McNamee is painting here is clearly an exclusive one. According to these early scripts, Vallée sang approximately twenty songs on each program, just as he had in his nightclub act, and he continued to do all of his own announcing of numbers. Vallée defined the romantic crooner of network radio as a classy, youthful, glamorous urbanite who, more than anything else, was a servant of the mass audience, especially its women. His early film appearances would do little to change this impression.

THE VAGABOND LOVER CAPTURED ON FILM

During summer 1929, with much fanfare, Vallée left New York for Hollywood. There he made his first star vehicle, *The Vagabond Lover*, for RKO. In the spring he had already shot a couple of short films for Vitaphone, *Rudy Vallée and His Connecticut Yankees* (released on 27 May 1929), and *Radio Rhythm* (released 9 August 1929). He also filmed a cameo in the Ziegfeld Follies variety film *Glorifying the American Girl*, which was released two weeks after *The Vagabond Lover* (on 25 November 1929).[82] The Hollywood that Vallée entered was transitioning from silent to sound film; all his films were very early talkies, technically limited and especially unsuited to doing much with a musical performer beyond a kind of "visualized Broadway." Importantly Vallée's film roles—unlike Crosby's subsequent roles—did nothing to establish him as a film actor. They instead attempted to reproduce the effects of his radio and concert performances.

Vallée's film appearances in 1929 reinforced the idea that he was a female-only attraction. Advertisements clearly framed him as of interest to women alone, and reviewers expressed bewilderment at his appeal, reaffirming the idea that men would not find him compelling. Paramount's *Radio Rhythm*, for example, begins with a close-up of a young woman caressing the radio dial while the broadcast voice promises her, "For the next few minutes, you will be entertained by Rudy Vallée and his Connecticut Yankees." The girl smiles as the camera tracks in on the initials "RV" on the radio, and the screen dissolves to Vallée and his band, placing him inside the radio itself and therefore reinforcing his association with radio rather than cinema.

In this short film Vallée and his band perform the two types of music associated with him: his best-selling ballad "Honey" and the provocative urban novelty song "You'll Do It Someday, Why Not Now?" "Honey" is a slow, yearning ballad, which Vallée performs in his typical style, with his head back and eyes closed to emphasize the intensity of his feeling, his voice thin and weak but heartfelt. As in a number of his ballads, the woman has left him alone and distraught, and he frequently begins lines on high notes he can't quite reach, suggesting the exhaustion of heartbreak. The tone then shifts to the naughty "You'll Do It Someday, Why Not Now?," which consciously mocks the type of man who would pressure a woman into having sex. These two pieces illustrate very well Vallée's tweaking of masculinity, and the film reinforced attitudes toward Vallée rather than attempting to reshape them.

Vallée's feminine appeal and female-serving persona were reiterated through his cameo in the Paramount film *Glorifying the American Girl*. He performs as himself in a Ziegfeld Follies vaudeville show (though he never performed with the actual Follies). Hand in his pocket, he clasps his saxophone and performs his famous number "I'm Just a Vagabond Lover." Again his cameo allies him with the male spectacle that characterized both vaude-ville and 1920s Hollywood films; *Girl* featured half-dressed, athletic-looking men (including Johnny Weissmuller in his screen debut) accompanying the female stars in production numbers.[83]

Vallée's final film appearance in 1929 was his first and only major feature film role for five years. In *The Vagabond Lover*, he played a would-be jazz bandleader who achieves success as a crooner and sings his way into the heart of a middle-class girl, played by Sally Blane. Although named "Rudy Bronson" here, Vallée was again playing himself, and he performed a number of his well-known ballads in the film. And again reviewers noted that the film was specifically targeting Vallée's female fans. Although today we would probably label the film a romantic comedy (Marie Dressler supplied the comedy), *Vagabond Lover* differs significantly from the snappy pace and witty dialogue that came to be associated with the screwball genre in the 1930s. It is more melodramatic than comic, and its story of mistaken identity—Vallée takes on the persona of a famous jazz bandleader to avoid arrest—is played more for pathos than for laughs.

Vallée's character was very much the sincere, sensitive, devoted lover his fans expected, and he was filmed as an object of female desire. His character feels immensely guilty that the woman he loves believes him to be someone else; at one point, after singing to her about how happy he would be if they could be together forever, he bursts out, "I've just got to tell you the truth!" There is a gravity pervading the film that suggests the lovers' depth of feeling and vulnerability toward one another. Vallée's love scenes with Blane are slow and invariably involve long takes of him holding her hands, singing a love song to her while she gazes at him, breathing heavily, her eyes full of tears. In these scenes Vallée is the object of Blane's adoration; she is given the only close-ups, and the audience is encouraged to view him through her eyes. These scenes also privilege Vallée's voice over his body, thus referencing his radio persona. In part because of the nascent sound technology of the time (before the traveling boom mic), the actors have to remain stiffly in place during most of their scenes so that the planted microphone can pick up their voices. Many reviewers noted Vallée's woodenness, but in some ways it served to accentuate his voice for audiences, who concentrated on its move-ment instead of his body.[84]

Vallée's songs in this film are some of his most pleading ballads, and he re-tains his iconic romantic crooner posture, open and submissive, head tipped back, mouth open, and eyes closed. He suggests his desire for and depen-

FIG. 4.19. Vallée and costar Sally Blane, publicity photo for
The Vagabond Lover. The publicity photos for the film feature
Blane in assertive poses, such as brushing his hair and holding
his head in her lap, highlighting Vallée's submissiveness to
women and presenting this romantic fantasy as highly pleasurable for both sexes. Reprinted by permission of Eleanor Vallée.
Courtesy of Rudy Vallée Collection, American Radio Archives.

dence on his love through drawn-out lyrics that repeat the phrases "I need
you, believe me, I need you," and "I'll find paradise and keep it for you." In a
reversal of Hollywood conventions, here the male is the spectacular attraction, while the narrative plot is driven by the female lead. When Dressler,
who plays Blane's mother, finds out he is an imposter, she threatens to have
him arrested, but his singing saves him from imprisonment. Ever the gentle-
man, Vallée is willing to "take the blame if you let the others go." The crooner
persona here respects rather than resents the company and authority of
strong women. First he wins over the daughter, then her middle-aged mom.

Film critics positioned *The Vagabond Lover* as a woman's film having little crossover appeal. They felt that Vallée was a stiff actor, and most of them denied being able to understand his attraction. The reviewer for *Variety*, for example, acknowledged that "New York gals, young and old, are nuts over this boy," but claimed to be mystified as to why and found it difficult to evaluate the film because of it: "Who can figure the feminine tangent? They threw flowers at him at the Riverside [a Manhattan motion picture house]. So, upon that deduction, this release classifies as an oddity."[85] Some critics echoed their vaudeville cousins by noting the distinctiveness of Vallée's voice and the contrast between it and his body. "The laddie's face is set in a sort of perpetual sorrow," noted Quinn Martin of the *Daily Mirror*, "and added to the fact that he seldom looks the camera in the eye, makes him seem like the wraith of some calamity walking through the scenes. Only the voice is virile, and quite alive."

Vallée's fans did not seem to mind these incongruities or his lack of acting chops, and the picture was a success. Helen Shea, for example, wrote to the *New York Graphic* to dispute Cal York's unenthusiastic review of the film: "Just because Rudy Vallée's picture wasn't the flop that Cal York thought it should be, because Rudy is so popular with women, Cal said the picture was SAVED by Marie Dressler. I don't think I ever laughed more than I did at Marie, but when I left the theatre, I wasn't thinking of HER! And neither were the girls who went with me! Rudy is a type all by himself, not only his music and his singing but his looks!"[86] Such defenses would become commonplace as Vallée's continued popularity suggested that neither he nor crooning was going to disappear anytime soon.

Vallée's new romantic crooning sound was soon dominant in national entertainment, pouring out from radios, gramophones, bandstands, and motion picture theater speakers. He remained the nation's top star for the next two years, while the music, radio, and film industries were completely saturated by Vallée-style imitators. By the end of 1930 Vallée and romantic crooning more broadly were clearly the people's choice for entertainment. In a tribute to Vallée, Gustave Davidson of the *Daily Mirror* acknowledged the power of the mass audience in his appeal:

Perhaps the stenographer, the salesgirl, the operator, the clerk, the mill or factory hand, lays claim, individually, to no special consideration. But *en masse*, are they not more powerful than princes—and more significant? You, in any case, are their idol. To you they look daily for heart's ease and "a dream come true."

Therefore we toast you.[87]

While some in the press were heartened by the populism of Vallée's appeal, other cultural authorities were beginning to be concerned. Vallée's designation as a woman-made star began to take on more sinister connotations as it became clearer that radio's audience was not merely swooning after some novelty but had taken over the reins of American culture. The efforts of social and cultural institutions to contain crooning's audiences and to establish masculine control over the new national soundscape would soon make crooning the subject of a very public, acrimonious, and wide-ranging set of attacks.

(((Five)))

"A SUPINE SINKING

INTO THE PRIMEVAL OOZE"

Crooning and Its Discontents, 1929–1933

Whining and crying as the singer does, there is no man
in America who would not feel disgusted. . . .
The man who whines that way—well, he just isn't a man.
—Cardinal O'Connell of Boston, January 1932

Have you noticed how slushy all the crooners' names sound?
Bing, Russ, Ozzie, Rudy, PHOOEY.
—*New York Telegraph*, 22 November 1931

"What have you got against Bunny Harmon, anyhow?"
"He's a crooner, ain't he? Ain't that enough?"
—Newspaper columnist Alvin Roberts's exchange
with his secretary in the popular film *Blessed Event*, 1932

In early 1931 Vallée's identification with the cultural feminine began to provoke more direct public attacks. In January a Harvard student threw a
grapefruit at him during a Boston concert; the incident garnered enormous attention and stoked crooning's dissenters. Columnists, fanning
the flames, reported that men throughout the land were happy about the
incident but distressed that the student missed his mark. *New York World*
reported, "The Harvard student who threw grapefruit at Rudy Vallée was

suspended for getting zero in marksmanship."[1] The columnists' hyperbole continued to emphasize Vallée's role as a home wrecker, evidenced by a New York woman who was charged with murdering her husband when he would not let her listen to Rudy Vallée.[2] The columnist Henry Clune enumerated the criticisms men supposedly felt for crooners, connecting them to a long line of male entertainers who were objectionably feminine: "He-men with red blood in their veins, as the saying is, detest cake-eaters, lounge lizards, dance hall sheiks, and crooners. The he-men . . . have generally said, in word or substance, 'Vallée and his type are a blot on American manhood.'"[3]

The grapefruit incident was the first volley in what would become, initially, a rhetorical war on crooners, one that drove them from popular ubiquity in 1930 to figures of widespread public derision by 1933. When crooners came to dominate mass culture in the early years of the Depression, they did much to reorient urban entertainment away from live, locally generated music by offering an inexpensive alternative that was available in one's home. Romantic crooners like Vallée represented not only a new form of popular music, however, but a new kind of male ideal whose pleading voice and sensitive persona emphasized the feminine-friendly aspects of both modern urban public culture (gender-fluid, sexually liberal) and New England and immigrant households (mother loving, sentimental).

It is fitting that the first widely publicized shot against crooners came from a Harvard man, since the rare accusations of effeminacy toward crooners in the 1920s had primarily occurred in elite institutions. Indeed he continued to be regarded as the people's representative, and letters to Vallée from his fans regarding the incident—including a remarkable one from soldiers on Governor's Island in New York—defend him as a "Regular guy" and lambast the Harvard student as a snob.[4] Nevertheless, as crooning's influence on national culture increased and the Depression worsened, these gender-policing concerns became more urgent to cultural authorities, and they sought to contain and control the crooner phenomenon. The Harvard attack symbolized a new level of cultural nationalism and mass media hegemony generally in the early 1930s, one that was rooted in the propaganda campaigns, increased nativism, and immigration restrictions of World War I and the postwar Red Scare. As the mass media, especially radio and film, became nationally prominent and powerful in the 1920s, nationalism (Americanism) became an important litmus test for star performers as well as ordinary citizens; concurrently, as concerns about racial mixing abated through industrial segregation and reduced immigration, gender normativity and heterosexual behavior emerged as key criteria for white American citizen-ship and status.[5]

The Depression intensified such concerns tenfold; the loss of jobs and masculine status for men indicated a destabilization of gender roles that crooners seemed to affirm. The crooner thus became a prominent target of criticism and a central figure in the narrowing of gender roles in the early 1930s. Crooners presented a particular challenge at first since they were not candidates for overt censorship. With little objectionable language or overt suggestions of homosexuality, it was the *sound* of crooners that was objection-able. And indeed crooners were far too profitable for radio networks or the recording industry to voluntarily regulate their content on the basis of class or taste, in the way that British state-owned radio regulated their appearances on the air.[6] Instead crooners became targets of growing public condemnation and ridicule across a broad range of cultural authorities: religious and sec-ular, urban and suburban, scientific and industrial, highbrow and lowbrow.

The alliance of these authorities against crooners and their female audi-ences in particular illustrates how gender concerns had come to dominate popular music. As I demonstrated in chapters 1 and 2, the feminization of the crooner was the result of racial, ethnic, and class assimilation and erasures in the standardization of American music. The crooning debates, however, rearticulated this process primarily in terms of gender transgression. The strength of crooning audiences as consumers potentially invested them with socially transformative power, a concern that cut across divisions of class, region, and politics. Powerful institutional leaders united as agents of social control. Religious leaders, educators, psychologists, musicians, social sci-entists, and engineers employed a variety of rhetorical strategies to attack crooners in print, while radio columnists, popular films, novels, cartoons, and songs ridiculed them in popular culture.

Institutional authorities of this era drew heavily on the new psychology, a moralized American interpretation of Freud that validated polarized gender roles and devalued the cultural feminine. According to this discourse, mas-culinity meant the rejection of the feminine; any man who did not reject the feminine was seen as weak, immature, and potentially homosexual. Vocalists became prime exemplars of this thesis, especially those males whose high pitch, gentle tone, emotional vulnerability, or intimate address suggested gen-der transgression. Discourses of authenticity converged with and reinforced these connections, helping to tie male vocal production to fixed gendered and sexual identities. The aesthetic shift from imitation to authenticity in the late nineteenth and early twentieth century in American culture was part of what defined modernity, and discourses of authenticity were employed to reinforce essentialist divides of race and class as well.[7] As the binary division of homosexual and heterosexual identity became more secure and such identities began to be viewed as stable and authentic, crooners' perceived feminine voices and personae increasingly became markers of homosexuality, making them susceptible to censorship, institutional regulation, and stigmatization.

The attacks against crooners were the first time that gender norms had been applied to voices on a national scale. The need for such regulation was unexpected. When radio and sound films burst onto the scene, there were no existing conventions regarding voices in mass media. This permitted the emergence and dominance of the crooner and allowed culture to be taken over, it seemed to many authorities, by the desires of swooning women. In reaction to radio crooners' popularity, new codes of normative white masculinity were developed specifically for pop's voices, and new rhetorical and regulatory strategies attempted to discipline the fans. The public condemnation of crooners thus functioned to belittle the cultural feminine and gender deviance in a commercial culture increasingly dominated by assertive female consumers and to encourage the development of hegemonic standards for gendered voices that would be broadly applied in mass media and in American life more generally.

TIPTOEING THROUGH:
CROONING DOMINATES POPULAR CULTURE

By 1930 crooning was no longer simply a specialty act, nor was Rudy Vallée an anomaly. What was once called "peculiar" was quickly becoming the norm. Crooning had transformed radio; Vallée and his imitators dominated the airwaves and set the performance standards for radio singers and other personalities. Crooning's new sound and the crooner's love-struck persona also strongly impacted other media and music performances. Romantic crooning songs dominated records, sheet music sales, and popular dance steps, and they were ubiquitous in early sound musicals; crooning singers, using microphones, continued to be ubiquitous in live performance as well. Radio and recording executives recognized a gold mine when they saw one, and they identified and publicized as crooners singers whose voices were in any way similar in softness, tone, or emotion to Vallée's. Being identified as a crooner was an advantage to any singer's career in 1929–30; promoters

Just call them Crooners

RUDY VALLÉE

CARMEN LOMBARDO

EARLE NELSON

SMITH BALLEW

DON PARKER

WILL OSBORNE

BERNIE CUMMINS

• These seven thrilling and irresistible young men are the most devastating crooners that ever melted a microphone; and their seven incomes, combined, amount to a million dollars annually.

The dramatic points of Rudy Vallée's career have been touched upon by all of the adoring journals. It remains for *Vanity Fair* to add a brief incident not so generally known—namely, that Mr. Vallée once played in a night-club collegiate orchestra conducted by Peter Arno (now cartoonist for the *New Yorker*). Rudy used to bring his megaphone along to the night-club every night in the wistful hope that Mr. Arno might let him sing; but Arno was adamant—Rudy could play the saxophone, and he could do nothing else. To-day Mr. Vallée's annual income from crooning is $350,000.

Carmen Lombardo made his crooning début at the age of sixteen, at the Mothers' Club in London, Ontario. Earle Nelson was a printer's apprentice who got a chance to sing one night over a small radio station. Smith Ballew, a Texan, learned to play the banjo by ear from an old Negro. Don Parker attended Stevens Institute, where he formed a lively collegiate orchestra. Will Osborne, perhaps Mr. Vallée's nearest rival, started singing in a small country hotel for twenty dollars a week and board; his present income is estimated at $200,000 a year. Bernie Cummins was a prize-fighter and a hoofer before he drifted into a Cincinnati night-club and discovered that crooning could do considerable profitable damage to a lady's heartstrings.

FIG. 5.1. This article identifies some of the many romantic crooning stars that emerged in the wake of Vallée's success, among them Carmen Lombardo, Will Osborne, Earle Nelson, and Smith Ballew. Although the writer describes these crooners as "thrilling and irresistible young men," the bulk of the article focuses on their large salaries, which became a point of attack as the Depression worsened. "Just Call Them Crooners," *Vanity Fair*, July 1930. Courtesy of Rudy Vallée Collection, American Radio Archives.

identified singers as the "Rudy Vallée of Rochester" and the "Rudy Vallée of China." When some audiences were unable to distinguish Vallée's voice from that of a young bandleader named Will Osborne, the newly formed network CBS hired Osborne and his band to compete with Vallée on NBC in the fall of 1929. Their widely publicized rivalry lasted through the spring, and the popularity contests they generated drew great publicity for both networks.

Networks and music promoters created crooners in two ways during the crooning explosion of 1929: they redefined existing singing stars as crooners, and they "discovered" new crooning singers. Most of these singers, such as Cliff Edwards and Seger Ellis, had employed crooning delivery styles before they were called "crooners," but crooning came to define them exclusively from this point on; other "new" crooners were often young bandleaders such as Osborne and Ozzie Nelson. These singers dominated popular music sales. Vallée had hit after hit in 1929–30. Gene Austin (whom NBC kept trying to woo into radio) had a best-selling song in February and March 1929, "Carolina Moon." Smith Ballew recorded an especially popular rendition of "I Kiss Your Hand, Madame," a song Vallée had made a crooning standard, and enjoyed success with a number of other crooning songs, including "Am I Blue?" (1929), "Miss You" (1929), "Why Do You Suppose?" (1929), and "(You're Always Sure of) My Love for You" (1930). Seger Ellis had a hit with the crooning song "There Was Nothing Else to Do." "Whispering" Jack Smith had several popular records, among them the pro-flapper number "A New Kind of Old Fashioned Girl." Everyone sang the soon-to-be crooning standard "Stardust." British crooners also found popularity on the U.S. airwaves, among them Harry Shalson, Sam Browne, and especially Al Bowlly, whose version of "If I Had You" was a U.S. hit in 1929.[8]

Crooning singing also influenced dance music. Vallée helped popularize the "off-time fox trot" that became prevalent and was, for a time, publicized as "The Rudy Vallée" dance. New York dance master Oscar Duryea attributed the new slower steps to Vallée: "He sings slowly. The music for his songs is slow. Therefore, if dancers want to step to the music he made popular, they must move slowly."[9] Other commentators felt Vallée's music was of a piece with a larger cultural turn toward slower dance music in sweet bands generally, best represented by the rising star bandleader Guy Lombardo. This change was largely interpreted as a return to more traditional values after the frenzied steps of the 1920s, but the slow dance was also modern because it increased intimacy between the dancers.[10]

·OKEH·
ELECTRIC RECORDS

· S M I T H   B A L L E W ·
· M A R C H ·

Ask her—she knows why—

The young lady who chooses Smith Ballew records knows what is lovely in rhythm and melody.

The young lady who dines in Whyte's Restaurant knows the joy of responding to his charming manner and refreshing dance music.

The young lady who listens to his broadcasting programs knows that his songs come nearer to her heart.

FIG. 5.2. Magazine ad for Okeh Records, in *Talking Machine World & Radio-Music Merchant*, February 1930. This ad for the crooner Smith Ballew is typical of those of romantic crooners of the time. It is entirely targeted toward the female listener and links Ballew's recordings with other kinds of performances—both public (nightclubs) and mediated (radio)—which indicated crooning's broad popularity and the growing corporate consolidation of entertainment industries in the wake of the Depression. Author's collection.

Hollywood quickly snatched up crooners, songwriters, and Tin Pan Alley publishing house catalogues, assuring the even greater reach and popularity of crooning songs; Hollywood's new financial interest in popular songs resulted in their inclusion in both musical and nonmusical films (often as romantic theme songs).[11] Many crooners were featured in the musical films of 1929, and these songs quickly became nationwide hits. The Broadway showman Charles King crooned one of the year's favorites, "You Were Meant for Me," in the Best Picture winner of 1930, *The Broadway Melody*. Cliff Edwards, Nick Lucas, "Whispering" Jack Smith, and Morton Downey all appeared as singing players or stars of early musical films, many of which were revue-style entertainments in which studios paraded their singing, dancing, and acting talent. Edwards's recordings of "Orange Blossom Time" and "Singin' in the Rain" from MGM's *The Hollywood Revue of 1929* were popular in the summer of 1929, and Lucas had a huge hit with "Tiptoe through the Tulips" from Warner Bros.' *The Gold Diggers of Broadway*. Crooner hits from radio were also featured in films, most notably Vallée's hit songs in *The Vagabond Lover*, and song pluggers for the film industry often paid radio crooners like Vallée to sing and promote a song that had appeared or was going to appear in a film.

The romantic crooner persona was so popular in 1929–30 that Hollywood even promoted some homegrown singers with crooning qualities. The silent screen heartthrob Ramon Novarro became a successful romantic tenor lead in early musicals from 1929 and 1930.[12] Billed as "the Golden Voice of the Silver Screen" in musicals that were ostensibly light operettas, Novarro interspersed crooning with operetta and serenading songs in a more popular vein, such as the song "Lonely" from *Call of the Flesh* (1930).[13] His romantic crooner voice sounded natural and untrained, and he quickly became a singing success in the Latin-lover vein. Novarro's films reveal his immense charm, sophistication, beauty, and desirability for both sexes. In *In Gay Madrid* (1930), for example, Novarro is beloved by both the heroine and, more subtly, her brother. He fits the crooner type of the attractive, passionate young man, and his singing voice is light and gentle. Not surprisingly Novarro would run into the same gender troubles that all crooners did after 1930, and his movie career dropped off.

Another Hollywood crooner type was the college boy, usually the star quarterback, whose masculine credentials were not compromised by a little sweet singing to win the girl. As F. Scott Fitzgerald's novels remind us, athletics and singing were not antithetical for the males of the late 1920s, and campus musicals were a popular subgenre. Stanley Smith in *Good News* (1930) is a good example of this crooning collegian, although his quarterback actually looks more like a lipsticked matinee idol than a bruiser. The most popular and fetching of the young male Hollywood crooners of the time was Buddy Rogers, whose striking beauty and string of successful musicals earned him the nickname "America's boyfriend." Rogers was often teamed with Nancy Carroll,

FIG. 5.3. Ramon Novarro and Dorothy Jordan in *Devil May Care*, MGM, 1929. Novarro's beseeching position here is typical for him; his musicals focused on his intense love and heartache, and his female leads often had greater emotional strength and physical dominance (note the riding crop Jordan is holding). Author's collection.

a popular new starlet who always played a modern, high-spirited girl. Their pairing typified the crooning song's gender-role reversals: she played the experienced flapper, while he was usually the well-intentioned innocent trying to win her over. The film historian Richard Barrios calls Rogers's persona "perilously close to male ingenue" but notes that audiences of the period loved his "guileless sincerity."[14] One production still from the Carroll-Rogers film *Close Harmony* is representative of their on-screen relationship and is an iconic pose of the period. Carroll has her leg lifted high in the air (a pose from the Charleston dance) while Rogers hunches down in contrast, playing a saxophone to woo her (fig. 5.4). In such shots the high kicking leg of the chorus girl dominates the frame, and the crooner or wooer cowers, cheerfully submissive, wanting to please and well positioned to put the "fast-tonguing" he learned on the saxophone to better use.

This new breed of Hollywood crooner would lose favor by the mid-1930s. Though largely forgotten, the crooning musicals from this period that remain available—the snippets from *Chasing Rainbows* and *Good News*, the Rogers-Carroll musicals, *The Broadway Melody*, the Vitaphone and Movietone shorts and revues—convey a freedom of expression and a lack of self-consciousness regarding gender behavior that is quite remarkable and indicative of the queer-friendly urban culture of the time, as well as pre-Code Hollywood. Judy Garland would famously lament her gender "in-between" status in song in 1938, but just a few years earlier such freedom from gendered boundaries was widely accepted and celebrated. The wit and drive of the musicals' heroines, the sweet unaffectedness of the crooner heroes, the jazzed-up energy, acrobatic skills, and sexual overtones of the dancers of both sexes (female dancers frequently perform forward roll-overs, baring their panties proudly to the world, and male dancers perform acrobatics while locked in an embrace) and the unaffected, delightful silliness of certain set pieces attest to a lack of creative or social constraints.

All of these elements combine in the two extant numbers from *The Gold Diggers of Broadway* in two-strip Technicolor: "Painting the Clouds with Sunshine" and Lucas's hit number, "Tiptoe through the Tulips." The former contains extraordinary acrobatic and homoerotic (from today's vantage point) dance numbers from both sexes, while the latter is a cousin to *The Wizard of Oz*. "Tiptoe" is set on a theatrical stage, where Lucas serenades one young lady at her window while two androgynous couples dance an easy soft shoe alongside them. Behind them, on several tiers, stand chorus girls dressed as tulips (anchored in pots), who begin to sing and "open" as they are watered by chorus boys dressed in green from top hat to toe. The sense of delight, even giddiness evident in this scene suggests not innocence but theatrical wit and sophistication that is extraordinarily naturalized. There is no winking at the audience because there doesn't need to be. The huge popularity of both the film and the song suggests the familiarity and ease of a mass, mixed audience with these kinds of representations; indeed both sexes in the audience within the film give the number a rousing ovation. It is this naturalization of blurred gender roles and queer content in national mass media that was making cultural authorities increasingly uncomfortable.[15]

FIG. 5.4. America's sweethearts Nancy Carroll and Buddy Rogers in *Close Harmony*, Paramount, 1929. The crooning collegiate and the dancing flapper were two of the most popularized images of the sexes in the 1920s, and the Carroll-Rogers pairing in several films of the time represented these roles very successfully. Note Carroll's Charleston leg lift countered by a bent Rogers looking up at her, an iconic pose of flapper power that will be considered too suggestive in Code-era Hollywood. (See also fig. 4.12.) Courtesy of the Academy of Motion Picture Arts and Sciences.

FIG. 5.5. Buddy Rogers, fashion publicity still, 1929. Rogers was a well-known clotheshorse, and this picture is typical of MGM's promotion of him as a fashion role model for men as well as a love interest for women. He wears the latest fashions, which are clearly influenced by the collegiate style: a light-weight, light-colored suit; tailored pants with a full, soft drape and a front crease; two-toned shoes; patterned tie; light shirt with matching pocket square; and fedora. His hands behind his back emphasize his role here as spectacle for the viewer, an object of display. Rogers's clean-cut, tailored appearance and beauty earned him the nickname "America's boyfriend." Courtesy of the Academy of Motion Picture Arts and Sciences.

GENDER LINES NARROW:
ANDROGYNY AND BEER, 1929–1931

As crooners grew in popularity, gender became increasingly central in the coverage of them; the press underlined their newly perceived feminine and androgynous qualities and continued to insist they had female-only audiences. While for much of the press and public, crooners still represented well-brought-up young gentlemen, certain radio columnists began to point to the feminine roots of crooning music in the mother's or mammy's lullaby. Leslie Allen in the *New York Sun* wrote in February 1930, "Crooning is as old as the hills. It is lullaby—no more, no less. And the lullaby is ingrained in the memory of every mother's son to us." Allen asserted that crooning may therefore appeal to some men whose mothers used to croon them to sleep every night.[16] The *Washington Star* agreed, noting in March 1930 that "while mammies also croon," crooning did seem to be "the secret of [Vallée's] success."[17] This connection did not initially spur negative comment, but it was in the first wave of press acknowledgments that crooners were men who sang in ways previously associated with women.

Radio industry practices reinforced this vocal ambiguity by promoting female singers as crooners, and audiences often could not distinguish women's voices from those of crooning males. One prominent Chicago orchestra exploited this ambiguity in its hotel broadcasts by concealing the crooner Harriet Lee's sex in a booth on the stage. As a result, newspapers widely reported that she had received several phone calls and mash notes from women who had mistaken her for a man.[18] There were no gender codes in place for these new disembodied voices; female singers were still called "crooners" just as men were often dubbed "torch singers" or "blues singers." The female singer Lee Morse was described as doing "husky-voiced crooning" in her 1930 Vitaphone short, while Ruth Etting was described as the "lovely crooner of low-down tunes." The overlap between blues and crooning also continued, with Etting promoted as a "blues crooner" and Morse "the peer of all blues singers."[19] The fact that songs were often recorded and played with the lyrics unchanged regardless of the sex of the singer did much to encourage these blurred lines.

Gradually, coverage of male crooners began to exhibit some unease with this gender fluidity; the press shifted from bemusedly describing crooners' perceived feminine qualities and female fans to criticizing crooners for the same. Again Vallée's career is exemplary. His press coverage continued to stress a female-only appeal, even while radio polls and fan club membership

Well, Well, Here's First "All-America Crooning Eleven" Choices

FIG. 5.6. This illustration reflects the fact that crooning was still an ungendered descriptor in 1930. Although the most famous crooners were men, female crooners were also very popular at the time. Singers such as Helen Morgan and Ruth Etting, both pictured here, were described regularly as "crooners," "blues singers," and "torch singers." Crooners football team, *Cleveland Plain Dealer*, 30 November 1930. Courtesy of Rudy Vallée Collection, American Radio Archives.

indicated that he had a large percentage of male fans. A national radio poll conducted in November 1930, for example, found that Vallée's program rated first among women and second among men in popularity (after *Amos 'n' Andy*). The broad popularity of his Thursday evening radio program also attested to his mixed-audience appeal, with reportedly over 10 million listeners tuning in weekly (40 percent of the U.S. broadcast audience and 8 percent of the U.S. population).[20]

In addition, his live appearances remained immensely popular across the country. His radio sponsor, Standard Brands, conducted an in-depth study of audience reactions to Vallée's national ten-week live tour, from January to March 1931, and found that his audiences were "very heterogeneous," with a variety of ages and sexes represented. Although women generally outnumbered men 60 to 40 percent, and the young women remained most demonstrably appreciative, male attendees were very enthusiastic as well; even those men who had been prompted to come by their wives or girlfriends, the study reported, "were very much surprised to find" that they were impressed with Vallée. The investigators concluded that the "degree of enthusiasm manifested by [Vallée's] fan following undoubtedly exceeds the following of any other stage or radio personality in this field by a good margin" and called him "a dominating influence in the entertainment world today."[21]

In spite of such national approbation, columnists continued to portray Vallée as a source of division between the sexes, such as this writer for the *St. Paul News*: "At the moment no young man is more popular with the ladies and more unpopular with the men than Rudy Vallée. I happen to be a member of the anti-Vallée sex so, of course, all my remarks about him are highly prejudiced."[22] The press increasingly treated Vallée's popularity among the female sex as more of a liability than an asset. His hit "The Stein Song" provides a case in point. The song, a jazzed-up version of a University of Maine drinking song, became a monster hit in 1930. Press commentators spent weeks mulling over its success, but they focused most on whether or not the song would help Vallée win the male audience, which they had spent so much time assuring their readers did not exist. A very young Ed Sullivan, then a columnist for the *New York Graphic*, asserted that Vallée was "the idol of men radio fans since he struck out into new fields with 'The Stein Song.'"[23] Others expressed greater skepticism about washing away the feminine taint with one song. The *New York Evening Post* newsman Russel Crouse commented, "Mr. Vallée's Stein Song may be all right, but in the old days you never saw a man crooning into his beer."[24] The mere fact of Vallée's being a crooner disqualified him, in Crouse's view, from manly status—beer or no beer.

By the fall of 1930 pointed speculations about Vallée's sexuality were becoming more frequent, and Vallée began to respond. In two interviews he angrily refuted press claims that his audience was exclusively female and asserted he didn't care if critics said he was "effeminate" or "queer" since his friends knew better.[25] The columnists who liked Vallée responded by characterizing him as a hardworking businessman and advised him to enlarge his repertoire of music. Vallée countered that although he tried to make his voice "as strong and masculine as possible" when singing certain martial and college songs, he would not vary his repertoire since "the majority wish me to stay in [romantic] character and sing the songs they most enjoy hearing me sing." When an interviewer tried to align Vallée with male pursuits by assuring his readers that Vallée was simply a businessman who "peddles . . . in heart-throbs and tender sighs," Vallée undid the attempt by pointing out how

"Turn off that radio, you brats! I can't do a thing while Rudy Vallee is crooning his stuff."

FIG. 5.7. The violence in this cartoon reflects the growing hostility
toward crooners and their perceived audiences as the Depression
worsened. The caption reads, "Turn off the radio, you brats! I can't do
a thing while Rudy Vallée is crooning his stuff." *Washingtonian*, 1931.
Courtesy of Rudy Vallée Collection, American Radio Archives.

romantic he was and how much he preferred the company of women to men,
asking the interviewer, "If you had the choice of attending a prize-fight or taking a girl out for a ride, you'd probably prefer to go to a prize fight." "Oh, yeah,"
responded the interviewer. Vallée continued by emphasizing both his softer
masculinity and heterosexuality: "But as for myself, I've never been to a prize
fight. I'd much prefer the company of a charming girl. To me that's the supreme
and only happiness." The chagrined interviewer noted, "This was the only time
during the tete-a-tete that your dear correspondent almost frowed up."[26]

By sticking to his audience's desires, which mirrored his own, Vallée became an especially easy target. But while these criticisms may have dam-
aged his career, they did little to diminish the popularity of crooning generally. Vallée never again achieved the success as a crooner that he enjoyed
from 1929 to 1931, yet crooning remained the dominant form of music on
the airwaves, and romantic crooners were more popular than ever. Both Bing
Crosby and Russ Columbo became radio stars in the fall of 1931, and as Vallée's

'I Enjoy Girls' Company!' Rudy Admits

GIRLS, GIRLS, GIRLS—Rudy Vallée (center) takes time out while rehearsing with a group of chorus girls in George White's "Scandals" to pose for a photographer. "Girls," he says in his own love story, "have played a prominent part in my life, and frankly I enjoy their company."

FIG. 5.8. As criticism of crooners began to accelerate, Vallée's preference for female company began to be viewed as a problem, indicating the growing unacceptability of his perceived femininity. Rudy Vallée with fans, *Cleveland News*, 28 July 1931. Courtesy of Rudy Vallée Collection, American Radio Archives

star began to fall under the criticism of effeminacy (spurred in part by a troubled marriage), theirs rose. For example, papers widely reported that 3,000 members of one Vallée Boosters Club switched their allegiance to Crosby because "he's more masculine. . . . The men in our club became disgusted with Vallée. . . . [Membership is] picking up wonderfully since we decided to go for Bing."[27] What's important about columnists' criticism of crooners is that they continued to emphasize a divided audience, making women's ("feminine") tastes a regular target for ridicule. They also provided some of the initial rhetoric with which later attacks on crooners would be carried out. But it would take a much larger, united effort to knock crooners off their pedestals.

POLICING AND CENSORSHIP
IN THE EARLY 1930S

The greater attention to crooners' femininity and sexuality in the press was concurrent with the greater policing of feminine-seeming men in the public sphere and mass media. As I discussed in the previous chapters, the rise of romantic crooners paralleled the rise and popularity of urban pansy acts and what today we might call a generally queer-friendly culture among many in the urban working classes as well as its sophisticates (especially its women). The presence of pansy acts in public space at first served to mitigate the crooner's feminine qualities, reflecting the broad range of acceptable gender positioning for men during the era. But the pansy craze ultimately made crooners and other feminine-coded men more vulnerable to attack by helping to codify emerging ideas about sexuality, gender, and performance. As the historian Chad Heap has shown, the figure of the pansy emerged at a time in which middle- and upper-class Americans, including some with same-sex desires, had begun to change the way they thought about sexual identity and to identify as either heterosexual or homosexual.[28] Many of the most cele- brated pansy performers, like Jean Malin, presented themselves unasham- edly as confident, assertive, same-sex-oriented men; the transgressive and titillating value of their performance therefore lay in being perceived as an enactment of *who they actually were* rather than their skillful *impersonation* of a sissy or a woman. As a result their feminine gestures, extravagant dress, or sliding pitch, long associated with vaudeville sissy performances, began to be understood as aspects of their authentic homosexual identity. The pansy craze therefore had important implications for vocalists, because it linked certain kinds of vocalizing not only with a queer performance *style* but with homo- sexuality. Nightclub and cabaret promotion and reviews of the time would often indicate the presence of pansy or butch female acts by referencing the voices of the performers, those "high soprano" men and "deep-voiced girls."[29] While such vocalizing had been present in popular entertainment for years, during this era such a description became a code for the presence of "real" homosexuals in the clubs. Such rhetoric did not cause a reaction until 1931, when the craze peaked and quickly dropped off as the New York mayor's office and several newspapers began a public campaign against pansy acts and gender transgression more generally.[30]

This reactionary change in attitude and policy was due in large part to a Depression-era backlash against urban excess, as well as rising concerns over men's loss of masculine status as a result of massive unemployment. In such an atmosphere, female impersonators, "lavender-tinged" emcees, and other insufficiently masculine male performers seemed like ideal scapegoats and were harassed by police to the point that they became liabilities for club owners. In February 1931 the RKO vaudeville circuit ordered their theater managers nationwide to prohibit performers from even using the words *fairy* or *pansy* in their routines. (New York State had already banned the depiction of "sex degeneracy or perversion" on the legitimate stage in 1927.)[31] The repeal of Prohibition in 1932 gave more power to opponents of gender transgression since public entertainments could be more easily regulated at a local level, and the state was able to institute stricter rules and boundaries regarding public behavior. The State Liquor Authority of New York began refusing to issue liquor licenses to establishments that permitted "disorderly conduct," which was defined to include the mere presence of lesbians or gay men.[32] Since most Americans (reinforced by regulating institutions) identified homosexuality as gender transgression, any nonnormative behavior was therefore suspect and subject to policing. As George Chauncey points out, the rules prohibiting gay culture thus served "to codify the proper dress, speech patterns, modes of carrying one's body, and subjects of intellectual and sexual interest for any man or woman who wished to socialize in public."[33] In such an environment, being a male crooner became a key marker of deviance.

Social critics also singled out the mass media for its presentation and promotion of such deviant and immoral social behavior, and calls for regulation became more pronounced.[34] The Depression-era turn to *national* censorship came out of the collapse of local, live entertainment and the rise of the homogenized and nationalized mass media as the primary entertainment source for most Americans.[35] As the historian Warren Susman notes, the sound era "helped create a unity of response and action not previously possible; it helped make us more susceptible than ever to those who would mold culture and thought."[36] In 1930 Hollywood established the Production Code, which banned "sex perversion," among other acts deemed immoral, and greatly curtailed sexual expression generally, particularly outside of marriage. The Code seemed particularly necessary to producers because of the introduction of sound film, which could not be as easily altered by local censors as silent film because of the need to synchronize sound.[37] The adoption of the Code was gradual during the early 1930s, but it would be fully enforced by 1934.[38]

Radio did not adopt a similar code, but content regulation became an important part of network policy by the early 1930s. Radio executives understood their place within the family home and did not want to jeopardize it by offending the morals of middle-class consumers or, more important, sponsors or federal agencies. Network executives and sponsors began paying closer attention to program content and the behavior of their newly created radio stars. The early years of the Depression saw a great influx of vaude-villians into the medium and the gradual shift from music-based to narrative programming. While ad-libbing had been common among radio performers in variety-based music programs like Vallée's in 1929–30, written scripts became the norm for all programs by the early 1930s. Network executives had to approve these scripts before airtime.[39] In addition, radio sponsors sought further control over their stars by introducing morality clauses into their contracts in 1932. Like their Hollywood counterparts, radio stars had to agree that they would "perform no act" that would elicit "public contempt, shock, or indignation." The *Radio Guide* explained why these contracts were necessary: "Radio goes directly to the heart of the home, and the American family insists that its entertainers be just as straight and clean as those who live in the home itself."[40]

With the disappearance of pansies from public life and the greater regulation of gender content in the media, crooning's perceived femininity and projected homosexuality became the focus of widespread public concern. But crooning offered a particular challenge because, unlike fairies on the street or pansies on the stage, radio crooning was invisible and crooners' songs could not be effectively censored in terms of content beyond "correcting" pronouns in love songs, which became the standard in all media during this time. Since objections to crooning centered on crooners' soft voices and general romantic appeal, gender norms were developed for male vocal performance and promoted rhetorically. Calls for the regulation of crooners initially took place in the public sphere, where the crooner's lack of masculinity became a subject of prolonged public discussion by institutional leaders.

BROAD INSTITUTIONAL ATTACKS, 1932–1933

In January 1932 Cardinal William Henry O'Connell, archbishop of Boston and dean of the Roman Catholic hierarchy in America, delivered the first major attack against crooning to come from beyond the radio columns in a public address about the corrupting influences of popular culture. He singled out crooning as particularly harmful and degenerate:

> There is no man who would lower himself to such art as that. . . . It is [a] sensuous, effeminate, luxurious sort of paganism, with which men of your age may not be influenced, but think of the boys and girls who are brought up with that idea of music. . . . If you will listen closely, you will discern the basest appeal

to sex emotions in the young. They are not true love songs. They profane the name. They are ribald and revolting to true men. If you will have music, have good music, not this immoral, imbecile slush.[41]

In many ways the cardinal's objections resembled those made against jazz music in the mid-1920s. The class and racial transgressions were clear: crooning music was bad art as well as immoral. It was lowbrow *because* of its sensuousness, a word long associated with the lower classes and non-whites. But the cardinal's speech also reflected the way gender—rather than race or class—had become the primary frame for critiquing crooners. The stigma of the feminine thus came to define the early crooner, and from this problem all others stemmed. The cardinal's speech also suggested that crooners presented new problems due to their status as dominant figures in a national mass medium. Because romantic crooners had more influence over popular music than any singers before them, they had the power to establish new national standards for musical performance that the next generation would perceive as normal. This fear of crooning's corrupting influence on the young caused the cardinal to frame his objections in nationalist rhetoric.

This attack opened the floodgates. Cardinal O'Connell was one of the most influential political figures at a time when the Catholic Church played a major role in the regulation of popular media, most famously in the film industry. His attack elicited similar diatribes from many educators, religious figures, and newspaper editors. Transgression of gender roles remained central to these critiques, as did worries about how crooners' immature, inartistic whining would be damaging to young people. Psychologists and philosophers found crooning infantile and potentially pathological; educators and music teachers focused on its untrained, uncontrolled quality and its corrupting influence; and voice experts and sound engineers claimed that it distorted the voice and did not permit a "natural" balance in the sound studio.

Like the commercial media industries it attacked, the Catholic Church was becoming more centralized, streamlined, and masculinist by the early 1930s. The Church's transformation had a national impact on American culture, and it developed new uniform national standards of "American" identity and behavior that were grounded in unassailably masculine, middle-class aesthetics and attitudes. The "social Catholic" who emerged in the early years of the Depression advocated progressive policies of economic reform and

CROONERS NOT MEN, SAYS CARDINAL

FIG. 5.9. This is one of many nationally syndicated articles publicizing Cardinal O'Connell's attacks on crooners and is representative in that the top crooners of the time are pictured: Rudy Vallée, Bing Crosby, Russ Columbo, Nick Lucas. "Crooners Not Men, Says Cardinal," *Cleveland Press*, 11 January 1932. Courtesy of Rudy Vallée Collection, American Radio Archives.

social justice but also a reactionary agenda regarding gender roles, women's rights, and sexual expression. With the increasing nationalization of popular sound cultures, including radio, recording, and talking films, Catholics became heavily involved in media policing in order to prove their patriotism and protect their own interests, helping to impose cultural standards for mass-media products that endured for many years.[42]

Cardinal O'Connell's targeting of crooners was part of this larger Catholic project to "clean up" popular culture for the common Catholic good, a program that asserted the "primacy of moral rather than economic reform."[43] By disaffiliating the Church from the compromised masculinity of romantic crooners, Catholic leaders could show their adherence to dominant gender standards and police their own constituents. The Church's agenda was especially ambitious given that the leading crooners were all Catholics and the bulk of largely urban-dwelling Catholics partook of the mass media under attack. Vallée, Morton Downey, Columbo, and Crosby were more representative of their fellow Catholics than the Church leadership at the time; they embraced the commercial media and, ostensibly, the modern attitudes toward sex and marriage it represented. Polls suggested that the Catholic public, unlike their leaders, largely did not support media censorship—indeed Vallée had performed a benefit for the Catholic Daughters of America months before the attacks—and many wrote to the New York papers defending crooners and calling for "a more liberal outlook on modern life" from "our priests and clergyman."[44]

Crooners were particularly popular among Catholics because they tapped into singing traditions that had existed for generations in Irish and Italian cultures, specifically a privileging of the young, emotional male tenor voice. The tenor most often sang in praise of a mother (epitomized by "Ave Maria" in classical music and the mother songs in secular singing), a reflection of both religious scripture and centuries of art that depict the Madonna as a powerful figure of strength and identification, protectively holding the vulnerable, wounded, or dead Jesus in her arms. The overlap of religious and romantic feelings was common among mass culture audiences (Vallée fans frequently claimed he had the "voice of an angel"), and it is thus not surprising that crooners resonated so strongly with Catholics. Yet Catholic culture's reverence for the passionate female protector and the exposed, vulnerable young man were what the cardinal was insisting needed to be sacrificed in order to adhere to the new, aspirational masculinity of a developing middle-class Catholic American identity. In criticizing crooners, O'Connell was thus communicating to Church members—especially the next generation of Catholics—that not just the crooners themselves but those who loved them were to be condemned. Being or loving a young, sensitive, romantic male popular singer, O'Connell asserted, was no longer acceptable behavior for a good Catholic.

Where O'Connell framed his objections to crooning's effeminacy in religious and moral terms, psychologists used a secular source to make the same points. Because it located gender as a site of psychic and social identity, Freudian psychology proved particularly important in providing a pseudo-scientific language with which to validate perceptions of crooners as emasculated and explaining crooning's damaging cultural effects. Such Freudian-inspired terms and concepts as *hysteria, inferiority complex*, and *sex appeal* had become staples of New York politics and culture in the 1920s. Ann Douglas asserts that "Freudian discourse, no matter how simplified and distorted, had by the 1920s eclipsed the Protestant pieties sovereign in America's official life until then. It had become the explanatory discourse."[45] Moralists, psychologists, and business leaders used Freud to reinforce masculine superiority and to pathologize and devalue femininity in both men (who were labeled homosexuals) and women (who were portrayed as gullible, infantile consumers).

While Freud both rejected and indeed abhorred the moralizing and commercial uses to which his work was put in America, New York moderns embraced him so intensely because there were genuine affinities between them and Freud, particularly in their attention to sex generally and their championing of masculine superiority.[46] Despite writings that suggested bisexuality was an inherent feature of the human psyche, Freud's work helped redefine a gender binary in American thought by suggesting that masculinity and femininity depended not only on proper gender identification but also on making the correct object choice. He made a distinction between identification and desire, with the implicit assumption that identification should be directed at the same sex and desire should be directed toward the opposite sex. American cultural authorities employed this distinction to flag media instances in which desire and identity overlapped. Needless to say, crooners and their audiences were prime offenders. Audiences both desired and identified with the crooner, and although the crooner did not explicitly desire men, he did identify with and desire women, muddying the line between the two sexes.

The designation of the crooner as homosexual thus proceeded in part from this binary system: a crooner is not properly heterosexual, therefore he must be homosexual. Freud was interpreted as privileging heterosexuality over homosexuality and as pathologizing homosexuality. Homosexuality, Freud suggested, represented a case of narcissistic "arrested development," a stage between the autoeroticism of the infant and the heterosexuality of the mature male in which pleasure is directed at an external object, a woman.[47] Such rhetoric of immaturity and narcissism was reiterated tirelessly by Americans in discussions of crooners in order to pathologize them.

Freud himself put great stock in masculinity and at times compared femininity in an unfavorable light to masculinity's virtues. This was another point that won him favor with the most influential moderns, the bulk of whom were rebelling against what they perceived as a female-dominated culture. Freud saw masculinity as representing self-denial rather than self-love (female narcissism) and therefore valued it more because he considered self-abnegation "the supreme value of the civilized man."[48] In its American adaptation, Freud's bifurcation of the sexes into the self-abnegating male and the self-indulgent female was projected onto commercial culture; women and homosexuals became identified as the pleasure-seeking consumers in society, while straight men could view themselves as self-denying producers, allowing them simultaneously to assume the moral high ground and de-emphasize gratifications they surely also found in the new consumer culture.[49] Although Freud himself regarded the producers of mass culture with as much disdain as he viewed its consumers, his American followers generally ignored this aspect of his work. Instead they appropriated his rhetoric to forge a link between sexuality, gender behavior, and the commercial economy.

Thus Freudian rhetoric was widely employed to characterize crooners as masturbating narcissists and their audiences as immature hedonists. Such a characterization was particularly effective regarding the radio crooner, whose autoeroticism was what most separated him from embodied, public performers. He was not visibly employing exhaustive physical labor for the approval of an audience, as Al Jolson did, or using technical proficiency, like Paul Whiteman. Instead the crooner acted in isolation, pouring out his soul to the mic; the crooner had a lack of emotional and physical control that psychologists agreed was damaging to the psyche as well as morals. Charles Diserens, a psychology professor at the University of Cincinnati, asserted, "[The crooner] depends for his 'effect' upon songs embracing self-pity, apology, misfortune, weakness and invariable frustration. From a psychologist's point of view, such an emotional stimulus can have only a deplorable result on crooner and croonee."[50]

Clearly crooning's audience was at risk, since their immature minds and undisciplined bodies were unable to resist the crooner's influence. Freud's concept of the unconscious proved especially useful here. Scientists' and psychologists' testimony concerning crooning's effects on the unconscious mind had frequently appeared in the press prior to this, including this warning from the New York Evening Graphic's unidentified "professional consultant": "The voice that catches on, so to speak, is, then, the voice that establishes contact with those unconscious emotional urges and tends to satisfy them. This is so, oftentimes, regardless of the refinements and culture of the voice, or lack of them. Technique and finish appeal to what I might call the conscious ear, but it is that other deeper and more primitive appeal that gets us when we hear certain singers. It is the unconscious ear that opens up the soul of the multitude to the voice which has that mysterious grip."[51] By connecting crooners with the unconscious mind and base desires, the consultant suggests that crooning is insidious, a thing not capable of being understood or, more important, resisted by the conscious mind. This assessment resonates historically with many commentators' views of early radio as an invisible, uncontrollable, and possibly threatening force. Most significant, however, it confirmed the perceived threat by the middle and upper classes from lowbrow popular culture. A crooner preys on people's more "primitive" impulses, a word that at that time was most often employed to describe African Americans and the "uncivilized" lower classes. While Tin Pan Alley songwriters had managed to whitewash popular music for the majority of its audiences, the residual associations of racial and class transgression would have remained in the minds of higher authorities, who linked the desire for crooning music to fears of cultural degeneration.

The ultimate target of such warnings was white females, upon whose desires rested the next generation of privileged citizens. Although the *Graphic*'s consultant suggests that everyone has primitive impulses, this kind of assessment encouraged the public to make distinctions among crooning's audiences based on their "strong" or "weak" mindedness. Unsurprisingly, white, middle-class men were seen as able to resist crooning's appeal with their strong minds, whereas the "immature" minds of crooning's audiences (women, children, lower classes) could not. "Rudy," noted the *Graphic* in a later article, "has that insidious off beat rhythm in his voice that does exactly what it is intended to do with adolescent females and others who are still that age emotionally and mentally."[52] In this scenario a crooner is nothing less than a sexual predator, threatening to corrupt the bodies and minds of the young by exposing them to modern sensual pleasures.

Music educators, including members of the influential New York Singing Teachers Association, were among crooning's most vocal critics. Their criticisms highlighted how much crooning was in opposition to the conventions of white middle-class singing that had been established at the turn of the century. Singing, they believed, should demonstrate technical mastery, strong muscles, proper hygiene, and control of the vocal instrument. In

FIG. 5.10. This widely reprinted article offers "scientific" evidence that only women were susceptible to Vallée's singing. The caption explains that when hooked up to a cardiograph while listening to Vallée, women's heartbeats increased by 35 percent, while men's heartbeats remained steady and unaffected. "Science Proves That Rudy's Singing Does Thrill the Girls," *Detroit Times*, 20 June 1932. Courtesy of Rudy Vallée Collection, American Radio Archives

return for the singer's hard work, singing would increase his health by "developing the lungs and purifying the blood by emptying the lungs more completely of used air." Singing would also "develop character" by increasing "poise and self-confidence" and encouraging the pursuit of "higher ideals . . . and therefore guide the life and thoughts away from other evils." In contrast, the Association asserted that crooning "corrupts the minds and ideals of youth" because "its devitalized tone . . . robs the voice of its ability to express higher emotions and . . . its inherent devotional quality."[53] Members also found crooning detrimental to "the development of the vocal mechanism."

A subsequent article in *Musical America* that was syndicated and reprinted in several major newspapers polled musicians, composers, and singing teachers who condemned crooning in words similar to those used to describe sex perversion: "an abomination," "belongs in the realm of pathology," "abnormal," "demoralizing," and "an offense against good taste." Frank La Forge, a voice teacher, called crooning a "perversion of the natural production of the voice" and "extremely injurious." When warned that, once injured, good singers could never again return to "real singing," the implicit parallel with both homosexuality and masturbation became particularly evident. These "words and sounds of the gutter," concurred another voice teacher, Percy Stephens, "emanate from only one impulse."[54] The threat the crooner's conflated bodily and musical transgressions posed for America is clear in a teacher's complaint that her students could not properly sing the national anthem because they had been too influenced by crooners' "sliding over the words" and "running notes together."[55]

In the view of these educators, the crooner's lack of bodily control connected him with the dangers of raced and feminine bodies, both of which have been historically characterized in terms of their impurity, their oozing fluids marking them as grotesques in relation to the closed, sleek, white masculine classical body.[56] In their critiques, however, music teachers mentioned racial associations only as additional proof of crooners' *gender* deviance. Charles Wakefield Cadman explained that crooning's "lazy repose" was "more of the Oriental temperament than of our own." Others compared crooning unfavorably with jazz music—a genre widely associated with African Americans—because its energizing aspects were considered more masculine. "I prefer a riot, even of galvanic, hiccoughing action [i.e., jazz], to a supine sinking into the primeval ooze [i.e., crooning]," claimed Will Earhart, the Pittsburgh public schools music director. Such distinctions reflected the masculinist values of the time and were perpetuated and naturalized in the years following because of the new raced and gendered musical divides. Cultural memory of a shared, mixed performance world disappeared, including acknowledgment of early crooners' affiliations with jazz and blues performance. Pop crooning and jazz performance would be constructed as oppositional musical and cultural categories, one commercial, feminine, and essentially white, the other artistic, masculine, and authentically African American.

For music teachers and trained singers, bad gender behavior equaled bad music, and bad music equaled bad gender behavior. Critics were far less concerned about female crooning, paving the way for the replacement of male tenors by female altos in the swing bands of the 1930s. Dean Harold Butler explained that female crooners like Kate Smith "are not quite as bad" because "they at least sound something like the way members of that sex should sing."[57] Commentators attacked the lyricists of crooning songs for making men sing such emasculating tripe: "There are lots of things more pleasant in the world than hearing a masculine voice sobbing about 'you dear' and 'the day we met,' and if crooners had any respect for themselves they'd soon inform the song writers that there are plenty of interesting subjects in the world other than love."[58] John McCormack, the most popular trained tenor of the time, complained that no one wanted to become a "legitimate" vocal artist anymore because crooning's "fake" singing was so popular; his own popularity had diminished because he didn't have the "sex appeal" now required to be a popular singer. Part of having "it," McCormack despaired, was having an androgynous appeal, being "slim and sylph-like and all that." He specifically blamed the commercialism of radio for permitting this state of affairs, noting that English radio allowed no advertising, and as a result "entertainment is a thing of general excellence there."[59] Like the music teachers, he assumed that crooning's immature listeners didn't know what was good for them and were being corrupted by consumer culture.

Two authoritative studies in the early 1930s reframed concerns about the voice and gender deviance in scientific and technical terms. The voice scholars Douglas and Alma Stanley released *The Science of the Voice* in 1929 and a second edition in 1932; their study details the anatomy of the voice and argues for its "proper" usage according to scientific rather than simply aesthetic principles. One of the Stanleys' aims was to develop some rules for voices that could benefit (and police) radio singers: "It is at last possible to bring science into the studio and to formulate many really definite laws of the technique of singing and speech." Of all the types of singers on radio, the Stanleys explicitly condemn only the crooner, whom they refer to as "that abomination, the radio tenor." They identify the problems with radio tenors in terms similar to those used by the music teachers: the sound crooners make is "weak" and "effeminate" because they have not properly developed their muscles and therefore cannot coordinate them with their breathing. Proper singers use their muscles to develop their upper (falsetto) range so that it is strong and maintains a "*pure* register," but a crooner does not, and a falsetto voice that is not properly developed will sound "thin, weak, effeminate, and rather unpleasant." Radio tenors do injury to their voices by muddying up their "pure falsetto" tones with improper breathing, producing instead "a light, throaty mixed-register tone which is most injurious." They suggest that "use of uncoordinated falsetto in performance is degenerate, inartistic, and utterly to be condemned." Similarly, they assert that only a well-trained singer with a well-developed voice should attempt to sing softly (pianissimo), since "it must be accomplished by means of a *pure* upper register co-ordination of the laryngeal muscles and a perfectly controlled *rigid* throat."[60] Their emphasis on the words *pure* and *rigid* throughout their discussion speaks to the crooners' implied lack of control, which makes them impure (immoral) and emasculated (flaccid).

Soon after the second edition appeared, Douglas Stanley produced another book with J. P. Maxfield, a leading sound engineer and a pioneer of phonography and film sound. *The Voice: Its Production and Reproduction* (1933) brings together "the sciences of acoustical engineering and of vocal technic . . . in order [that] they may advance together hand in hand." This collaboration was initiated because, they assert, "faulty reproduction" and lack of vocal education had led "to the glorification of an inartistic and most vicious form of voice production known as crooning." Stanley's contribution emphasizes the social, psychological, and physiological dangers of crooning, suggesting the three have become conflated. Both Freudian psychology and nationalist rhetoric is evident in Stanley's concern that psychologically abnormal people may not only be singing crooning songs but teaching crooning to children. He asserts that besides being trained musicians, voice teachers "must be normal, healthy individuals both physically *and psychologically.*" He writes, "My friend introduced me to a group of about five extremely effeminate men who taught singing." These men "dislike free, full, mellow tones," claiming to prefer "the sound of the effeminate, mixed falsetto tones of the crooner to the glorious ringing tones of a Caruso. Any real volume of tone distresses their 'sensitive ears.'" Worse yet, these teachers pass on their "pathologically biased" tastes to their students: "Not only do they make their male pupils sound effeminate, but they also 'whittle down' the voices of their female pupils to a mere squeak." The ideal singing voice, he asserts, is not only "forceful," "powerful," "vibrant," and "loud" but is also "free" and announces itself in "glorious ringing tones." Stanley's anecdote inadvertently affirms the existence of male crooning fans and also of male teachers who clearly dissent from the leaders of their field; his nationalism indicates his anxiety, suggesting the real stakes and importance of the crooning debate for music educators. Ironically, "freedom," according to Stanley, can be achieved only by disciplining the singing body, ignoring the "majority opinion" regarding popular singers, and purging nonconforming music educators from the ranks. Finally, Stanley employs the rhetoric of authenticity: "There is no such thing as a real voice of good quality without power and vibrancy."[61]

Although less histrionic in his feelings about crooners, Maxfield was no less invested in obliterating them from the studio. His critique specifically promotes a reading of crooning as inauthentic, unnatural, and artificial, a "distorted form of voice production" made possible through the misuse of technology rather than a sincere sound produced by an actual body: "The frequency characteristics of the microphone, the reverberation of the studio and the lack of dynamic range in reproduction have caused such voices not only to sound pleasant, but have also made them easy to reproduce. These conditions lend a false, 'sweet' quality to the voice of the 'fake' singer whose lack of dynamic range makes him unable to sing forcefully."[62] Sound engineers like Maxfield had a conflicted relationship with modern technology and were very concerned with what they considered to be a "realistic" depiction of sound that reproduced, as closely as possible, the binaural experience of acoustic hearing within a live space of performance (such as a concert).[63] While recognizing that such an effect is itself an "illusion" created within the studio space, Maxfield uses the terms *natural* and *natural balance* to describe his construction of the sound of proper singing, while depicting crooning's sound as unnatural. Because Maxfield wanted to reproduce his own idea of "realistic sound," he did not value the intimacy achieved by crooners and viewed it as a "distortion" of the voice. He seems particularly concerned about what would become known as the "proximity effect," made possible by the regular use of directional mics in late 1931; when singers sang close to this mic, as crooners swiftly learned how to do, it enhanced the warmth and depth of their sound and gave it increased intimacy. Maxfield laments that because crooners' "voices are so weak" that they have to be close to the microphone in order to be audible, "it is impossible to attempt a natural balance." This "microphone technic," asserts Maxfield, "fails to give the listener the emotional value that is obtained by real concert or operatic singing," which he describes as having a great range of volume and "full, free power and color." Like Stanley, Maxfield dismisses the emotional satisfaction that crooners provide their audiences. He then offers engineering and studio techniques to help singers and technicians undo the "poor, thin, 'fuzzy'" crooning tone.[64]

By opposing his ideas of realism and naturalism to the crooner's artificiality, Maxfield buttresses his own claims and promotes "natural"-sounding radio singers. Other radio technicians provided further evidence for Maxfield's and Stanley's assertions by claiming that crooners had small, almost nonexistent voices. In January 1932 Colin O'More, a program supervisor for CBS, reported in the *Musician* that crooners in fact "have no voices," that they are the sole products of amplification: "In the studio, they are actually inaudible."[65] In making it possible for unnatural voices to have more sexual power and a greater effect on women than "real men," crooners upset "natural" sex roles and encouraged "unnatural" appetites. Thus Stanley and Maxfield's book helped to define proper masculinity for voices in the early 1930s and provided radio engineers, scientists, and music teachers with ways to sonically support dominant ideologies. But it would be up to the producers of commercial culture to try to convince a reluctant public to readjust their attitudes toward their favorite singers.

DAMAGE CONTROL: DENIALS, DEFENSES, AND DIVISIONS

By 1932 anticrooner rhetoric had pervaded public discourse, and the commercial media were forced to respond. Unlike cultural authorities, however, popular culture producers depended on crooners for their livelihoods and could not afford to do away with them completely. Crooners had represented a musical breakthrough for the radio and phonograph industries and had helped keep the latter alive during the early years of the Depression; they had also proved very popular in early sound films. Moreover, the popularity of crooners among the broad public remained high during the attacks. After initially denying that their singers were crooners, which persuaded no one, radio networks and other mass-culture industries began to alter their production, promotion, and coverage of crooners to respond to the attacks. Producers tried a number of ways to redefine the crooner persona for the mass public during the next couple of years. Although much of the producers' rhetoric parroted the masculinism and homophobia of the attacks, there were also key differences that allowed for the crooner's continued presence and profitability in mass culture.

Initially, however, industry leaders panicked. Radio sponsors were the first to abandon even the most prominent crooners in the wake of institutional attacks. Columbo's and Crosby's programs, although still extremely popular, had trouble finding sponsors in the spring of 1932 and remained sustaining (network-sponsored) programs.[66] Prominent radio bandleaders and many crooners distanced themselves from the term. Paul Whiteman, who had long been a supporter of Vallée, declared the death of crooning. He hired a new singer for his band, Red McKenzie, who he assured audiences was "not a crooner," and columnists interpreted this as a sign of the return of the "male voice" and the "he-man singer"; Whiteman also began hiring more female singers, including Jane Vance and Irene Taylor, helping to set the new national trend of replacing feminized men with women.[67] Likewise, the bandleader Vincent Lopez, who had always had a crooner in his band, stated that, although he did not believe crooning was "purposely vulgar," it was "an insinuating form of song presentation, utterly devoid of cultural aspects." He hoped that improved microphone technology would soon make possible an increased interest in "strong, straight singing."[68] In April 1932 Nick Lucas (of "Tiptoe through the Tulips" fame) declared he was not a crooner, even after he had been billed for years as "the Crooning Troubadour."[69] Will Osborne, who had tried for so long to establish himself as the first radio crooner, now tried to distance himself from crooning, declaring that he was a baritone, not a crooner.[70] And in case anyone was wondering, Kate Smith and the Boswell Sisters also declared that they were not crooners and should no longer be referred to in that way.[71]

Cardinal O'Connell's attack had been especially awkward for the networks' four top crooners—Vallée, Crosby, Columbo, and Downey—all of whom were Catholic. The stars did not want to disagree with the cardinal, but they also did not want to be perceived as immoral. Broadcasters insisted that Downey was a tenor and Crosby a baritone, so they couldn't be crooners, causing one columnist to note that a crooner seems to "be between these two."[72] Both Crosby and Downey echoed this sentiment, specifically distancing themselves from the emasculating falsetto. Crosby said, "A crooner is a person who sings with a half voice and takes the top notes with a falsetto. I always sing in a full voice." Downey went even further and had his voice scientifically tested to prove he was not a crooner. Dr. William Baird White, the same "accoustical researcher" who declared New York an effeminate-sounding city, tested Downey's voice with a projection oscilloscope and declared, "He is the possessor of a pure and legitimate light lyric tenor of extremely unusual range. There are no artificial notes, and there are no falsetto qualities in his voice."[73]

Vallée and Columbo took slightly different tacks, initially defending their style in ways that suggested their bewilderment (in Columbo's case) or rejection (in Vallée's) of the gender norms being imposed on voices. In his defense Columbo noted the connection between crooning and the mother's lullaby: "Mothers from time immemorial have crooned to their babies, and nothing is sweeter than that."[74] The *Boston Transcript* radio editor responded that Columbo's work "is far from being like the soft lullabies of tender mothers. It seems to be a kind of distorted or jazzed sentimentalism, perhaps immoral only in the sense that low-grade sentimentalism is apt to run towards immoral subjects. . . . It is evident that crooning should be passed back to the mothers."[75] Vallée was the only crooner to dispute the narrow gendering of the voice in these attacks, asserting that "nobody can tell a man by the pitch of his voice."[76] Walter Winchell backed Vallée up on this point, further stating that the heavyweight champ Jack Dempsey "still talks in falsetto" and that the premiere pansy performer, Jean Malin, "talks bass."[77] Other columnists threw open the question to the public.

The radio industry was not only influenced from above; it used the radio press to monitor public reaction to the crooning attacks and to conduct surveys on public taste.[78] Crooning's continued popularity on the airwaves and on recordings indicated to the networks that the public was not finished with crooners, and letters to the radio press confirmed it. Most letters, from both men and women, defended crooners.[79] Many writers pointed out that the public had created crooning and that listeners did not appreciate their choices being belittled. Crooning fan clubs continued to proliferate; many had become accustomed to defending their stars. One of the purposes of the Brooklyn Vallée Rooters, explained President Dorothy Yosnow, was "to encourage understanding people to answer all unfriendly remarks in the public press about Rudy."[80]

In addition, when New York radio columnists polled audiences about the cardinal's assertion that crooners were not men, the responses from both men and women indicated that listeners were not disturbed by the crooner's less than normative masculinity. Their comments are instead reminiscent of Winchell's statement from 1929 about crooners having "it," defined as neither masculine nor feminine. Nathan Ritter, a steward, remarked, "Radio crooners are men, but not he-men. . . . I believe that they have many feminine traits with enough of the masculine to save them from being called effeminate."[81] Such statements suggest that many members of the public were not unduly concerned about the fact that crooners occupied space "in between" gender roles. These responses worried cultural authorities but encouraged mass-media producers to retain crooners.

New York radio columnists, many of whom also wrote novels and screenplays about crooners, were largely responsible for reconstructing the crooner's popular image and distinguishing it from the one offered in more cultured institutional discourses. No columnist was more vocal and influential than the future film producer Jerry Wald, whose series of attacks on Vallée's persona in the fall of 1931 and winter of 1932 identified the crooner characteristics that would be most commonly represented in the popular culture of 1932–33. Wald's attacks on Vallée made him famous, and the next year he moved to Warner Bros., where he provided stories and screenplays for several crooning films before becoming a successful producer; his own attacks were immortalized in the 1932 Warner Bros. film *Blessed Event*.

Wald found Vallée effeminate, narcissistic, immature, and unsophisticated. He called him an "incompetent performer," "an ungrateful parasite," a "whimpering cry baby," and a "megaphoney"; he referred to him in infantilizing and feminizing terms, such as "darling," "Mr. Wavy-locks," "Our own little Curly Locks," and "Poor 'ittle Wudy." More significantly, Wald suggested that Vallée was a publicity monster who was no longer in touch with his audience and that his recent marriage was a sham created for publicity purposes. Vallée had married Faye Webb in July 1931, and at the time critics suggested that the move might help him be seen as more masculine (the assumption being that if one is married, one must be heterosexual). Wald's attacks were unusual in their viciousness, but his tone reflected the more general press response. The opposing views of the columnists Wald and Winchell were also representative of the lack of unity among the radio press regarding how to address criticism of what was, for many, their livelihood.

Angry fans fought back, accusing Wald of attacking Vallée for his own publicity purposes and pointing out that it was the public, not Wald, who had made Vallée famous. "So it was Broadway that really made Vallée, was it?" wrote Virginia from Brooklyn. "I had always thought it was a great many people all over the United States, some of whom have never seen Broadway and have no such desire."[82] Wald countered by suggesting that Vallée was no longer one of them, noting that he has "more money than you or I" and detailing an extravagant lifestyle. By painting Vallée as an elitist and attempting to undercut fans' belief in his sincere service of them (an essential aspect of Vallée's romantic crooner image), Wald attempted to distance Vallée from his fan base. But in his belittlement of Vallée, he suggested that the romantic crooner persona was not threatening, just annoying.[83]

In September 1932 a new, menacing tabloid devoted to sex scandals, *Hush: New York*, published an article asserting that both Vallée and his wife were homosexuals, using the term *Hush* readers would recognize: "degenerates." Although the publication was quickly shut down by local authorities, the damage had been done to Vallée's reputation, and he did lose at least some fans because of it. The radio columnist Nick Kenny passed on a letter to Vallée he received from some outraged Vallée fans who believed the charges, and he advised Vallée to "go after those 'Hush' bastards." These fans identified themselves as the South Brooklyn Daffydils and wrote, "An immoral and normal act on [Vallée's] part would not have shocked us. We never thought him anything but human. But to find out that he is abnormal. . . . We turned him on tonight on the Fleischmann

Hour but tuned him out right away. We couldn't listen to him knowing what he is. . . . We want to forget him, and as quickly as possible, before the morbid thought muddies our minds."[84]

Given the legal and cultural crackdown on homosexuality in the public sphere, these fans' response is not surprising. Rather it indicates that new discourses about homosexuality had begun to influence fan culture: divisions between "normal" and "abnormal" sexual behavior and fear that the mind and body could both be corrupted by exposure to sexual deviance. This view of crooners as dangerous was still much more a product of cultural authorities than of popular culture, but it did increasingly inform its subtexts.

THE PANSY AND THE PLAYBOY

In the wake of the attacks, two new variations of the young romantic crooner archetype emerged in the popular culture of 1932–33, both of which emphasized the crooner's gender and sexual deviance: the pansy and the playboy. Cardinal O'Connell had criticized crooners for being both effeminate *and* sensuous because such qualities were not antithetical in the popular culture of the 1920s; popular representations of crooners in the early 1930s, however, divided these objectionable qualities between the two types: the crooner's gender transgressions made him either ineffectual and juvenile or predatory and amoral. As a central character in popular media texts, the pansy was a proto-sissy, without the confidence, humor, or erotic allure that marked many star nightclub pansies.

In such texts the pansy crooner is always effeminate and immature, his immaturity evident in his narcissism and stupidity. He has no real sex appeal, is not threatening to men, and elicits chiefly maternal feelings in women. His fame is most often the result of luck or a mistake rather than his own talent or hard work, but he is so stupid that he believes his own publicity and thinks he's an "artist." In these narratives the crooner is also frequently self-hating and abhors the romantic music he is forced to sing by money-hungry promoters. But the pansy crooner is ultimately still redeemable as long as he gives up crooning, which is antithetical to a happy personal life; he must stop singing to millions of women as a romantic idol and object and instead embrace normative heterosexuality and masculinity by marrying one woman. He must also turn to some more masculine profession where he can be his own boss and with which he can properly support a wife and family. In Freudian terms, he must "grow up."

The pansy romantic crooner was satirized as the central figure in a number of popular texts, including many songs and cartoons, the play *Heigh Ho Everybody* (a.k.a. *Coast to Coast*), the novels *Crooner* and *The Great Crooner*, and several films, most prominently those starring the new young crooner Dick Powell.[85] Popular songs proved to be an excellent venue for crooner satire. Although popular singers frequently did impressions of each other to show off their versatility, the imitations of Vallée and other crooners that proliferated during this period were most often ridiculing in tone and manner.[86] Film parodies of crooners by trios such as the Three Radio Rogues as well as by young girls like the child star Baby Rose Marie were especially common. The success of the satiric song "Crosby, Columbo and Vallée" led the way for the mockery of crooners in many popular song lyrics. This song appeared in the fall of 1931, just prior to the major attacks, and remained popular for over a year, inspiring its own cartoon. The song made fun of women's devotion to crooners from the point of view of the abandoned male: "Listen, all you bachelors, all you married men / There's too many crooners, too many megaphones / Breaking up our happy homes."[87]

This same condescending tone was adopted in plays, novels, and films and generally applied as much to crooning's deluded female fans as to the crooner himself. Review synopses of the Broadway play *Coast to Coast* (initially titled *Heigh-Ho Everybody* after Vallée's radio program theme song) note how the crooner Buddy Baxter, a thinly disguised portrait of Vallée, starts to croon only when he catches a bad cold, underlining the abnormal, diseased nature of the crooning sound. It turns out, however, that the sound he makes is so popular with the ladies that his manager keeps a perpetual draft blowing on him during his broadcasts. Buddy's marriage falls apart because of his crooning, yet the crooner is redeemable; being kidnapped by gangsters toughens him up enough to make him a respectable hero by the end (as long as, of course, he ceases to croon).[88]

The crooner hero of Clarence Buddington Kelland's novel *The Great Crooner* (1933) starts out hating crooning, but his mother and music teacher force young Claude to sing solos when he would rather sing in a more manly quartet. Kelland particularly indicts women for leading this young man astray and feminizing him. Claude is presented as a mollycoddled boy whose music teacher forced him to sing soprano and take on female roles in his songs ("like where he's a young mother, and the fairies are puttin' his baby to sleep," sneers one townsman). He gets taken advantage of by a gold digger and an opera diva, both of whom want to marry him for his money and fame.

Most important, Kelland characterizes crooning's radio audience as entirely young and female, and he underlines the ridiculousness of their worship by making Claude's crooning voice the result of a freak accident during throat surgery. Like Buddy Baxter's in *Coast to Coast*, Claude's voice is unnatural, out of control. The "waywardness" of his voice mirrors the way he has wandered from masculine standards of effectiveness and control. Instead Claude's crooning voice is repeatedly referred to as "swooping," "sliding," and "gulping," words that suggest a vocal deviance that becomes conflated with sexual deviance in the minds of the men listening to him. Men hearing Claude deduce that he is a homosexual and hate him, which embarrasses him. The only solution is another trip to the doctor, where his "normal" voice is restored so that he no longer is the subject of mass female adoration and can retire to the country with his faithful girlfriend, who, of course, had always disliked his crooning sound.

The crooner comes off even less sympathetically in films of the period, which reflected Depression-era reassertions of traditional social values and idealizations of rugged working-class masculinity. As gender roles became more regulated on-screen and censorship of queer-seeming characters took hold, the more assertive, usually working-class pansy supporting characters were replaced by ineffectual, usually upper-class, often silly "sissy" characters. The portrayal of the crooner in the early 1930s often conflated the pansy and sissy character traits in their young men, who may start off being working class but, because they croon, are emasculated and develop delusions of high-culture grandeur and elitist tastes. A character's "sophistication" became more and more suspicious in films of the period; *Variety* reported in 1933 that studios were concerned about driving straight men away from the movies because they found them too sophisticated.[89]

In the films *Blessed Event* (1932) and *International House* (1933) the crooner is a narcissistic boob. *International House* is the lesser critique, since the entire film is a good-hearted parade of perversions; nevertheless, Vallée's cameo as himself reaffirms the crooner's self-love in no uncertain terms: in his trademark silk pajamas and robe, Vallée sings a love song to "my first love," an unseen bedroom companion who is revealed to be none other than his own megaphone. *Blessed Event* is notable for its central portrayal of the crooner-hating New York newspaper gossip columnist Alvin Roberts (Lee Tracy), a combination of Winchell and Wald. Tracy's nemesis is the crooner Bunny Harmon (Dick Powell), clearly based on Vallée, whom he refers to as a "megaphonie," a "saxophonie," and, repeatedly, in the language of this pre-Code film, a "pansy." (Even his name, Tracy points out, is an "inversion"; his real name is Herman Bunn.) Here the crooner is portrayed as a mindless, elitist young man set against the working-class masculinity of Tracy, a common opposition in Depression-era films where "real men" are working class while pansy or sissy characters are invariably identified with the elite. Harmon is identified not only strictly with female fans, particularly mothers, but with commercial exploitation; the crooner's insincere "selling" is part of the film's critique of the crooner and of consumer capitalism. The film displaces the responsibility for consumer culture away from the masculine hero and onto a much easier target: pansy singers and their gullible female listeners.

Although Powell's character in *Blessed Event* is portrayed as a supercilious fool, Powell was a hit with audiences, and the success of the film resulted in his getting a long-term contract from Warner Bros. His appearances in the famous Busby Berkeley musical films from 1933—*42nd Street* (screenplay by Rian James, who wrote *Crooner*), *Gold Diggers of 1933*, and *Footlight Parade*—follow the same trajectory in their portrayal of the crooning singer as do other representations of the period. In all three films, Powell starts off as a crooning object for women but ultimately rejects crooning to embrace the normative masculine roles of devoted boyfriend or professional provider. "There's no future in singing," Powell's character declares in *Footlight Parade*.

In contrast to emasculated, pansy crooners like Powell, who are portrayed as immature but harmless and capable of reform, the playboy crooner, who has sexual allure, represents more of a threat. The playboy films, which were produced by all the major studios of the time, usually foreground the point of view of their desiring central female characters; they function as prescriptive texts that warn young women against their attachment to crooners and emphasize their need for traditional feminine roles. The playboy crooner is a dissolute figure, an uncaring seducer; these traits are portrayed as especially dangerous because the cultural emphasis of a good husband has shifted from a good lover to a good provider, signaling a 1930s rejection of 1920s companionate marriage's focus on erotic compatibility. Films of this type focus on the crooner's insincerity and unreliability. In MGM's *Going Hollywood* (1933), starring Bing Crosby, the crooner is an insincere playboy whom the female star must redeem. In both public and private life, as I demonstrate in chapter 6, Crosby represented the epitome of this persona.

In MGM's *Sadie McKee* (1933), redemption is possible only with the playboy crooner's death. *McKee* was a successful vehicle for Joan Crawford, a major star, who is faced with the choice of three men in the film: a weak and amoral crooner (played by Gene Raymond), a drunken millionaire, and a respectable middle-class lawyer (played by Franchot Tone). Audiences were meant to identify with Sadie's need to outgrow her attachment to her ethnic Irish, working-class roots, represented by her crooner boyfriend, Tommy, and embrace the assimilated, hardworking, middle-class values of the lawyer Michael. Both the film's narrative and its press book emphasize that the crooner is "naturally" an immature narcissist (Sadie herself calls him "a baby" and "a boy") who shirks hard work and responsibility. Tommy seduces Sadie with songs and then abandons her. His weakness of character is translated into physical weakness when he contracts tuberculosis, a feminine-coded wasting disease; although on his deathbed Tommy apologizes for hurting Sadie, it's clear that his sickness makes him pathetic and an unsuitable husband.

Other films in this vein are predicated on the need for women to embrace normative gender and social roles lest they emasculate their husbands to the point that they start crooning in nightclubs. In Columbia's *Ann Carver's Profession* (1933) Ann Carver (Fay Wray) is a successful lawyer whose husband, Bill (Gene Raymond), is a former football hero who becomes a drunken playboy crooner when she becomes too involved with her career. While performing at a nightclub, Bill gets (chastely) involved with a drunken woman and is wrongly put on trial for her murder. Ann defends him, claiming that Bill's troubles are her fault because she did not devote herself to him; she renounces her career in order to become a proper wife and mother, while he becomes a successful architect. In this film female careers are equated with male crooning as socially toxic forms of gender deviance; what is fascinating about this particular interpretation is that, in other ways, the film foregrounds the artificiality of gender and racial boundaries—racial passing, both vocal and physical, is a major subplot—and it's clear throughout that Ann is very good at her job and enjoys it. Instead of asserting essential gender differences, the film argues that women must make the *conscious choice* to assume traditional feminine roles if they want to preserve the greater social order and find happiness in their personal lives. In the Depression era, national concerns with male emasculation outweighed modern women's social freedom and professional progress.

The consequences for women of making a bad choice are well illustrated in the most devastating portrayal of the playboy crooner in this film cycle, Twentieth Century Fox's *Bondage* (1933), a cautionary tale for Depression-era women like its heroine, Judy Peters (Dorothy Jordan). Peters is a smart, cautious woman who works in a record store at the film's beginning; we know she's sensible because she does not moon over the latest crooning recording star, Earl Crawford (Edward Woods), as her silly female coworkers do. Peters is a 1930s heroine; she's not a flapper but believes in traditional values, waiting to date "until the right fella comes along." But she is nevertheless doomed. Crawford the crooner reappears, and although she finds him pretentious and vain, he succeeds in getting her into bed by lying to her about his sincere love for her, and then he abandons her when she becomes pregnant. Her life goes into the downward spiral of the early 1930s "fallen woman" films: a sadistic charity home, a dead child, and an arrest for streetwalking. By the end of the film she is hopelessly and irrevocably downtrodden. Although this social message movie contends that Jordan's fall is a product of "society's evils," that evil is primarily manifested in the crooner.

CROONER

By far the most publicized and most popular crooning film with both critics and audiences was Warner Bros.' 1932 screen adaptation of the columnist Rian James's 1932 novel, *Crooner*, and it is worth examining in detail. Both the novel and the film present the crooner as an antihero and a victim of exploitation who must prove his masculinity. The novel is remarkable for how it rewrites the story of Vallée's rise to fame through the character of Teddy Taylor. Taylor, like Vallée, is described as having "brushed, curly hair, peaches and cream complexion," and singing with his eyes half-closed. As a radio columnist for the *Brooklyn Eagle*, James had covered Vallée's rise to fame, and his novel emphasizes just how much promoters, columnists, and nightclub owners took advantage of early crooners. Far from enjoying crooning, Taylor is an unhappy, emasculated man whose effeminate persona almost ruins his life. He considers himself a saxophonist rather than a singer, and James indicates that he is correct in thinking he has no singing talent. James defines the crooner's audience as entirely fluttering females, further devaluing any artistic or social value that might have been attributed to the crooner's voice. Taylor's appeal to women is portrayed as asexual, thereby erasing any need for men to feel jealous of him. Instead James describes Taylor's appeal almost entirely in maternal terms: women coo over his "neat golden curls" and refer to him as a "helpless little boy." A gold digger trying to nab him calls her boyfriend after Taylor leaves her apartment because she "wants a man!"[90]

In the novel columnists, Taylor's manager, and other authority figures refer to Taylor as a "pansy," a "nance," and other common contemporary terms for homosexuals. They call his photo shoots "pansy poses" and talk worriedly about the "town's turning pansy." James also fictionalizes the Catholic Church's attacks, notably eliding the charge of sensuousness; its representatives instead label crooners "sexless beings who glorify masculine weakness."[91] James compounds Taylor's feminization and his alienation from the masses (here defined, like much Depression discourse, solely as working *men*) by emphasizing Taylor's "mama's boy" qualities (no smoking, drinking, or bad language) and his belief in the "art" of his work. By connecting Taylor's narcissism to highbrow pretensions, James, like Wald, furthered the unsuitability of the romantic crooner as a mass audience idol.

While it might seem difficult to recuperate such a character, or even to achieve a happy ending, James's portrayal cleverly borrows from popular Freudianism and suggests that crooning (and the emasculation that comes with it) is just a phase in a boy's life. Taylor's immaturity implies that he can grow out of his emasculation, and he does by the novel's end. Upset at the jibes, he hits a heckler who calls him a pansy during a performance, and he receives wild applause. He then goes backstage to beat up and fire his manager, proving that he *can* be a self-made man—a criterion for manhood, his girlfriend assures him—rather than depend on other men for financial support. One can imagine the appeal of such an idea for unemployed men during the Depression. Like *Coast to Coast*, *Crooner* also employs a gangster kidnapping to masculinize its singer. Taylor proves stronger than expected under torture and, in the end, achieves additional masculine credibility when he risks his career to protect the gangster's moll, who saves him. At the end of the novel, he gives up crooning, marries his girlfriend, and becomes the manager of another up-and-coming young singer. Because he has both a woman and other men dependent on him, he officially achieves manhood. As a final nail in the crooner's coffin, Taylor even admits, in the novel's final pages, that he really hated singing those love songs all along.

The film, directed by Lloyd Bacon, adheres to James's narrative for the first two-thirds but breaks from the book in its climax and denouement to reflect a Depression-era "common man" nationalism in which there is no place for crooners. The heckler that Taylor attacks in the crowd is now a crippled war veteran; thus instead of proving his masculinity by beating him up, Taylor is further knocked down for attacking a "real man" who, unlike Taylor, has fought for his country. As a result of his action Taylor loses what is left of his popularity. The gangster subplot is entirely absent in the film version, so Taylor cannot prove his manliness in that way either. Instead his fans turn

FIG. 5.11. In this publicity still for the popular Warner Bros. film *Crooner*, 1932, the crooner Teddy Taylor (played by David Manners, center) is so suffocated by his female fans that he cannot properly court his girlfriend. By 1932 cultural authorities and the media decried crooners as threatening to the normative "companionate" couple. Courtesy of the Academy of Motion Picture Arts and Sciences.

on him and thoroughly humble him, reducing him to playing music in cheap clubs. Only at this point does his girlfriend return to him—on condition, as in the novel, that he give up crooning.

Crooner both references and rewrites Vallée's rise and his appeal to a mass, mixed audience. Its nightclub and radio scenes emphasize that crooners have an exclusively feminine appeal; from Taylor's first to his last crooning scene, women are his chief and almost exclusive admirers. Most men are interested in him only as a commodity to be exploited; otherwise he is as an irritant to them. When Taylor starts to sing, male patrons retreat to the washroom, which notably fills to capacity. Remarkably, however, although the film reduces crooning to a strictly feminine appeal, it also demonstrates how crooning crossed lines of class, race, and sexual identity in a way that Code-era films would not dare to do, thus inadvertently revealing a much broader audience for crooning. Both female nightclub patrons and female working

FIG. 5.12. A queerly marked couple listen to Taylor's crooning in *Crooner*, 1932. This is one of the few instances in popular film where male appreciation for crooning is made visible, and that appreciation breaks down here over lines of gender rather than sex. The masculine-coded woman dislikes Taylor ("He's lousy!"), while the feminine-coded man likes him ("I think he's superb!").

staff are enthralled by the crooner, including the black female washroom attendant (played by Hattie McDaniel, uncredited), who flutters her eyes happily and sighs over Taylor's "soft and low!" style. Most significantly, *Crooner* portrays, however disparagingly, a gay male audience for crooning, underlining the fact that it's the cultural feminine that is the target of ridicule here, not simply the female sex. At one nightclub table, a feminine-coded man (nasal voice, excessively groomed) sits with a masculine-coded woman (large, severe short hair, monocle), listening to Taylor (fig. 5.12). The man is most appreciative ("I think he's superb!"), but the woman retorts decisively, "He's lousy!" While these scenes are meant to comically illustrate the susceptibility of the weak (feminine) mind to crooning, they instead suggest crooning's appeal to diverse groups who themselves were marginalized and devalued by a straight, white male culture.[92]

Crooner is also notable for its persistent and fairly successful attempt to take away the pleasures of crooning vocals. While women respond strongly to Taylor's singing, their reaction seems unjustified because his crooning is very flat, unemotional, and inexpressive; only one song, "Three's a Crowd," was publicized in the film's press book.[93] *Crooner* promotes the idea that crooning is not legitimate singing, that when it is heard above a whisper it is unbearable. One long sequence depicts the now pretentious Taylor trying to learn opera, screeching and honking in a loud and obnoxious voice. The film also undercuts the appeal of crooning's intimate sound by focusing on Taylor's initial rise in a nightclub rather than on the radio, and suggests that the sincerity of both the crooner and his fans is a sham cooked up by publicists: Taylor is in fact an insincere lover who cheats on his girlfriend, and his fan letters are shown to have been written by his publicists.

Crooner received exceptionally good reviews for its trendy subject matter, fast pace, and satiric edge, although reviewers insisted that the film was made to appeal specifically to the Vallée-hating crowd.[94] Jack Bryan of the *Memphis Press Scimitar* remarked, "Warner Brothers leaves no shred untorn to disparage the vocal prestige of our modern bathtub Caruso. . . . But *Crooner* is done with such a flash and flourish that it is impossible not to enjoy it even if it should hurt Mr. Vallée's feelings."[95] Most reviewers, however, were more concerned about fan reaction. The syndicated columnist Ken Barry wrote that the film wants "women to laugh at their own worship of an idol" and wondered how they would respond.[96] In fact the film displeased many crooner fans, and reviewers around the country noted that their papers had received large amounts of mail protesting both the film's unflattering portrait of Vallée and their paper's own positive reviews of the film.[97]

Film advertisements and promotion affirm the extent to which Vallée specifically and the cultural feminine more generally were the primary targets of the film's satire.[98] The crooner's only audience in these ads is women and crying babies; men despise him: "He wrecks happy homes!" The ads clearly caricature Vallée in the shape of his face, his drooping eyelids, long eyelashes, and blond wavy hair; in fact the drawings resemble Vallée much more than David Manners, the actor who plays Teddy Taylor.[99] One ad even advises customers to "kindly check your grapefruit at the door." The ads also present the film as exposing "the truth" of the crooner's sexuality: "Are they he-man or heliotrope? This picture tells you all you want to know about your favorite radio star."[100] The answer is obvious in the ads, since they effectively "out" the crooner as a pansy. The most blatant ad depicts a limp-wristed crooner wearing eye shadow and handcuffed to a wall, with the tagline "We've captured the public enemy" (fig. 1.3) More signs of the crooner's femininity are indicated by the ads' references to the crooner's stupidity and narcissism: "The actual story of the bimbo who put sex-appeal in a megaphone—and fell in love with himself!"

FIG. 5.13. This publicity still for *Crooner*, 1932, shows the crooner, Teddy Taylor (played by David Manners), using throat spray to improve his voice, indicating his increasing pretentiousness and narcissism. Taylor's crooner is often shown in bed, wearing striped pajamas, deliberately evoking Vallée's public imagery. (See fig. 4.10.) Courtesy of the Academy of Motion Picture Arts and Sciences.

FIG. 5.14. This still from *Crooner*, 1932, shows the crooner's female fans behind bars in a recording studio scene and is indicative of the film's ridicule of crooning audiences, which amused critics of the film but annoyed many crooning fans. Courtesy of the Academy of Motion Picture Arts and Sciences.

FIG. 5.15. This advertisement for *Crooner*, 1932, emphasizes the film's satire of Rudy Vallée in particular through an instantly recognizable caricature of him, one that was widely circulated in the film's publicity: drooping eyes and brows, long eyelashes, open mouth. The ad also reflects the growing concerns regarding Vallée's gender and sexuality (and that of crooners generally)—"Are they he-men or heliotropes?"—and notably ties the crooner's perceived gender deviance to the perceived racial inferiority of African Americans by invoking minstrel stereotypes. (See also fig. 1.3.) Author's collection.

Like other popular culture portraits of the crooner, the film version of *The Crooner* characterizes him as having pretensions to highbrow culture, thereby conflating high culture and effeminacy in a way that further alienates him from his mass audience. Reviewers reported that the biggest laugh came in the middle of the film when, "at the height of his popularity, (the crooner) goes aesthetic and arty."[101] Like the radio columnists, *Crooner*'s producers wanted to appeal to some of the same mass audience as the crooners themselves did, while at the same time offering a new type of crooner persona that would satisfy crooning's critics.

While such satires of crooners encouraged audiences to view aspects of male singing and male identity as unacceptable and ridiculous, they did not offer a coherent or lasting solution that would preserve romantic crooning as a cash cow and mitigate the crooner's image problems. In the last shot of *Crooner*, for example, a new crooner has taken the air, Bang Busby (an obvious reference to Bing Crosby). Taylor throws a bottle at the radio to indicate that crooners in any form are despicable. The message here, as in other crooning narratives of the time, is that crooning characters could attain masculinity only if they abandoned crooning. But this message merely avoided the problem. Even as popular culture texts ridiculed the romantic crooner, their manufacturers recognized their audience's desire for crooning songs, and they knew that crooning music could continue to be a big money maker for the radio, music, and film industries if its more objectionable aspects could be eliminated. In order to keep profiting from crooning's huge audience, the industry had to develop popular singers who would satisfy the demands of both profit and ideology. The strategies these industries developed for dealing with crooners' perceived deviance would come to shape and define each of them, beginning, as modern crooning began, with radio.

REHABILITATING THE RADIO CROONER: THE VARIETY SHOW AND FAMILY VALUES

The radio industry fought back against these critiques and attempted to rehabilitate its crooners' images along a number of fronts between 1932 and 1933. Radio's response was not to erase the crooner, since so much of its Depression revenue depended upon him, but instead to manage his image by reducing his role in individual programs and promoting a more acceptable Depression-era masculinity for him. The rapid development of commercial network programming and concerns about crooners converged, resulting in more structured fare, especially during prime-time evening hours. The networks greatly reduced the large chunks of airtime allotted only to one individual crooner (from hour-long to fifteen-minute slots) and developed evening variety programs, spearheaded by the massive success of Vallée's revamped *Fleischmann Hour*, which showcased a number of performers and transitioned the crooner into either a master of ceremonies figure, like Vallée, or a supporting player. The radio press, fan magazines, and short radio promo films of 1932–33 trumpeted these changes and offered revised narratives of crooners that emphasized their strong work ethic, family values, and athletic abilities.

As the biggest target, Vallée was most in need of an industrial makeover to assuage crooning's critics. *The Fleischmann Hour* advertisers' decision to turn him into the showman-facilitator of a variety program rather than its central performer resulted in the creation of the most influential variety show in radio's history. Radio historians have identified the J. Walter Thompson agency's decision as a key moment in broadcasting history, one prompted, I am arguing, in part by the industry's need to accommodate and redefine radio crooners.[102] Vallée's "elevation" to maestro-conductor of a commercially sponsored variety show successfully downplayed his crooner image by limiting him as a figure of mass appeal.[103] The high-culture promotion of his show set him apart from the common man of the Depression era, as did its urban setting. Although Vallée was one of the original proponents of crooning as a democratizing art form, his persona in the 1930s as a man of cultivation made him seem out of touch. At the same time, however, radio offered him a place to continue to thrive as a star even after the emasculating attacks. His survival was based in part on the unique properties of radio as a medium, specifically its privileging of and need for distinctive and familiar voices. Vallée's celebrity voice, with its trace of New England gentility, was a known quantity and provided the class signifier NBC wanted. He could thus maintain some cultural authority on radio without exactly fitting normative masculine standards, so long as he was not too dominant a figure. But public visibility in other media remained a problem for Vallée, and he never regained popularity as a leading man in film, although he made some attempts. In *George White's Scandals* (1934) and *Sweet Music* (1935) he played a band director much like himself, but his signature intimate appeal is missing in the fast pace of these musical comedies. Over time Vallée's past as a romantic idol became a cultural joke, and his popular Preston Sturges comedies of the late 1940s satirize his previous romantic persona to great effect.

The fact that J. Walter Thompson retained Vallée during the crooning attacks is a testament to how much romantic crooners had changed the landscape of radio broadcasting and popular music between 1929 and 1932. In February 1930 JWT advertising executives discussed plans to drop Vallée when his contract expired in September. They felt they had "gotten him at the height of his career" and could now replace him with an artistically superior product ("the best orchestra of that type in the U.S.").[104] Within two years, however, their standards had changed. The popularity of romantic crooners generally had convinced the agency that musical standards of excellence were not as important to radio audiences as a friendly personality and soothing songs, provided they could be acceptably regulated.

Therefore, instead of replacing Vallée, JWT at first combined his romantic crooning with comedy. Unlike crooning, comedy was a known category of performance, already familiar to and accepted by critics and the public. The success of satires like *Crooner* had shown that the public would accept comic crooners because the humor would deflate the crooner's cultural threat as a sexual rival. Moreover, in the fall of 1931 Vallée himself began appearing in the stage version of *George White's Scandals*, a musical variety revue in which he parodied a fellow singer, Maurice Chevalier, and engaged in other comic shtick, largely supported by the Broadway press.[105] But JWT did not immediately find a successful format for his radio show. The agency first paired Vallée with previous guest star Ray Perkins, a popular comic and musician, from January to June 1932, and then with the vaudeville comedy team Olsen and Johnson during the summer. The results were mixed. Although Vallée's comic exchanges with Perkins undercut his earnest crooning—often directly, as Perkins continually ridiculed Vallée's romantic music and his huge appeal for female audiences—Perkins's mocking style did not prove popular with the sponsor or audiences. In the extant scripts, Perkins suggests the gender transgression typical of a vaudevillian in that he places himself in the position of a swooning fan in his satire; like some performers of pansy routines, however, the nastiness of his approach reaffirms straight masculine superiority and gender hierarchies (not surprisingly, Perkins was considered a more popular performer with men than with women).[106] Vallée's pairing with Olsen and Johnson, broad comedians in the Marx Brothers vein, was more successful with audiences, but the program lacked coherence as it seemed oddly split between the two very different acts, and the team's anarchic visual style did not translate well to radio.[107] The sponsor was not pleased, and these comedians made their last appearance in fall 1932.

Nonetheless, Vallée proved to JWT that he was "a good program builder" who could facilitate an integrated variety show format in which his romantic crooner would link together different aspects of the program.[108] With this in mind, the agency refashioned Vallée's image into that of a master of ceremonies and promoted him as the person responsible for discovering and organizing new talent. While Vallée and his Connecticut Yankees still sang some romantic songs, thus satisfying his fans, the agency refocused the show around his numerous guest stars, all "close personal friends," Vallée assured his listeners. The agency hoped Vallée could bridge listeners' tastes: "The omnipresence of Vallée takes away the impression of unrelated acts. Each one seems to grow out of the one that preceded it and presage something still more interesting to follow. So that the listener, especially the listener who likes Vallée, is more or less willing to put up with an act he doesn't like."[109] This redesigned variety hour debuted on 9 October 1932 and became the blueprint for all variety programs on network radio. The program appealed to a mixed audience by offering something for everyone (although notably *less* for some listeners than they had before) and also reinforced the idea of radio as a family-friendly medium whose talent constituted a community of people who knew and liked each other.

The presentation of Vallée as the "author" of *The Fleischmann Hour* allowed JWT to exploit his appeal while in fact undercutting his control over the program. Vallée's image as a showman worked because it drew on the populist musical practices he had brought to radio, which audiences associated with him. Staff meeting minutes make clear that Vallée's showman image was being carefully constructed and controlled by the agency: "All the theatrical publications are now hailing Vallée as the greatest showman on radio. . . . The facts are that Vallée doesn't know now what is going to be rehearsed this afternoon. He doesn't write one word of the script. All of the things about how he first met these people, etc., we make up for him."[110]

Designating Vallée as the author of the program helped JWT sell it commercially but also promoted the high-culture concepts of authorship and individual genius.[111] Attempting to preempt government regulation, NBC promoted some of its programming as educational or at least "high culture." JWT emphasized Vallée's Yale pedigree and knowledge of languages, promoting him as a man of erudition at a time when low-culture vaudevillians were flooding the airwaves (especially at the rival upstart network, CBS), making sponsors nervous. Vallée's difference from much of this new talent was most obvious in his voice; his perfect diction and lack of slang combined with his accent marked him as middle to upper class (a northeastern elite) at a time when class was a key vocal signifier for radio audiences.

However, based on the existing scripts and recordings, the actual content of *The Fleischmann Hour* was a mix of highbrow and more popular fare. But the program's tone of urban sophistication gave it a compelling allure, a glamour that appealed to listeners without being too "high hat" or involving morally objectionable content. *The Fleischmann Hour* drew from Broadway, Hollywood, and the New York music scene, all of which were international in scope and diverse; its featured performers enjoyed a national platform, and the show helped create many stars. Broadway stars frequently performed scenes from their current successes, as did Hollywood stars if the material was considered sufficiently literary; Bette Davis, for example, performed a scene from her breakthrough performance in the film version of Somerset Maugham's *Of Human Bondage*. A typical show balanced highbrow talent with the most successful acts from vaudeville, film, music, and radio. A program on 9 March 1933, for example, featured the torch singer Helen Morgan, the Broadway and radio comic actor George Givot, the Broadway actress Edith Barrett, English actors A. E. Matthews and Reginald Carrington, and vaudeville's great Bert Lahr. Not surprisingly, such a diverse cast led to some fascinating juxtapositions of material that were held together by Vallée's gentle enthusiasm and soothing music.

In promoting *The Fleischmann Hour* the industry disavowed catering to a female listening audience. Vallée's modified persona allowed him to continue singing romantic songs, yet he was no longer promoted as a sexually desirable figure. While female fans continued to constitute a large portion of his audience, the new terms set by the press and the industry regarding his image forced women into the position of endorsing his program for its edifying qualities. For example, the National Women's Radio Committee, an influential organization of middle-class housewives, was a big supporter of Vallée and his program throughout the 1930s, but its members always couched their support in terms of the program's "educational value" rather than the pleasure it gave them.[112] This organization's endorsements carried great weight with advertisers because its members claimed to represent the interests of "the American family," although clearly they used that power to support programs that appealed specifically to them.

Such indirect tactics were now necessary because female radio audiences had lost much of the power to set the terms for radio popularity that they had enjoyed when they first made Vallée a star. The separation of high-culture from low-culture programming led to the bifurcation of the radio day, in which "women's" programming was relegated to daytime while the patriarchal family group listened in at night. As Michele Hilmes has written, the daytime hours "became the venue for a debased kind of commercialized, feminized mass culture in contrast to the more sophisticated, respectable, and masculine-characterized arena of prime time."[113] Because crooners remained a part of nighttime variety aimed at both sexes, their position as woman-made stars was obscured, and their influence on radio programming was more easily denied. Crooners became an expected staple of variety programs, either as permanent sidekicks in comedy-variety, such as Dennis Day on *The Jack Benny Show* or Kenny Baker on *The Fred Allen Show*, or as guests on music variety programs. Day's and Baker's characters (both Irish tenors) were split between their comedic side, based on their adolescent stupidity (beyond which they never matured), and their romantic crooning duties; thus crooning's erotic effects were continually compromised by the silliness of the characters.

The radio press knew how much was at stake for both Vallée and radio itself in the rehabilitation of the crooner. As the *Pittsburgh Press* noted, "Vallée wants to become serious, dignified, to command the respect of the male as well as the female public. He's on the spot, facing the test of his life. He must become the master of ceremonies of an entirely different program and if he flops (and we hope he doesn't), Rudy's shoe string will have burst and his fame shot to ——."[114] Fortunately the new program and Vallée's new image were smashing successes. Vallée's was rated the third most popular program within a year, and within two it had become the number one program, very popular with both sexes until the end of the 1930s.[115] All was forgiven by the radio press, who rushed to endorse Vallée as Broadway's newest showman. "Rudy Vallée Still among Radio's Great" and "Rudy Vallée Just Staged Big Comeback," proclaimed headlines. "Thank Heavens," sighed *Radio Art*, "Rudy Vallée is restored to grace with a new set-up for the Fleischmann program!" "The Dialist" radio columnists at the *New York Daily News* declared, "Where do all the good crooners go when they die? They turn into showmen! At least that's true of the only good crooner we ever listened to, Rudy Vallée."[116]

The palpable relief in Vallée's coverage attests to the eagerness of the radio press to end the gender controversy and construct a new, acceptable masculine persona for Vallée. Indeed the hyperbolic nature of some of their prior coverage appears to have been directly inspired by James's novel *Crooner*, published earlier that year. The radio press floated a rumor that, like the hero of the novel, Vallée had been kidnapped by a gang and "threatened with death" before paying a hefty ransom and agreeing to tell no one.[117] They also reported that, like James's hero, Vallée punched a male concertgoer who questioned his masculinity. Newspaper columnists relayed that Vallée no longer wanted to be photographed only with female autograph seekers.[118] Once the revamped program was assured of success, however, columnists were able to praise Vallée for his business acumen, his career longevity, and his "new ideas."[119] For their part, radio fan magazines like *Radio Guide* and *Radio Stars* published a succession of articles about Vallée in 1932–33 that insisted he was no "dandy" but rather a "regular guy," a "manly fellow," and "the hardest worker we ever heard of."[120] The *Guide*'s editors even attempted to underline Vallée's manliness by floating a rumor that his estranged wife, Faye Webb, was pregnant.

As part of revising Vallée's star image, the radio press and fan magazines also identified and promoted Vallée's newly discovered masculine vocal qualities. This new voice was "stronger, better than ever," reported one columnist.[121] Others noted that he was singing with less "reediness" and "nasality" and more "virility" and "deeper tones."[122] The romantic crooner's passivity was a thing of the past, as the press asserted, "Rudy seems to be reaching out with a more dominant personality."[123] "Rudy," assured *Radio Guide*, "has discarded his emasculated style."[124] The perception of Vallée's voice as lower and deeper in early 1932 likely had technological as well as ideological roots; NBC's introduction of the bidirectional ribbon microphone in the fall of 1931 (replacing the previous condenser mics fully by 1932) significantly altered the sound of vocals on radio and records, resulting in a warmer, richer, fuller sound.[125]

Vallée, of course, was hardly the only crooning singer to require rehabilitation by the radio press; male singers still primarily valued for "singing murky love lyrics" on radio variety programs needed their images revamped to better fit Depression-era masculine norms. Throughout 1932–33 the radio press worked hard to establish crooners as industrious, modest, monogamous men who did not want to be figures of sex appeal, and they flooded radio fan magazines with pictures of crooners either at work in the studio or with their girlfriends, wives, and children—in contrast to prior images of crooners as the freakish target of throngs of swooning female fans. *Radio Stars* reported with approval that the popular crooner Carmen Lombardo refused to perform in the studio until the "wives and sweethearts" of his band mates were removed, saying, "Take 'em away! I won't sing with all those women glaring at me."[126] A *Radio Stars* regular feature promising "intimate shots of your favorites"

FIG. 5.16. Morton Downey and his wife, Barbara, and child, *Radio Stars*, 1933. Star publicity photos of crooners like this one were representative of the shift in radio star publicity that attempted to establish a crooner's masculine bona fides by focusing on his normative family life. Courtesy of Rudy Vallée Collection, American Radio Archives.

Mr. Morton Downey, Mrs. Morton Downey (Barbara Bennett, you know) and Master Downey. That wide-eyed look on the baby's face is due to the fact that he's just been told that he is the nephew of Joan and Constance Bennett and the grandson of Richard Bennett. Downey's in London now.

shifted its focus from pictures of performers lounging on beaches to shots of them at work in the studio, grabbing lunch, or attending public events.[127]

In addition, instead of profiles focusing on crooners' romantic availability, stories centered on their monogamous relationships. Fan magazine writers created narratives that situated crooners within a normative family group, either as the product of a family ("one of eleven children," in the case of Russ Columbo) or as husbands and fathers themselves, such as Morton Downey and Bing Crosby. They also portrayed romantic crooning idols as scrappy, mischievous little boys at heart rather than sophisticated or sensitive men; for instance, Downey was characterized as an incurable practical joker who pulled school fire alarms as a kid and still played jokes on his colleagues. At times revisionist narratives foregrounded the crooner's rehabilitation through the love of his wife and family. Little Jack Little's profile in *Radio Stars*, "Little Jack's Little Secret," portrayed him as an errant, drunken playboy ("a riotous, unnatural existence") who had since learned the error of his ways and become a dignified professional singer and songwriter. Dramatic scenes featured Little's long-suffering wife, trying in vain to wake him after a night of carousing with the boys, and his mother, far away on her Iowa farm, listening to her son on the radio and writing him the concerned letter that turned his life around. However, the author makes a point to assure readers

FIG. 5.17. Rudy Vallée and Claudette Colbert in *The Palm Beach Story*, Paramount, 1942. This image of Vallée as a prissy aesthete in film and musical comedies would become the dominant one in public memory. Author's collection.

that Jack, though reformed, has not been emasculated: he's "still a good fellow but not *too* good a fellow."[128]

Just as films played a central role in critical send-ups of the crooner image, they also played important roles in attempting to rehabilitate this figure for popular audiences. Many former radio columnists, including Rian James and Jerry Wald, became directly involved as writers and producers in shaping crooner images in early sound films. Wald launched his successful film career by producing and hosting a series of six radio short films made by Vitaphone in 1932–33, *Rambling Round Radio Row*. Wald's attacks on Vallée's perceived narcissism and effeminacy had made him (in)famous and earned him an opportunity to help revise the crooner's image on film. This series is one of the most interesting transitional portrayals of radio crooners because Wald was attempting to *promote* rather than simply denigrate radio crooners, still radio's biggest stars. As such, the crooner remains both a central figure and a curiosity in these shorts, defined by his identity as a crooner and his physical attractiveness to women more than by his performances. Unlike the shorts' other radio stars, however, the crooning male singers either sing very little or don't sing at all; instead Wald emphasizes their normative masculine bodies. For example, *Rambling Round Radio Row* #3 features the top popular crooner Carmen Lombardo and his three brothers, including bandleader Guy, who are introduced as female heartthrobs but, paradoxically, are not called upon to perform music; rather they are shown walking on a beach and water-skiing. This seems like a misguided attempt to masculinize the Lombardos by divorcing them from commercial spaces and emphasizing their physical prowess and athleticism, although what the scenes most succeed in doing is proving their value as bodily spectacle.[129]

Despite such disparate efforts to convince the public of crooners' rehabilitation, only one romantic crooner from this era, Bing Crosby, would survive the attacks of the 1930s and remain a major crooning star across the mass media. While Vallée's transition from crooner to showman was successful on radio, efforts to masculinize him in other media were not. His later film career testifies to the way crooning permanently emasculated him. The films he made in the late 1930s and 1940s, especially his films with Preston Sturges, confirmed his new comic-sissy status, pitting him as the undesirably pompous, foolish, or emasculated male competing for the girl against the likes of Tyrone Power, Joel McCrea, Rex Harrison, and Cary Grant.[130] In these roles Vallée is most famous for his prissiness, which remained tied to his image for the rest of his career and eclipsed memories of his amplified megaphone and his sensual saxophone.[131] While he does sing from time to time in these movies, his singing is either insincere (he fakes being in love with a girl by singing to her in 1938's *Second Fiddle*) or a catalyst for other couples rather than furthering his own romantic inclinations (as in 1942's *The Palm Beach Story*). The power of his voice is negligible. "Why, you have a nice little voice," remarks Claudette Colbert to Vallée in *The Palm Beach Story*. "Yes, I used to sing when I was in college," Vallée replies.

Vallée's career trajectory provided a cautionary tale for the crooners who followed, suggesting the difficulty in maintaining one's masculinity after exhibiting an unmanly amount of vulnerability and spending too much time serving women. To succeed as a leading man in multiple media, a crooner would need to have an acceptably masculine persona. No one learned this lesson better than Bing Crosby.

(((Six)))

"THE KIND OF NATURAL

THAT WORKED"

The Crooner Redefined, 1932–1934 (and Beyond)

The twenties were great years of "naturalism," but their idea
of natural differed drastically from any that has come since—and
Crosby represents the line of demarcation. He was the one who came up
with the kind of "natural" that worked: the warm B-flat baritone with a little
hair on it, the perfect balance between conversational and purely musical
singing, the personality and the character. Crosby was the first singer to
truly glorify the American popular melody. —Will Friedwald, *Jazz Singing:
America's Great Voices from Bessie Smith to Be-Bop and Beyond*, 1990

Bing Crosby is definitely not the matinee idol type. . . . He's the boy
next door, the fellow that lives across the street—folksy, familiar, utterly
lacking in self-consciousness or self-conceit. —*Liberty*, 25 March 1939

Bing Crosby has won more fans, made more money than any entertainer
in history. Today he is a kind of national institution. —*Life*, June 1945

By the middle of 1932 it appeared that the romantic crooner's days were num-
bered. Institutional attacks and ridicule in the popular media had taken their
toll, and press reports everywhere proclaimed the crooner's demise.[1] Even
radio fan magazines stated that "the fickle public is crying for something
new. . . . The tide has shifted towards the he-man type of baritone, and the

wisest of the air favorites are sailing with the tide."[2] There was only one problem with this rhetoric: many of "the public" were still not on board. As much as the press asserted that "the people" wanted change, ratings for all radio crooners (tenors and baritones alike) remained high, and their recordings continued to be top sellers. Crooners also continued to be popular in other media, especially in sound films such as Bing Crosby's breakthrough, *The Big Broadcast* (1932), and the Busby Berkeley musicals featuring Dick Powell.

In their attempts to meet audience demand for crooning music and to placate critics, between 1932 and 1934 the radio and movie industries, along with their newly acquired record and sheet music subsidiaries, experimented with ways to mitigate the power of the romantic crooner and construct an acceptably masculine identity for him. New York–based network radio had been able to diminish the influence and centrality of the romantic crooner by absorbing him into a variety program, as exemplified by Rudy Vallée's revised *Fleischmann Hour*. The revue-style film musical, however, had waned in popularity by 1931, so a variety show format was not the answer in feature films. Likewise, films like *Crooner*, which narratively suggested that the only good crooner was one who ultimately denounced crooning, did not exactly allow for the film industry's long-term investment in male singing stars. If the musical was to be sustained as a genre, it would need a male singer who could be an acceptable leading man, a star, and a romantic crooner; Bing Crosby ultimately proved to have the necessary ingredients.

During the first wave of attacks against crooners in January 1932, however, Crosby was especially vulnerable. He was the latest romantic crooning idol, arguably the biggest one since Rudy Vallée, and he had become a national star in the fall of 1931 by deliberately embracing the fervent, devotional song style that would soon become the target of public condemnation. Crooners were known quantities in 1931, at the peak of their popularity, and promotional procedures were in place for building up new stars. Crosby's star rose quickly and simultaneously across media; his baritone voice—a novelty at the time—was everywhere that fall. Songs such as "I Surrender, Dear" and "Just One More Chance" were on records, on the radio, and central to his short films. His daily network radio show over CBS was immensely popular, and *Variety* reported in December 1931 that Crosby was "leading in all radio favorite contests, evidently succeeding Rudy Vallée."[3] As a result of his popularity and well-publicized playboy persona, Crosby was thus at the forefront of criticism when the backlash hit. He was specifically singled out—along with Vallée and Russ Columbo—in all the institutional attacks on crooners outlined in the previous chapter. Crosby's radio sponsor, Cremo Cigars, panicked and dropped him within a month of the attacks, despite his unflagging popularity with the public.

Crosby's biographers have revised historical events to serve their masculinist narrative of him and the larger culture, and these attacks on him are either marginalized or misrepresented in most biographies of him. Even Crosby's most thorough chronicler, Gary Giddins, places the attacks on crooners in 1929 rather than 1932 and devotes only a few paragraphs to them; he assures readers that Crosby was not the subject of criticism because he was so "virile" that the "cardinals of the world could never tag him with imputations of effeteness."[4] Crosby was, in fact, considered one of crooning's prime offenders, repeatedly named and charged with effeminacy. For example, the widely quoted comments by Dean Harold Butler of Syracuse University in January 1932 identified Vallée and Crosby as the top two culprits, calling them "emasculated, effeminate whiners whose efforts cannot be called singing."[5]

Yet alone among the romantic crooners of his time, Crosby survived and persisted as a multimedia star, the first crooning film star and, within two years, one of the top film stars in the world. His lone ascent is due to a number of social, industrial, and technological factors that this chapter seeks to identify. While most discussions of Crosby's success focus on his talent as a singer and actor, talent alone doesn't create a star. Crosby became a crooning star when other talented singers around him did not because his particular kind of "natural" singing and his particular performance of masculinity suited the shifting values of his time, which were becoming more socially conservative. Crosby was the exceptional crooner who became the rule; he set a new standard for male singers that aligned perfectly with a culture that was becoming at once more national and nationalistic, more standardized and institutionalized, and more narrow, censored, and limited. Unlike most romantic crooners of his age, Crosby benefited from these social and industrial changes.

Although a target of attack early on, Crosby quickly distanced himself from other romantic crooners, denying that he was a crooner and deliberately promoting a more masculine image. He worked with his record producer, Jack Kapp, to broaden his repertoire of songs, revising old standards to encourage a sense of familiarity and nostalgia from a pre-1920s social era, and recording songs that associated him with home, family, and his roots in the rugged West rather than the sophisticated East. His delivery of romantic vocals had always been more confident than that of his peers, and he emphasized this

FIG. 6.1. The term *crooner* became so toxic that *Photoplay* initiated a contest in May 1934 inviting its readers to send in new terms to describe Crosby's singing style. The article affirms that Crosby is not a crooner because he sings a variety of music rather than singing "only sentimental lyrics"; he is an "artist" because he doesn't "slide over the tune with love-sick wailings." Bing Crosby, "No More Crooners!," *Photoplay*, May 1934. Author's collection.

quality by pulling back on his emotional intensity, reviving the more assured, detached, and relaxed style he had developed with Paul Whiteman's sweet jazz band in the 1920s. His "more masculine" baritone voice already gave him an advantage over the majority of popular singing males, who were tenors, and the introduction of new microphones in 1931–32 helped emphasize his lower register even further, giving his voice added warmth and intimacy without his needing to "emote."

Crosby's early film narratives were also crucial to transforming his crooner persona. His slapstick-comedy shorts for Mack Sennett from 1931 to 1933 were his first starring screen roles, and they did much to help him mitigate and disavow the associations of the crooner with femininity and passivity, introducing more acceptably masculine characteristics—aggressiveness, physical activity, emotional detachment—that would begin to differentiate him from his peers.[6] These films remain transitional, however, displaying modern attitudes toward sexual expression in other ways that mark them as "pre-Code" films, those sound films released before the full implementation of the Hollywood Production Code in 1934. In contrast, Crosby's feature films show a more obvious progression from the romantic crooner and modern sexual mores that characterize his first film, 1932's *The Big Broadcast*, to the Depression-era "regular guy" image and traditional sex roles that define his fourth and final pre-Code film, 1933's *Going Hollywood*. The changes in Crosby's film persona mirrored those of his personal life, which were widely publicized and became key to his rehabilitation with institutional leaders, including the Catholic Church. Getting married and having children allowed Crosby to be viewed as "mature" in the Freudian psychosexual ideology of the day; he was perceived as having outgrown his "immature" phase as a romantic crooner to embrace a more normative gender identity as a responsible family and business man.

By 1934 Crosby's dissociation with the gender troubles of the romantic crooner persona of 1929–32 was complete, and fan publications such as *Photoplay* had disconnected him completely from the toxic term that *crooning* had become (fig. 6.1). His film characters and his star image had changed from a playboy to a responsible patriarch who fully embraced white masculine middle-class values in his public and private life. In affirming this image, Crosby and his managers drew on a number of tropes of white masculinity to help naturalize the disturbing effects of the crooning male: heterosexual monogamy, white superiority, devoted Catholicism, a preference for sports and horse racing, earned wealth, homeownership, and, most important, patriarchy and the traditional family. Because Crosby was able to successfully combine these qualities and masculinize the crooner, he set a new standard for popular singers across the mass media, helping Depression-era America to distance itself from the excesses of the 1920s and effectively appeasing crooning's biggest critics.

Crosby became the last crooner standing as a multimedia star; thus examining his rise helps to make more visible the magnitude of the cultural changes—the losses, repressions, and deletions—that framed and accompanied it. The vocal variety that had existed throughout the 1920s and early 1930s had all but disappeared by 1934; vaudeville had collapsed, and media conglomerates had largely completed consolidating and classifying their holdings, tying particular song genres and performance practices to a performer's race, class, and, finally, gender. Technological and industrial changes further reinforced the public erasure of 1920s popular culture; shifts in microphone technology, in particular the development of the directional microphone, meant that singers in the early and mid-1930s sounded substantially different from their predecessors, creating a new definition of "natural" singing that has largely persisted—unacknowledged—to this day. Finally, the Depression-era focus on the hard times of the "common" (white, heterosexual) man marginalized queer and nonwhite performers even further and reinforced gender hierarchies that would reverberate throughout popular culture and in American society at large for decades to come.

CROSBY, THE JAZZ BAND SINGER

Like his romantic crooning peers, Bing Crosby emerged out of the college culture of the 1920s. Also like his rival Rudy Vallée, Harry Lillis Crosby was born to an Irish Catholic middle-class family, but on the West Coast, which would become an important distinction between the two.[7] He earned the nickname "Bing" because of his devotion to a humor feature in his Spokane, Washington, Sunday paper called the *Bingville Bugle*.[8] He was very well educated; he received a classical education at his Jesuit-run high school and studied prelaw at the Jesuit Gonzaga University (although he left college just a few months shy of graduation). He would later point to his experiences at these two schools, particularly the influence of specific priests, as the reason for his continuing religious faith. By all accounts a charming, ingratiating student who excelled at elocution, he was not a particularly ambitious one. Crosby came from a musical family, and he sang and whistled constantly from an early age, qualities that were not seen as antithetical to his love of sports and other, more masculine pursuits. He was particularly attached to the family phonograph and kept up on all the latest records. Although he admired the Irish tenor John McCormack for, in part, his "sincerity" of expression, his idol was the blackface minstrel Al Jolson, whose energy, charisma, and comic timing inspired him.[9]

Crosby's early success depended on many of the same ingredients that his later stardom would: an attractive collegiate appearance, movie house appeal, musical novelty and proficiency, and being in the right place at the right time. His actual start in the music business was less a product of planning than a fortuitous meeting with the younger musician Al Rinker, who needed a drummer for his new band. Crosby joined his amateur band in Spokane as both drummer and singer, complete with megaphone. When the band broke up, Rinker and Crosby stayed together as a duo, with Rinker playing piano and chatting with his fellow singer Crosby. Like many nascent crooners, Crosby had his first success working with Rinker in motion picture houses, where they learned how to choose songs that would be good thematic fits with the film's narrative. Their success in local theaters convinced them to move to Hollywood in 1925, where the pair, billed as Two Men and a Piano, found work at venues in Los Angeles and San Francisco. *Variety's* first review of the duo's appearance at a San Francisco picture house referred to them as "young and clean cut," terms generally associated with collegiate, attractive, ethnically assimilated performers, and noted that their "blues of the feverish variety" proved very popular with audiences.[10]

The use of the term *blues* in this review speaks to the way that Crosby and Rinker's material reflected the vocal variety of the 1920s, which had not yet become entirely institutionally segregated or gendered. Like other crooners, Crosby began his musical career as a sweet jazz musician and singer, performing all the latest Tin Pan Alley hits, especially those of the top performers Gene Austin and Al Jolson. Minstrel music, blues, early crooning, and hot jazz also heavily influenced him. In his act with Rinker, Crosby frequently included jazz scat singing, humming, whistling, and kazoo sounds in the manner of top picture house crooners such as Cliff Edwards and Johnny Marvin, and the two also engaged in the kind of banter associated with minstrel shows and vaudeville "dialect" singing duos like Van and Schenck. In 1926 the duo got their big break when the celebrated sweet bandleader Paul Whiteman hired them, making them the first performers hired by a prestigious band as singers. Eventually they teamed with an even more energetic songwriter-arranger, Harry Barris, and renamed their act the Rhythm Boys.

During the late 1920s Crosby toured the country with Whiteman and the Rhythm Boys, and he recorded many songs with Whiteman's orchestra. Barris wrote several compositions for the group that became standards, including their first national hit, the fascinating "Mississippi Mud," first recorded in 1927. "Mud" draws from all of Crosby's influences; although it is clearly minstrel and nostalgic in theme and lyrics ("when the darkies beat their feet on the Mississippi mud") and the singers engage in spoken banter reflective of minstrel acts, they do not sing or speak in dialect. Instead their initial recording of the song combines well-articulated close vocal harmonies with a fast tempo, jazz scatting, banter, and, most remarkably, an interpolated contemporary ballad Crosby sings about leaving his girlfriend standing in the mud, which becomes a humorous interlude.[11] The mix of musical styles anticipates Crosby's later inclusion of a variety of musical referents in his pop songs, as well as his signature blend of melodic richness with a carefree, optimistic, even somewhat indifferent affect, what the music scholar David Brackett calls Crosby's "emotionally detached" early style. Brackett's perception of Crosby as emotionally remote is grounded in his reading of Crosby's rhythmic abilities and delivery style as primarily influenced by minstrelsy and vaudeville, especially Jolson.[12] Brackett's reading is different from the dominant discourse of Crosby biographers and journalists, who interpret Crosby's detachment admiringly as evidence of "masculine cool" and connect his rhythmic abilities to his innate understanding of jazz rhythms and nascent swing.

The Rhythm Boys' delivery suited Whiteman because they were both more interested at that time in style and sound experimentation than a song's narrative content. "Mud" reflects the high spirits and rhythmic drive of jazz band versions of popular songs generally at this time, although Crosby's recordings with Whiteman are particularly upbeat. He recorded an up-tempo, downright peppy version of "Ol' Man River" that, although technically innovative, exhibits a startling disconnect from the suffering expressed in the song's lyrics: Crosby doesn't seem in the least "tired of living" or "scared of dying."[13]

The Rhythm Boys' dedication to playful rather than emotional versions of popular songs hurt them with some audiences at the time, although their live performances and recordings were popular with critics. The trio's lack of emotional involvement with the narratives of their songs put off some motion picture audiences, who expected and wanted their stage performers to be "in character" and to exhibit more intensity of feeling. Audiences on the East Coast also valued the gender fluidity of the New York scene, and they appreciated young male performers who took care in their appearance and were willing to be emotionally vulnerable and generous. The qualities that would later be referred to admiringly by Crosby biographers as his masculine "cool" and his "hipness" were off-putting to these audiences, who perceived the Rhythm Boys in the late 1920s as "cocky" and emotionally cold.[14] Since picture houses were Whiteman's bread and butter, he was forced to put the trio out on the vaudeville circuit in late 1928, although they were still billed as Paul Whiteman's Rhythm Boys.

To become a national commercial success, Crosby had to—and did—amend his style to give these audiences the emotional intensity, sensitivity, and narrative involvement they desired. When Whiteman changed record companies to Columbia in 1929, his new contract permitted his employees to do solo recordings. Looking to cash in on Vallée's success, Columbia permitted Crosby to record his first solo records, mainly love songs, in March and May 1929. Crosby's early recordings remained more up-tempo sweet jazz than the slow romantic crooner style that Vallée was popularizing. Yet on the popular hit "I Kiss Your Hand, Madame," Crosby slowed his pace somewhat and employed more vibrato than he usually did at the time; he also utilized the Irish mordent, a vocal swirl or quaver on particular words to solicit emotional engagement (like the "do" in "things I'll do").[15] But Crosby was still his casual self on this record; he scatted and whistled on the vocal more like Johnny Marvin than like Vallée, and was declarative rather than passionate. Although Crosby's 1929 records were not best-sellers, they established his potential as a solo singer; his next venue would give him the opportunity to soar as a romantic soloist.

Crosby made his transition into romantic crooning singing back on the West Coast, splitting from Whiteman and debuting as a soloist with Gus Arnheim's Orchestra at the prestigious Cocoanut Grove nightclub in Los Angeles in 1930. While with Whiteman, Crosby and the Rhythm Boys had been tremendously successful with both Hollywood's elite and the radio audiences listening to the orchestra's nightly two-hour broadcasts via KNX all over the West. *Variety* declared, "Never in their varied and cosmopolitan career in the effete east did the trio enjoy the popularity it now has out here. They are the collective Rudy Vallée of the ether west of the Rockies."[16] As the broadcasts continued, Crosby's solo singing began to have its own following, making him a regional sensation within a few months. Romantic crooning was in vogue because of Vallée's swift rise. Grove audiences enjoyed the intimacy permitted by slow dancing, while radio audiences loved the domestic companionship of a soft-voiced lover.

Crosby's breakthrough romantic recording, written by Harry Barris and released in January 1931, was "I Surrender, Dear." Music historians have written that the recording was artfully arranged to accommodate both big band instrumental solos and Crosby's forceful vocals. The song is equally if not more notable, however, for Crosby's adherence to its narrative line and rhetoric of romantic submission. His passionate and sincere delivery indicates a significant break from his casual jazz band persona, and the lyrics reinforce that change, claiming that his cool and contained image ("I may seem proud") has been a façade ("just a pose"), and he's just a love-struck guy now realizing he can't live without his beloved:

We've played the game
Of stay away
It costs more than I can pay
Without you I can't make my way
I surrender, dear.

Crosby's emotional exposure here is reinforced by his use of the mordent— most markedly on the last word of the title—and by the unusually dramatic swoops and dives of the arrangement; for example, in the last stanza his final pledge of surrender "to you my life, my love, my all" vocally descends along with the music, as if he is falling into the arms of his beloved. Crosby could not have planned the timing and choice of this recording any better. "I Surrender, Dear" was a big hit with both critics and youthful consumers, and it was widely covered and parodied. The recording cinched Crosby's career as a solo singer and earned him his own record deal with Brunswick in March.

Crosby's hit recordings over the next several months were dominated by slow-paced romantic crooning tunes that shared the sincere performance style of "I Surrender, Dear" and were clearly "in character"; they continued to offer a narrative of Crosby as a reformed playboy, one now devoted to loving a single person, whom he directly addressed as "you." He sang with a new passion and narrative commitment that created the impression that it was costing him energy, physically and emotionally, to do so. Largely absent are the jazzed-up minstrel tunes and the vocal variety that characterized the 1920s jazz-age Crosby, as a brief survey of his song titles from this period (all recorded between March and August 1931) indicates: "Thanks to You," "If You Should Ever Need Me," "Were You Sincere?," "I'm Through with Love," "At Your Command," "I Apologize," "Dancing in the Dark," and "Stardust." His biggest hits were the pleading "Just One More Chance" and the devotional "Out of Nowhere." "Chance" repeats the mantra of "I Surrender, Dear" almost exactly, with Crosby asserting, "I'd bury my pride" for "just one more chance" and admitting that he did wrong and deserves punishment. As was the style of the day, Crosby employed vibrato to indicate emotional involvement more consistently in these recordings than any before or after them, and his mordents were also more frequent, appearing, for example, on both syllables in "nowhere." His apologies endeared him to listeners on two levels: narratively he was offering his song's beloved numerous apologies for bad behavior and promises of eternal fidelity, but he was also exposing himself as a singer, apologizing to his listeners for his own previous perceived arrogance in performance and his lack of narrative faithfulness.

Crosby's revised persona was a big success. As a result of his radio, recording, and Grove work, he became a regional celebrity by summer, with a large female following and offers to perform in film and on network radio. His first big break came when the director Mack Sennett heard him at the Grove and signed him in the summer of 1931 to do musical comedy short films, a new venue for cultivating and publicizing young talent. Crosby walked out on his Cocoanut Grove contract to make these shorts for Sennett, and he also accepted CBS president William Paley's offer to broadcast nightly as a soloist in New York City. In the fall of 1931, after the release of his first short film and the debut of his national radio program, Crosby emerged as a national star.

Crosby's shift in attitude and genre on these records represents a defining moment of his career and, in retrospect, his most culturally transgressive, the moment when a singer who would become an icon of American masculinity became a star by adopting a song style soon to be identified as emasculating, deviant, and un-American. As chapter 5 details, crooners were identified as feminized, "pansies," likely homosexuals. These attacks, precipitated by the social changes discussed in previous chapters, would bring about the gendered divides in popular music that by 1934 would make Crosby the last remaining crooner as a crossover media star. But his recordings and radio work from 1930 to 1932 are representative of these few final years when the gender transgressions of romantic crooners were still naturalized and helped make them wildly popular. Indeed the cultural ubiquity and normalcy of devotional crooning songs and their "feminine" positioning is reinforced by the fact that Crosby, America's future "everyman" singer, embraced them. Today, however, it is startling to listen to recordings in which Crosby puts himself narratively in the role of the pining male whose happiness is dependent on his beloved, or delivers a heartfelt rendition of the popular hit "Just a Gigolo" from the perspective of a has-been male prostitute. His use of the gender-neutral "you" in his songs and their lack of identifying details, typical of the romantic crooning genre, also made all his songs open to queer readings in being inclusive of male-male desire (an interpretation sheet music often reinforced); certainly his recording of "Gay Love" would have done nothing to discourage same-sex appreciation for his music at the time, although *gay* as a term for homosexuality was not yet in mainstream parlance.

FIG. 6.2. This piece of sheet music reflects the beginning of Crosby's turn toward a more male-oriented, less romantic persona in the early 1930s, although this shift ironically made some of his cultural production more open to homoerotic readings (particularly in the pre-Code era). Sheet music, Bing Crosby, "I Only Want a Buddy . . . Not a Sweetheart," 1932. Author's collection.

Even with shifts in attitude and genre, however, these records are still distinctively Crosby's; certain characteristics of delivery style, tone, and attitude carry across his song history and distinguish him from other crooners. A comparison with Gene Austin, the most popular crooning singer of the 1920s, is instructive here. Both were products of the first ethnically unmarked generation of white male singers and masters of the microphone; their romantic recordings share loving sentiments, folksy charm, and melodic accessibility, which made them broadly popular. (For example, both frequently employed whistling interludes and nonsense syllables.) Austin's songs, however, were influenced more by blues and Crosby's more by sweet jazz and minstrelsy. Austin's attitude was one of yearning, lamentation, and often despair—blues qualities audible in the way he slid between notes, indicating regret, hurt, and longing, and his fast-fade final ascending notes (feminine endings)—made more poignant by his high-pitched tenor voice, indicating waning strength of heart.

In contrast, there was no inherent despair in Crosby's attitude or delivery; even at his most plaintive, he sounded confident, not vulnerable. Part of this steadiness came from the lower pitch of his voice, but his attitude was also more assured and upbeat, a reflection of his preference for sweet jazz rhythms; he sang as if he believed his love would forgive him and return to him. Unlike Austin (and certainly unlike Vallée's romantic crooner), Crosby largely did not employ feminine endings and did not tearfully slide between notes to indicate emotional turmoil; he hit them, sustaining them or bouncing quickly off them, without self-doubt or hesitation. Even his use of the mordent was consistent and assured. Crosby would strike the notes forcefully without fading out, employing a wide vibrato that flooded the mic, suggesting the self-confidence of a man who makes pledges and demands rather than begs or wallows. When Crosby asked for "one more chance," it was as much an order as a plea, and when his desires were thwarted, as in the song "Through with Love," he became angry rather than sad. While Austin's narrator was uncertain of the future and given to melancholia or fantasy, Crosby's narrator realized his mistakes, apologized for them, and looked to a future that he clearly believed would improve. Crosby's affective resilience was likely reflective of his privileged social position as a member of the educated white middle class (unlike Austin), and the optimism and expectation that came from that. These qualities were also characteristic of the collegiate type in the 1920s and early 1930s, typified by the band Waring's Pennsylvanians, and would become key markers of Crosby's Americanness in later years. In combination with Crosby's other, more conservative personal qualities, this performance attitude would help him to withstand the crooning attacks.

CROSBY, THE PLAYBOY CROONER

Crosby's ascension in the crooning ranks inaugurated the second wave of romantic crooning idols, which the press referred to dramatically as "the battle of the baritones." Crosby on CBS and Russ Columbo on NBC were the top singers, rivaling Vallée in popularity for the first time and dominating popular music in the fall of 1931. Crosby and Columbo were considered at the time to be manufactured stars in a way that Vallée had not been, stepping into the prefabricated romantic crooner image and formula for success.[17] While crooners were heard on radio during the day and in the evenings, both Crosby and Columbo were assigned the most prestigious time slot for a network singer: the early evening. This was a star-building time slot that had quickly become a nightly staple of the early network era, and both men were promoted as the next (or at least newest) big thing in popular singing. Due to the thorough integration of mass media and live performance venues by the early

1930s, both Crosby and Columbo became multiplatform stars very quickly. The mass media was desperately looking for a novel twist with these early Depression stars, and *baritone* crooners fit the bill—even better, rival ones.

Although both singers benefited from massive network promotion, neither was allowed as much power to program content as Vallée and other early radio singers had enjoyed in the pre-network era. Each man sang every night for only fifteen minutes (Vallée had originally sung for a full hour in 1929), and neither was allowed to speak, only to sing; a network announcer framed their performances. They were also expected to perform only their best-selling romantic recordings, and they were initially equally promoted in the press as "sexy singers" and "handsome lads."[18] Both were also feature attractions during the day at the Paramount Publix movie theaters in Manhattan and Brooklyn, singing their hits between film presentations to generally enthusiastic response. Little attempt was made, initially, to distinguish one from the other; most publications lumped them together, asserting, "They are so much alike that unless you know what station you've dialed, you'll wonder which is which."[19] They proved to be ideal song pluggers, and their recordings continued to be big sellers. Both were named by *Variety* as new stars of radio for 1931.[20] They were sold to newspapers and radio fan magazines as glamorous playboys in fashionable dress, matinee idols of the air to be eagerly consumed by the (solely female, the promotion insisted) obliging masses.

There were other, less obvious reasons for the rise and staying power of the baritone voice at this particular time. At first they were primarily novelties, dubbed "barytones" and "baricrooners" by the New York press that fall. Tenors still ruled, especially as soloists, as they had for decades. The baritone sound was new to the national airwaves and especially East Coast audiences, so much so that the National Broadcasting public relations man had to assure the New York press that he meant no "insulting intention" by describing Columbo as "something like Vallée but 'lower.'"[21]

But the baritones held on through the fall, and their popularity remained high with the public in the face of the attacks in January and February 1932. Certainly there were cultural shifts at work that benefited them in the long run. Both Crosby and Columbo came to New York after becoming regional solo stars broadcasting with Gus Arnheim's Cocoanut Grove Orchestra—although music critics disagree about who influenced whom for crooner performance styles—and their ascent was part of the transition of the center of American popular culture from New York to Hollywood in the early days of the Depression. The tightening gender norms also favored the baritones, even before the direct attacks in January 1932. One prominent fan club switched allegiance from Vallée to Crosby in the fall of 1931 because "he is more masculine." The critic Sidney Skolsky reported in the *New York Sunday News* in December, "At the Friar's Club the other eve, Rube Bernstein told Bing that he was Rudy Vallée with a man's voice."[22] After the attacks on crooners, of course, tenors had a tougher battle for rehabilitation than baritones and, in fact, never recovered their dominance. The industry shifted toward lower-pitched crooners who could be more easily promoted as properly gendered, having not an "in-between" voice but one that was "naturally" more potent and masculine than the tenor.

Just as significant, however, were developments in microphone technology in the popular rise of the baritone voice, possibly prompted in part by sound engineers' public dislike of crooning tenors. The lower pitch and perceived "warmer, richer sound" enjoyed by baritone audiences was the result not only of a change in singers and shifting cultural expectations of gender norms but also a technological shift. While attacks on effeminacy helped to marginalize those high-pitched crooners of the 1920s, the technology itself was against them by 1931–32. The introduction of two new types of microphones in 1931 accompanied Crosby's and Columbo's popularity and undoubtedly helped make it possible. Dynamic (moving-coil) and bidirectional (ribbon) microphones had an enormous impact on popular singing, replacing the condensers that had been used in radio and record studios since the days of the crooning pioneers. The dynamic microphone was a transitional mic for singers, first introduced by Western Electric in January 1931. Like the condenser, it was omnidirectional (picking up surrounding sound), but where the condenser was often perceived by audiences as making voices sound higher because of its exceptional reproduction of higher frequencies, dynamic mics could be built to favor certain frequencies; most dynamics were built with a frequency boost at the lower end, which resulted in voices being perceived as lower and richer than they had been on condensers. This change in microphones particularly served voices in the midrange, as baritones were, enhancing their sound.

The bidirectional ribbon microphone was introduced in the summer of 1931 by RCA and directional mics became the new industry standard by 1932, although several improvements would be made during the following few years. The directional mic was the biggest and most totalizing shift in the reproduction of vocal sound, introducing the microphone sound that we recognize today as more "natural" compared to voices recorded on nondirectional

FIG. 6.3. This representative crooning song cover is notable for its open-shirted, glamorous, matinee-idol portrait of the lovely "Latin" crooning star Russ Columbo. The cover identifies him as "The California Radio Star" because, like Crosby, he earned his reputation as a romantic crooner on the West Coast before he became a national star over New York's NBC station in the fall of 1931. Sheet music, Russ Columbo, "Why Do I Care For You," 1931. Author's collection.

FIG. 6.4. This cover is typical in foregrounding the attractiveness of its young crooner, although Crosby's crossed arms indicate less vulnerability and openness than his crooning peers. However, there is a halo effect on his blond hair that emphasizes his whiteness and suggests that he should be revered for his white masculine superiority rather than his romantic appeal. Sheet music, Bing Crosby, "The Blue of the Night," 1931. Author's collection.

condenser microphones. Directional microphones were more sensitive and had better pickup, frequency range, and dynamic range, which greatly improved sound quality, especially of softer, lower sounds. They were "directional" because they privileged the voice coming from only one direction over the surrounding sounds. (A bidirectional ribbon accommodated two voices, front and back.) When singers sang especially close to these mics, they increased the bass and vocal resonance in their voices, giving them a warmer, fuller, more "close up" sound, although engineers initially discouraged vocalists from taking advantage of it because they considered it a "distortion." The "proximity effect," as it became known, gave an even stronger impression of vocal intimacy than earlier microphones had, and Crosby skillfully employed it, helping set the standard for those who followed him.[23]

It is difficult to ascertain the exact moment when NBC and CBS began using dynamic and bidirectional mics, although radio trade magazines and anecdotal evidence suggest they were both in place by the summer of 1931 and certainly by the fall. CBS employed Western Electric technology, so Crosby most likely would have used a dynamic microphone in his star-making early months, although CBS may have also acquired directional microphones by that time. Because both of these new mics favored bottom rather than top frequencies, they had a significant, noticeable effect on vocal transmission. All of Crosby's biographers make note of the period in September 1931 when Crosby missed several shows and that, when he returned, the radio press, audiences, and his handlers perceived his voice as being "a tone or two lower" than before.[24] His biographers attribute the change to a medical condition, but the perceived difference in pitch and richness was most likely due to the introduction of a dynamic mic and, in other contexts, directional ribbon microphones. Rival network NBC, allied with RCA, began employing the bidirectional ribbon in the summer of 1931, before CBS; radio listeners and reviewers noted a deeper sound in the voices of the NBC stars Vallée and Columbo by early 1932.[25]

The change in microphones dovetailed with the new discourses advocating more masculine singing, and critics applauded Vallée for his new sound, although it was likely the result of the microphone shift. Certainly the fact that Crosby's career as a star crooner began with dynamic and directional microphones and their enhanced lower frequencies and warmer, fuller sound accounts in part for the perception of him as a more "masculine" singer. The fact that these microphones became the industry standard also meant that Crosby's sound would quickly come to be perceived as more "natural" than that produced by previous technologies, an idea that has persisted for decades.[26] I am arguing, alternatively, that Crosby's exploitation of the directional mic's proximity effect should be understood as a key moment in the often conflated industrial and cultural constructions of "natural" and "masculine" that characterized this new era in sound media.

While both Crosby and Columbo benefited from the new preference for baritone crooners, Crosby differed from Columbo both in his network affiliation and, increasingly as the months passed, in his star persona. Crosby's association with the underdog network CBS rather than the prestigious and often pretentious NBC, for example, made him the singer more likely to be viewed as a "man of the people." William S. Paley's strategy for developing CBS as a rival to NBC included hiring more popular performers, some of whom, such as ex-vaudeville stars, were considered too lowbrow by NBC, which prided itself on the "highest quality" productions. As a result CBS was snappier and more innovative, taking risks in programming and grabbing up whatever sponsorship it could get. (Laxative ads were common.) CBS's emphasis on a mass rather than class audience would have especially attracted newer listeners; radio sales catapulted during the Depression, and the wide availability of the cheaper "midget radio" sets starting in 1931 allowed for many more people of limited means to buy radios. Crosby's voice over the populist CBS therefore was likely the first radio crooning that many people heard at home. The network's perceived populism, commercialism, and underdog status would serve Crosby well, especially as his Depression-era "common man" persona developed in 1932–33.[27]

In addition, Crosby's public image emphasized the playboy aspects of the romantic crooner more than Vallée's or Columbo's did. The crooner as drinker and womanizer, which Rian James had fictionalized in his novel *Crooner*, was reflective of Crosby's life. Crosby had a reputation for missing performances because of his drinking, including his solo spot in the 1930 film *The King of Jazz*, when he was jailed for drunk driving. (The role was recast.) He also missed the first two days of his CBS radio contract, for which drinking was widely held to blame. His 1931 radio contract was rumored to have been amended after his debut to include a "no drinking" clause. This amendment was widely publicized, prompting Sidney Skolsky to comment wryly in the *New York Daily News*, "There is also a *law* that forbids drinking."[28]

Crosby's widely publicized marriage to the Twentieth Century Fox star Dixie Lee in September 1930 was in trouble by March 1931, when she left him in a shower of publicity, charging "mental cruelty." While she eventually returned to him (in part to help his career by keeping him sober), rumors of divorce and drinking circulated heavily in the press during the fall of 1931. *Radio Guide*'s November 1931 profile of Crosby focuses on his vices: "[Crosby] smokes, more than he should. Drinks . . . moderately . . . at least he hopes that's what people call it."[29] The *New York World-Telegram*'s December interview is even bolder, identifying the "broken bottles and unpaid bills" that Crosby has left in his wake.[30] The photograph accompanying the article shows Crosby as a dissolute young playboy with waved hair, a wrinkled suit, and a cigarette hanging lazily from one hand (fig. 6.5). These characteristics, so different from Vallée's and Columbo's clean-and-sober images, were damning evidence of Crosby's connections to immoral urban life. Otherwise the press treated Crosby with the same amusement and mild condescension (he was a "bad boy") with which they covered other crooners.

When crooning attacks achieved full force in January 1932, Crosby was an obvious target, and his troubled personal life provided ammunition for moralists. He had to deal with charges of both immorality and effeminacy. Yet, unlike Vallée and his peers, Crosby ultimately emerged from these attacks changed but largely unscathed. Certainly they provided him with direction in constructing a more masculine crooning persona. The changes he began to make at this time, both personal and professional, would eventually help him become an acceptable standard-bearer for American popular song and American masculinity.

Initially Crosby denied that he was a crooner and tied his type of singing to public rather than private space: "I wish I could croon. . . . It would be a lot easier on my throat than the way I sing now. I tried it once or twice—in private—when I had a throat breakdown, but I was not satisfied with it." He argued that while crooning was easy, his singing took real "work"; it was not masturbation. Finally Crosby separated himself from the crooner's effeminacy by explaining that crooners sang in "half voice, singing the top notes in a falsetto," whereas he always sang "in full voice" and therefore did not need to employ falsetto, a vocal technique that had increasingly become a primary indicator of crooners' emasculation.[31]

Although other crooners made similar denials, Crosby succeeded in a way that others did not. Part of the reason may be that he was older than most crooners, and he was unusually well organized and well managed. He had allied himself with important men who were essential to guiding his career and shaping his image: Mack Sennett in films, Jack Kapp of Brunswick and then Decca Records, and William S. Paley of CBS radio. His stardom was also a family affair. Crosby's brother Everett negotiated his lucrative radio and

In Which Bing Crosby Debunks Himself; Broken Hearts? No, Just Broken Bottle[s]

"I Was One of the Three Rhythm Boys in Whiteman's Orchestra," He Says—"I Was Pretty Bad; I Got in Fights and Things Like That—Whisky Got Me Five Times."

By JOSEPH MITCHELL,
World-Telegram Staff Writer.

Bing ("Romantic Singer of Songs You Love") Crosby is a forthright, easily bored young man who would rather talk about automobile wrecks, Harlem night clubs or fishing than discuss the possibility that he soon will be a more popular singer of Broadway folk-songs than Vallee or Downey.

"People who compare me with Vallee and the other mugs are more interested in me that I am myself," he said today. "I like for people to be interested in me. Sure. But they say I left a trail of broken hearts behind me when I left California for New York. Now, I wouldn't do a thing like that. The fact is—I left a trail of broken bottles and unpaid bills."

Laughs at Ballyhoo.

He likes to sing sentimental songs, but he would just as soon sing old bayou, swamp edge, low-down jazz songs—the blues, the St. James Infirmary variations, or "hot songs" like "Ding Dong Daddy" or "Minnie the Moocher." He laughs at the ballyhoo which quickly grows up and surrounds a popular radio singer.

"There was a song published recently by the name of 'Crosby, Columbo and Vallee.' They had my picture on the cover. I made them take it off. Then Vallee made them take his picture off. I didn't want my picture on a song like that. It wasn't funny. Songs have to be romantic or sentimental or funny or hot."

Half the Work.

"I'd like to be able to sing like the crooners. The reason is — a crooner gets his quota of sentimentality with half his natural voice. That's a great saving. I don't like to work. In fact, there's been some talk about that."

Crosby—his real name is Harry Lillis Crosby—became a singer when, as a law student at Gonzaga College, in Seattle, he needed money to get himself paid out of an expensive automobile wreck, and was offered a job in an orchestra. He kept it. He precipitated himself into other

FIG. 6.5. Bing Crosby's drunken playboy persona was the focus of this feature story. Crosby's past drunken behavior—including his tendency to get into fights—ultimately helped his image during the attacks on crooners because it made him seem more masculine than his romantic crooning peers. "In Which Bing Crosby Debunks Himself," *New York World Telegram*, 23 December 1931. Courtesy of Rudy Vallée Collection, American Radio Archives.

Paramount contracts, and his brother Larry helped protect his image from criticism by acting as his publicist. On the advice of his brothers and lawyers, Crosby incorporated himself very early in his career, giving him more control over his image than other singers had. Thus when Crosby saw the handwriting on the wall for romantic crooners, he and his managers quickly responded, emphasizing certain aspects of his image while trying to eliminate others. He was concerned about the need to reform his persona from the time he began broadcasting in the fall of 1931, initially because of his reputation for drunkenness, and he hired Larry to "redefine his reputation as one of professionalism and sobriety."[32] In interviews he was careful to talk in the past tense about his objectionable personal behavior. While he admitted to his five years of drunkenness with Whiteman and at the Cocoanut Grove, he continually emphasized that his bad behavior was "in the past."

More significantly Crosby's past, specifically his drunken behavior, was less objectionable in the new masculinist popular culture than was being a sensitive teetotaler. Drinking was, ultimately, something working-class men were expected to do when they were young, like playing sports. Crosby's "wild past" ultimately helped give him a masculine legitimacy with popular audiences that neither Vallée nor Columbo ever attained. While moralists deplored such behavior, urban audiences in the 1920s had no respect for the Prohibition law they felt had been unfairly imposed on them, and national sentiment had begun to shift in that direction as well; Prohibition was revoked within the year (1933). Crosby's past defiance of that law served both popular opinion and cultural authorities: his past behavior allied him with the "modern" rebels of the 1920s, and his current behavior assured 1930s critics that his days sowing his wild oats were far behind him.

In the press Crosby came off as more mature compared to his rival Columbo, whose untimely death in 1934 preempted a promising film career that might have equaled Crosby's. While the press claimed that Crosby "was a bad, bad boy," profiles of Columbo were titled "A Little Boy—Russ Columbo," and referred to his having "a cherub's smile and the mannerisms of a well-bred child. . . . Russ is like that song he popularized, 'Sweet and Lovely.'"[33] Although their singing voices were considered remarkably similar, Columbo was clearly the more easily feminized of the two in profiles. He was younger (twenty-three to Crosby's twenty-nine) and more attractive; in his picture house debut, *Variety* predicted his success because he was both entertaining and good-looking.[34] Columbo also enjoyed his "Latin lover" title and shared Vallée's love for women, tailored clothes, and New York nightlife. While Crosby also notably reported enjoying Harlem nightclubs in his leisure time and wore plenty of tuxedos in his public appearances, he claimed to prefer nonurban, working-class masculine pursuits such as fishing, football, baseball, prizefights, and discussing automobile wrecks.

Although both Crosby and Columbo were Catholic, their ethnic differences were also emphasized in the press to favor Crosby at a time when the "common man" clearly denoted a white man. Crosby was described as "the blond, blue-eyed, stocky, football playing Nordic," while Columbo was "the suave, smoldering-eyed, smooth-haired Russ, a Latin."[35] Although early profiles indicate that the public was equally enthralled with both these young singers, such distinctions must be seen within the racial hierarchies of the time. Even though Columbo represented an assimilated ethnicity (Italian), and therefore a permissible love object for American women, he was noticeably olive-skinned compared to Crosby, and the "Latin lover" descriptive exoticized him further. He was frequently compared to Rudolph Valentino, whose feminizing characteristics (racial and class-based) had been widely attacked only a few years before and were now distinctly out of favor. As if to emphasize this difference further, newspapers reported that Columbo preferred brunettes and Crosby blondes, allying Columbo with "dark women" (the flapper of the 1920s) and Crosby with the "all-American girl" (the platinum blonde heroine of the 1930s).

Crosby's "Nordic appearance," preference for curvy blondes, and appreciation for sports helped him forge an image that was not available to Vallée or Columbo. Crosby also helped establish and promote gendered singing, making distinctions between types of songs based on gender affiliations. He was quick to separate himself from Columbo's style of singing as early as October 1931, when he claimed, "Columbo is a sexy, torchy singer, while I go for ballads."[36] The aural distinction between a ballad and a torch song was negligible at the time; Crosby's own crooning voice had often been described in the press as both sexy and torchy, but the term had begun to be more gendered in its application.[37] Women were most often described as singing torch songs, men increasingly less so. Crosby's use of the term *ballad* indicated that he was trying to distance himself from any associations with 1920s gender-bending, sensual singers; ballad singers had existed before crooners and notably before male singers were openly identified as sex objects.

Three articles from 1932 fan magazines demonstrate the remaking of Crosby's star image. Two weeks after Cardinal O'Connell's condemnation of crooning, *Radio Guide* ran a front-page story about Crosby that rewrote his marital problems to completely exonerate him from any wrongdoing. It blamed the Crosbys' brief separation on "Hollywood gossips" and Dixie's interfering friends. The editors assured readers that Crosby had quit drinking once he married and that his separation was the result of Dixie's friends' insistence that she reactivate a film career she had given up for marriage: "Perhaps because he was more mature than Dixie, [Crosby] knew how to treat the 'kind friends.' . . . [He] promptly told them where to put their advice. . . . Crosby's home life is ideal. Bing's ambition is to make as much money as possible, and then to retire for a while and just pal around with Dixie. They are both fond of sports. They both love children. . . . And so the story draws to a close. Bing and Dixie happy together, Bing working hard and to good effect, Dixie so content to be Mrs. Crosby."[38] Exemplary of Crosby's new coverage, this article presents his marriage as a model of polarized gender roles. It emphasizes the male's dominant position as the breadwinner and hard worker, while his wife is both dependent on him and less mature. Cheesecake photos of Dixie and descriptions of her as "the grandest bit of femininity Bing had ever seen" further served to reinforce Crosby's masculinity and returned the crooner's "girl" back to the position of passive object rather than the aggressive flapper of the Vallée era.

Subsequent fan articles continued to promote the "traditional" Crosby family and therefore Crosby's suitability for "leading man" status. The fan magazine *Pictorial Review* named Crosby the "Clark Gable of the air. In other words, Crosby is our most masculine radio singer."[39] This article made the distinction that Crosby was not a "glamorous" figure like Vallée or Columbo. Within six months *Radio Guide* went further: "Never has anyone pointed the finger of scorn at him. Why? Because Bing is happily married to Dixie Lee. Their romance has been untouched, unbroken."[40] *Radio Guide* thus effectively rewrote Crosby's history, erasing his playboy crooner days and his brief marital separation, even going so far as to assure readers that he had no need for a morals clause in his contract.

While the fan magazines worked on Crosby's persona, his style of singing changed as he enlarged his repertoire. Although he continued to sing romantic songs with pleading crooner lyrics during the early 1930s, the pitch of his songs sounded lower in 1931–32 (likely due to the microphone change), and he did not visibly strain to reach high notes as those before him (most notably Vallée) had done. His decision to broaden his range of songs was primarily due to the influence and opinion of the music producer who would remain with him throughout his career, Jack Kapp. Crosby originally signed with Brunswick Records and began working there with Kapp in 1931. When Kapp left Brunswick in 1934 to form Decca Records, Crosby went with him. Kapp encouraged Crosby to sing a variety of different types of songs in an attempt, as Will Friedwald claims, to "turn him into all things for all people."[41] Thus Crosby's repertoire expanded to include pre-1920s standards, western folk songs, nostalgic minstrel tunes, hymns, and popular songs that spoke of the benefits of home and family rather than big city living.[42] If Vallée's early songs were notable for the repeated use of the word *love*, Crosby's songs from 1932–33 privilege the term *home* almost as much. Taking a page from earlier western crooners like Johnny Marvin, Crosby recorded several traditional and western folk songs that celebrated the great outdoors and small-town values (family, home, religion) over urban values, among them "What Do I Care, It's Home" (1933), "Cabin in the Pines" (1933), "The Last Roundup" (1933), "Home on the Range" (1933), and "Let's Spend the Evening at Home" (1933).[43]

The influence of the minstrel plantation song is also a distinction of Crosby's oeuvre and helped distance him from the romantic crooner figure. Showing the early influence of Jolson, Crosby's new repertoire contained a large number of minstrel tunes. Early crooners had shown a wide range of attitudes toward the appropriation of culturally coded black music and of minstrel songs; the vocal diversity of performance culture meant that blues, jazz, and minstrelsy were all popular genres from which early crooners borrowed, although by the early 1930s the recording industry had become firmly racially segregated, and live performance had begun to follow suit. Crosby had borrowed more from minstrelsy than other genres in his early years, although, like other pioneer crooners, he had not sung in blackface. Romantic crooners in the Vallée mold, however, generally did not sing minstrel music at all, so Crosby and Kapp's choice to record songs like "Shine" (1932) and "Cabin in the Cotton" (1932), both of which employed standard minstrel dialect and featured Crosby waxing nostalgic over "ma massa" and "those piccaninny days," was significant.[44] These minstrel songs aligned Crosby specifically with white men and their shared adherence to racial hierarchies in a way that Vallée's and Columbo's songs did not.

Crosby presented himself as "one of the people," and as such he became affiliated with the common (white) working man who came to represent "the people" in 1930s popular culture. His 1932 hit song "Brother, Can You Spare a Dime?" indicated the suitability and effectiveness of this populist persona for him.[45] "Dime" is one of Crosby's most interesting recordings because it draws from the emotional intensity of romantic crooning but channels it into anger rather than devotion; it was one of the few popular song hits to deal explicitly with a social problem—the Depression—and to offer a critique of class inequality. Crosby never again expressed such anger or pain on a record as he does on "Dime"—indeed the recording is shocking in that respect—and his version of the song became an immediate anthem for unemployed men of the 1930s. Even though his persona would evolve as cool rather than hot, "Dime" did the work it needed to do in helping to rehabilitate his aural reputation. With "Dime," Crosby succeeded in performing a new kind of masculinity, one that could still be both broadly appealing and viewed as gender-normative (a suitably "American" male sound). Depression-era politics supported notions of a democratic, accessible song style that would bond white men from different classes by reinforcing rather than challenging the traditional masculine roles that were now threatened by a collapsed economy. Before this shift could be complete, however, the crooning body had to be visibly masculinized.

REMAKING THE CROONING MAN: CROSBY'S EARLY FILMS, 1931–1933

While romantic crooning made Crosby a national star, film is what kept him there. Hollywood established a lasting star image for him by effectively restoring the crooner's white, straight, masculine body. Stars' images often bring together conflicting and complex aspects of their society in ways that naturalize them.[46] Crosby's persona rests on a central paradox that was essential to the crooner's being perceived as acceptably masculine: his warm, comforting voice did not come from the body of a particularly warm, comforting, or emotionally accessible man, especially when compared to the vulnerable, unabashedly romantic crooners who had preceded him. Crosby's early films established and helped naturalize this paradox: his enhanced singing voice did the work of indicating his character's sincerity and emotional investment, while his masculine body, active and often emotionally detached, served to balance and therefore effectively mitigate his soft, intimate sound. This balance was not immediately achieved, however, but evolved over a series of Mack Sennett comedy shorts between 1931 and 1933 and in Crosby's first feature films, particularly *The Big Broadcast* (1932) and *Going Hollywood* (1933).

Crosby made his first short films before he became a national radio star in the fall of 1931, and his film appearances are very different from Vallée's early work in film. Vallée was a star spectacle in his film appearances; there was little attempt to narrativize him. His radio persona, already well established by his radio programs and public appearances, was merely exploited by Hollywood. In contrast, Crosby's persona on radio was being established at the same time as his first short films were released. While Vallée's intimate, bedroom voice captivated radio listeners across the country in 1928–29, Crosby caused no such shock when he began his national radio career in the fall of 1931; he stepped into an industrial context in which romantic crooners were known quantities. While Vallée's body was considered an "oddity" on film, audiences would not have felt the same disjunction between voice and body in Crosby, and they would have associated his voice with an already established romantic, playboy-crooner narrative that his films both exploited and revised in important ways.

In addition, Sennett's films emphasized comedy over romance. They were known for their slapstick, a fast-paced and punchy comic style very different from Vallée's seriocomic drama *The Vagabond Lover*. Thus Crosby did not begin his film career playing the earnest leading man, and he rarely played his love scenes for pathos. His early films would forgo the emotional connection of the romantic couple and the centrality of the ballad in favor of action and familiar comic characters and situations, such as madcap heroines, car chases, cross-dressers, zoo animals, and pansies (precursors of Code-era "sissy" characters). The presence of the pansy or sissy is especially vital to Crosby's film persona generally, and it marks an important difference from Vallée. In *The Vagabond Lover*, all other male characters are more conventionally masculine than the sensitive Vallée. In Crosby's films, the more effeminate men buttress Crosby's own masculinity, making him the obvious choice for the desired girl's affection without his actually having to make love to her or indeed display any of the crooner's characteristic emotional vulnerability. Crosby's short films typically contained at least two queer men, one the friend who helps him win the girl, the other his rival. (The rival was twice played by the soon-to-be-familiar, archetypal 1930s sissy actor Franklin Pangborn.) These early films did not abandon the crooner character so much as they reframed and reshaped him through comedy and Crosby's more confident, aggressive persona. Unlike the passive Vallée, the object of women's affections, Crosby was the active pursuer of the women in his films, the confident playboy who easily seduced women.

The activity of Crosby's body was key to establishing his masculine persona. Whereas Vallée was typically passively immobile and wooden on-screen, Crosby was in constant motion. Crosby himself felt much more at ease during filmmaking if he could move around, and technological advances such as boom microphones, directional mic'ing, and on-set playback and postproduction sound served him well, making possible the movement he desired.[47] The sound clarity and warmth of new directional mics, which were in general use by 1932, also greatly enhanced his singing. A comparison between the singing scenes in *The Vagabond Lover*, which were full of ambient sound, and Crosby's early films, which were not, makes this distinction

FIG. 6.6. Bing Crosby in *I Surrender Dear*, 1931. The all-American Bing Crosby engages in comic swordplay with a "foreign" rival for his girl's affections in his first Mack Sennett comedy short film. Author's collection.

very clear. This improved sound film technology greatly assisted Crosby's masculine image by allowing him to be physically active—even violently aggressive—on-screen.

Crosby's films also downplayed romance, so that his characters' seductions were portrayed as more competitive than romantic. The plots revolved around Crosby happily plotting how to get the desired girl away from her fiancé or overprotective parent. (Crosby's crooner appeals only to young girls, not to their mothers, differentiating between the generations and setting women against each other.) Unlike Vallée, Crosby exhibited little passion or sincerity. His characters did not really need (much less love) the women he pursued, nor did they in turn seem as attached to him as Sally Blane was to Vallée in *Vagabond*. Crosby's publicized lack of interest in women generally was evident in these early films.[48] Even his ballads in these shorts rarely involved him singing directly to his girl. The ballads were mitigated by sight gags involving radio broadcasts of the song or by Crosby's own slapstick performance of them. In *I Surrender Dear*, for example, Crosby makes fun of his own rendition of "You Came Out of Nowhere" when it comes on the radio, suggesting the silliness of the sentimental song and its emotional excess. Whereas Vallée poked fun at masculinity in his performances, Crosby ridiculed femininity.

Yet the differences between the Vallée and Crosby crooners are often subtler and more playful in Crosby's early films than later in his career. While these pre-Code films posit a masculinity more in keeping with traditional gender roles, Crosby's crooners are hardly moralists; rather they are allied with the impulsive youth of the jazz age and their desire for sexual freedom. The frivolous, comedic, and hopeful tone of these shorts undercuts Crosby's emotional blankness and the hints of homophobia and misogyny in their narratives. For example, a cross-dressing college boy pairs up happily with Crosby's sissy pal at the end of *Billboard Girl* instead of being punished for his gender deviance.

The transitional nature of the crooner here—the uncertainty regarding proper gender conventions—was especially evident in Crosby's first full-length feature film, the lively satire *The Big Broadcast*. In this film Crosby played himself as a drunk, undependable radio crooner, a characterization that mirrored public knowledge of his past. His first scene encapsulates perhaps better than any other the publicized appeal of the radio crooner for women. As Crosby steps out of his taxi, young and old women begin shouting "Bing!," then surround him and tear at his clothes. When he finally makes it to the studio microphone, his face is covered with lipstick, his clothes are torn, and he barely has the energy to get out the words "I Surrender, Dear" (fig. 6.7). Women's adulation of Crosby is shown to be as widespread within the studio as outside of it: the telephone operators and secretaries are equally infatuated with him, and his lack of responsiveness is attributed to his drunken bewilderment rather than a lack of interest in women. His character is happily in love with an ambitious young brunette flapper named Mona Low (Sharon Lynn), and he pays little attention to his work because he is so excited about their impending marriage.

After his opening radio performance, Crosby's character befriends a sensitive Texas oilman (Stuart Erwin) who has just been jilted by his girl; the friendship they form is mutually affectionate and respectful. In fact after Crosby finds out that his own girl has jilted him, the two friends decide to go home together. There, after an aborted suicide pact, they decide to give up on women and live together, looking at women as "only the toys of an idle

FIG. 6.7. In this still from the set of *The Big Broadcast*, 1932, Bing Crosby's clothes are in disarray and his face covered with fans' lipstick. What is equally noteworthy, however, is the presence of the carbon "button" mic within the film's frame as a prop and the actual recording microphone above it, out of the frame, on a boom. The traveling boom mic gave Crosby more freedom of movement than stars had in earlier sound films, and the development of the directional ribbon mic gave him a clearer, richer, smoother recorded sound than the carbon, a sound that would become the industry standard. Courtesy of the Academy of Motion Picture Arts and Sciences.

hour." After spending the night in their side-by-side twin beds, Erwin gets up and offers to make breakfast, already the good wife to Crosby's crooner. In this and in many other instances throughout the film, Erwin's character performs routine sissy shtick: he demonstrates a curious knowledge of women's clothes, he puts on women's clothes by mistake, and he fusses over Crosby.

The same homosocial humor that would serve to ridicule such effeminate men in Crosby's later *Road* pictures with Bob Hope was at this time comparatively complex in portraying emotional bonds between men. When the pair become enmeshed in a love triangle with an office secretary, played by Leila Hyams (she loves Crosby, Erwin loves her, Crosby is fond of both), rather than compete, they all agree to remain friends—a resolution that would not occur in a Code film bent on exclusive coupledom.

The Big Broadcast, made as the attacks on crooners were just beginning, differs from other crooning films before and after it. Although it reproduces the situations that most worried crooning's critics—the crooner's possible homosexuality (or queerness) and his poor work ethic—it complicates them in unexpected ways. The film attempts to reassure the audience that Crosby is still a man's man *despite* his voice. An exchange between Erwin and Hyams makes this point plain:

HYAMS: It's funny, there's something about Bing that reminds me of you. . . .
It's that funny little catch in his voice when he sings.
ERWIN: I'll have to practice that.
HYAMS: You do it, anyway, sometimes, when you talk.

Here *The Big Broadcast* suggests that the sufficient masculinization of the body *can* mitigate the feminizing effects of the crooning voice. Hyams indicates that it is the emotional vulnerability of the crooning voice that she responds to—an emotionality she associates with sensitive men like Erwin rather than men like Crosby. The "catch" in Crosby's voice (that Irish mordent) is significantly not indicative of his overall masculinity, especially in comparison to the sensitive Erwin. Against expectations, the film ultimately pairs Hyams with the sissyish Erwin, while Crosby is reunited with an old girlfriend, Sharon Lynn. Lynn's character is a demanding woman who gets herself into fistfights with Crosby; her lack of femininity implies that gender conventions have not yet become rigid in 1932. Sensitive or feminine men can still get the girl, and aggressive women can attract men.

While *The Big Broadcast* plays more loosely with gender roles than any other crooning film, it does reinforce patterns established in Crosby's shorter films that will continue to characterize his 1930s features: crooning is linked with comedy more than drama or romance, and Crosby is paired with a more feminine man who doubles as both buddy and rival—a role Bob Hope would most famously play in later films. As in all his films, Crosby prefers the company of men to women, and there are no love scenes between him and Lynn. In fact the only semiromantic scene between them is the film's conclusion, where Lynn appears brandishing a black eye apparently given to her by Crosby, who tried to ditch her to go to the studio to fulfill a promise to Erwin. Thus the film endorses Crosby's work ethic, loyalty to men, and masculine aggression, presenting them as comedy, at the expense of his romantic relationship.

Two more Crosby films from this period present key developments in his persona: *Dream House*, a short film released in 1932, and *Going Hollywood*, a big-budget MGM musical released a year later. *Dream House* references and reworks some of the romantic aspects of the Vallée crooner, combining them with Crosby's more confident, traditional common-man persona. Crosby's character starts out as a lovelorn crooner, a naïve plumber whose fiancée's mother has whisked her off to Hollywood to prevent their marriage. After following them to Hollywood, Crosby dons blackface and impersonates a "slaveboy" to get onto the studio set to see his fiancée, who is starring in a picture called *Hot Kisses*. After singing a ballad to her in blackface, he leans over and kisses her. She is horrified until she realizes it is Crosby, and they both get burnt cork smeared all over their faces. After they both quickly wipe it off, the chase starts, with Crosby and his fiancée in the obligatory car chase with her mother in pursuit. When the film ends they are safely on their way home to the "dream house" that he has built for them in their old hometown.

Several elements in *Dream House* diverge from Crosby's other short films. His use of blackface, although comic, inevitably links him with its tradition of white male superiority and paternalism; it signifies that Crosby's crooner is *not* offering a new, alternative white masculinity, as the Vallée crooner did, but is seeking to legitimize crooning by connecting it with historical performances of white masculinity. This connection became much more obvious in later Crosby uses of blackface in feature-length films. In addition, the ending of *Dream House* suggests still another strain of traditional masculinity that will become more and more integral to Crosby's films and his star persona: his preference for country living, small-town life, and traditional values.

Crosby's crooner image did not change overnight, but his film roles for Paramount reflect the naturalization of his singing and his increasingly straight-man persona. His early films gradually moved him away from the sophisticated, lipsticked crooners he played in his three 1933 films to the more independent, common man surrounded by less common "others" in a number of romantic settings: the Old South of Mississippi, the tourist paradise of Hawaii, and the upper-class hotel where he seduces and "tames" the invariably temperamental rich heroine. These integrated musicals abandoned the backstage formula of previous film musicals and naturalized musical performance within a variety of story lines and characters, helping Crosby distance himself even further from the romantic crooner figure. They promoted him instead as a musical "everyman" for the Depression era, playing a number of different characters with similar masculine Crosby attributes. In this way he could drive the narrative action rather than be an "attraction" himself, and he could narrativize his singing in a way that further naturalized it for audiences (singing to his horse, say, instead of on a bandstand). Although he still played a modern crooning character in the pre-Code transitional films *Too Much Harmony* and *College Humor*, both notably place him in settings where he sings without a diegetic (visible) microphone, and, because of movie boom mic'ing, he appears not to need a microphone to project his voice. The illusion of film sound thus presents Crosby as a "legitimate" singer rather than a microphoned crooner; his sound is completely naturalized.

Crosby's final film to address the problem of crooning directly and in any detail, 1933's *Going Hollywood*, was also the one that made him a top-ten box office star. The film was the last significant transition for the Crosby crooner; not coincidentally it was also his last film before the full implementation of the Production Code in 1934. The plot is similar to *The Big Broadcast* but reflects the values of *Dream House*. Marion Davies, Crosby's first blonde love interest, plays a crooning fan who falls in love with Crosby's voice on the radio and tracks him down in Hollywood, only to find out that he is a drunken playboy, not the sincere lover his songs suggest. His character is eventually redeemed in the course of the film by the small-town values of this good woman—unmistakable parallels with Crosby's own life, especially his marriage. The tolerance with which his previous films handled queer characters is handled very differently here; though still present in this film, gender deviance is no longer embraced. There is no warm friendship between Crosby and the more feminine male, again played by Stuart Erwin, and neither he nor other gender-deviant characters (Davies's tough-girl friend Patsy Kelly and aggressive French girlfriend, Fifi D'Orsay) make matches with the central

FIGS. 6.8–6.9. Bing Crosby and Marion Davies in *Going Hollywood*, MGM, 1933. Hollywood films of this time often used lap dissolves (one image fading directly into another) to make dramatic connections between scenes. In this remarkable shot Crosby fan Davies fantasizes about the two of them "making hay while the sun shines" as Crosby sings. This is one of the few instances on film where female pleasure and romantic fantasy as triggered by a crooning male's voice is actually portrayed, although the more normative gender politics of the remainder of the film do much to try to recuperate the threat of female self-pleasure. Tellingly the content of the fantasy itself is tied to normative coupling and gender roles, as well as "old fashioned" values.

FIG. 6.10. Fifi D'Orsay in *Going Hollywood*, MGM, 1934. This lap dissolve demonstrates the poisonous influence of the flapper girl. The dissolve from her to two drinks makes her directly responsible for the Bing Crosby character's alcoholism. D'Orsay, who is playing a French flapper, is pointedly contrasted with Marion Davies's wholesome, blonde, all-American girl, a contrast that reflected the increasing xenophobia of the time as well as the end of the flapper era.

couple. Marking a significant shift in representations, the crooner "problem" is negotiated by emphasizing that the newly demonized flapper figure (also, significantly, French and foreign) leads the crooner astray; her strength, sensuality, and cosmopolitanism are corrupting rather than empowering influences. This new indictment of the flapper is most obvious in a remarkable scene in which Crosby drunkenly sings "You Are Temptation" to D'Orsay, who keeps plying him with alcohol.

In *Going Hollywood*, crooners are portrayed as insincere and aligned with the artificiality of the city and of Hollywood. Davies's character makes this point in the film's strong indictment of Crosby: "This is Hollywood, isn't it? Everything's a motion picture set. It's all artificial, the costumes, the scenery, the people. You're just part of this, possibly you're just as fake as the scenery. You're really no more sincere than those songs of yours about love and moonlight, or whatever else you've been crooning about. You're just a voice that croons about something that once was real. You're not real. You're just a fake!" Although *Going Hollywood* indicts crooners, it also suggests that playboy crooners can be reformed into proper leading men, even role models, so long as they can be adequately masculinized. Unlike earlier crooning films (such as *Crooner*), which suggested that the crooner must give up crooning to become masculine, *Going Hollywood* offers another possibility through Crosby, the reformed, remasculinized crooner. This process could be achieved both through changes in the crooner's physical body—properly disciplined, muscular, active, emotionally contained—and through values associated with white Protestant (and increasingly Catholic) hegemony: a good work ethic, morality, family, and small-town living. These characteristics would come to define the Crosby star crooner of the Code era.

AMERICA'S CROONER, 1934–1944

The Hollywood in which Bing Crosby became a star was a changed place from what it had been only a year or two before. The implementation of the Hollywood Production Code in 1934 shut the door, decisively, on the kinds of fluid gender and sexual expressions that had been common in American popular culture for decades. Hollywood's producers, anxious about declining Depression receipts and threatened by Catholic Church boycotts and possible government regulation, agreed to ban "sex perversion" (tied to gender transgression) from the screen and instituted moral standards of sexual behavior on- and offscreen for its players. The Code had such an enormous, long-lasting impact on the public's conception of normative gender roles, in part, because the Depression had largely wiped out live performance alternatives. As a result Hollywood's ideological positions reverberated throughout the entertainment world, and the new gender standards dictated by the Code resulted in fundamental changes to film texts and a massive turnover in star players. The Code was also the final, perhaps most visible strike against queer behavior in American public life that had been building since the late 1920s.[49]

For popular singers, the situation in 1934 was especially dire. Although *Variety* regularly referred to both male and female singers as "torching" and "crooning" songs as late as 1932, by 1934 the terms had become gendered, a reversal that helped establish gendered standards for voices that have largely persisted to this day. These newly instituted binaries meant that low-voiced women and high-pitched men were personae non grata in popular media; most crooning tenors' careers ended by 1934, and female crooners like Lee Morse and Harriet Lee also found themselves out of work. Female altos or small groups largely replaced male tenors as the lead singers in the big bands. Radio still provided work for some male crooning singers, most often in variety programs, but film producers found the physical appearance and high-pitched vocals of most male crooners unsuitable for celluloid. In his discussion of Code changes, William Mann notes that high-pitched male voices were actively censored; in one instance Code monitors found violence against a child unobjectionable but did object to a man's "fairly feminine voice."[50] "Pretty" male singing stars like the popular Ramon Novarro disappeared. A front-page story in *Variety* in October 1934 emphasized Hollywood's "big need" for "he-men crooners": "Looks count; he must be around six feet and have femme appeal. It's no joke. There are a dock of young lads around who can croon, but they lack the face or physique that fits. . . . If only Clark Gable could sing!"[51]

The lack of acceptably masculine crooners created a void that Crosby filled, and Paramount did its best to keep him working, churning out three or four star vehicles for him each year in the mid-1930s, as well as devoting massive amounts of promotional energy into making him a star. His films for the next ten years continued to build on the type of masculine persona that emerged at the end of *Going Hollywood*. Because Crosby's voice made him more vulnerable to accusations of emasculation than other screen stars, his persona offered a white masculinity that was extreme in its evacuation of emotion or desire, especially when compared with prior romantic crooners. While he pursues the heroine in these films with the intention of marrying her, there is never anything remarkable about her or especially loving in his attachment to her. Indeed his courtship is often marked by anger and violence; high-class women need to be taken down a notch, while working women need to get their priorities straight: Crosby humiliates Shirley Ross by pushing her off a pier at the beginning of *Waikiki Wedding* (1937); he slaps Carole Lombard and ties her to a stake in *We're Not Dressing* (1934), and he ridicules working woman Madge Evans in *Pennies from Heaven* (1936) as a "nosy social worker" whom children are shown to despise as intensely as they worship Crosby. His characters often don't even do their own proposing, requiring his sidekick (most frequently Bob Burns) to do the asking. He is frequently nonchalant to the point of indifference and coldness, using his singing to romance women without indulging in sincere devotion or reverence.

The film *Mississippi* (1934) has a particularly brutal narrative for a musical and provides the strongest contrast with the earlier softness of the crooning image. Although Crosby's character is a pacifist when the Old South narrative begins, his belief marks his independence rather than a genuinely

FIG. 6.11. *We're Not Dressing*, Paramount, 1934. By the time this film was released Bing Crosby's film image had changed considerably. He had largely lost his collegiate, stylish wardrobe and adopted plainer, more overtly masculine clothes, and the variety of characters he was able to play broadened his appeal. As this still demonstrates, his new film characters were also frequently aggressive and violent (toward women as well as men), a clear contrast with the romantic crooner image. Courtesy of the Academy of Motion Picture Arts and Sciences.

nonviolent nature. He is billed as "the Singing Killer" on a riverboat for publicity reasons, but when a heckler throws a knife at him during a number, Crosby shoots him with his own gun. He later holds men off at sword-point, explaining to his stepfather, "I've learned there are some things [a] man has to fight for." He then breaks down a door and forcibly abducts his love interest, Joan Bennett, who has refused to see him because of his new embrace of violence. For Crosby, sometimes you gotta fight to be a man.

Tellingly, the narratives of Crosby's films repeatedly have him sing romantic or comforting songs without looking at his intended, nor she at him. In *Rhythm on the Range* (1936), for example, Crosby's cowboy sings a love song to Frances Farmer while doing various activities to prepare the campsite. He keeps his head down or looks off into the sky while he sings, and she stands some distance away the entire time with her back to him. The narrative thus does everything possible to de-spectacularize Crosby, making it look like

FIG. 6.12. *Rhythm on the Range*, Paramount, 1936. This scene is a good example of how Bing Crosby managed to deliver the requisite love song to his love interest without compromising his masculinity. Here he sings to Frances Farmer without making eye contact with her and from a distance.

he's not singing but simply talking to himself (fig. 6.12). The viewer doesn't even know if Farmer has heard him until the end of the song. He also frequently sings the requisite love ballad to children or animals and is simply *overheard* by his intended. Because he is not sensitive or sensual, he's not autoerotic in these moments so much as he seems utterly self-involved. His narcissism is also evident in his relationships with men. Although Crosby is more comfortable in a homosocial environment, he shows very little strong feeling for his male buddies either (unlike his early film *The Big Broadcast*).[52]

The need to reinforce the masculinity of the crooning male and keep him from becoming a spectacle did much to structure the classical Hollywood musical. Crooner films were the first to require the establishment of what became the classic double bind of musical men in Hollywood cinema: in order not to seem too effeminate as performers, they must surround themselves with sissies or oafs, but they cannot show too much interest in the heroine either, lest they seem too emotionally vulnerable. This problem results in love triangles like those in Gene Kelly's films, where the leading man ends up spending much more time with other men and seems to have much closer emotional bonds with them. In Crosby's 1930s films, however, the relationship between him and the other sissy men is competitive rather than mutually supportive, and homosocial attachments are made fun of through constant ridicule of the feminine. His sidekick in these 1930s films is Bob Burns (also his radio sidekick), who is stupid and infantile rather than effeminate. His devotion to Crosby is implicit but never underlined; Crosby treats him with amused condescension and sends him his castoff girls.

As in *Going Hollywood*, aggressive or independent female characters who depart from their passive gender roles are routinely spectacularized and humiliated in Crosby's films. In his early films, Ethel Merman played this role; her strong voice and stage presence served to further naturalize Crosby's singing and his narrative absorption. The young comedienne Martha Raye took this role to extremes in three of Crosby's most successful 1930s films, *Rhythm on the Range*, *Waikiki Wedding*, and *Double or Nothing*. The films foreground her characters' loudness, overt sexual desire, directness, and unfeminine appearance in numerous scenes in which she gets drunk, pratfalls, is trod on by horses, mistakes a chimp for her boyfriend, falls in a tub of liquor, and responds to a call for a pig to the delight of a crowd. (She then makes loud noises that frighten the pigs away, amusing the crowd still further.) Other characters, including Crosby, constantly refer to her undesirability and ugliness. When, in *Waikiki Wedding*, Crosby realizes he has mistakenly sung to her window rather than his intended's, the horror on his face is palpable. He asks Burns, "Did I bring *that* over here?" and pawns her off on Burns with a "This one's for you." Raye is also the most obvious "performer" in these films, the person who sings on a stage for the amusement of the crowd. Again, making her the spectacle rather than Crosby deflects attention from his singing, naturalizing it and his masculinity even further by conflating visual spectacle and excess—stagey performers, comedians, sexual objects—with the female sex.

This kind of gendering succeeded in reinforcing Crosby's masculine image. Tellingly, critics applauded his lack of emotional intensity and credited him, approvingly, with "not acting" in his films. Bosley Crowther, a longtime reviewer for the *New York Times*, was a big Crosby fan. In one typical review, he praised Crosby's screen presence: "One thing about Bing, you never catch him acting. He is always himself."[53] This carefully constructed "authentic" self affected music critics as well, who similarly praised Crosby's microphone technique for the way they felt he did not appear to depend on the technology for his sound, even when this was obviously the case. The music critic

Martin Williams wrote in 1968, "Crosby doesn't sound like a singer using a microphone for some of his most telling effects. The microphone in effect, overhears him. To say that he is effortless, natural, intimate, as is often said, is to say that he uses the mic to reach members of his audience more directly."[54] Thus Crosby's reconstruction of the crooner was deemed successful because he allowed for the classical Hollywood ideal of technological transcendence, erasing the technology that could be seen as "artificially amplifying" or "distorting" him in the public's mind.

These critics' comments suggest the extent to which Crosby successfully drew on tropes of white masculinity to belie and indeed erase crooning's roots, both technologically and culturally. His persona seemed to restore the physical boundary of straight white masculinity that had been violated by the gender-queer 1920s, particularly its urban popular music. By emptying his body of emotion, he indicated that those qualities had not penetrated and feminized him—and what is more, that they never had. Unlike previous romantic crooners, whose vulnerability and emotional excess transgressed social boundaries, Crosby's lack of intense, expressive emotion signified naturalness because it continually reaffirmed and reproduced boundaries of gender and race. The noted jazz historian Will Friedwald's praise of Crosby's singing is most clearly contingent on his proper performance of white middle-class masculinity when he compares him to Louis Armstrong: "Armstrong's great strength was his ability to express emotion, and the key to Crosby's singing is the way in which he controlled emotion."[55]

Crosby's films also continued to build on the idea of him as "America's supreme musical patriarch" and erase any previous version of the crooner through their increasingly conservative politics, "exotic" locations, treatment of women as objects, and the regular presence of people of color and children as loyal servants and background singers to Father Crosby.[56] These tropes are most obvious in the series of *Road* pictures he made with Bob Hope beginning in 1940, but they are notably present in several 1930s films, including 1935's *Mississippi*, set in the antebellum South, 1936's *Pennies from Heaven*, set in the Depression era, and 1937's *Waikiki Wedding*, set in a tourist's Hawaii. *Mississippi* reinforces Crosby's patriarchal whiteness by having him sing "Swanee River" in front of a black chorus; in *Pennies* he is the stand-in patriarch to orphaned and poor children, whom he serenades (his chief romance is with the ten-year-old orphan Patsy, who claims to "fall in love" with him after he regularly sings her to sleep); *Waikiki* sets Crosby's whiteness and

FIG. 6.13. Bing Crosby singing to a bear in *We're Not Dressing*, Paramount, 1934. Crosby frequently sang more directly to children and animals than women in his films, undercutting his feminization and eroticization by making him more patriarchal and less of a sexual object. This comic scene nonetheless implies his ability to tame wild beasts with his voice.

more masculine singing against a group of "exotic" natives whose musical performances are more spectacular and feminized.

Waikiki Wedding is particularly notable for producing the song "Sweet Leilani," one of the biggest hits of the decade. The song contrasts his voice with that of the Hawaiian Lani McIntyre and his popular band (and fellow Decca recording artists), the Hawaiians.[57] Significantly, McIntyre sings in falsetto or very high tenor, thus ensuring Crosby's more masculine sound and underlining the point that men of color singing in very high-pitched, emotionally intense voices would continue to be perfectly acceptable, even desirable, in American popular culture. Nevertheless, the masculine naturalizing of voices has become so taken for granted by now that critics retrospectively often find McIntyre discomfiting and project their anxieties onto 1937 audiences. Crosby's biographer Gary Giddins, for example, wonders if audiences of the time were anxious when McIntyre's voice begins the recording ("Did people wonder if Crosby had joined the castrati?"), though happily "seventy-seconds into a three minute side, the exotic vocalist is suddenly supplanted by the reassuring virility of Bing's dulcet baritone." Again Giddins's concern here is very much a product of our own era, rather than that of the 1930s mass audience; he finds it unfathomable that part of the reason audiences might have liked this particular record so much was, in fact, that it also featured the kind of high-pitched male voice they had so enjoyed in the past but had been deprived of in mainstream films for several years.

Crosby's use of blackface performance in his later films reinforced his connection with dominant white masculinity. Although he did not perform in blackface in *Mississippi*, he continued to employ the occasional blackface performance in films such as *Holiday Inn* (1942) and *Dixie* (1943); blackface was generally less common but still acceptable in the studio era. Like many other musicals of the time, blackface musicals of the 1930s and 1940s were about national unity and integration, the coming together of white and black; that coming together, however, was always predicated on the idealized South of the plantation song, in which racial hierarchies were naturalized and unthreatening.[58] As "America's crooner," Crosby was a white patriarch masquerading as a common man, a very successful persona for an American star.

This persona was reinforced by Crosby's enormously popular radio program, *The Kraft Music Hall* (NBC, 1935–45). This variety show was based in Hollywood rather than New York, and Crosby's now-standardized masculine voice contrasted with every kind of guest star, including Hollywood and Broadway talent, country singers, opera stars, concert performers, and child stars. He also continued to feature minstrel music; one 1947 radio program featured Crosby with guest Al Jolson (his early hero) "revisiting the good old minstrel days."[59] Crosby's variety program notably supplanted Vallée's (both were sponsored by J. Walter Thompson) in the ratings in 1936, the year when most network programs moved to the West Coast, as Hollywood continued to overtake New York as the center of popular culture. Eventually Crosby would further distance himself from the live shock of the original crooner by becoming the first radio performer to institute the use of transcription rather than live performance in postwar radio. His programs were recut and spliced for maximum effect, although they appeared to be spontaneous.

Crosby's studio and fan magazine promotion continued to portray him as a devoted family man who had achieved the American dream of wealth and fame without letting the sweat show.[60] He also more clearly aligned himself with country over city living as the 1930s advanced, which was easier to do as a Hollywood star than a New Yorker. He claimed disinterest in nightclubbing ("I'm a homebody now") and instead celebrated the traditional values of small-town living (family, hard work, religious practice). *Photoplay's* writers credited Crosby with helping to spur an interest in ranching and farming among Hollywood's elite, and profiles of him were accompanied by photos of him and his family "down on the ranch."[61] They also stressed how much he enjoyed involving his four boys in traditional male pursuits such as sports, horse racing, and fishing.[62] Crosby no longer appeared publicly in tuxedos, claimed he didn't "like to dress," and instead wore an old cap and sweater for publicity photos and on set.

Reporters no longer questioned Crosby's virility and masculinity, since procreation and fatherhood represented the ultimate deflection of emasculation.[63] Just to be sure, though, studio and fan magazine profiles continually emphasized his role as patriarch and frequently quoted him giving parenting advice. A kidnapping threat against his son resulted in especially reverent press coverage, in which Crosby was lauded as a concerned father praying for his son's safety. Like crooners past, Crosby often credited his mother with his success, but with a key difference: she was no mollycoddler, and he would not sing any mother songs in her honor. Crosby's mother, he asserted, had insisted that he learn the benefits of hard work, self-discipline, and competition. "She could have turned young Bing into a sissy," insisted one writer, "and handicapped him for life. But she influenced him in the other direction, in athletics, in competition with other boys." Crosby claimed in these profiles that mothers like his "make this country glorious" because "they instill patriotism, fear of God, and unselfishness in their children."[64] Discourses of patriarchy, family, masculinity, and nationalism are firmly tied together in profiles that ground Crosby's "he-man" masculinity in his family's status as "hardy Americans from away back."[65]

Ironically, although he was the subject of continual, intense promotion by Paramount and fan magazines, Crosby himself remained distant from his fans and reduced their access to him. Although most radio comedy-variety programs worked with studio audiences, Crosby refused one for *The Kraft Music Hall* and turned his back on audiences when doing guest spots on other shows, claiming that people distracted him. He rarely spoke of his fans in interviews, and when he did, he reflected the paternalistic concerns of psychologists and educators of the day who viewed pop culture as harmful if it encouraged youth—particularly young women—to dream of alternatives to normative values and gender roles. Unlike previous romantic crooners who enjoyed the attention of female fans and often identified with their desires, Crosby asserted to one fan magazine interviewer that fans' attachments were unhealthy, and he encouraged his female fans to forget about him and instead to find a good man and start a family.[66] What's fascinating about Crosby's attitude is that he was so firmly entrenched in the mass-mediated world he decried. Yet such contradictory rhetoric served his image as a "natural" star whose popularity and success were based on his talent and laudable character rather than on promotional machines, and whose personal behavior displaced any possible concerns about his emasculation as a romantic object onto his psychologically immature, vulnerable female audiences.

Crosby's continual assertion of the importance of old-fashioned values was usually accompanied by details of his own strong work ethic, rooted in his upbringing. Crosby would insist that he did not "work really hard" and then sit back as the writer praised his modesty by reeling off his numerous films, recordings, and personal appearances. His "laziness" was clearly disingenuous, but it reaffirmed his masculine credentials; comparing him to the working-class men they asserted (incorrectly) hated crooning, journalists declared that Crosby was "too smart to take his singing seriously" and understood that it's not "real work."[67] His common-man persona was also reinforced by growing attention to his Irishness; Crosby referred to his four sons, for example, as "the Irishers," spoke often of his Irish roots, and eventually played an Irish priest in Going My Way (1944) and The Bells of St. Mary's (1945). At the time Irish Catholics like Crosby were becoming scions of the middle class and a powerful influence on American public life, but the Irish were still generally portrayed in American popular culture as working-class outsiders with traditional values. Crosby's ethnic affiliation became an ideal of unthreatening assimilation as the 1930s became the 1940s, and his story emblematic of the rise of the white ethnic outsider to a place of acceptance.

Indeed Crosby's religious affiliation aided rather than hurt his ascent. He was a well-known, devout Catholic, a fact that was publicized more in the mid-1930s than earlier in his career. Once he had sufficiently separated himself from the romantic crooner persona, he was quickly embraced by the Catholic Church as an ideal representative of the new homogenized, nationalist "American" Catholic Church, whose members have been described by the historian Charles Morris as "disciplined, rule-bound, loyal to church and country, unrebellious, but upwardly mobile and achievement-oriented."[68] Crosby cemented his Church loyalties in 1935 by enlisting the help of its motion picture ratings organization, the Legion of Decency, in his campaign against his casting in a film version of the Broadway show Sailor Beware! The Legion did indeed enthusiastically support Crosby, publicizing his protest in the Catholic press and praising him for resisting his casting in a production "widely condemned for immorality" and "one of the bawdiest, most suggestive shows that has appeared on Broadway in a long time." In these discussions the Legion contrasted the "sophisticated," wealthy Broadway audience with the vast, "heterogeneous" motion picture audience, suggesting that Crosby and the Legion represented a mass rather than class audience.[69] Crosby won his case against Paramount and did not have to make the film, an unusual triumph for a screen actor under studio contract and one that demonstrated the increased clout of the Catholic Church in the film industry.

Religious adherence, especially Catholicism, came to be foregrounded more and more in Crosby's film and recording career over the next decade. His playboy-crooner persona was entirely forgotten when he put crooning in the service of religious praise; his devotional albums sold very well, and his two best-selling records were Christmas songs, "Silent Night" and "White Christmas." His Academy Award–winning 1944 film, Going My Way, presented the ultimate Crosby crooning image. His lack of sensuality and his emotional reserve perfectly suited the role of a Catholic priest, a prime representative of the "superpadre" of the classical film era: "virile, athletic, compassionate, wise."[70] Notably, the Academy Award–winning song Crosby sings in the film, "Swinging on a Star," is not a love song but a cautionary tune that echoes the middle-class masculine norms of the pre-jazz age in its advice to young boys to "be better than you are": to go to school, stay clean, and mind your manners, lest you grow up to be pigs, mules, or monkeys. Religious figures around the country were so impressed with the film that they sent him congratulatory letters. Pope Pius XII saw the picture several times and sent Crosby a letter in which "he described his enjoyment of the film, and said he thought it good to have the priesthood so humanized."[71] Going My Way thus established the crooner as a cultural and even religious icon. In order to mitigate the disruptive effect of the crooning voice, Crosby's screen persona effectively disciplined the body to the degree that it was no longer human but expressionless, unemotional, undesiring. Going My Way thus served as the ultimate repudiation of the 1920s crooner on behalf of a new standard of white masculinity.

The changes in Crosby's life and career enabled him to reinvent the crooner image in a way that ensured its mass appeal while minimizing the emasculating aspects of male popular singing. He represented the final stage in an evolution in popular song that began with the minstrel mammy's lullaby. While the soft tone of his voice remained a direct legacy of the

FIG. 6.14. *Going My Way*, Paramount, 1944. In this scene, Crosby performs his famous song "Swinging on a Star," promoting middle-class values of hard work, education, and cleanliness to the impressionable male youth under his guidance so they won't grow up to be "mules," "pigs," or "monkeys." Author's collection.

crooning mammy figure, his masculine body successfully erased its feminine and racialized connotations from the public's mind, at least where he was concerned. For this reason Crosby indeed represents the "line of demarcation" that music critics have claimed for him. His singing set the aesthetic and social standard for male popular singing and did much to shape how the music, broadcasting, and film industries and the critics of each have judged popular music ever since. His early musical roles successfully narrativized the male singer in a way that influenced the shape of the American film musical for decades. He dominated popular recording and took the mantle of radio variety from Vallée; his *Kraft Music Hall* program remained radio's top variety show for ten years. Crosby also set the tone for fan magazine and press coverage of crooners; stories about crooners in the 1930s emphasized their wives and children, frequently showing them holding pictures of their babies. This kind of coverage worked to de-glamorize and demystify the crooner and his magnetic effects.

The desires of the crooner's original audience for his soothing songs were validated and fulfilled, although at quite a cost. Crosby came to represent a new, homogenized American popular song that drew on a variety of traditional American musical sources (especially Tin Pan Alley) yet was generic enough to have broad appeal. The standards he established ensured the dominance of crooning music in national culture and set the narrow gender norms against which subsequent male popular singers would be measured. Crosby's crooner did not offer an alternative masculinity, as previous crooners had done, but sought instead to legitimize crooning by connecting it to traditional notions of white masculinity: a good work ethic, patriarchy, religious belief, white superiority, and contained emotions. The balance that Crosby achieved, however, was not as easily maintained by the singers who followed him; society's continued unease regarding the crooner reflects the ongoing struggle between gender norms and audience desires that have marked popular male singers' careers throughout the twentieth century and beyond.

CONCLUSION

FRANK SINATRA: "Why do you run after girls all the time?"
GENE KELLY: "I'll tell you when your voice changes, Junior."
—On the Town, MGM, 1950

In Gus Van Sant's 1991 independent film *My Own Private Idaho*, the main character is a young queer street hustler named Mike (River Phoenix). In an early sequence, Mike stands on a street corner waiting for a pickup. The opening bars of Rudy Vallée's signature 1929 crooning song, "Deep Night," begin their staccato descent as Mike takes his position on the corner; their punchy gravity is similar in tone to the soundtrack of a cheap 1930s horror film: something pleasurably queer is about to occur. A German john (Udo Kier) with a cleaning fetish takes him home and dances in anticipation as he watches and listens to Mike scrub his house. Vallée's thin, pleading voice emerges to accompany him. The voice is soft and the singer strains to reach each note, but both the lyrics and Vallée's emotional intensity make clear how urgent his need is:

Come to my arms my dear one, my sweetheart, my own
Vow that you'll love me always, and be mine alone . . .
Kind night, bringing you nearer, dearer, and dearer
deep night
deep in the arms of love.[1]

The use of this song in *Idaho* tells us much about the place of early crooning music in American culture since the mid-1930s. It allies Vallée and his desire with that of sexual outsiders: gay people, prostitutes, fetishists, foreigners. Critics did not interpret the juxtaposition of this young man singing sadly of his desire to be "deep in the arms of love" and the bouncing fetishist and his "little Dutch boy" as ironic but rather empathetic. Many reviewers commented on the appropriateness of the song as a way to suggest the young hustler's marginal existence and his unrequited desire for love.[2] The hope the singer expresses is affecting here because both the situation it accompanies and the song's minor key suggest the futility and absurdity of actually finding love. It is a song about desire, and its placement early in the film underscores *Idaho*'s primary story arc: Mike's thwarted attempts at love with Scott (Keanu Reeves).

Many critics considered *My Own Private Idaho* one of the most important films of 1991, a defining text of New Queer Cinema, because they felt its story of unrequited love suggested a larger critique of the people who had been shut out of Reagan-Bush's America. The critic Amy Taubin suggests that the desire for love expressed by "Deep Night" goes hand in hand with Mike's "unrealized desire for the 'brotherhood' represented in the film by a pedal steel guitar rendition of 'America the Beautiful.'" Mike is one of America's outsiders because he's queer and poor, but he still desires connection: "Betrayed countless times, those romantic yearnings are never vanquished."[3]

The use of Vallée's romantic crooning in *Idaho* reflects the way early crooning's queer sounds also were culturally marginalized in the decades following the 1930s, to the extent that their presence in popular culture since then has served to evoke the subversion of gender or sexual norms for either dramatic or comic effect. Significantly, the most notable prior use of Vallée's "Deep Night" occurred in 1967, when it was chosen to play under the black-and-white photos that serve as the opening credits for *Bonnie and Clyde*, the groundbreaking film about social outsiders and sexual deviance that ushered in the new Hollywood cinema of the late 1960s–70s. One year later Tiny Tim's hit revival of Nick Lucas's very popular 1929 song, "Tiptoe through the Tulips," was received largely as a freakish novelty number. Tim's falsetto voice, vibrato, and use of the soprano ukulele were framed as sources of amusement on comedy and talk shows, although he was a proficient and talented singer and musician. His unusually high-pitched voice, incongruous with his lanky stature (his moniker was ironic), reinforced—to an absurd degree—the association of male performance from the 1920s era with strange, "queer" sounds. While Tin Pan Alley standards have become staples of heteronormative romance since the 1930s, most notably in romantic comedies in the vein of *When Harry Met Sally*... (1989), early crooning songs and performances by stars like Vallée, Cliff Edwards, Russ Columbo, and even early Bing Crosby have remained either marginalized or signifiers of marginalization.

FIG. C.1. *Gosford Park*, USA Films, 2001. One of the more interesting portrayals of the crooner as social outsider is Jeremy Northam in *Gosford Park*, directed by Robert Altman and set in 1932. Northam portrays Ivor Novello, an actual British romantic crooner and actor of the era. The film makes a point of showing the intense appeal of crooning music for the servants and middle classes of the time, both male and female, and many of the elite characters' disdain for it. One unhappy middle-class wife, Mabel Nesbit (played by Claudie Blakley), in particular, embraces the pleasure offered her by Novello's singing, suggesting the transporting possibilities of crooning music for some fans.

THE VOICE OF AMERICA

The norms for white masculine vocal performance that began to be enforced on a mass scale in the wake of the crooning crisis initially applied to popular music performance, connecting a male pop singer's high pitch (or use of falsetto), emotional vulnerability, and demonstrative female audiences with his effeminacy, arrested development, likely homosexuality, and, consequently, his critical devaluation. However, as I indicate in the introduction, because of the increasingly federalized homophobia of World War II and the cold war, these new standards reverberated well beyond the world of popular performance; they were regularly utilized in evaluations of everyday speech and were institutionalized in American political and education systems for decades. Although in recent years legal homophobia has decreased and gay culture has become more mainstream, these masculinist vocal norms persist and have largely continued to ensure the effeminizing stigma of high-pitched male voices and the related devaluation of young female ("feminine") and queer tastes, desires, and behaviors. At the same time historical and social changes have also impacted the degree of cultural anxiety surrounding male vocal performance. While I cannot offer a comprehensive survey here, I will briefly demonstrate how such attitudes have evolved since the 1930s, concluding with recent signs of a fundamental and hopefully enduring shift away from these narrow vocal codes by a younger generation of performers and their audiences.

From the late 1930s through the early 1960s, the golden age of Hollywood cinema, the crooner was most often portrayed as an arrested, idealistic, and sexless adolescent whose lampoon of the romantic crooner persona was central to his popularity. Part of the reason Crosby was unrivaled as "America's crooner" for so long was that no one else could successfully combine current codes of masculinity with a romantic crooning voice. Instead, men who sang romantic songs to women in films or in pop music were almost always constructed as college boys (Dick Powell, Ozzie Nelson, Dick Haymes) or innocent, earnest, often simpleminded young men (Frank Sinatra, Eddie Fisher, Frankie Avalon), all of whom would presumably grow out of their childish crooning phase. In the meantime their daydreaming and their music were a joke readily available for commercial exploitation but never taken seriously.

Sinatra is the most obvious case in point. As the epigraph suggests, a crooner needed to wait until his voice changed before he could attain adult masculinity, which is defined in *On the Town* (and other films) as the desire to aggressively "chase after" women—as Kelly does—rather than passively adore them.[4] The fact that Sinatra could be portrayed as an unsuitable mate because of his immaturity at the very moment he was the "swooner crooner" idol of millions of adoring women is evidence of how well established these conventions had become by the late 1940s. Sinatra would eventually be able to attain "adult" masculinity, but only by winning over straight men in the 1950s by drawing on discourses of Method acting and "authentic" Italian bel canto singing in order to legitimize the intense emotion of his performances; at the same time, his persona changed to reflect more hypermasculine behavior: womanizing, drinking, gambling, and rumored Mafia ties.[5]

Because gender roles were so strongly polarized in American cold war culture, and because homosexuality was still widely tied to gender presentation, any hint of femininity in men made them sexually suspect. The stakes of being perceived as effeminate—and therefore gay—threatened the life and livelihood of young men during this period; gay and lesbian persons were considered mentally ill and social deviants who could be fired from their jobs for no cause beyond suspicion and no redress. They were legally forbidden from holding federal office. Thus to be a youth or man with a high-pitched or falsetto voice, either in singing or in speech, was as much a marker of possible homosexuality as "feminine" gestures, and just as dangerous.[6]

Indeed feminine-marked speech was institutionally pathologized through-out the cold war era according to these same masculine vocal norms. From the 1950s to the 1980s, adolescent boys with high pitch or other effeminiz-ing vocal markers ("hissy s," lisp) were regularly assigned to speech pathol-ogy classes in public schools in order to "treat" their vocal "disorders." *The Handbook of Speech Pathology* (1957, 1971), the standard text in the field, regarded high-pitched voices in adolescent and adult males as "one of the most distressing of vocal defects" specifically because of its social stigma and presumed evidence of mental disease: "The resemblance to the female voice suggests a lack of masculinity. It is this implication, with its psychosocial sequelae, which creates the seriousness of the disorder, since the voice proper does not interfere with communication, nor would it be unpleasant if produced by a female."[7] The *Handbook* explicitly ties high-pitch to sexual identity: "The pitch a person uses reflects his sexual identification. . . . Such individuals are psychologically different from other members of their sex."[8]

The *Handbook* is only the most authoritative of the many books written by well-regarded speech pathologists that sought a popular audience of parents and teachers. In one of the most widely employed and reprinted of these books, *The Voice and Its Disorders* (1957), Margaret Greene devotes an en-tire chapter to the "problem" and treatment of persistent *puberphonia*, that is, the continuing "instability" of boys' pitch after adolescence. For many decades, puberphonia was understood primarily as a psychological malad-justment that indicated potential homosexuality. Greene employs a detailed Freudian framework in which she attributes puberphonia to "an Oedipus or Narcissus complex" that results in neurosis and homosexual affiliations that are marked by high pitch, falsetto, stammering, and other "infantile" habits. Like so much of the medical discourse of this period, Greene's assessment of pathology is rooted in deviance from masculine social norms; she lists one of the primary causes of puberphonia as the "fear of assuming a full share of adult responsibility or of losing maternal protection with consequent uncon-scious assertion of immaturity."[9]

The recommended treatment in all these guidebooks is "vocal psychotherapy," which is clearly grounded in the same Freudian-based psychotherapy techniques used at the time to try to make troubled gay men function as straight by altering their behavior. The focus of vocal psychotherapy was on training the male patient to value and appreciate his "lower tones," to view them as more "clear" and "natural" than his higher tones. Patients often found their lowered voices repulsive, and therapists observed that it usually took a long time to break down their resistance and make them accept their "new voices." In fact Greene asserts that vocal therapy would not work with the unwilling patient since "he needs a sincere desire to acquire a normal voice." She cites the case of one sixteen-year-old patient who had been rejected from a dramatic society because his voice was considered "unsuitable" and whose "manner and dress is well understood in colloquial parlance as a 'pansy' or 'sissy.'" He had a particularly wide singing range, which Greene was pleased to be able to narrow and stabilize to a tenor, but it took "endless discussion and argument" to persuade him "to speak normally outside of the clinic." However, when he favorably impressed a girl at work with his new voice and also found that the men who had previously "'ragged him' unmercifully" now ceased to do so, he was convinced to stay with it. Greene reports with satisfaction that this youth's "homosexual trends were arrested in time by speech therapy."[10]

These manuals also state that family members or educational authorities frequently advised and often forced these adolescents into speech therapy.[11] The institutionalization of these norms in the public education and medical systems as well as popular culture thus ensured that the social stigma of high-pitched voices would be entrenched early in a child's life, often causing acute distress for boys with such voices and justifying their bullying and harassment from students and teachers.[12] It is not surprising therefore that such voices would inspire loathing among young people, and self-loathing among those who possessed them. Proto-gay boys were particularly aware of being marked as different and the dire social consequences it meant for them. As a gay youth growing up in the 1960s, the scholar Wayne Koestenbaum recalled how acute his abhorrence of high-pitched, falsetto voices was because of the threat it represented to him: "I have always feared the falsetto: voice of the bogeyman, voice of the unregenerate fag; voice of horror and loss and castration; floating voice, vanished voice. With a grimace I remember freak pop singer Tiny Tim tiptoeing through the tulips with his ukulele."[13]

By the 1990s, following the gay liberation movement and the activism during the AIDS epidemic, the association of high pitch and homosexuality was largely de-institutionalized, ending enforced speech pathology in schools and medical establishments. The de-pathologizing of homosexuality, which began with its removal from the *Diagnostic and Statistical Manual of Mental Disorders* of the American Psychiatric Association in 1973, did not, however, end the pathologizing of perceived effeminate qualities in boys. In fact throughout the 1980s and early 1990s the American Psychiatric Association continued to list male effeminacy as a Gender Identity Disorder, conflating sex and gender roles to privilege normative masculinity, thus perpetuating effemiphobia among all men, both straight and gay.[14] Similarly, speech handbooks officially de-pathologized homosexuality while continuing to view high male pitch as a "vocal disorder" because of its violation of social norms, specifically those of age, gender, and sex. While an explicit pathologizing framework has been removed in assessments of puberphonia, traces of it remain in some popular texts that continue to describe the condition as a result of both psychological and sexual "immaturity."[15]

Work by sociolinguists in the 1990s and 2000s has confirmed the continued cultural association between "feminine-sounding" men and homosexuality by parsing the specific ways that public *perception* of sexual identity is based on vocal cues. While their studies have found no evidence that gay-identifying men have higher-pitched voices than straight-identifying men, such beliefs persist among the general public so that whatever sounds "feminine" in male speech also "sounds gay." Linguistic studies have found, for example, that male actors reify this association by altering their voice in various ways (including raising their pitch) when playing gay characters.[16] Perceived "gay speech" relies on a variety of vocal cues, including higher pitch, greater clarity, intonation variability (more rise and fall of the voice), the articulation and duration of specific speech sounds, and speech rate. Recent studies suggest some men's association with culturally feminine speech is a result of gender nonconformity in childhood (for any variety of reasons), but that such speech is not a predictor of sexual behavior in adults.[17]

Nevertheless, the connection between perceived feminine male gender behavior and sexual identity has persisted well into the twenty-first century and is perpetuated in a variety of ways in Anglo-American culture, most obviously by an entertainment industry that often champions gay rights but continues to devalue the cultural feminine. Indeed effemiphobia has replaced the direct homophobia that is no longer acceptable in mainstream popular culture, although effemiphobia is itself a form of homophobia.

Within the music industry, masculinist vocal standards have continued to be applied most stringently (although certainly not exclusively) to young white male singers of mainstream pop. Such singers and their most demonstrative fans—young, primarily female audiences—can't be ignored because they are often hugely profitable. And yet music critics dust off and reapply the same old gendered norms to both devalue these singers and to police the cultural power of their audiences, who are figured as mindless, tasteless consumers. Singers whom young women adore have been routinely dismissed as feminine (vain, emotional, probably gay), artistically suspect, and developmentally immature ("arrested").

Indicative of cultural shifts of the late 1960s and 1970s, the biggest commercial pop star of the decade was the sun-kissed white teen idol David Cassidy of television's *The Partridge Family*. Cassidy was roundly dismissed by music critics as a "bubblegum" star with a crazed teen girl fan base, even though his androgynous appearance represented the liberal turn toward a softer, more "sensitive" straight masculinity in the decade. His famous naked *Rolling Stone* cover in 1972, complete with armpit hair, did nothing to masculinize him to the dominant culture.[18]

Musically, the 1970s also offered more cultural fluidity and diversity, exposing the shared influences and interdependence among musicians and performers across racial, class, and gender lines that had been largely unacknowledged since before the 1930s. Motown produced a wildly popular crossover African American boy band, the Jackson Five, whose precocious young lead singer, Michael, became the first mainstream African American teen idol. Jackson's use of falsetto and other queerly marked vocal sounds postpuberty offered a gender "in between" and nonwhite young icon to a broad and diverse American public for the first time. In particular, he offered an important alternative "space of dreaming" to nonwhite and reluctantly assimilated white ethnic adolescent girls who didn't fit—or who resisted fitting—into the social norms of their environment.[19] Although the use of falsetto has always been more acceptable in black performers because of its perceived "authentic" roots in black culture (gospel, soul, and rhythm and blues music), Jackson's emergence as a crossover, highly commercial pop idol distinguished his stardom and has remained unequaled since.[20]

In terms of the visible codes of gender, 1970s androgyny gave way to 1980s conservatism and masculine "power ballads," shifting even falsetto signifiers in glam and hair metal from queerness to avowed heterosexuality.[21] Although the social movements of the 1970s opened up enormous industrial potential for queer music—a potential marked by the peak year of 1981—this potential was largely shut down, or at the very least closeted, by the conservative political shift of the 1980s and the cultural backlash that accompanied it.[22] This backlash had profound consequences for both commercially mainstream pop and queer vocalizing at all industrial levels and helped to stoke the general cultural homophobia and effemiphobia of earlier eras that would only intensify with the AIDS crisis. Although the 1980s did not shut down the production of queer or romantic crooning sounds, it closeted, masculinized, or disparaged them in various ways that continued as dominant paradigms for decades, even through the "gay 1990s."

A review of a John Mayer album, *Heavier Things*, in *Entertainment Weekly* in 2003 provides a typical example of such rhetoric; the reviewer describes Mayer's female-only appeal ("firmly in the sensitive-singer-songwriter-whom-chicks-dig division") and adds, "Male opinion [of Mayer] is near monolithic and goes something like this: He's all right, I guess, but I'd rather listen to Dave Matthews Band, Man." Effeminacy, of course, is underlined and ridiculed; Mayer's voice is described as "airy-fairy, and the resulting sounds could be dubbed fey contempo (or perhaps Oy Fey)."[23] Almost a decade later, this same publication—one that has notably long supported gay and lesbian representation in popular culture—routinely deployed misogynist and effemiphobic perspectives in its repeated references to the top teen idol Justin Bieber as a "girl."[24]

Likewise, crooning's female audiences have continued to be characterized as brainless, emotionally unstable, sex-crazed, and immature. An image of a Justin Bieber fan went viral in 2012 and became one of the most seen Internet images of the year; *Entertainment Weekly* described the image as "Overly Attached Girlfriend: An overly ardent Justin Bieber fan became the face of emotional clinginess."[25] Earlier in the year the publication jokingly diagnosed "Bieber Fever": "a serious illness that affects one in three adolescent girls, and one in eight of their mothers."[26] Although such slights may seem harmless enough and are presented as jokes, they are indicative of a larger cultural discourse of patronizing, trivializing, sometimes hostile rhetoric consistently directed at this particular audience like no other in the mainstream media; this attention both acknowledges the consuming power of this audience and tries to contain the threat it represents to gender, sex, and taste hierarchies.[27]

Such portrayals have functioned for decades to contain crooning's social impact while keeping it profitable; since the 1930s the entertainment establishment has also made sure that crooners themselves understand that having a huge following of teen girls is a critical and industrial liability to any hope of an enduring, critically respected singing career. As a result, every time a new, young white singer with a soft voice attracts attention, the cycle of containment begins anew: critical ridicule or dismissal, charges of effeminacy or emasculation, and calls for masculine rehabilitation, if possible. Unlike most other contexts in which a performer is at the top of his or her profession, profiles and reviews of such singers, almost always white, consistently suggest ways for them to dissociate themselves from the very qualities and audience that have made them stars and to "grow up" enough to become legitimate artists worthy of critical respect; this "arrested development" rhetoric attests to the persistence of cold war masculinist psychosocial frameworks and is an assessment that is notably never applied to female pop singers or people of color who are the same age.[28]

This nonsensical, punitive process has been so naturalized that it is largely unquestioned; indeed it is expected that critical evaluation of each new generation of white pop singers will be based largely on their degree of perceived masculinity or their popularity with men. The select few young crooners who have managed to sufficiently accumulate enough masculine bona fides to mature into mainstream critical acceptance have done so by moving beyond pop and tying their performances to accepted artistic or ethnic traditions or more masculine-coded, often black-associated genres, and by developing their star personae and music to be more macho and less female-friendly.[29] I am not taking the position that change or reinvention itself is problematic—far from it. But the message communicated to young white male singers is that the *only* acceptable way to change is by first distancing themselves from their female fans and embracing masculine-identified styles, genres, and attitudes.

In recent years it has been common for white male singers to ally themselves with black producers and reference musical genres that white male critics and consumers will perceive as "authentically" African American and therefore gender-cool. Justin Timberlake's solo debut, *Justified* (2002), distanced his star image from his days as a member of the boy band 'N Sync by establishing his relationship with the hip-hop producer Timbaland. He was also repeatedly photographed bare-chested, a strategy that simultaneously presented him as an objectifiable male and attested to his newly "masculine" physique (muscles, defined abs). His subsequent releases, *FutureSex/LoveSounds* (2006) and *The 20/20 Experience* (2013), have continued his hip-hop associations and, importantly, featured him in menswear: suits and ties. Critics have praised his "beat-heavy tracks" that "sound worlds away from those of his wildly popular old group, 'N Sync"; they have also used authenticity discourses to validate his shift into critically respectable vocal production: he's "the boy-band graduate who has turned out to be the real deal."[30]

Bieber has become the latest teen crooning idol to attempt to masculinize his image by incorporating masculine-coded musical elements to critically legitimize his stardom. Using rhetoric very similar to that of the *Entertainment Weekly* reviewer from six years earlier, *People's* critic wrote approvingly, "He's already got his beliebers, but Justin Bieber is on a mission to convince the unconverted that he's the real deal on his new album. To that end, he takes a page from another Justin—Timberlake—who went from teen-pop heartthrob with 'N Sync to grown-up artist in his solo career by adding elements of R&B and hip-hop. While transformation isn't complete for Bieber at just 18, he smoothly makes some similar strides into manhood."[31] In the choice between being spoken of as a "girl" or a man, it is not surprising in which direction—as of this writing—Bieber seems to be headed.

The gendered discourse surrounding discussions of crooning singers and their audiences has also exposed, however briefly, the social controls and myths upon which the crooner paradigm has always rested and which have kept it in constant need of renegotiation as the historical context has changed. This cycle of containment has continued for so many decades because the desire for these kinds of voices and the alternative masculinities they represent has never gone away. On the contrary, the most recent developments in U.S. popular culture suggest that a larger paradigmatic shift from merely *exposing* these masculinist norms to *critiquing* and *disrupting* them may at last be under way; these competing discourses—audience desires for long-suppressed queer voices pushing against their cultural gatekeepers—are in many ways more present in the mainstream, as of this writing, than they have been since the 1920s.

NEW DIRECTIONS

What immediately struck me about the photo of *Glee's* Chris Colfer (as Kurt Hummel) and Darren Criss (as Blaine Anderson) from *Entertainment Weekly's* 28 January 2011 cover story (fig. C.2) is that this image might easily have been taken in the late 1920s, but it would have been unlikely to appear in the mainstream press after that time. Attractive young men in collegiate attire, sporting ukuleles or megaphones, singing to each other and to their adoring public in high-pitched voices was a mainstay of 1920s American popular culture. Even the easy, unselfconscious homosociality (and homoerotic possibility) of a boy positioned between another boy's legs dates back to popular images of the 1920s. Although the intention of this image and others from that same article was to illustrate "gay teens on television"—therefore explicitly tying these images to gay identity, as 1920s popular culture did not—the magazine's framing of the story was clearly celebratory. This image of a joyous, ukulele-strumming prep school crooner and the adoring countertenor boy who loves him was part of the increasing variety of exultant images of gay and lesbian people, both fictional characters and newly marrieds, in mainstream American culture of the late 2000s and early 2010s. This political and cultural mainstreaming began in the late 1990s and has gradually helped open up a space for the increased visibility and audibility of high-pitched, gender-queer "boy" singers not seen since Rudy Vallée's heyday.

As I have argued, although the decrease in outright homophobia has not yet had an equivalent effect on the effemiphobia and casual sexism that continue to underpin America's cultural hierarchies, it has put those inequities into greater relief, especially for young people. American youth today have grown up in a less homophobic, more femme-friendly culture and are generally more accepting of gender fluidity and sexual nonnormativity as a result; for example, many more youth identify as transgender, an identity category that critics consistently erase in their discussions of popular culture's youth audiences and that represents one of the many ways young people today are revising decades-old sex and gender binaries and boxes.

These cultural shifts converged with major industrial changes that have foregrounded boy crooning stars and "girl power" princesses in popular culture. The millennial generation grew up with Disney musicals and *Animaniacs*, animated fantasy texts that accessibly mixed pop and Broadway musical scores and in which vocal representation was less bounded by embodied conventions of gender. As tweens and teens they directly participated in, indeed ensured the pop dominance of 'N Sync's and the Backstreet Boys' high-pitched crooners by consuming their songs and voting for their music videos to be played on MTV's highly influential daily television program *Total Request Live* (1998–2008).[32] For many of these adolescents, their intense, formative emotional investments in individual boy band members, within

"They're kind of like the Joanie and Chachi of our generation," says Colfer. "When we made the announcement that Kurt was getting a boyfriend, people went bats---."

FIG. C.2. This photo featuring *Glee*'s Darren Criss as Blaine Anderson and Chris Colfer as Kurt Hummel suggests a return of the 1920s collegian in style and attitude. These attractive young men wear clothes that replicate collegiate styles, are posed with a ukulele (see resemblance to fig. 2.6), and are positioned in a way that reflects the easy, unselfconscious homoeroticism and queer inclusion of the pre-Code era. "Gay Teens on TV," *Entertainment Weekly*, 28 January 2011.

a more receptive cultural climate, contributed to their embrace of gender-queer vocal stars as adults.[33]

While the pop music world largely continues to operate according to the crooner paradigm, audience-driven television programs like *Total Request Live* have emerged as sites of more progressive change in male pop performance. Like radio audiences of the 1920s who marginalized highbrow fare to embrace commercial singers such as Vallée as their stars, television's audiences have made their voices heard by making singing shows the most popular programs for more than a decade. The first of the prime-time pop singing competition shows, *American Idol*, proved an immediate, nationwide hit upon its debut in 2002; its success surprised many in the industry, who realized the broad audience that existed for pop singers previously assumed to be of interest only to teenage girls. *American Idol* inspired thousands of young people to sing in order to emulate their favorites and compete on the program. Vocal risk-taking did not come quickly, however; for many years *American Idol* primarily promoted performers who fit the gendered, raced, and classed industrial categories and cultural assumptions that had existed for decades. As a result, boys with high-pitched or falsetto-heavy voices were often figures of ridicule in the show's audition clips, rarely moving forward, and gay contestants were kept in the closet. But this situation changed decisively when a singer emerged who challenged these categories and, with broad audience support, was able to impact the national vocal landscape. Adam Lambert's competitive season during the winter and spring of 2009 represented a Vallée-like debut in American popular culture, a gender-queer pop/rock voice whose national exposure provoked a similar kind of hopeful euphoria across a broad spectrum of the public.

Lambert's competition performances shattered masculine vocal norms. He combined masculine- and feminine-coded qualities, eroticizing femininity in his performances like a Valentino-style matinee idol; his huge vocal range (including an unapologetic, throbbing falsetto) and emotional intensity impressed the male judges and left the female judges visibly panting. He sang every musical genre equally well, exploding gendered and raced industrial divisions. He also regularly changed his persona, although his signature look was glam-rock (heavy eyeliner and makeup, earrings, theatrical costuming). Lambert announced his gender-queerness in no uncertain terms and yet was discouraged from coming out by the show's producers until after the competition ended.

Early on, the only white, straight male judge—the program's ostensible star personality, Simon Cowell—criticized Lambert for being too "theatrical" (as opposed to "authentic," "real"), which was his preferred coded language for "too gay." But Lambert's charm, easy eroticism, and extraordinary vocal range—honed, ironically, in musical theater—made him so intensely appealing that he was able to transform *Idol*'s previously highly gendered program into a queer space. Cowell was forced, for the first time, to couch any criticism of Lambert as his "personal taste," a remarkable marginalization of masculine norms that lasted for the duration of that season. Lambert's finale performances on 19 May of "Mad World" and "A Change Is Gonna Come," in which the young audience's enraptured voices rose along with his, emphasized fans' identification with his point of view and the desire for change they felt he represented. Lambert suggested an alternative vocal order in American culture: the return of the young, beautiful falsetto king; the queerer Lambert presented himself and the higher he sang, the better the audience liked it. Although he placed second in the final program—reflecting his position as a challenging cultural figure—he was the season's inarguable star and immediately appeared on the cover of *Rolling Stone*. Lambert provided a popular, accessible, genuinely alternative performance of vocal and visual masculinity for an audience eager to embrace him. Most important, his success was not a fluke and opened the door for others.

Indeed Lambert's eager audience did not have long to wait. As the journalist Rae Votta reminded me, the evening of 19 May 2009 was perhaps the single most resonant moment for the gender-queer male voice in American pop history, since it marked both Adam Lambert's final competition performance and the premiere of *Glee* directly following it on the Fox network.[34] *Glee*, a fictional hybrid of comedy, drama, and musical, presented itself as the story of misfits who represented marginalized voices in American culture (notably on a pre-Lambert *Idol*): the "feminine" gay kid, the plump black diva, the Asian goth chick, the Jewish girl who refused a nose job, the disabled kid. For these underdogs, singing was an act of self-determination, a way to help them cope with bullying and fuel their dreams of getting out of their provincial Ohio town.[35] From its beginnings, *Glee* acknowledged the emasculating stigma of male singing (the jocks regularly assert that "singing is gay") while providing a compelling counternarrative that promoted pop singing as liberating and empowering for *straight men* in particular, as well as society at large. Its immediate, immense popularity—the cast eventually broke records set by the Beatles on the *Billboard* charts—demonstrated, as Lambert's popularity had, that the show addressed unmet, profound desires in its audience.

Like Lambert's, the countertenor voice of Chris Colfer (Kurt) was marked as gender-queer from the beginning of *Glee* because of his high pitch and unusually wide range. But the breakout moment for the character and the actor was Kurt's performance of the witch Elphaba's song of liberation, "Defying Gravity" from the musical *Wicked*, in the show's ninth episode. In Colfer's hands, this song became a manifesto for a new generation of queer kids. In *Glee*'s narrative, Kurt protests not being allowed to sing the song because "it is a girl's song" (a plot lifted directly from Colfer's own high school experience). Kurt defies the dominant gender norms that would keep his voice from taking flight, as well as defying the gender binaries of American mainstream culture that would prevent him from playing a girl's role. "Defying Gravity" was the beginning of Kurt/Colfer's gradual erosion and queering of the gendered and sexed norms surrounding popular singing, which *Glee* most often presented through Kurt's reclamation of the diva for boys.

"Defying Gravity" began *Glee*'s practice of having Kurt reinterpret selections from the gay-fan canon of female diva performances, most of them from Hollywood and Broadway. Kurt sings numerous solos in traditionally female vocal ranges, including "Le Jazz Hot" from *Victor/Victoria*, which, the character explains, allows him to "embrace my male and my female sides." Kurt showed that boys did not have to be ashamed of their high voices, that the culturally reviled "feminine" boy could and *should be* his own diva and make these traditionally "girl songs" their own as singers as well as fans. Kurt's embrace of the cultural feminine made him an icon of identification and passion for the girls (and many queer kids) who could sing along with him, in his range, and who shared his feelings of cultural marginalization and his desire for the disruption of gendered social norms and roles.

Colfer himself was a gay adolescent when the show began, only eighteen, with a long history of being bullied in school for his high-pitched voice. His character's development mirrored his own, and in the fall of *Glee*'s second season, Kurt's arc synched up with the national grassroots campaign against gay bullying ("It Gets Better"). Colfer's star discourse emphasized the way, as a youth, he had embraced his own difference by working hard to preserve his countertenor voice. While most adolescent boys are relieved to lose the stigma of femininity associated with a high pitch, Colfer fought to keep his by practicing songs in high ranges; he also preserved the vibrato equally associated with effeminacy, which became one of the most poignant, affecting aspects of Kurt's vocal production.

Kurt/Colfer's immediate success with audiences (he was the most popular actor in the cast's first nationwide tour in 2010) opened the door for further progress in the show's second season, represented by the introduction of Blaine Anderson (Darren Criss), a gay crooning tenor who became Kurt's boyfriend. The very first moment Kurt is introduced to Blaine and the Warblers, the a cappella club at Blaine's all-boys prep school, they are performing a cover of Katy Perry's "Teenage Dream" to a group of equally enthusiastic young men. The song choice is appropriate in that it posits Blaine as a romantic and erotic dream object for Kurt, and it presents the school as a fantasy, aspirational space in which the feminine associations of male singing are both desired and regularly celebrated. "Teenage Dream" was the first *Glee* single to debut at number one on iTunes, immediately making Criss a star, and "Klaine" the show's most popular power couple.

Blaine's character both honored and reimagined the crooner for the new millennium. As this book demonstrates, the pop crooner has been operating both in the commercial mainstream and on the fringes of gender normativity for decades and has been culturally stigmatized because of both associations. But Blaine is first introduced in a boys' school where normative American gender expectations and roles have been suspended and gender hierarchies largely reversed. *Glee* celebrated the crooner for the very qualities that masculinist America did not: his alignment with the cultural feminine through his preference for romantic songs and commercial pop, his status as an erotic object for male and female audiences, his beauty and sensitivity, his emotional openness and transparency. And the producers cast an actor, Darren Criss, whose star persona emphasized and extended these same qualities to a remarkable degree. Blaine/Criss retains the sincerity of the crooner even as he performs beyond the boundaries of a fixed or normative gender identity. Criss himself occupies queer cultural space in that he identifies as straight but plays gay, represents a men's grooming company, writes and performs songs from female as well as male points of view, identifies as a fan and champions "feminine" mass culture and female audiences, loves his mother (calling out "I love you, Mom!" during performances), and is more than happy to be an erotic object for both sexes.

Just as Kurt turned his Blaine fantasy into a reality, *Glee* effectively realized its own revision of male singing in a multitude of scenes that were equally new to American popular culture: young men unironically singing pop songs to other young men, both gay and straight; teen boys falling in love with other boys as they sing to them; boys singing pop songs without changing the lyrics from "him" to "her" to accommodate gender norms; boys regularly singing songs associated with female divas; and the restoration and celebration of the countertenor sound and singer.[36] Colfer's rapturous countertenor and Criss's velvety crooner became *Glee*'s most popular characters, and they were celebrated as role models for a new order of male vocal performers.

Glee's cultural position as a challenge to traditional gender hierarchies was not without detractors, and effemiphobia was central to such critiques. Media coverage of Colfer and Criss remained tellingly distinct based on the actors' affirmed sexual identities, their vocal normativity, and their gender presentations. On social media sites, Kurt/Colfer's countertenor voice became a site of both euphoria and anxiety. Many male auditors, both gay- and straight-identified, objected to the gender fluidity and ambiguity of his voice; Colfer's "feminine" register was always a prominent thread in discussions on websites ranging from YouTube to popular gay-specific blogs such as Towleroad, and his perceived femininity was frequently framed as a problem ("He's got a good voice, but he sings like a girl" or "He's the worst gay stereotype"). Colfer's deviations from masculine vocal norms also spurred dismissive reactions to his "inauthentic" style and allegations of Auto-Tuning, as well as bewilderment regarding his intense popularity with young women. In a *New York Times* profile of Colfer, the author declared himself mystified as to the attraction; while the paper of record has little trouble understanding why gay men might love female divas, it has yet to appreciate or validate cross-gender identification and love when it is directed at "feminine" or gay-identified boys and comes from young women.[37]

In contrast, Criss's more gender-normative appearance and straight identity make his croony tenor, adoring female fandom, and painted nails more acceptable in a masculinist culture.[38] As the media commentator Racheline Maltese wrote on her Tumblr when comparing press coverage of Colfer and Criss, "When the screaming girls get talked about re: Criss, the press frames that as the burden of being a heartthrob star. . . . [However] re: Colfer, there's often an implication that those girls don't count, that he can't be a mainstream heartthrob, and that he's somehow failing at being a gay role model because he's not surrounded by screaming queer teen boys."[39]

Yet the naysayers only reinforced Colfer and Criss's cultural significance, both as characters and as stars, to an international fandom that valued their gender fluidity and appreciated their devotion to their female fans. In particular, fans adore Kurt's countertenor voice and Blaine's crooning devotion to him; this gendered inversion in which the more normatively masculine male worships the culturally feminized male ("Kurt deserves Blaine singing to him") is a key aspect of fan pleasure in this pairing and an example of fandom as an act of social criticism. As I noted in the introduction to this book, women's queer fan affect is rarely noted or valued for the culturally challenging, *feminist* act it is. Like Vallée's fans from the 1920s, these fans reflect the complex nexus of devotions involving identification, fantasy, and many kinds of love—erotic, romantic, rapturous, grateful, proud, often experienced simultaneously—that have fueled countless social media sites, thousands of fan fictions and art, and many other kinds of cultural production worldwide.[40] It is noteworthy that, in the more than eighty years since Vallée's popularity, female fans still gravitate toward more feminine-friendly male performers, suggesting the continued narrowness and oppressiveness of normative masculinity, and they employ rhetoric similar to Vallée fans when describing ecstatic reactions: they talk of falling in love; praise the beauty of their idol's "angelic" voice; shake, shiver, and weep compulsively; signify their virtual (or actual) orgasms listening to his voice with the term *eargasms*; and indicate the active nature of their desire by claiming to repeatedly "rape the replay button."[41]

Criss and Colfer's popularity coincided with the advent of social media sites such as Tumblr and Twitter, which have made more visible the diversity and complexity of their audiences. Although most print-media reviews of their performances cite the amorphous "teen girl" fans without further differentiation, such monolithic assessments are much less easy to defend in the age of social media, which readily reveals a diverse fandom composed of people of all ages, non-Americans, people of color, ethnic and religious minorities, and many people who identify across a broad range of sex and gender identities, including queer, transgender, lesbian, gay, bisexual, and panromantic. Likewise, fan production has made clear the variety of nonnormative pleasures and fantasies that the Colfer and Criss fandom engenders and supports, reflecting the cultural and political value for queers, for feminists, and for gender outsiders of this fandom's championing of the still-demonized feminine boy and his boyish lover.

The success of Lambert, Colfer, and Criss and of singing television programs generally has led to greater vocal variety on American screens. *The Voice* debuted in 2011 on NBC, and its massive success (it eclipsed *Idol*) has given a great deal of exposure to singers who expressly do not fall into essentializing, commodified, gendered and raced vocal categories. *The Voice*'s hook is its blind auditions, in which four industry stars (referred to as "coaches") determine the singers' promise by the quality of their voices alone. This portion of the program proved most popular with viewers, who enjoyed the surprised reactions of the coaches to a white boy from Nebraska who sang excellent rhythm and blues ("I thought you would be black!") or boys who "sing like girls." By the third cycle of the show, however, the "freak" novelty effect began to wear off as it became increasingly clear to producers that the "freak" singer was in fact *not* uncommon at all but simply representative of a diverse, porous American vocal culture otherwise rarely acknowledged on a national mass-media platform. *The Voice*'s contestants subvert and collapse boundaries of genre, age, race, class, gender, ethnicity, region, and nation that have been central to the American music industry since the 1920s; for example, Cody Belew, a white, queerly marked, country pop contestant impressed the coaches with his version of Dolly Parton's hit "Jolene"—which he performed without changing the pronouns—and confessed that vocally he feels "like the reincarnation of an old black woman."[42]

Singing programs such as *The Voice* thus offer hope that the long-entrenched gendered and racial norms for popular voices can eventually be eroded. For example, the show's coaches regard high-pitched male performers as valuable artistic *and* commercial commodities and do not intend to be insulting when they describe them as "singing like a girl" (unlike the press descriptions of Bieber as a "girl"). Adam Levine, a *Voice* coach and pop idol, became famous for his falsetto and frequently praises male singers who perform it well. *The Voice* is evidence of a paradigmatic shift away from effemiphobia and opens up a space for developing new ways of talking about voices in popular culture. It is very clear from *The Voice*, however, that even the show's industry veterans don't know how to describe a high-pitched male voice without that binary characterization because such voices are still so rare in American popular culture. Both they—and we—need to develop and incorporate new ways of describing a vocal production that moves past these long-established, oppressive social and industrial divides.

AMONG THE MANY recent crooning performances that have seemed to evoke and pay tribute to an earlier vocal era, one in particular has been especially moving and resonant for me. After early crooners were banned from most visual media in the 1930s, many of them went on to provide voices for Disney musicals. The most famous of these was Cliff Edwards, who sang the Oscar-winning song "When You Wish upon a Star" in *Pinocchio* (1940) as Pinocchio's friend and "conscience" Jiminy Cricket.[43] Edwards's weary but hopeful delivery of this song rises and ends on a high B ("your dreams come true") that hangs in the air and then fades away rather than coming to rest, echoing the 1920s crooning style of a "feminine ending" that finishes on an ascending rather than a descending note to suggest unmet longing. Edwards was going through hard times when he recorded this song, and you can hear it in the fatigue of his voice, the effort the song costs him to control his affecting quick vibrato throughout. For me, that fatigue mirrors the cultural marginalization of early crooners, voices that were largely lost to the public when the new norms took hold. The great success of "When You Wish upon a Star" suggests not only that the general public remembered Edwards the star but that their love for this high-pitched, yearning male voice continued despite the repressions of the 1930s. Like so many crooning pop songs, it is inherently democratic ("makes no difference who you are") and yet, at the same time, its lyrics imply that its listeners' desires have had to remain "secret" for some reason, privately rather than publicly acknowledged or perhaps even completely unexpressed. Edwards's song is validation for those listeners and a glinting of hope.

Glee's crooner Darren Criss has recently revived the song "When You Wish upon a Star," making it his signature song at the end of his concerts, when he is spent and blissed out—his eyes often closed, head back, mouth open, in the iconic romantic crooner pose.[44] Criss considers himself part of the "Disney generation," someone who grew up singing and playing songs from Disney musicals, and this song was formative for him. For me, his choice of this song, and his performance of it at major public events, including President Barack Obama's 2012 inaugural ball, indicates that the queer crooning voice that Edwards and others were forced to hide for years behind animated characters can finally be performed and celebrated again, unmediated, for an audience that never went away. Criss, an unusually optimistic youth, notably follows the high falsetto ending note of the song with a descending, reassuring one in his warm tenor, as if to affirm that the crooner's "secret longings"—and those of his audience, who also need to believe that change is possible—will finally be publicly acknowledged, appreciated, and, hopefully, fulfilled. "If your heart is in your dream / no request is too extreme." All we need to do is keep wishing upon our crooning stars.

NOTES

INTRODUCTION

1. Gilbert Swan, "The Voice of New York Is Effeminate," *Baltimore (MD) Post* (syndicated), 11 December 1931, Vallée Scrapbooks, vol. 33, Rudy Vallée Collection, American Radio Archives, Thousand Oaks Library, Thousand Oaks, California (hereafter RVC). A word about this book's organization: the first section of the introduction tells the story of this era chronologically, as do the chapters; the successive sections of the introduction and the conclusion lay out the book's larger scholarly and historical contexts.

2. *Oxford English Dictionary* online, accessed 12 September 2012.

3. Susman, *Culture as History*, 159.

4. I use the term *homosexual* throughout this study because it is the historical term used to describe both male and female sexual deviants at the time and is therefore the most inclusive term; it also underlines the importance of the heterosexual/homosexual binary that became entrenched during these years and was specifically used to stigmatize and pathologize crooners. My use of the word *queer* is less historically specific, and I employ it primarily to indicate gender and sexual behavior that would have been considered nonnormative or "between" at the time or since, depending on the audience. Although much of 1920s popular culture could be described by this term, such perceptions varied a great deal by social position, and therefore performances that would have seemed unobjectionable to mass audiences and young people would often have been considered nonnormative and objectionable to the upper classes (and increasingly objectionable to many in the middle classes, as this book describes).

5. Scholarly work on American popular voices has been largely interdisciplinary but most prevalent in musicology, film, radio, and sound studies. See, for example, Lawrence, *Echo and Narcissus*; Hilmes, *Radio Voices*; Douglas, *Listening In*; Loviglio and Hilmes, *The Radio Reader*; Smith, *Vocal Tracks*; Weheliye, *Phonographies*; Sterne, *The Audible Past*. Since I began this project more work specifically addressing pop vocal masculinity has emerged, most prominently Jarman-Ivins, *Oh Boy!*; see also Royster, *Sounding Like a No-No*; McClary, "Soprano Masculinities"; Harrison et al., *Perspectives on Male Singing*. Neverthe-

less, pop stars are international commodities, and most scholarly work on this subject has been and is still produced by those working outside of the United States. Popular criticism has also been a key site of cultural analysis regarding pop star vocals generally; see, for example, Wilson's remarkable study *Let's Talk about Love: A Journey to the End of Taste*.

6. In popular culture studies the most comprehensive study of whiteness remains Richard Dyer's *White*, which focuses on visual culture.

7. America's early crooners have since the 1930s been more popular with and written about by Canadian, European, and Australian consumers and scholars. See, for example, Whitcomb, "The Coming of the Crooners," 1–49; David Brackett, "Family Values in Music? Billie Holiday and Bing Crosby's 'I'll Be Seeing You,'" in *Interpreting Popular Music*; Doyle, "From 'My Blue Heaven' to 'Race with the Devil'"; Stanfield, *Horse Opera* and *Body and Soul*. Notable exceptions include Thomas A. DeLong, a radio historian who covered the anxiety over radio crooners in *The Mighty Music Box*, 67–88; Michael Pitts and Frank Hoffman, *The Rise of the Crooners*, a valuable survey of early crooners; and the musician and writer Lenny Kaye's lovely novelistic appreciation of early crooners, most prominently Russ Columbo, in *You Call It Madness*. The advent of YouTube has made these early singers' recordings much more accessible than they were when I first began this project.

8. There are many intriguing cultural parallels between the gender-transgressive voices and the personae of opera's castrato stars and radio's romantic crooners, not least of which is the strong backlash against both groups, which resulted in a focus on more normatively "masculine" singing among the upper classes more than a century before similar norms were imposed on crooning's mass audience. See Purvis, *Masculinity in Opera*, especially essays by McClary and Jarman; Senelick, *The Changing Room*, 193–96.

9. This tremendous variety in New York City entertainments in 1930–31 is vividly described in Shaw, *Nightlife*.

10. Waters and Samuels, *His Eye Is on the Sparrow*, 73.

11. See Radano, *Lying Up a Nation*; Miller, *Segregating Sounds*. See also the music historian Elijah Wald's *Escaping the Delta*.

12. "Oakland Wins Over Richman in Contest," *Variety*, 23 December 1925, 4. Oakland's ethnic appeal as a well-known Irish singer and former minstrel put him over the top; the paper notes he was "strongly supported by the police."

13. Frith, "Pop Music," 97–98.

14. *Variety* regularly used *pop* as a descriptor for cheap, lowbrow entertainment in the early and mid-1920s ("pop priced"), most frequently in relation to small-time vaudeville theaters ("pop vaudeville") but also in relation to music ("pop number," "pop blues," "pop ballad"). See, for example, references to "pop vaudeville" and "pop jazz tunes," *Variety*, 14 January 1925, 23, 30, 45, and "pop priced record," *Variety*, 11 February 1925, 7. Therefore when *Variety* referred to the song plugger and early crooner Jack Smith as a "pop song salesman" in its review of his debut recording in 1925, it was underlining his exclusively commercial intent ("Disk Review: Jack Smith," *Variety*, 9 December 1925, 51). Over the next year, however, the term would begin to be employed more specifically to refer to crooning

performances of popular love songs, and by Vallée's time it would be exclusively used as a descriptor for the nascent music genre. On the growing popularity of the "pop" sound by early crooners, see *Variety*, 8 December 1926, 53.

15. Gunning, "The Cinema of Attraction," 229–35, famously argues for a move from spectacle to narrative-based content in early cinema's aesthetics. Audio culture in the 1920s similarly shifts from vocal virtuosity (wonder) to sincere narrative (affect) as the dominant style of singing performance and audience response. Smith, *Vocal Tracks*, 81–162, also details the way the advent of the microphone and its intimacy changed vocal acting styles.

16. See Studlar, *This Mad Masquerade*; Anderson, *Twilight of the Idols*; Nash, *Geraldine Farrar*.

17. My discussion of the social construction of whiteness during this period owes much to Carter, *The Heart of Whiteness*, and Bederman, *Manliness and Civilization*.

18. A note on my use of *Variety*: I rely on *Variety* chiefly for historical information regarding players, performance styles, audience tastes, and critical standards. I reviewed all issues in their entirety between 1925 and 1929 and many single issues before and after those years. The well-known hyperbolic tendency of its writers was useful in spotting trends, as *Variety* invariably identified an act's approach as "new" when it became popular and commercially profitable, not when it originated.

19. Sterne, *The Audible Past*, 9; Thompson, *The Soundscape of Modernity*. Such gendered discourses regarding American technology were not new; see Marvin, *When Old Technologies Were New*.

20. *Oxford English Dictionary* online.

21. See Radano, *Lying Up a Nation*, 168–73. Crooning sounds fit very well into the minstrels' repertoire, which was heavily influenced by folk music, particularly the Irish melodies Thomas Moore first popularized in the early nineteenth century and which, along with the songs of Stephen Foster, became the most popular songs of the century.

22. Hamm, *Yesterdays*, 50.

23. Although individual affective responses to music are often multiple and simultaneous (romantic *and* spiritual, etc.), the expressive language available to describe them varies according to social and historical contexts. For a nuanced discussion of these changing affective frames in the nineteenth century United States, especially among the middle classes, see Cavicchi, *Listening and Longing*.

24. Spaeth, *A History of Popular Music in America*, 261.

25. See McClary, "Same as It Ever Was," 29–40.

26. The American Academy of Teachers in Singing, "Reasons for Studying Singing." See also Koestenbaum's discussion of the history of racism and homophobia in early singing manuals, *The Queen's Throat*, 167–75.

27. Quoted in Cooke, *Great Singers on the Art of Singing*, 218.

28. I am making a distinction between trained singers who performed primarily classical music according to middle-class singing directives and singers who may or may not have had some training but who largely performed popular songs in venues where the

middle classes were the highest (rather than the lowest) audience rank. While there was a great deal of crossover in public entertainment (opera stars performing in vaudeville, for example), these standards of evaluation were broadly accepted.

29. Martin Hansen of Decatur, Illinois, first-prize winner in the *Radio Revue*'s contest for the best letter explaining Rudy Vallée's popularity. "Mere Man Wins First Prize in Rudy Vallée Contest," *Radio Revue*, January 1930, 27/47, Vallée Scrapbooks, vol. 167, RVC.

30. Letter to Rudy Vallée from a remarkable album sent to him by blind listeners, edited and put into Braille by his blind fan Margaret Long, bound volume, 1934, RVC.

31. For discussions of modernity's masculinist turn in the 1920s across high and popular culture, see, for example, Huyssen, *After the Great Divide*; Jacobs, *The Decline of Sentiment*; Douglas, *Terrible Honesty*; Oja, *Making Music Modern*; Penner, *Pinks, Pansies and Punks*; Hatch, *Shirley Temple and the Performance of Girlhood*; Marchand, *Advertising the American Dream*. Modernity, both then and now, is a highly contested term that was often employed to mean anything new, urban, or technological; women's enfranchisement and their sexual expression, for example, were considered modern developments. Certainly the tensions over modern romantic crooning reflected the larger cultural tensions and contradictions surrounding the use of the term. For a nuanced discussion of gender and modernity, see Felski, *The Gender of Modernity*.

32. Radano, *Lying Up a Nation*, 2; Miller, *Segregating Sounds*, 2, chapters 6 and 7. The music industry also presented genres as fixed when they were in fact constantly shifting according to market trends and political changes; Wald, *Escaping the Delta*, 3–42, refers to blues music as "working class pop music," which underlines the way commercial music and its performers were racially segregated but performed similar music.

33. Anderson, *Twilight of the Idols*, chapters 3 and 4.

34. Jacobson, *Whiteness of a Different Color*, 8. Jacobson makes the point that the word *race*, not *ethnicity*, was used to distinguish groups like Italians and Irish at the time. I have generally used *ethnicity* to avoid confusion. For more about these distinctions, see Heap, *Slumming*; Roediger, *Working towards Whiteness*; McGreevey, *Parish Boundaries*.

35. Most "star" crooners in the pre–World War II period were Irish, Italian, German, or southern or western working-class whites. After World War II, however, Jewish and African American star crooners emerged as well, such as Eddie Fisher, Mel Tormé, Nat King Cole, and Johnny Mathis.

36. See Carter, *The Heart of Whiteness*, 6, chapter 2; Jacobson, *Whiteness of a Different Color*, 82–87; Kline, *Building a Better Race*; Simmons, *Making Marriage Modern*. While some social scientists and physicians were genuinely invested in promoting women's sexual equality and pleasure, their more progressive views were marginalized in marriage discourses by the mid-1930s. See Terry, *An American Obsession*.

37. Marchand, *Advertising the American Dream*, 108–10.

38. For a more detailed discussion of the relationship between the human sciences—psychology, sociology, and anthropology—and sexual identity and social deviance in the 1920s, see Anderson, *Twilight of the Idols*; Carter, *The Heart of Whiteness*; Terry, *An American*

Obsession. Douglas, *Terrible Honesty*, 122–55, notes the prominence of Freud as explanatory discourse generally for the most influential moderns of the 1920s.

39. Editor, "'Crooning' Caustically Stigmatized by Majority of Twenty Musical Notables in Lively Symposium," *Musical America*, 25 May 1932, 8–9, Vallée Scrapbooks, vol. 168, RVC.

40. O'Leary, *To Die For*, 242.

41. Blake, *How New York Became American*, 131, describes how New York neighborhoods were newly balkanized in the wake of the intensified nationalism, and their citizens promoted as separate identity groups—recognizable by specific physical traits as well as cultural practices—in travel literature for tourists.

42. Review of Bing Crosby's film *Too Much Harmony* (Paramount, 1933), *Newsweek*, 30 September 1933, 47.

43. Sam Costa, quoted in Friedwald, *Jazz Singing*, 9.

44. For a detailed discussion of the effects of the Production Code on Hollywood's gays and lesbians, see Mann, *Behind the Screen*, 121–60.

45. Giddins, *Bing Crosby*, 7.

46. Quotes from Friedwald, *Jazz Singing*, 30–53; Giddins, *Bing Crosby*, 7. See also Pleasants, *The Great American Popular Singers*; Giddins, *Riding on a Blue Note*; Giddins, preface to *Call Me Lucky*; Lees, "The Sinatra Effect," in *Singers and the Song*; Hemming and Hajdu, *Discovering Great Singers of Classic Pop*, 9.

47. See, most prominently, Ann Douglas's assessment of crooners, *Terrible Honesty*, 360–61.

48. Hubbs, *Rednecks, Queers, and Country Music*, argues that country music has been likewise denigrated by cultural elites as a way of policing the working classes and its "queer-working class alliance" similarly erased.

49. It is not unusual that so many people in crooning's mass audience should reject the new psychosexual politics of the upper and middle classes. The internalization of and adherence to gender and sexual norms among working-class people especially has always been uneven. Chauncey, *Gay New York*, 76–86, notes, for example, that many Irish and Italian men did not fully internalize the concept of exclusive sexual binaries until after World War II.

50. *New York News*, 15 January 1932, Vallée Scrapbooks, vol. 59, RVC.

51. Simmons, *Making Marriage Modern*, 200–209. See also Fass, *The Damned and the Beautiful*, 78–83.

52. McGovern, *Sold American*, 15.

53. Julie W., Chattanooga, 8 February 1931, Correspondence: Fan Mail, RVC.

54. For discussions of affect theory, see, for example, Gregg and Seigworth, *The Affect Theory Reader*, especially the introduction, 1–25.

55. Lawrence Grossberg, "Affect's Future," in Gregg and Seigworth, *The Affect Theory Reader*, 327. For a relevant study of queer fan affect, see Bennett, "Flaming the Fans."

56. Butler, *Undoing Gender*, 29.

57. Ehrenreich et al., "Beatlemania," 524. See also Douglas, *Where the Girls Are*. For more on the feminist and queer politics of female pop audiences, see Coates, "(R)evolution Now?," 50–51; Railton, "The Gendered Carnival of Pop"; Wald, "'I Want It That Way'"; Halberstam, *In a Queer Time and Place*, 174–79.

58. I employ the term *effemiphobia* (*effeminaphobia* is equally correct) throughout this study to indicate the specific derogatory, antifeminine, sexist, and homophobic character of the objections to male crooners and pop idols (both then and now). This term is based in *effeminate*, a pejorative descriptor for men who exhibit qualities associated with women (such as "weakness, softness, delicacy") and are therefore considered "unmanly" (*Oxford English Dictionary* online). *Effemiphobia* is not, as yet, a widely employed term. I am defining it broadly to mean "fear of effeminacy in male-identified persons" of whatever sexual preference, which is more applicable to this study. Although the ideological connection between perceived femininity in males and homosexuality is at the core of this book, as this study also shows, this cultural bias has been widely used to police all male behavior since the 1930s. The conclusion of this book traces the persistent effemiphobia in current U.S. culture. Indeed, homosexuality's growing acceptability has put effemiphobia's related roots in sexism and classism—most manifest in gendered cultural hierarchies of "taste"—into greater relief. See Connell, "The Social Organization of Masculinity."

One PUTTING OVER A SONG

1. Sheet music, "Crooning to the Baby," lyrics by Mark Thyme, music by Claud Nugent (London: Francis, Day and Hunter, 1884).

2. Sheet music, "In My Merry Oldsmobile," lyrics by Vincent Bryan, music by Gus Edwards (New York: M. Witmark and Sons, 1905).

3. Radano, *Lying Up a Nation*, 2.

4. See Levine, *Highbrow/Lowbrow*; Rabinovitz, *For the Love of Pleasure*; Peiss, *Cheap Amusements*; Erenberg, *Steppin' Out*; Nasaw, *Going Out*; Allen, *Horrible Prettiness*; Kibler, *Rank Ladies*; Stamp, *Movie-Struck Girls*; Butsch, *The Making of American Audiences*; Brown, *Babylon Girls*; Rodger, *Champagne Charlie and Pretty Jemima*.

5. Rogin, *Blackface, White Noise*, 102; Roediger, *The Wages of Whiteness*, 117.

6. Lott, *Love and Theft*, 156; Allen, *Horrible Prettiness*, 48–50. Minstrels were regarded with particular disdain by the more educated classes, an estimation that crossed racial lines; see Handy, *Father of the Blues*, 10–11, 33.

7. Toll, "Social Commentary in Late Nineteenth-Century White Minstrels" and *Blacking Up*.

8. Hamm, *Yesterdays*, 136–39.

9. Saxton, "Blackface Minstrelsy," 67–85.

10. Vinson, *The Voices That Are Gone*, 200–208; Toll, "Social Commentary in Late Nineteenth-Century White Minstrels," 86–110; Hamm, *Yesterdays*, 254.

11. Sheet music, "Carry Me Back to Old Virginny," lyrics and music by James Bland (Boston: Oliver Ditson, 1906). Originally published 1878.

12. Toll, "Social Commentary in Late Nineteenth-Century White Minstrelsy," 103–4.

13. *Oxford English Dictionary* online; McElya, *Clinging to Mammy*, 4–8.

14. *Oxford English Dictionary* online; Robert Burns: "Let se how ye croyne. Can ye bark at the mone?"

15. Radano, *Lying Up a Nation*, 233. See also Hamm, *Irving Berlin*, 70–76.

16. David Pilgrim, "The Mammy Caricature," Jim Crow Museum of Racist Memorabilia, October 2000, edited 2012, http://www.ferris.edu/jimcrow/mammies/. See also Turner, *Ceramic Uncles and Celluloid Mammies*, 43–49; McElya, *Clinging to Mammy*.

17. Sheet music, "The Darkies Cradle Song," lyrics by H. G. Wheeler, music by J. W. Wheeler (Boston: BF Wood, 1895); sheet music, "Kentucky Babe," lyrics by Richard Henry Buck, music by Adam Geibel (Boston: White-Smith, 1897).

18. The mammy characters in Harriet Beecher Stowe's *Uncle Tom's Cabin* (255–83) are often seen as the basis of the iconic mammy, but minstrels revised these characters in the postbellum era to serve their points of view rather than Stowe's abolitionist agenda.

19. See Turner, *Ceramic Uncles and Celluloid Mammies*, 45–49; McElya, *Clinging to Mammy*, 15–37; and, more generally, Manring, *Slave in a Box*.

20. Sheet music, "Little Alabama Coon," lyrics and music by Hattie Starr (New York: Willis Woodward, 1893).

21. Sheet music, "Sleep L'il Chile Go Sleep: A Pathetic Mammy Song," lyrics by G. V. Hobart, music by Frank L. Bristow (Cincinnati, OH: Geo R. Jennings, 1900).

22. Sheet music, "Mammy's Little Alligator Bait," lyrics by Sidney Perrin, music by Henry Wise (Milwaukee, WI: Charles K. Harris, 1899).

23. For Rosamond Johnson's decision, see Vinson, *The Voices That Are Gone*, 235. Miller, *Segregating Sounds*, 129–36, details a similar deliberate "softening" of the coon song and the turn toward more romantic content by the black songwriter Bob Cole, who often collaborated with Johnson and his brother James. Regarding black protests against coon songs by black songwriters, see Eugene Levy, *James Weldon Johnson*, quoted in Riis, *Just before Jazz*, 53. For a discussion of black songwriters' incorporation of nonracist street slang and vernacular language, see Jasen and Jones, "The First Black Composers on Broadway," in *Spreadin' Rhythm Around*.

24. On William and Walker's employment of authenticity discourses, see Krasner, "The Real Thing," 99–123.

25. Sheet music, "Mammy's Little Pumpkin Colored Coons," lyrics and music by Sidney Perrin and George Hillman (New York: M. Witmark and Sons, 1897).

26. See, for example, discussion of the white singer Artie Hall in Abbott and Seroff, *Ragged but Right*, 12; see also Kibler, *Rank Ladies*, 111–42; McElya, *Clinging to Mammy*, 38–73.

27. Quoted in Abbott and Seroff, *Ragged but Right*, 23. See Brooks's discussion of the complex vocal styles of black female minstrel and nascent blues performers in "'The Voice Which Is Not One,'" 47–49.

28. Charles Hamm has famously asserted, "Tin Pan Alley did not draw on traditional music — it created traditional music" (*Yesterdays*, 325). For histories of Tin Pan Alley, see Suisman, *Selling Sounds*; Ewen, *The Life and Death of Tin Pan Alley*; Goldberg, *Tin Pan Alley*; Jansen, *Tin Pan Alley*; Starr and Waterman, *American Popular Music*, chapters 2–4; Hamm, *Yesterdays*, chapters 13–14. See also the memoirs of two Tin Pan Alley publishers: Marks, *They All Sang*; Witmark and Goldberg, *The Story of the House of Witmark*.

29. The wholesale value of sheet music more than tripled between 1890 and 1909. Sales of parlor pianos and player pianos also jumped during the turn of the century. Singing around the piano became a national pastime in middle-class (and aspiring middle-class) homes, although it is worth noting that New York City itself did not see the same boom, since more of its population generally went out for entertainment. Sanjek, *Pennies from Heaven*, 22–23; Suisman, *Selling Sounds*, 92; Witmark and Goldberg, *The Story of the House of Witmark*, 124.

30. Melnick, "Tin Pan Alley and the Black Jewish Nation," 29; Tawa, *Supremely American*, 4–5; Goldberg, *Tin Pan Alley*; Hamm, *Yesterdays*, chapter 14.

31. Suisman, *Selling Sounds*, 48–50; Hamm, *Yesterdays*, 290; Tawa, *Supremely American*, 15–18.

32. Marks, *They All Sang*, 176. By 1910 there were more than a million Jewish people in New York City, making up more than a quarter of the population. Hamm, *Yesterdays*, 328.

33. Witmark and Goldberg, *The Story of the House of Witmark*, 68.

34. Radano, *Lying Up a Nation*, 271–72, chapter 5.

35. Tawa, *Supremely American*, chapter 1; Melnick, "Tin Pan Alley and the Black Jewish Nation," 37; Mooney, "Songs, Singers, and Society"; Spaeth, *A History of Popular Music in America*.

36. Sheet music, "Mammy's Angel Chile: A Pickaninny Croon," lyrics and music by J. R. Shannon (Detroit: Grinnell Brothers, 1911).

37. Sheet music, "Mammy's Little Sugar Plum," lyrics and music by Benny Davis and Ernie Erdman (New York: Jerome H. Remick, 1920).

38. For Gillham and Anderson, see Abbott and Seroff, *Ragged but Right*, 23, 243. Sophie Tucker helped popularize "Mammy's Chocolate Soldier" (Mitchell and Gottler); her picture is on the sheet music's cover published by Waterson, Berlin and Snyder, 1918. Adele Rowland continued to sing crooning songs through the 1920s; her later vaudeville character act, "Stories in Song" (1928), is included on *The Jazz Singer Deluxe Edition* DVD (2007).

39. Jasen and Jones, *Spreadin' Rhythm Around*, 184, 190. Black performers frequently took on Irish accents and sang Irish songs. See also Abbott and Seroff, *Ragged but Right*, 322–23; Radano, *Lying Up a Nation*, 5n14. Sheet music, "Mammy O' Mine," lyrics by William Tracey, music by Maceo Pinkard (New York: Shapiro, Bernstein, 1919).

40. Sheet music, "I'd Love to Fall Asleep and Wake Up in My Mammy's Arms," lyrics by Sam M. Lewis and Joe Young, music by Fred E. Ahlert (New York: Waterson, Berlin and Snyder, 1920).

41. Hamm, *Irving Berlin*, 54–55, chapters 1 and 4 generally.

42. In their extant 1920s Movietone and Vitaphone film performances, the duo Gus Van and Joe Schenck communicate a variety of ethnic and racial types (Chinese, Italian, Jewish, African American, and Irish) through small changes in their vocalizing and gestures. See *Metro Movietone Revue I* (1929); *Van and Schenck: The Pennant Winning Battery of Songland* (1926) (on *The Jazz Singer Deluxe Edition* DVD).

43. Some historians have argued that ethnic stereotypes in popular songs diffused tensions, exposed social oppression, and aided in assimilation; these positive aspects primarily benefited white-identified groups, however, since African Americans and Asian immigrants were often not even permitted in the audience. See discussions in Hamm, *Irving Berlin*, 31. Some performers of color worked within the dominant caricatures of their racialized group to challenge or complicate their meanings. See Chude-Sokei, *The Last Darky*; Moon, *Yellowface*, chapter 6. Successful "coon-shouters" such as Bessie Smith and Sophie Tucker shifted into blues styles and "hot" music when the word *coon* went out of style, but they retained the strong female point of view and sexually explicit material of coon songs. See Abbott and Seroff, *Ragged but Right*, 22; Erenberg, *Steppin' Out*, 193–99.

44. Hamm, *Irving Berlin*, 166.

45. Sheet music, "Winter Garden Glide," lyrics and music by Henry J. Volz (New York: E. J. Murray, 1916). "Crooning Lullabies," lyrics by Al Dubin and Herman W. Weise, music by William F. Caesar (New York: M. Witmark and Sons, 1921).

46. This transition in the use of the word *croon* was also evident in the acoustic recording career of the era's most prolific star, Billy Murray (1877–1954). Murray started his career in blackface, traveling with minstrel troupes, but he became a recording star singing every kind of popular song from 1905 to 1925, including many romantic crooning songs and "In My Merry Oldsmobile." Gracyk, "Billy Murray," in *Popular American Recording Pioneers*, 233–50; Hoffman et al., *Billy Murray*.

47. Sheet music, "Bring Me a Ring in the Spring," lyrics and music by Irving Berlin (New York: Ted Snyder, 1911).

48. Jennings, *Theatrical and Circus Life*, 374.

49. On vaudeville, see Nasaw, *Going Out*, chapter 3; Snyder, *The Voice of the City*, especially chapters 2 and 4; Kibler, *Rank Ladies*, especially 46–54; Glenn, *Female Spectacle*; Butsch, *The Making of American Audiences*, chapters 7–8; Lewis, *From Traveling Show to Vaudeville*; Caffin, *Vaudeville*; Laurie, *Vaudeville*; Gilbert, *American Vaudeville*.

50. The designation *feminine tastes* came into use as women became the new target audience for popular culture and was regularly employed by media trade papers to signify the female sex through the 1930s.

51. Women were often barred from public singing by religious and secular laws. See "Singing," "Castrato," "Jewish Music," and "Anglican and Episcopalian Church Music," in Stanley, *The New Grove Dictionary of Music and Musicians*; Slobin, *Chosen Voices*, 119. For a detailed discussion of men playing women's parts in opera (and the reverse), see Senelick, *The Changing Room*, 189–205, 216–27.

52. On Thackeray, see Lott, *Love and Theft*, 187; on Twain, see Saxton, "Blackface Minstrelsy," 82. Both authors deemphasize the importance of European-derived sentimental music to male audiences.

53. Senelick, *The Changing Room*, 298–300.

54. Rabinovitz, *For the Love of Pleasure*, 6; Allen, *Horrible Prettiness*, 50. The very presence of a lone woman could mark an entire establishment as disreputable well into the 1880s and 1890s.

55. Chesnut, quoted in Radano, *Lying Up a Nation*, 183. For more on the changing language and frameworks for descriptions of musical affect in the nineteenth century, see Cavicchi, *Listening and Longing*.

56. Marks, *They All Sang*, 60–68. For a contrasting view of this lifestyle, see Senelick, *The Changing Room*, 297–302. Because adolescent boys' voices were so valuable, their exclusive training was common across social groups. Young Jewish meshoyer (choirboys), for example, were apprenticed from young ages by the Hazzan (cantor) and also led similarly "itinerant lifestyles" within homosocial environments. Slobin, *Chosen Voices*, 33–34.

57. Jennings, *Theatrical and Circus Life*, 371.

58. Toll, *On with the Show*, 242–44; Senelick, *The Changing Room*, 298, 300–302.

59. Jennings, *Theatrical and Circus Life*, 288–90.

60. Jennings, *Theatrical and Circus Life*, 372–73.

61. See Benson, *Counter Cultures*; Rabinovitz, *For the Love of Pleasure*; Erenberg, *Steppin' Out*, especially chapter 3; Nasaw, *Going Out*; Peiss, *Cheap Amusements*; Allen, *Horrible Prettiness*, especially 185–93; Kenney, *Recorded Music in American Life*, chapter 5; Kitch, *The Girl on the Magazine Cover*; Kibler, *Rank Ladies*, chapters 1 and 2; Stamp, *Movie-Struck Girls*, introduction and chapter 1; DeCordova, *Picture Personalities*. For urban working-class women's experience, see Peiss and Ewen, *Immigrant Women in the Land of Dollars*.

62. Hamm, *Irving Berlin*, 22–29; Levine, *Highbrow/Lowbrow*, 195–98; Snyder, *The Voice of the City*, chapters 1–2; Butsch, *The Making of American Audiences*, chapters 7–8.

63. Ewen, *The Life and Death of Tin Pan Alley*, 37.

64. Witmark and Goldberg, *The Story of the House of Witmark*, 88.

65. Handy, *Father of the Blues*, 37.

66. Handy, *Father of the Blues*, 37. It was common in minstrelsy for adult men to sing female parts in popular performance.

67. Marks, *They All Sang*, 67–68.

68. Marks, *They All Sang*, 60; Gracyk, *Popular American Recording Pioneers*, 198–206. Will Oakland (1880–1956) became the popular favorite after Jose; he began recording in 1908, and his career overlapped directly with early radio crooners. He remained popular on radio throughout the 1920s.

69. Broadway musical comedy and acoustic recording provided new performance opportunities for former minstrel singers. Musical comedy's brightest star was an Irish

tenor, Chancellor "Chauncey" Olcott (1858–1932), whose biggest success, "Mother Machree," reflected the continued popularity of mother songs and Irish tenors.

70. Witmark and Goldberg, *The Story of the House of Witmark*, 55.

71. Witmark and Goldberg, *The Story of the House of Witmark*, 219. Suisman, *Selling Sounds*, 58–72. Although Suisman refers to pluggers primarily as "young men," working-class adolescent males left school (if they attended at all) and began work typically between the ages of twelve and fourteen.

72. Whitcomb, *After the Ball*, 48–49.

73. Ewen, *The Life and Death of Tin Pan Alley*, 73, argues that the heavy use of boys as song pluggers started in 1893. See also Marks, *They All Sang*, 129, 152–53.

74. Witmark and Goldberg, *The Story of the House of Witmark*, 219–24.

75. Witmark and Goldberg, *The Story of the House of Witmark*, 116–18. Song-slide presentations, also known as "illustrated songs," were popular in vaudeville from the mid-1890s to the early 1900s and as preshows in nickelodeons from 1908 until about 1913. Rick Altman, "Cinema and Popular Song," 19; Altman, *Silent Film Sound*, 181–93; Abel, "The Most American of Attractions, the Illustrated Song," 143–55; Abel, *Americanizing the Movies*, 127–39. Early cinema drew a higher proportion of female audiences than vaudeville of the same period.

76. See Ewen, *The Life and Death of Tin Pan Alley*, 73; Harris, *After the Ball*, 254; Jessel, *So Help Me*, 8–10.

77. Mildred Luber, quoted in Gabler, *Winchell*, 13–15.

78. In Richard Abel's 2006 study of midwestern song-slide presentations, he notes that female presenters had given way to men by the early 1910s; however, boys dominated song-slide presentations in New York, where many did double-duty as song pluggers (*Americanizing the Movies*, 133, 135). For male adolescent worship, see Senelick, *The Changing Room*, 280; Vicinus, "The Adolescent Boy."

79. Women were the primary consumers of sheet music and records, many times on behalf of the family. They made these minstrel tenors the biggest recording stars of the late nineteenth and early twentieth centuries. See Gracyk, *Popular American Recording Pioneers*; Kenney, *Recorded Music in American Life*, chapter 5.

Two CROONING GOES ELECTRIC

1. "Confidential Tenors' New Cabaret Item," *Variety*, 11 February 1925, 35.

2. "Cabaret Reviews," *Variety*, 7 October 1925, 51; "Yacht Club Boys," *Variety*, 24 March 1926, 45.

3. Wilder, *American Popular Song*. David Horn's more recent assessment of torch singing's roots is that it "drew musical influences from jazz, blues, sentimental Anglophone ballads and the chansons of Parisian café-culture, and developed within the closely related industrial contexts of Tin Pan Alley, Hollywood and Broadway" ("Torch Singer").

4. See introduction, note 14.

5. "Picture House for 'Best Plug,'" *Variety*, 6 October 1926, 85.

6. Miller, *Segregating Sounds*, 3–4. On authenticity's importance to understandings of modernity, see Orvell, *The Real Thing*, xv–xvi.

7. Within the first five months of 1922, the number of licensed stations rose from twenty-six to ninety-nine. Douglas, *The Early Days of Radio Broadcasting*, 32. See also Balk, *The Rise of Radio*, 40–47.

8. Lockheart, "A History of Early Microphone Singing"; Bowlly, *Modern Style Singing*, 13–16.

9. Bowlly, *Modern Style Singing*, 10–11.

10. See Sterne, *The Audible Past*, 239–40; DeLong, *The Mighty Music Box*, 28, 31, 34, 54–55; Bowlly, *Modern Style Singing*, 14; Dragonette, *Faith Is a Song*, 69–70, 81; Peters, *Speaking into the Air*, 213–14.

11. It was not until the late 1920s that larger radio stations and the networks began to incorporate studio audiences for many radio music and comedy programs.

12. Some of De Leath's Edison recordings are available online at archive.org; see also these collections: *The Original Radio Girl*, Diamond Cut, 1997, CD; *Ukulele Lady*, ASV Living Era, 2006, CD; *Dancing the Devil Away*, Document Records, 2006, CD; *Vaughn De Leath: Original Recordings, 1925–1929*, Bygone Days, 2012, CD.

13. "The Whisper Song: When the Pussy Willow Whispers to the Catnip" (lyrics and music by Cliff Friend, Edison, 1927, CD) is a good example of De Leath's mastery of many vocal effects.

14. Some recording historians and authors of liner notes have attributed same-sex address in sung lyrics to copyright laws, but I have found no evidence for that. Pronouns gradually shifted from third-person gendered (*him* or *her*) to second-person direct-address (*you*) in the romantic crooner era (1928–33).

15. Douglas, *The Early Days of Radio Broadcasting*, 170. Radio broadcasters of the early 1920s emphasized the importance of "a voice with personality" in making hiring decisions for announcers. Hilmes, *Only Connect*, 59.

16. "Radio Ramblings," *Variety*, 29 September 1926, 50; *Variety*, 7 April 1926, 43; *Variety*, 15 December 1926, 44; *Variety*, 5 January 1927, 50.

17. Scannell, *Radio, Television and Modern Life*, 24–25.

18. Quoted by Craig Maier in liner notes to De Leath, *The Original Radio Girl*, CD.

19. For more on Lucas, see Pitts and Hoffman, *The Rise of the Crooners*, 131–58; Peter Dempsey in liner notes to Nick Lucas *"The Crooning Troubadour": Tip Toe thru the Tulips*, ASV Living Era, 2000, CD; and several transcribed and audio interviews with Lucas from the early 1970s at "Nick Lucas Interviews," Nick Lucas, accessed 15 April 2012, http://nicklucas .com/biography-interview1974.html.

20. For 1920s song plugging, see Suisman, *Selling Sounds*, especially chapter 2; Sanjek, *Pennies from Heaven*, 80; Hilmes, *Radio Voices*, 64–69; Razlogova, *The Listener's Voice*, 75–

80. See also fan letters sent to plugger and early radio star Wendall Hall, State Historical Society of Wisconsin, Madison.

21. On Gillham, see Whitcomb, "The Coming of the Crooners," 16–21; "Art Gillham, the Whispering Pianist," accessed 15 April 2012, http://lwhisper.home.mindspring.com /ArtGillham.html.

22. Whitcomb, "The Coming of the Crooners," 14.

23. "Disk Review," Art Gillham, *Variety*, 9 September 1925, 39; "Disk Review," Jack Smith, *Variety*, 9 December 1925, 51.

24. At this point, pluggers were doing what was known as "indirect advertising" by performing songs on the air; commercial broadcasting would not be explicitly permitted by the courts until 1925. On radio song plugging, see Whitcomb, "The Coming of the Crooners," 14–34; Sanjek, *Pennies from Heaven*, 80–81 and the chapter "A Simple Radio Music Box," 74–90.

25. Bowlly, *Modern Style Singing*, 15–16.

26. Quoted in DeLong, *Radio Stars*, 167.

27. O. M. Static [pseudo.], "Radio Voice Has Critics Baffled: Microphone Develops New Groups of Stars, with Distinctive Mannerisms," *Boston Post*, 4 May 1925, quoted in Lockheart, "A History of Early Microphone Singing," 372.

28. Frank Biocca, "Media and Perceptual Shifts," 7.

29. In 1926 nearly half of homes had phonographs, compared to a quarter with radios. Sanjek, *Pennies from Heaven*, 69.

30. Sutton, *Recording the Twenties*, 131–44.

31. Wurtzler, "The Social Construction of Technological Change," 219. Douglas, *The Early Days of Radio Broadcasting*, 46–48; Douglas, *Listening In*, 77–78. Electrodynamic loudspeakers, more powerful and soon to become standard, replaced cone loudspeakers in 1925. My account of technological developments in this section also draws from Sutton, *Recording the Twenties*; Horning, "Chasing Sound" and *Chasing Sound*; Millard, *America on Record*; Thompson, *The Soundscape of Modernity*; Gelatt, *The Fabulous Phonograph*; Welch and Burt, *From Tinfoil to Stereo*.

32. Sales of the "talking machine industry," as *Variety* referred to recording, dropped significantly from 1923 to 1925; although *Variety* reports that sales officials did not blame radio directly, they did note that sales of radio sets increased 261 percent during that same period. *Variety*, 17 November 1926, 45.

33. Horning, *Chasing Sound*, 39. Edison, the fourth major phonograph producer of the time, resisted electrical recording for several years and was bankrupt by 1929 (Millard, *America on Record*, 194). Many smaller companies could not afford the new technology either; some merged with major labels, while others continued to produce acoustic records and eventually went bankrupt. Electrical recording helped to further the consolidation of the record industry and, by the end of the decade, the record industry's merger with the radio and film industries.

34. Maxfield, quoted in Horning, *Chasing Sound*, 37.

35. "Disk Reviews," *Variety*, 17 June 1925, 41.

36. Baur, cited in Gracyk, *Popular American Recording Pioneers*, 41. In late 1926 *Variety* reported that one singer, Frank B. Walker, for Columbia was able to "can" twenty-eight songs in a single day. *Variety*, 10 November 1926, 45.

37. Victor Music director Nathaniel Shilkret, interviewed in *Phonograph Monthly Review*, May 1927, cited in Gracyk, *Popular American Recording Pioneers*, 2. Within five years, with the notable exception of the traditional tenor John McCormack, all the most famous Irish singers would be crooners (but not promoted as Irish): Rudy Vallée, Bing Crosby, and Morton Downey.

38. Suisman, *Selling Sounds*, 141, 125–49. The historian John Potter describes Caruso as "manly and powerful, yet sweet and lyrical—everyone's ideal of Italian manhood in tenor form" (*Tenor*, 83).

39. Gracyk, *Popular American Recording Pioneers*, 13.

40. My understanding of early microphones has been helped enormously by my interview with Jim Webb, sound engineer and mixer and microphone historian, 12 December 2009.

41. *Variety*'s "Disk Review" section from 1 December 1926 is representative of the turn in the aesthetic tide; all ten reviewed records have vocals, all the vocalists are men, all are singing pop songs, and all are evaluated by new standards for microphone recordings.

42. Sutton, *Recording the Twenties*, 195–202.

43. See "Art Gillham, the Whispering Pianist"; Pitts and Hoffman, *The Rise of the Crooners*, 16–26.

44. This assimilationism affected live performance venues as well, indicating the general hegemonic shift. See, for example, the vaudeville review of the young male vaudeville team Mario and Lozan: "The foreign sounding names are not an asset and as both youths appear to be American born, something more local and euphonious would be a trade asset" (*Variety*, 10 June 1925, 13).

45. See Miller, *Segregating Sounds*. On "hillbilly" music and the industrial development of country, see Pecknold, *The Selling Sound*.

46. Smith and Gillham, along with fellow piano man Little Jack Little, were the most worldly-wise and world-weary of the early crooners, their melancholy often laced with an acerbic wit. None of these three singers would survive as crooning performers beyond the early 1930s. See Whitcomb, "The Coming of the Crooners," 16–29; "Whispering Jack Smith Comes Back," unidentified clipping, Whispering Jack Smith file, Margaret Herrick Library, Academy of Motion Picture Arts and Sciences, Beverly Hills.

47. Nick Lucas, "Sleepy Time Gal," lyrics by Joseph Alden and Raymond Egan, music by Ange Lorenzo and Richard Whiting, Brunswick, 1925, CD.

48. Pabst and Austin, *Gene Austin's Ol' Buddy*; Pitts and Hoffman, *The Rise of the Crooners*, 51–83. See also Peter Dempsey, liner notes, *Gene Austin: The Voice of the Southland*, ASV Living Era, 1996, CD.

49. Song success was based on both record and sheet music sales. While sheet music sales are difficult to measure, Austin's biggest records sold around the half-million mark,

which was the top-selling range for Victor, while his regular songs sold around a quarter million copies, the average for top stars. Sutton, *Recording the Twenties*, 309.

50. Pabst and Austin, *Gene Austin's Ol' Buddy*, 144.

51. Pabst and Austin, *Gene Austin's Ol' Buddy*, 10. See also Miller, *Segregating Sounds*, 217–18; Harkins, *Hillbilly*, 71–75.

52. Pabst and Austin, *Gene Austin's Ol' Buddy*, 84.

53. Miller, *Segregating Sounds*, 189–97, 221–27; Pecknold, *The Selling Sound*, chapter 1.

54. Pabst and Austin, *Gene Austin's Ol' Buddy*, 67–68. Elijah Wald has shown that "blues" was primarily a marketing term for a variety of music styles, often overlapping with other music labeled "minstrel," "hillbilly," and "crooning"; he describes blues of the era as "working class pop music," which fits Austin's sound well. My use of "blues" in relation to Austin comes from the general understanding of "blues feeling" as melancholy, his own designation of his emotion and sound as "blues," and the low-class connotations his music choices held for Victor records. Wald, *Escaping the Delta*, 3–42.

55. Austin is such a hybrid singer by today's standards that he has been categorized any number of ways since his death; his biographers refer to him as the "first white soul singer," while the cowboy singer Gene Autry regarded him as a key inspiration in the cowboy/country-western genre. As of this writing, iTunes currently lists Austin as a country singer, although the label did not exist in his day, and music historians generally associate him with pop.

56. Pitts and Hoffmann, *The Rise of the Crooners*, 58. "Yearning (Just for You)," lyrics by Benny Davis, music by Joe Burke, Victor, 1925, YouTube.

57. *Variety*, 10 June 1925, 39.

58. In employing McClary's famous term *feminine endings*, I am extrapolating from her general argument in *Feminine Endings* rather than her specific employment of the term in reference to gendered cadences in classical music. I am also drawing on feminist media critics who have argued that "feminine" texts such as soap operas are marked by their emotional excess and lack of narrative closure. McClary, *Feminine Endings*, 7–19.

59. "The Lonesome Road," lyrics by Gene Austin, music by Nathaniel Shilkret, Paramount, 1927, CD. Austin's style had much in common with that of the early blues singer Ethel Waters, whose soft and low delivery of the blues, focusing on clear enunciation of lyrics and intense feeling, set her against the "shouter" blues singers and helped initiate a new era in blues recording in the mid-1920s. As I noted in the introduction, there were numerous similarities and alliances between male crooners and female blues singers who were institutionally segregated by race and eventually by gender but sang much of the same music and were the product of many of the same influences, sensibilities, and motivations. See Waters and Samuels, *His Eye Is on the Sparrow*.

60. "My Blue Heaven," lyrics and music by Walter Donaldson, Victor, 1927, CD.

61. Tommy Lyman's popularization of the song in New York cabarets in 1927 and Victor's recording of it that same year reflect the overlap of cabaret culture and mass media in the 1920s.

62. Pabst and Austin, *Gene Austin's Ol' Buddy*, 102. For scholarly analyses of this song, see Starr and Waterman, *American Popular Music*, 68–71; Doyle, "From 'My Blue Heaven' to 'Race with the Devil'"; Hamm, *Yesterdays*, 369–71. On popularity, see *Variety*, 17 April 1929, 1.

63. Gomery, *The Coming of Sound*, 43.

64. See *The Vitaphone Release Index* written by Warner Bros. for its theater chain, October 1928, archived at the Margaret Herrick Library, Academy of Motion Picture Arts and Sciences, Beverly Hills; Liebman, *Vitaphone Films*. My analysis in this section also draws from Barrios, *A Song in the Dark*; Crafton, *The History of American Cinema*; Gomery, *The Coming of Sound*.

65. My analysis of Vitaphone derives from three kinds of sources: the original films, especially those collected on the Warner Bros. DVDs *The Jazz Singer Deluxe Edition* (2007), *Vitaphone Varieties* (2011), and *Vitaphone Varieties*, vol. 2 (2012); the Warner Bros. *Vitaphone Release Index*, instructions from the studio to its exhibitors regarding presentation of the Vitaphone shorts; and reviews of these shorts in *Variety*.

66. "The Croonaders," *Vitaphone Release Index*, 72. The Yacht Club Boys, the Croonaders, the Revelers, the Aristocrats, and the Gotham Rhythm Boys were all examples of attractive, youthful male quartets featured in early Vitaphone shorts. On the Croonaders' attractiveness, their "clean-cut" and "spiffy" appearance, see *Variety*, 12 January 1927, 20, and 2 March 1927, 34—the latter from *Variety*'s "Woman's Page."

67. *Variety*, 13 April 1927, 25. In the same issue, *Variety* notes that Smith was currently playing in "opposition to himself" at a New York City Keith vaudeville house, appearing both onstage and in his Vitaphone short; the paper notes that Smith's appearance indicates that Keith was already being forced to break its two-week-old ban on featuring players in vaudeville who had appeared on Vitaphone because of Smith's popularity. *Variety*, 13 April 1927, 1.

68. My analysis of Movietone films is based on the original films, which are parts of five different revue collections: *A Movietone Divertissement* (1928), *Metro Movietone Revue I* (1929), *Metro Movietone Revue II* (1929), *Metro Movietone Revue I* (1930), and *Metro Movietone Revue II* (1930).

69. Wolfe, "On the Track of the Vitaphone Short," 38–39.

70. Barrios, *A Song in the Dark*, 49–53; Gomery, *The Coming of Sound*, 56.

71. Vogel, *The Scene of the Harlem Cabaret*, 65. This section also draws from Heap, *Slumming*; Wilson, *Bulldaggers*; Erenberg, *Steppin' Out*; Chevigny, *Gigs*; Lerner, *Dry Manhattan*.

72. Studlar, *This Mad Masquerade*, 150–98.

73. For specific examples of queer and sexually explicit performance (and suggestions of prostitution) in the cabarets of the time, see *Variety*'s "Cabaret Reviews" column for 1925–26; for example, 11 November 1925, 46; 28 October 1925, 46; 4 November 1925, 45; 25 November 1925, 44; 30 December 1925, 206; 13 January 1926, 18, 47. "Pansy," "fop," and gender-queer performance was ubiquitous in vaudeville as well, and suggests the more general circulation of such acts (since performers often overlapped venues). The pop-

ular queer performer Jack Osterman, for example, moved between vaudeville and cabaret; 9 September, 1925, 17.

74. *Variety*, 7 October 1925, 51.

75. *Variety*, 28 July 1926, 46; *Variety*, 26 January 1927, 51.

76. *Variety*, 8 February 1923, 37.

77. "Nightclub Reviews: Salon Royal," *Variety*, 14 September 1927, 56. See also "Manhattan Madness," *Variety*, 31 August 1927, 54.

78. "Disk Reviews," *Variety*, 29 July 1925, 41; *Brooklyn Daily Eagle*, broadcast listings, 17 June 1927, 15.

79. Chauncey, *Gay New York*, 306.

80. "Confidential Tenors," *Variety*, 11 February 1925, 35.

81. "Whisper Low Nightlife," *Variety*, 15 December 1926, 1.

82. *Variety* notes that the new laws were inconsistently enforced depending upon the local inspector, since the police in Mayor Walker's administration operated according to "former Tammany standards" of payoffs; "Inside Stuff: Jimmy Walker on Nightclubs," *Variety*, 7 July 1926, 42. For growing concern about the effects of the laws on the city's financial and moral wellness, see "Hotels Now Most Popular Nightspots," *Variety*, 22 December 1926, 47; "Night Clubs Seem in Bad Way," *Variety*, 5 January 1927, 1, 53; "Morality Investigation of Night Club Applicants," *Variety*, 12 January 1927, 1; "Broadway's Under Cover Nightlife," *Variety*, 19 January 1927, 1, 32; "At 3:00 A.M.," *Variety*, 26 January 1927, 1. See also Chevigny, *Gigs*, 54–57; Lerner, *Dry Manhattan*, 164–66; Peretti, *Nightclub City*, 65–72 and chapter 4; Vogel, *The Scene of the Harlem Cabaret*, 58–59, 75.

83. "Lyman at Ambassador," *Variety*, 26 January 1927, 51; "Nightclub Reviews: Salon Royal," *Variety*, 14 September 1927, 56.

84. "Straight Dance Bands without Chance with Only Straight Music," *Variety*, 9 June 1926, 41.

85. "Inside Stuff: Singing Orchestras and Records," *Variety*, 14 October 1925, 45.

86. White bands could more easily cross this divide, and some played in a "hot" style. See ad for Ben Pollack's band, *Variety*, 23 June 1926, 45. See also Ogren, *The Jazz Revolution*; Peretti, *Jazz in American Culture* and *The Creation of Jazz*; Leonard, *Jazz and the White Americans*.

87. See, for example, "King Jazz and the Jazz Kings," *Literary Digest*, 30 January 1926, 37–42; Paul Whiteman, "Jazz," *Saturday Evening Post*, 27 February 1926; "The Anatomy of Jazz," *Harper's*, April 1926, 578–85. For a detailed history of sweet jazz bands and Whiteman, see Wald, *How the Beatles Destroyed Rock 'n' Roll*, 60–110.

88. "King Jazz and the Jazz Kings," 38.

89. Jazz bandleaders like Ben Pollack, Ted Weems, Ben Bernie, and Earl Burtnett crooned for their bands, as did band singer-musicians like Tom Waring, Jack Fulton, Carmen Lombardo, Phil Neily, Scrappy Lambert, Orlando Roberson, Parker Gibbs, Fran Frey, Charles Kaley, Russ Columbo, and Fred MacMurray (yes, that one).

90. See, for example, the tenor Orville Rennie's appearances with the Edgewater Orchestra in Chicago; he was also working in local picture houses. *Variety*, 14 July 1926, 44.

91. Crosby, *Call Me Lucky*, 83. See also, for example, "Review: Ted Weems and Orchestra," *Variety*, 16 June 1926, 21. For doubling in bands, see also *Earl Burtnett (Collegiate Jazz Artist) and His Biltmore Hotel Orchestra* (1928) (on *Vitaphone Varieties* DVD), and the soon-to-be famous crooner Russ Columbo playing violin and singing in *Gus Arnheim and His Ambassadors* (1928) and *Paul Tremaine and His Aristocats* (1929) (on *The Jazz Singer Deluxe Edition* DVD).

92. "Bands as Attractions," *Variety*, 5 January 1927, 48; see also *Variety*, 9 June 1926, 41.

93. "Bands as Attractions," *Variety*, 5 January 1927, 48.

94. See Starr and Waterman, *American Popular Music*, 39–61; Fass, *The Damned and the Beautiful*, 300–306.

95. Collegiate-themed bands included the Yale Collegians, directed by Rudy Vallée (*Variety*, 16 June 1926, 22); Johns Hopkins' Enoch Light's Collegians (*Variety*, 7 July 1926, 20); the Collegians (*Variety*, 1 September 1926, 50); the Maryland Collegians (*Variety*, 22 September 1926, 21). Others are reviewed in the following issues: 17 November 1926, 20; 26 January 1927, 23; 9 March 1927, 46; 27 April 1927, 1. Collegiate characters were also plentiful in vaudeville and cabaret acts of the time; see, for example, *Variety*, 5 May 1926, 24.

96. Thompson, *The Soundscape of Modernity*, 239–41.

97. An examination of several hundred pieces of sheet music from the mid- to late 1920s indicates the growing reliance on a song's affiliation with an individual male singer, either a record soloist or a bandleader-singer, especially from 1927–28 on. The songs before this period are more associated with the acoustic quartets and duos that were so popular in vaudeville. The songs become even more romance-minded in the late 1920s, and, as to be expected with crooning songs, the relationships between men and women are foregrounded. The songs range from those celebrating male-female domestic bliss (as in "Sleepy Baby," 1928) to those mourning a man's loss of his lady love. The increasing importance of women in men's lives and fate is particularly obvious in some of the sheet music covers, in which the woman's image is much larger than the man's. See fig. 3.3, "If I Had You" (1928), and "That's How I Feel about You" (1928), "Blue Evening's Blues" (1928), "My Fate Is in Your Hands" (1929), and "I'm Referin' Just to Her n' Me" (1929).

98. Crosby, *Call Me Lucky*, 75–76; Pabst and Austin, *Gene Austin's Ol Buddy*, 143.

99. Coilin and Staveacre, *Al Bowlly*, 4.

100. Coilin and Staveacre, *Al Bowlly*, 20.

101. *Variety* began regularly reviewing these motion picture house presentations in 1925; see also Gomery, *The Coming of Sound*, 11–14.

102. "Theaters 97 Percent Pictures," *Variety*, 12 May 1926, 1, 14; "New Audiences, New Acts," *Variety*, 12 May 1926, 24; *Variety*, 27 October 1926, 1, 103; 24 November 1926, 27; 16 March 1927, 22. Some vaudevillians resented dumbing down their acts to please "the lowest common denominator." *Variety*, 11 May 1927, 1, 51.

103. *Variety*, 9 June 1926, 35; Thompson, *The Soundscape of Modernity*, 248–50, 260.

104. *Variety*, 6 October 1926, 85.

105. Gomery, *Shared Pleasures*, 48.

106. On Ukulele Ike, see *Variety*, 12 May 1926, 19, 24; 9 June 1926, 35.

107. *Variety* reviews of Jack Smith: 29 September 1926, 22; see also 27 January 1926, 35; 6 October 1926, 58; 9 March 1927, 21; 7 April 1927, 46.

108. "New Acts: Howard Preston," *Variety*, 15 September 1926, 24.

109. "Dick Lucke and the Arcadians," *Variety*, 7 April 1926, 12; "Raymond Baird," *Variety*, 21 April 1926, 14; *Variety*, 15 December 1926, 19.

110. See Rich Conaty, liner notes to *Fred Waring's Pennsylvanians: The Collegiate Years 1925–1928*, Old Masters, 2000, CD; Waring, *Fred Waring and the Pennsylvanians*, 44–45, 51–52.

111. Waring, *Fred Waring and the Pennsylvanians*, 40.

112. *Waring's Pennsylvanians* (1927) (on *Vitaphone Varieties*, vol. 2, DVD). For contrast, *Earl Burtnett (Collegiate Jazz Artist) and His Biltmore Hotel Orchestra* (1927, 1928).

113. "Film House Reviews: Mark Strand, Brooklyn," *Variety*, 5 January 1927, 20.

114. *Variety*, 7 April 1926, 25; Waring, *Fred Waring and the Pennsylvanians*, 42, 50, 77.

115. *Variety*, 26 May 1926, 49; "4,000 for Photos for Fans," *Variety*, 12 January 1927, 44; *Variety*, 18 May 1927, 28; 29 June 1927, 28; 8 June 1927, 47.

Three FALLING IN LOVE WITH A VOICE

1. This collection of letters from 1928 has been preserved at the Rudy Vallée Collection, American Radio Archives, Thousand Oaks Library, Thousand Oaks, California (hereafter RVC). All quotations in this chapter come from this collection; I use partial names to protect the writers' anonymity. See Scrapbooks–Fan Mail 1 and 2.

2. Frith, *Sound Effects*, 37; Frith, "Pop Music," 97–98.

3. For more on the way listener letters influenced the technological development of radio broadcasting, see Razlogova, *The Listener's Voice*. On the historical importance of audiences as producers as well as consumers of new media, see Lisa Gitelman, "How Users Define New Media."

4. Carter, *The Heart of Whiteness*, chapter 2; Fass, *The Damned and the Beautiful*, chapters 6–7.

5. Information regarding Vallée's background comes primarily from two of his three autobiographies, *Vagabond Dreams Come True* and, with Gil McKean, *My Time Is Your Time*, as well as periodical sources in the Rudy Vallée Collection.

6. Fass, *The Damned and the Beautiful*, 46. See also Schrum, *Some Wore Bobby Sox*; Modell, *Into One's Own*, chapters 2–3; D'Emilio and Freedman, *Intimate Matters*, 239–42, 256–60.

7. D'Emilio and Freedman, *Intimate Matters*, 256.

8. Fass, *The Damned and the Beautiful*, chapter 6 and 69–70, 260–90, 306–10; Coontz, *Marriage*, chapter 12; Clement, *Love for Sale*, chapter 7. F. Scott Fitzgerald popularly

dramatized petting in his novel of college life, *This Side of Paradise*, 66–67, 72–73, 75. On contraception, see Davis, *Factors in the Sex Life of Twenty-Two Hundred Women*, 14.

9. Fass, *The Damned and the Beautiful*, 13–52; Deutsch, "From Ballots to Breadlines," 430.

10. "Bands as Attractions," *Variety*, 5 January 1927, 48.

11. On Dickerman, see Burton Peretti, *Nightclub City*, 5, 13–18. Sometime during 1928 Dickerman required Vallée to change the name of his band to the Connecticut Yankees, since some attendees at the exclusive nightclub complained that band members "didn't look like Yale men" (anti-Semitism was common in elite Manhattan nightclubs). I have used "Collegians" in this chapter to avoid confusion, since most fans used that name in their letters. Vallée and McKean, *My Time Is Your Time*, 69.

12. Douglas, *Listening In*, 58–78; Spigel, *Make Room for TV*, 26–29; Hilmes, *Radio Voices*, 37–39, 132–36; Butsch, *The Making of American Audiences*, 180–86.

13. Goldsmith and Lescarboura, *This Thing Called Broadcasting*, 223.

14. Thompson, *The Soundscape of Modernity*, 239.

15. Douglas, *Listening In*, 78. *Variety* notes that radio sales increased by 261 percent between 1923 and 1925. Estimates have suggested that one-fourth of households had radios by 1926, and one-third by 1930 (double the number that had telephones). *Variety*, 17 November 1926, 45; Sanjek, *Pennies from Heaven*, 69; "Census," *Radio News*, 15 October 1931, 15; Douglas, *Listening In*, 131.

16. Sterne, *The Audible Past*, 226–30.

17. Whether or not advertisers should invade the private sphere was hotly debated in the early 1920s. Marchand, *Advertising the American Dream*.

18. Hilmes, *Radio Voices*, 32–33; Goldsmith and Lescarboura, *This Thing Called Broadcasting*, 222–31.

19. Smulyan, *Selling Radio*, 87.

20. "Speaking on Radio," *Journal of Home Economics*, November 1932, 952. Regarding similar concerns over the introduction of the telephone and electricity to domestic family spaces in the late nineteenth century, see Marvin, *When Old Technologies Were New*, 67–81.

21. Douglas, *Listening In*, 88. Douglas notes that the number of female music attendees and students "prompted magazines like *Current Opinion* to ask, 'Is Music an Effeminate Art?'" See also Oja, *Making Music Modern*, chapter 12.

22. Théberge, *Any Sound You Can Imagine*, 97–100.

23. Hilmes, *Radio Voices*, 18.

24. Susan Kippax, "Women as Audience," quoted in Kenney, *Recorded Music in American Life*, 91. See all of chapter 5 in Kenney.

25. Gitelman, "How Users Define New Media," 65; Siefert, "The Audience at Home," 189–90.

26. Douglas, *Listening In*, 83–85.

27. On the significance of liveness on radio, see Peters, *Speaking into the Air*, 218.

28. Vallée, *Vagabond Dreams*, 104.

29. All major cities provided radio hookups in their most popular nightspots, and local bands built their followings through radio exposure. See, generally, *Variety*'s "Radio Ramblings" column, 1926–27; "Orchestra Leaders Pay for Radio Time," *Variety*, 23 June 1926, 1; and the following issues: 21 April 1926, 43; 18 August 1926, 87; 17 November 1926, 44. In a survey of current jazz bandleaders from 26 October 1931, 75 percent attributed their rise to radio; *New Orleans Times-Picayune*, Vallée Scrapbooks, vol. 32, RVC. Radio remote hookups were particularly important for black bands, as Valliant notes; while broadcasting segregation practices gave white bands the majority of studio airtime, "most of the black music on radio came from live music remotes in black and tan clubs" (*Sounds of Reform*, 136).

30. Vallée, *Vagabond Dreams*, 87.

31. Since the 1910s Hollywood had used music to support the film narrative; this was particularly important during silent films, where music helped compensate for the lack of voices. Use of musical scoring would become an integral part of the classical Hollywood film style, which peaked from the 1920s through the 1950s. See Flinn, *Strains of Utopia*; Altman, *Silent Film Sound*, especially chapter 18.

32. Vallée, *Vagabond Dreams*, 32–33. Vallée anticipated and influenced Hollywood musicals of the 1930s, which depended on the "democratic" accessibility of songs. Altman, *The American Film Musical*, 171.

33. Vallée, *Vagabond Dreams*, 98–100.

34. Vallée, *Vagabond Dreams*, 32–33.

35. Vallée, *Vagabond Dreams*, 41.

36. D'Emilio, "Capitalism and Gay Identity."

37. Simmons, *Making Marriage Modern*, 200–209, provides a detailed analysis and critique of these books. For major primary sources, see Van de Velde, *Ideal Marriage*; Groves and Ogburn, *American Marriage and Family Relationships*; Calverton, *The Bankruptcy of Marriage*; Lindsey and Evans, *The Companionate Marriage*.

38. Groves and Ogburn, *American Marriage and Family Relationships*, 37–38; Fass, *The Damned and the Beautiful*, 260–90, 306–10, 69–70; Modell, *Into One's Own*, 97. See also Simmons, "Modern Sexuality and the Myth of Victorian Repression," 164–65; Faulkner and Pruitt, *Dear Dr. Menninger*, 157.

39. Simmons, *Making Marriage Modern*, 212–13. For "genital kissing," see Van de Velde, *Ideal Marriage*, 140. Oral sex increased markedly in the 1920s and early 1930s. In 1930 regulatory changes allowed marriage manuals to become even more sexually explicit in order to help couples achieve a mutually orgasmic sex life. According to the Kinsey report on female sexuality, the rates for both kinds of oral sex increased with the birth cohorts born after 1900 and 1910. Over 50 percent of these interviewees reported practicing cunnilingus; indeed the rates of cunnilingus outpaced fellatio. Kinsey et al., *Sexual Behavior in the Human Female*, 281, 361–65, 399.

40. Fass, *The Damned and the Beautiful*, 79.

41. Deutsch, "From Ballots to Breadlines," 435.

42. Vallée's importance for disabled listeners is confirmed by an album of fan letters from blind listeners all over North America, edited and put into Braille by the young blind woman Margaret Long in 1934. Bound volume, RVC.

43. Frith, "Pop Music," 96, 107. See also Frith, *Sound Effects*, 37–38; Potter, *Seeing the Blossom*, 68.

44. Frith, "Pop Music," 96.

45. For more on Arnold's "idealist aesthetics" and its relation to modernism, see Moi, *Henrik Ibsen and the Birth of Modernism*, 256.

46. See Studlar, *This Mad Masquerade*; Chauncey, *Gay New York*; Anderson, *Twilight of the Idols*.

47. Showalter, *These Modern Women*, 4.

48. Simmons, *Making Marriage Modern*, 206–8.

49. See Simmons, "Companionate Marriage and the Lesbian Threat," 162–73; Duggan, "The Social Enforcement of Heterosexuality and Lesbian Resistance in the 1920s"; Rapp and Ross, "The Twenties' Backlash"; Laqueur, *Solitary Sex*, 359–97.

50. Simmons, *Making Marriage Modern*, 208.

51. Marchand, *Advertising the American Dream*, 175–85.

52. See Hansen, *Babel and Babylon*; Higashi, *Cecil B. DeMille and American Culture*, 163–65; Studlar, *This Mad Masquerade*, chapters 2–3; Anderson, *Twilight of the Idols*, 4–5 and chapters 1, 3, 4; Deutsch, "From Ballots to Breadlines," 435.

53. Scannell, *Radio, Television, and Modern Life*, 58–59.

54. Dyer, *Only Entertainment*, 21–23.

55. Sheet music, "Georgie Porgie," lyrics and music by Billy Mayerl and Gee Paul (London: Scherberg, Hopwood and Crew, 1924).

56. Simmons, "Companionate Marriage and the Lesbian Threat," 169–70.

57. Vicinus refers to the adolescent boy as the "femme fatale" of the turn of the century; his liminality meant that he could "reflect a variety of sexual desires and emotional needs" ("The Adolescent Boy," 91).

58. Davis's study of women's sexual lives at the time, *Factors in the Sex Life of Twenty-Two Hundred Women*, reported that between a third and one half of young women had some same-sex experience or feelings.

59. Simmons, *Making Marriage Modern*, 194.

60. Davis, *Factors in the Sex Life of Twenty-Two Hundred Women*, 95.

61. Calverton, *The Bankruptcy of Marriage*, 156.

Four "THE MOUTH OF THE MACHINE"

Epigraph: Excerpted from Martha Gellhorn, "Rudy Vallée: God's Gift to Us Girls," *New Republic*, 5 August 1929. Gellhorn's biographers generally interpret her review as a satire of Vallée and his audience, although it is in keeping with other reports of public reaction. This review became very well known, and the press frequently used the phrase "God's Gift to Us Girls" to refer to Vallée. See several such references in Rudy Vallée Scrapbooks, vol. 6, from the fall of 1929, Rudy Vallée Collection, American Radio Archives, Thousand Oaks Library, Thousand Oaks, California (hereafter RVC).

1. Vallée, *Vagabond Dreams Come True*, 122–31; Vallée and McKeon, *My Time Is Your Time*, 74–79.

2. Between 1925 and 1928 numerous radio-made acts appeared in vaudeville and motion picture houses. Vaudeville houses depended on these radio stars for much-needed cash during the institution's dying days. See, for example, *Variety*, 11 November, 1925, 37.

3. Publications from this time include *Radio Broadcast, Radio News*, the *New York Radio Program Weekly, Broadcast Listener*, and *Radio Digest*. Vallée's rise in 1929 ensured the viability of exclusively fan-oriented radio magazines; by the early 1930s there were several such national publications, including *Radio Guide, Radio Mirror*, and *Radio Stars*.

4. Unattributed clipping, Vallée Scrapbooks, vol. 1, February 1929, RVC. See also *Variety* review, 13 February 1929, 45. Vallée's initial rise to stardom is primarily covered in Vallée Scrapbooks, vols. 1 and 4, which cover winter and spring 1929.

5. Vallée, *Vagabond Dreams Come True*, 125.

6. Vallée, *Vagabond Dreams Come True*, 127.

7. *The New York American*, Vallée Scrapbooks, vol. 1, RVC.

8. *Brooklyn Eagle*, 1 September 1929, Vallée Scrapbooks, vol. 4, RVC.

9. Watts, *New York Herald Tribune*, [undated]; *Detroit (MI) News*, 24 March 1929; Vallée Scrapbooks, vols. 4 and 1, respectively, RVC.

10. *Variety*, 13 March, 1929, 56; *Lewiston (ME) Journal*, April 1929, Vallée Scrapbooks, vol. 1, RVC.

11. *New York World* (undated); *Dallas Herald*, 26 August 1929, Vallée Scrapbooks, vol. 4, RVC.

12. *Variety*, 17 April 1929, 1, 69. In 1929 a "freak" attraction meant having no discernible talent, and a "femme" meant appealing to female interest only rather than indicating effeminacy. There are many similarities in the appeal of Vallée and Valentino, which their press coverage makes more clear. Valentino has been extensively studied; see Anderson, *Twilight of the Idols*, chapters 3–4; Hansen, *Babel and Babylon*, chapters 11–12; Studlar, *This Mad Masquerade*, chapter 3.

13. Anderson, *Twilight of the Idols*, 66, 100–101, observes that Valentino's substantial male audience was likewise ignored by the press.

14. Dyer, *Heavenly Bodies*, 19.

15. See, for example, *New York Evening World*, 24 April and 7 May 1929, Vallée Scrapbooks, vols. 4 and 1, respectively, RVC.

16. Marguerite Tazelaar, *New York Herald Tribune*, 29 March 1929, Vallée Scrapbooks, vol. 1, RVC.

17. Frith, "Pop Music," 95.

18. In Vallée's discussion of his appeal to J. Walter Thompson Agency ad men on 31 March 1930, he defines his "average" taste as "middle class taste" and distances himself from the southern vernacular of Gene Austin's songs (which reads today as a pop versus

country distinction). See Staff Meeting Minutes, J. Walter Thompson Archive, Duke University, Durham, NC.

19. Eleanor Clarage, *Cleveland Plain-Dealer*, 4 August 1929, Vallée Scrapbooks, vol. 4, RVC.

20. Vinson, *The Voices That Are Gone*, chapter 1.

21. *College Humor*, fall 1929, Vallée Scrapbooks, vol. 166, RVC.

22. Douglas, *Terrible Honesty*, 360–61.

23. Vallée, *Vagabond Dreams Come True*, 126, 130. Vallée notes that he was particularly well received in Washington Heights and the Bronx. Irish Catholic immigrants made up much of Washington Heights in the 1920s, but the Jewish population was also substantial and would increase in the 1930s and 1940s. During the 1920s, the Bronx was increasingly dominated by Irish, Italian, and especially Jewish immigrants, and to a lesser degree by Germans and Poles, many of whom were also Catholic. See 1930 census, accessed 8 August 2011, http://mapserver.lib.virginia.edu/. He also received fan letters from all other boroughs, as well as New Jersey and surrounding towns and states. Although it is hard to know how many of his fan letters came from people of color, Vallée's upcoming performances in Harlem were promoted in the black press, attesting to his popularity there; one black newspaper, for example, notes that his appearance "will give the Harlem younger set a real thrill." "Vallée in Harlem," *The Afro-American*, 12 October 1929, 16.

24. The backlash against Victorian popular culture and the devaluation of the cultural feminine generally in the 1920s and 1930s has been well documented by Huyssen, *After the Great Divide*; Douglas, *Terrible Honesty*; Oja, *Making Music Modern*; Jacobs, *The Decline of Sentiment*; Marchand, *Advertising the American Dream*.

25. "Mother Tells of a Rudy Vallee Who Stayed at Home of Nights to Hold Hands with Her," *Boston Globe*, 11 April 1930, Vallée Scrapbooks, vol. 17, RVC.

26. For discussions of the matriarchal aspects of Irish, Italian, and Jewish households, see Diner, *Erin's Daughters in America*, 18–19, 43–69; Orsi, *The Madonna of 15th Street*, 129–35; Antler, *You Never Call!*, 15–45.

27. *Variety*, 17 April 1929, 1, 69.

28. *New York Evening World*, 27 April 1929, Vallée Scrapbooks, vol. 1, RVC.

29. See, for example, his multipart biography in the *Daily Mirror*, 21, 28–29 June 1929, and "ideal girl" articles, Vallée Scrapbooks, vols. 4 and 166, respectively, RVC.

30. *Dallas Herald* (syndicated), 26 August 1929, Vallée Scrapbooks, vol. 4, RVC.

31. *Outlook*, 23 October 1929, vol. 166, RVC.

32. On my use of Susan McClarey's term *feminine endings*, see chapter 2, note 58.

33. Vallée and McKeon, *My Time Is Your Time*, 60; Vallée, *Vagabond Dreams Come True*, 33–35.

34. *Newark Evening News* (syndicated), 6 April 1929, Vallée Scrapbooks, vol. 1, RVC.

35. George Davis, "Your Broadway and Mine," *Cleveland Press* (syndicated), Vallée Scrapbooks, 1929, RVC.

36. On Roosevelt's ideal of the strenuous life, see Gail Bederman, *Manliness and Civilization*, 170–215; Rotundo, *American Manhood*, 235–36, 268–69, 282–83; White, *The First*

Sexual Revolution, 1–15. On the Great Migration, see Gregory, *Southern Diaspora*; Grossman, *Land of Hope*. On gay men's community, see Chauncey, *Gay New York*, 232–35.

37. White, *The First Sexual Revolution*, 17–27; Fass, *The Damned and the Beautiful*, 286–87. While being clean-cut will later denote militarism and conservative values in wartime and cold war America, in the 1920s it was about maintaining a boyish, clean, vulnerable, soft, and kissable masculinity in order to be appealing to women.

38. White, *The First Sexual Revolution*, 16–35; Lerner, *Dry Manhattan*, 161–62. On Runyon, see Gabler, *Winchell*, 89. On the FBI and Dillinger, see Burrough, *Public Enemies*, 156, 373, 392.

39. White, *The First Sexual Revolution*, 36–44. Other influential novels with male flapper heroes are Floyd Dell, *Moon Calf* (1920), and Percy Mark, *The Plastic Age* (1924).

40. Broun refers to the Fitzgerald type as a "male flapper," as does the 1920 review by the *Chicago Daily News*. Both quoted in "Critical Excerpts," in Fitzgerald, *This Side of Paradise*, 313, 315.

41. Douglas, *Terrible Honesty*, 519.

42. Many of these songs reflect what would later be perceived as a "gay sensibility" because of the way they and their performers (as Dyer writes) combine theatricality with authenticity and strong feeling with irony. But such contradictory sentiments were not necessarily queer in the 1920s; instead they were thought of as modern or sophisticated. Some of the most influential songwriters, including Cole Porter and Lorenz Hart, were gay, but most were not. For more on gay sensibility, see Dyer, *Heavenly Bodies*, chapter 3.

43. For discussions of late 1920s live entertainment through 1931, especially in New York City, see Shaw, *Nightlife*; James, *All about New York*; Chauncey, *Gay New York*; Heap, *Slumming*; Vogel, *The Scene of the Harlem Cabaret*; Wilson, *Bulldaggers*; Mordden; *Make Believe*; Brown, *Babylon Girls*; Latham, *Posing a Threat*; Peretti, *Nightclub City*; Chevigny, *Gigs*; Drutman, *Good Company*.

44. Such vocals are often mentioned in *Variety*'s "New Acts This Week" section. See, for example, these issues: "Kitty O'Connor," 4 November 1925, 44; "Pitter-Patter Revue," 1 September 1926, 21; "Fay Templeton," 10 June 1925, 5; "Francis Renault," 8 April 1925, 10; "Margaret Ford," 19 August 1925, 15; "Joey Ray," 13 January 1926, 36; "Hatch and Carpenter," 2 September 1925, 15; "Marion Claire," 18 August 1926, 63.

45. Chauncey, *Gay New York*, 311–13.

46. Heap, *Slumming*, 234–35.

47. For extant pansy performances, see the comedian and dancer Jack Waldron, *A Little Breath of Broadway* (1928) (on *Vitaphone Varieties* DVD), and the "lavender emcee" Harry Rose in *Metro Movietone Revue I* and *II* (1929).

48. Unattributed press clipping, Vallée Scrapbooks, vol. 4, June 1929, RVC.

49. Herbert Corey, "Manhattan Days and Nights," *Louisville (KY) Courier* (syndicated), 4 September 1929, Vallée Scrapbooks, vol. 5, RVC. See also unattributed press clipping, "This Rudy Vallée Thing," Vallée Scrapbooks, June 1929, vol. 4; Arthur Groman, "Microphone Musings," *Pittsburgh Press*, 28 December 1929, Vallée Scrapbooks, vol. 9, 1929.

50. Nanette Kutner, *Dance Magazine*, September 1929, 23, 57.

51. Dyer, *Only Entertainment*, 103–19.

52. Dyer, *Only Entertainment*, 116.

53. See *Vanity Fair*, July 1929, 47; *Literary Digest*, 19 October 1929, 46; *Outlook*, 11 September 1929, 58.

54. Senelick, *The Changing Room*, 280. See also Vicinus, "The Adolescent Boy."

55. In the film *International House* (1933), Vallée's attachment to his megaphone is satirized by having him sleep with it. By 1933, this pose is portrayed for laughs as a sign of narcissism and possible sexual perversion.

56. Rudy Vallée talk at the J. Walter Thompson Company, his program's sponsor, on 31 March 1930, Staff Meeting Minutes, 25, J. Walter Thompson Archive, Duke University, Durham, NC. The descriptor "regular" was currently in transition from "not elitist" to "not effeminate"; it could mean either or both in this context.

57. Walter Winchell, *Daily Mirror*, 18 January 1930, Vallée Scrapbooks, vol. 6, and DAC *News*, Vallée Scrapbooks, vols. 11 and 4, respectively, RVC.

58. James, *All about New York*, 281–91. The section epigraph is from Gross, *I Looked and I Listened*, 80.

59. The most in-depth discussion of New York columnists and newspaper culture from this period is Gabler, *Winchell*. See also Kenny, *Conducting a Successful Radio Column*, 4.

60. "About Broadway," *New York Sunday News*, 19 May 1929, Vallée Scrapbooks, vol. 4, RVC.

61. When Winchell called him on it, Hellinger admitted he had "never seen Vallée perform." "Small Talk from the Big Street," DAC *News*, Vallée Scrapbooks, vol. 4, RVC.

62. Fan letter in Ben Gross's *Radio Review* column (undated); Winchell letter in Vallée Scrapbooks, vol. 11. See columnists generally, spring 1929, Vallée Scrapbooks, vols. 1 and 4, RVC.

63. "Voice of the People," *New York Daily News*, Vallée Scrapbooks, vol. 4, RVC.

64. Arthur Pollack, *Brooklyn Eagle*, 20 June 1929, Vallée Scrapbooks, vol. 1, RVC.

65. Where previous popular radio personalities like Vaughn De Leath, Sam "Roxy" Rothafel, and Wendall Hall had had strong followings and a degree of national fame within the nascent network system, their stardom had peaked by the time Vallée emerged. Coverage of Wendall Hall's star power has been particularly extensive because fan letters still exist. See Hilmes, *Radio Voices*, 60–68; Razlogova, *The Listener's Voice*. The term *national* here is relative, since networks skewed toward audiences in large urban centers, with more stations located on the East Coast and in the Midwest than in the South and West. Due to different time zones, "live" programs were rarely heard simultaneously across the country. Russo, *Points on the Dial*, 21–26.

66. Vallée and McKeon, *My Time Is Your Time*, 71–72.

67. Hilmes, *Only Connect*, 69, 76; Vallée, *Vagabond Dreams Come True*, 132.

68. In contrast, CBS, much more strapped for cash, worked to sign already established stars, primarily from vaudeville. Hilmes, *Only Connect*, 70–78.

69. *Radio Digest* estimated Vallée's fan mail at ten thousand letters per day in November 1929; see Gene Mulholland, "Rudy Vallée First Radio Vamp," *Radio Digest*, November 1929, 9, Periodicals, RVC.

70. "Radio Guide Makes Debut," Vallée Scrapbooks, vol. 168, RVC.

71. *Variety*, 6 February 1929, 65; Berlin letter, Vallée Scrapbooks, vol. 1, RVC.

72. Hilmes, *Radio Voices*, 65.

73. Accurate estimates of song sales are difficult to make for the 1920s since they were largely not made public, and in any event the popularity of a single song was the result of sheet music and record sales by any number of artists. It is clear, however, that radio play increased song sales generally and that Vallée's radio program spawned a likely unprecedented number of popular hits; association with him helped song sales. Both Bing Crosby and Russ Columbo likewise originated a huge number of popular hits in 1931–32, when they began their radio programs. See Sutton, *Recording in the Twenties*, 307–10; Wald, *How the Beatles Destroyed Rock 'n' Roll*, 85, 92–96. I have also consulted Whitburn, *Pop Memories*, 426–27; Whitburn bases his data on record label best-seller rankings, sheet music sales, trade publications, and ASCAP. Vallée top sellers from 1929 include "Sweetheart of All My Dreams," "If I Had You," "Marie," "Weary River," "Deep Night" (his most enduring song, for which he wrote the lyrics), "Lover, Come Back to Me," "My Time Is Your Time" (his radio theme song), "I'm Just a Vagabond Lover," "Lonely Troubadour," and "Heigh-Ho, Everybody, Heigh-Ho" (his radio greeting).

74. *New Yorker*, Vallée Scrapbooks, vol. 1, RVC.

75. Details of Vallée's benefit appearances can be found in Vallée Scrapbooks, vols. 4–12, 23 24, RVC. For Vallée's work with the musicians union, see articles from *Variety*, *Zits*, *Daily News*, *Orchestra World*, *New York American*, and *Daily Mirror* from November–December 1930, Vallée Scrapbooks, vols. 23 and 24, RVC.

76. Coverage of his Washington appearance made headlines in every Washington paper on 25 February 1930. See Vallée Scrapbooks, vol. 12, RVC.

77. Hilmes, *Only Connect*, 79–80.

78. Regional New York programs like *Roxy and His Gang* (1922–25) and *The Eveready Hour* (1923–30) pioneered the radio variety format. Hilmes, *Radio Voices*, 60–68.

79. For Randolph's letter of 28 November 1930, see Vallée Scrapbooks, vol. 24, RVC. For NBC's antiunion stance, see Elizabeth Fones-Wolfe and Nathan Godfried, "Regulating Class Conflict on the Air: NBC's Relationship with Business and Organized Labor," in Hilmes, *NBC*, 61–77.

80. For promotion and reviews of the *Fleischmann Hour* premiere, see Vallée Scrapbooks, vol. 8, RVC.

81. Vallée's *Fleischmann Hour* scripts, 1929–36, Vallée Collection, RVC.

82. *Rudy Vallée and His Connecticut Yankees* 771 (1929); *Radio Rhythm* (1929) (on *Hollywood Rhythm* VHS); *Glorifying the American Girl* (1929); *The Vagabond Lover* (1929).

83. Barrios, *Screened Out*, 43–44.

84. Vallée's stiffness would contrast markedly with Crosby's freedom of movement in his early Sennett short films, made after development of the movable boom mic, in 1931–33.

85. "Film Reviews," *Variety*, 4 December 1929, 15.

86. Helen Shea, letters, *New York Graphic*, 12 December 1929. See other film reviews and discussion in Vallée Scrapbooks, vols. 6 and 7, RVC.

87. Gustav Davidson, "Toast to Rudy Vallée," *Daily Mirror*, 8 December 1930, Vallée Scrapbooks, vol. 22, RVC.

Five "A SUPINE SINKING INTO THE PRIMEVAL OOZE"

1. Graham Wyer, *New York World*, 31 January 1931.

2. *Washington Capital*, 25 February 1931 (and others), Vallée Scrapbooks, vol. 35, Rudy Vallée Collection, American Radio Archives, Thousand Oaks Library, Thousand Oaks, CA (hereafter RVC).

3. The term *cake-eater* abounds in the 1920s but disappears by the mid-1930s. It was originally defined in the 1920s as a certain type of "sheik," a dandy or gigolo, who wore tight jackets, skinny ties, and bell bottoms; by the early 1930s, cake-eaters (and sheiks) had become associated with toxic gender deviance, and therefore with homosexuals. "Dance hall sheiks" are a specific reference to "tango pirates," whom women paid to dance with them in dance halls; Valentino had worked as a sheik. Wald, *How the Beatles Destroyed Rock 'n' Roll*, 61; Henry Clune, *Rochester (NY) Democrat-Chronicle*, 31 January 1931, Vallée Scrapbooks, vol. 35, RVC.

4. These self-described "hard-boiled, hard-drinking, rough-neck" soldiers praise Vallée's vocals and note that they have been "denied the 'culture' that is credited as going with a college education." Their use of the term *regular guy* in this context likely means "nonelitist," although this descriptor was being culturally redefined along the lines of gender/sexuality to indicate "not effeminate" (and, therefore, not gay). Letter to Rudy Vallée on 23 January 1931, signed by "The Boys of the 16th U.S. Infantry," Governor's Island, New York, Vallée Scrapbooks 35, RVC.

5. O'Leary, *To Die For*, 51–53.

6. Doctor, *The BBC and Ultra-Modern Music*, 25–32; Baade, *Victory through Harmony*, 131–52.

7. Orvell, *The Real Thing*, xv–xvi, 141–42, 154–55; Miller, *Segregating Sounds*, 3, 5–6.

8. All information regarding song popularity comes from Whitburn, *Pop Memories*; Mattfield, *Variety Music Cavalcade*. Although Whitburn's exact numbers are not always reliable, these songs appear on many CD compilations of 1920s favorites, and they were all widely promoted in *Variety*.

9. *Baltimore Sun*, 14 October 1929, Vallée Scrapbooks, vol. 7; *Cleveland (Ohio) Press*, 3 February 1930, Vallée Scrapbooks, vol. 11; *New York Sunday News*, 20 July 1930, Vallée Scrapbooks, vol. 20; *Washington (DC) News*, 3 September 1929, Vallée Scrapbooks, vol. 9, RVC.

10. "Battle of the Blues," *Radio Digest*, May 1930; *Milwaukee (WI) Leader*, 17 June 1932, Vallée Scrapbooks, vols. 167 and 62, respectively, RVC.

11. Katherine Spring, *Saying It with Songs*, 41–68.

12. Novarro's singing career began with the immensely successful "Pagan Love Song," the theme from his 1928 MGM film *The Pagan*.

13. See *Variety*, advertisement for Novarro's *Devil May Care*, 18 December 1929, 24; Barrios, *A Song in the Dark*, 277–78; Hirschhorn, *The Hollywood Musical*, 39, 55, 59, 84, 99.

14. Barrios, *A Song in the Dark*, 84–85.

15. "Painting the Clouds with Sunshine" from *Golddiggers of Broadway* (1929); as of this writing, the "Tiptoe" scene is on YouTube.

16. Leslie Allen, "The Lull from Lullaby Makes 'This Crooning Business,'" *New York Sun*, 1 February 1930, Vallée Scrapbooks, vol. 11, RVC.

17. *Washington Star*, 7 March 1930, Vallée Scrapbooks, vol. 17, RVC.

18. *Detroit (MI) Times*, 8 September 1929, Vallée Scrapbooks, vol. 9, RVC.

19. See Vitaphone Release Index (exhibitors' promotional material) produced by Warner Bros., 1928, 149, 173, 189, archived at the Margaret Herrick Library, Academy of Motion Picture Arts and Sciences, Beverly Hills.

20. Reported in *Memphis Commercial Appeal*, 23 November 1930; this was a national poll, widely covered. See also "Rudy Has Audience of 10,000,000," *Buffalo (NY) News*, 22 November 1930. Both articles in Vallée Scrapbooks, vol. 23, RVC.

21. Standard Brands, Inc., "A Study of the Public's Reaction to Rudy Vallée during His Ten Weeks Tour of the Paramount Publix Theatres," Rudy Vallée Correspondence, RVC.

22. Alton Cook, "The Voice Off Stage," *St. Paul News*, 6 January 1930, Vallée Scrapbooks, vol. 11, RVC.

23. Ed Sullivan, *New York Graphic*, 2 June 1930, Vallée Scrapbooks, vol. 18, RVC.

24. Russel Crouse, *New York Evening Post*, 7 May 1930, Vallée Scrapbooks, vol. 15, RVC.

25. Interviews with Vallée from *Louisville (KY) Times*, 6 September 1930, and *Buffalo (NY) News*, 14 November 1930, Vallée Scrapbooks, vols. 21 and 23, respectively, RVC.

26. Hugh Russell Fraser, "As I See It," *Albany (NY) Knickerbocker Press*, 27 December 1930; Bill Cunningham, *Boston Post*, 25 July 1930, Vallée Scrapbooks, vol. 23, RVC.

27. *New York World Telegram*, 7 December 1931, Vallée Scrapbooks, vol. 33, RVC.

28. Heap, *Slumming*, 232, 231–76 generally.

29. Heap, *Slumming*, 235, 249.

30. Chauncey, *Gay New York*, 331; Terry, *An American Obsession*, 268–72.

31. Chauncey, *Gay New York*, 352–53.

32. Chauncey, *Gay New York*, 334–37.

33. Chauncey, *Gay New York*, 346.

34. Maltby, "The Production Code and the Hays Office," 51.

35. For lengthy discussions on the shift from live to canned entertainment, see Erenberg, *Swingin' the Dream*, 3–34; Cohen, *Making a New Deal*, 323–33.

36. Susman, *Culture as History*, 160.

37. Maltby, "The Production Code and the Hays Office," 45.

38. For further discussion of the Production Code and its effects, see Mann, *Behind the Screen*, 121–60; Barrios, *Screened Out*, 55–80.

39. Networks also censored or rejected scripted songs as contrary to "public morals." Staff Meeting Minutes, 14 April 1931, J. Walter Thompson Agency Papers, Duke University. See also Smulyan, *Selling Radio*, 117–22; Murray, "'The Tendency to Deprave and Corrupt Morals.'"

40. "Are Air Stars Immoral?," *Radio Guide*, 6 November 1932, 1, 7; "Get Off the Air," *Radio Stars*, October 1933, 16–17, 61.

41. *Literary Digest*, 30 January 1932, and *Buffalo (NY) News*, 11 January 1932, Vallée Scrapbooks, vol. 59, RVC.

42. Maltby, "The Production Code and the Hays Office," 54. The National Catholic Welfare Council had been established during World War I, originally in response to the nation's wartime need for religious personnel and counsel. It became involved in film censorship during the war and continued afterward to advocate for film censorship and monitor the representation of Catholicism in mass culture. It helped set national standards for Catholic identity and culture generally in this period. See McGregor, *The Catholic Church and Hollywood*, 1–43; Walsh, *Sin and Censorship*, 4–94; O'Brien, *Public Catholicism*, 158–94; Morris, *American Catholic*, 113–64; Doherty, *Hollywood's Censor*.

43. Maltby, "The Production Code and the Hays Office," 54. For specific Catholic censorship of sex and sexuality, see McGregor, *The Catholic Church and Hollywood*, 77–106.

44. Brooklyn residents Joseph Mandula and Arthur Dix, "Letters to the Editor," unidentifiable New York paper, both responding to Cardinal O'Connell's remarks, January 1932, vol. 59, RVC; Vallée Catholic benefit, 7 May 1931, RVC. See also Walsh, *Sin and Censorship*, 19, 28, 48, 80.

45. Douglas, *Terrible Honesty*, 127.

46. Douglas, *Terrible Honesty*, 147; Abelove, "Freud, Male Homosexuality and the Americans."

47. Warner, "Homo-Narcissism," 192.

48. Douglas, *Terrible Honesty*, 236.

49. Warner, "Homo-Narcissism," 202–4.

50. *New York Post*, 18 January 1932, Vallée Scrapbooks, vol. 59, RVC.

51. Julia Shawell, *New York Evening Graphic*, 21 February 1931; see also *Washington (DC) News*, 24 March 1931, Vallée Scrapbooks, vols. 27 and 28, respectively, RVC.

52. *New York Graphic*, 18 July 1931, Vallée Scrapbooks, vol. 31, RVC.

53. *New York Times*, 23 February 1932, and *Musician*, March 1932, 3, Vallée Scrapbooks, RVC. Ironically, this group's members widely publicized these views in 1933 in a series of talks over NBC, home to Vallée and Columbo; they then published them in book form as American Academy of Teachers in Singing, *Singing, the Well-Spring of Music*.

54. "'Crooning' Caustically Stigmatized by Majority of Twenty Musical Notables in Lively Symposium," *Musical America*, 25 May 1932, 6–8; there are numerous reprints of this article from different newspapers. Professional musicians, including the NBC orchestra conductor Walter Damrosch, were no less scathing; see *Washington (DC) Star*, 12 June 1932. Both articles in Vallée Scrapbooks, vol. 168, RVC.

55. *Pittsburgh Press*, 21 April 1932, Vallée Scrapbooks, vol. 60, RVC.

56. *Musical America*, 25 May 1932, vol. 168, Vallée Scrapbooks, RVC. See also Russo, *Female Grotesques*; Douglas, *Purity and Danger*.

57. *Syracuse Journal*, 4 March 1932, Vallée Scrapbooks, vol. 59, RVC.

58. "Broadening the Attack," unidentified news clipping, February or March 1932, Vallée Scrapbooks, vol. 59, RVC.

59. *Boston Post*, 7 November 1931; *Boston Globe*, 20 November 1931, Vallée Scrapbooks, vol. 33, RVC.

60. Stanley and Stanley, *The Science of Voice*, 5, 16–17, 11. Douglas Stanley also published in the popular press as an expert; *Tower Radio*, July 1934, 40–41, 93.

61. Stanley and Maxfield, *The Voice*, 39–40, 185–86, 49, 48.

62. Stanley and Maxfield, *The Voice*, 40.

63. Maxfield encountered similar problems when working on film sound. See Wurtzler, *Electric Sounds*, 266–75.

64. Stanley and Maxfield, *The Voice*, 242, 246, 251–54. See also chapter 6.

65. *Musician*, January 1932, 17.

66. "Sustaining" programs usually were those that could not find a sponsor because they represented more highbrow fare or public service programming. John Dunning, *On the Air*; *New York Journal*, 26 April 1932, Vallée Scrapbooks, vol. 60, RVC.

67. "Paul Whiteman Moves to Replace Crooners," *Akron (OH) Beacon-Journal*, 8 February 1932, Vallée Scrapbooks, vol. 59, RVC; *L.A. Record*, 10 February 1932, Vallée Scrapbooks, vol. 58, RVC; *Radio Guide*, 20 November 1932, 5, 10.

68. "Broadway Left Limp," *New York Telegram*, 12 January 1932; *Pittsburgh Press*, 12 January 1932 (syndicated), Vallée Scrapbooks, vol. 59, RVC.

69. *Cleveland Press*, 29 April 1932, Vallée Scrapbooks, vol. 60, RVC.

70. "Crooner's Day Over," *Zits*, 22 October 1932, Vallée Scrapbooks, vol. 64, RVC.

71. Unidentified news clipping, Vallée Scrapbooks, vol. 60, RVC.

72. *New Haven Register*, 12 January 1932, Vallée Scrapbooks, vol. 59, RVC.

73. *Brooklyn Eagle*, 10 March 1932, Vallée Scrapbooks, vol. 60, RVC.

74. *Pittsburgh Press*, 12 January 1932, Vallée Scrapbooks, vol. 59, RVC.

75. *Boston Transcript*, 16 January 1932, Vallée Scrapbooks, vol. 59, RVC.

76. Vallée quoted in Walter Winchell's column, *New York Mirror*, 8 February 1932, Vallée Scrapbooks, vol. 59, RVC.

77. Walter Winchell, *New York Mirror*, 8 February 1932, Vallée Scrapbooks, vol. 59, RVC.

78. In Vallée's case, both he and his radio program retained a devoted and broad audience throughout the attacks on crooners. Dartmouth undergraduates (distinct from Ivy-Leaguers) voted him their number one star in 1932; see "Dartmouth Poll," 25 May 1932, Vallée Scrapbooks, vol. 62, RVC. He also retained popularity as an orchestra leader: "Rudy Vallée Leads New Radio Poll: Nobody Seems to Know Exactly Why," *Buffalo (NY) Times*, 25 December 1932, Vallée Scrapbooks, vol. 64, RVC.

79. There are many letters to editors in defense of crooners; see, for example, "Men Are Rudy's Sole Defenders," *Pittsburgh Press*, December 1932, Vallée Scrapbooks, vol. 64, RVC; and Vallée Scrapbooks generally, vols. 59–60, RVC.

80. *New York World-Telegram*, 4 December 1931, Vallée Scrapbooks, vol. 33, RVC.

81. *New York News*, 15 January 1932, Vallée Scrapbooks, vol. 59, RVC.

82. Virginia P., Brooklyn, letter dated 31 December 1931, Rudy Vallée Correspondence, RVC. My assessment of fan response is based on printed excerpts of fan letters published in Wald's column and copies of the letters fans wrote to Wald defending Vallée that they then sent to Vallée.

83. See columns by Jerry Wald in the *New York Graphic*, especially 20 November 1931, 30 November 1931, 31 December 1931, 28 January 1932, 17 February 1932; all in Vallée Scrapbooks, vol. 33, RVC. There is no evidence to suggest that Vallée's marriage was a publicity stunt. The press frequently asked Vallée how he planned to prove he was a "real man." See, for example, *Cleveland Press*, 1 October 1932, Vallée Scrapbooks, vol. 67, RVC.

84. Fan letter sent to radio columnist "Uncle Nick," Nick Kenny, by the South Brooklyn Daffydils, dated 13 September 1932 and forwarded to Vallée by Kenny. See in Rudy Vallée Correspondence, RVC. *Hush New York* ceased publication after the indictment. *Broadway Brevities*, another more established gossip tabloid targeted at gay men, had never shown much interest in Vallée, which the *Brevities* scholar Will Straw attributes to the fact that the editors knew he wasn't same-sex-oriented, but he was also of very little interest to their readers as an icon of masculinity. Thanks to Will Straw for sharing his research on these magazines.

85. The important transitional crooning films of Bing Crosby are discussed at length in chapter 6.

86. Maurice Chevalier's imitation of Vallée imitating him seems to have been among the most successful and least mean-spirited of these parodies. See *Variety*, 27 October 1931, and *New Haven (CT) Times*, 15 October 1931, Vallée Scrapbooks, vol. 32, RVC.

87. Sheet music, "Crosby, Columbo, and Vallée," lyrics by Al Dubin, music by Joe Burke (New York: M. Witmark and Sons, 1931). The cartoon version appears under the same title and was released by Vitaphone in March 1932.

88. My description of the plot is based on a number of mixed reviews of the play, in Vallée Scrapbooks, vol. 62, RVC.

89. "Films Too 'Wise' for Men: Sophistication Explains Drop [in receipts]," *Variety*, 28 February 1933, quoted in Mann, *Behind the Screen*, 126.

90. James, *Crooner*, 14, 134.

91. James, *Crooner*, 279.

92. Notably, all-female bands are also presented in the film as "novelty acts," who, like crooners, take away jobs from legitimate male musicians.

93. See the press kit for *Crooner*, New York Public Library film archives.

94. *New York Times*, 2 September 1932, Vallée Scrapbooks, vol. 63, RVC.

95. *Memphis Press Scimitar*, 20 August 1932, Vallée Scrapbooks, vol. 63, RVC.

96. Ken Barry, *Portland (ME) Express*, 9 August 1932, Vallée Scrapbooks, vol. 63, RVC.

97. See, for example, *Brooklyn Times Union*, 22 and 25 August 1932; *New York Mirror*, 8 August 1932, Vallée Scrapbooks, vol. 63, RVC.

98. See ads in Vallée Scrapbooks, vol. 63, RVC; *Crooner* press kit, New York Public Library.

99. David Manners was one of the many outwardly gay actors who relocated to Holly-wood in the early 1930s from the New York stage. Although Manners played a number of "straight" roles in films, he is best known as the hero of 1930s horror films like *Dracula* (1931), *The Mummy* (1932), and *The Black Cat* (1934)—horror being a niche genre for gay actors and directors. See Mann, *Behind the Screen*, 108, 110–11.

100. The word *heliotrope*, which technically means "lavender plant," was often used as the equivalent of *pansy*.

101. *Boston Record*, 5 August 1932, Vallée Scrapbooks, vol. 63, RVC.

102. See Hilmes, *Radio Voices*, 118, 213–14; Smulyan, *Selling Radio*, 113–14; Douglas, *The Early Days of Radio Broadcasting*, 118.

103. *The Fleischmann Yeast Hour* aired on Thursdays from eight to nine, October 1929 to 1936; Thompson switched its sponsor in 1936, and the program aired as *The Royal Gelatin Hour* from 1936 to 1939. Vallée had several more radio programs during the 1940s, although none was as popular as this original radio hour. Various "Rudy Vallée" shows aired on NBC in 1940–43, 1944–46, and 1946–47, on WOR in 1950–51, and on CBS in 1955. Not surprisingly, Vallée's mantle as musical variety host passed to Crosby, whose Hollywood-based *Kraft Musical Hall* program, also on NBC, aired from 1936 to 1946.

104. Staff Meeting Minutes, 13 February 1930, J. Walter Thompson Agency Papers, Duke University, Durham, NC.

105. See, for example, Gilbert Swan, "Rudy Vallée Dons False Mustache and Winks Boldly to Forestall the Eclipse of Coy Glances and Crooning," *New York World-Telegram*, 29 December 1931, Vallée Scrapbooks, vol. 33, RVC. Swan asserts: "Rudy Vallée is a big boy now. He has grown up. He has learned how to clown."

106. On Perkins, see *Rochester (NY) Journal*, 8 April 1931, Rudy Vallée Scrapbooks, vol-ume unclear, RVC; *Radio Stars*, October 1932, 26–27. The original scripts and recordings are housed in the J. Walter Thompson archives at Duke University and in the RVC.

107. *Variety*, 12 July 1932; *Albany (NY) News*, 7 July 1932, Vallée Scrapbooks, vol. 63, RVC. Original recordings of these programs are in RVC.

108. Staff Meeting Minutes, 14 April 1931, J. Walter Thompson Agency Papers, Duke University.

109. Staff Meeting Minutes, 21 December 1932, J. Walter Thompson Agency Papers, Duke University. See also "The Hour That Made Radio History," *Tower Radio*, October 1934, Rudy Vallée Scrapbooks, vol. 171, RVC.

110. Staff Meeting Minutes, 21 December 1932, J. Walter Thompson Agency Papers, Duke University.

111. Hilmes, *Radio Voices*, 213–14.

112. *New York Times*, 21 May 1935; *Newsweek*, 25 January 1936, 45.

113. Hilmes, *Radio Voices*, 154.

114. *Pittsburgh Press*, 3 October 1932, Vallée Scrapbooks, vol. 67, RVC.

115. For program ratings, see Summers, *A Thirty-Year History of Programs Carried on Na-tional Radio Networks in the United States*. Ratings were produced and sold to advertisers

and networks by companies who polled households with telephones in urban areas, privileging middle-class audiences. Eileen Meehan, "Why We Don't Count."

116. See *Boston Record*, 17 October 1932; *Worcester (MA) Telegram*, 23 October 1932; *Bridgeport (CT) Sunday Herald*, 16 October 1932; *Radio Art*, October 1932; all in Vallée Scrapbooks, vol. 64, RVC. "The Dialist," *Newark (NJ) News*, 10 December 1932, Vallée Scrapbooks, vol. 65, RVC.

117. This report was nationally syndicated; see, for example, *Chicago American*, 20 October 1932, and *Los Angeles Times Herald-Express*, 20 October 1932, Vallée Scrapbooks, vol. 67, RVC.

118. See *Bridgeport (CT) Post*, 23 April 1932, and various *Pittsburgh Press* articles from 3 and 4 October 1932, Vallée Scrapbooks, vol. 67, RVC; see "heckler" coverage, such as *Cleveland (OH) Press*, 19 August 1932, in Vallée Scrapbooks, vol. 66, RVC.

119. "Rudy Vallée's Variety Show," *Radio Guide*, 16 April 1933, 12–13, 23; see also *Brooklyn Eagle*, 4 December 1932; *Screenland*, June 1932, 60–61, Vallée Scrapbooks, vols. 65 and 168, respectively, RVC.

120. Mike Porter, "Reviewing Radio," *Radio Guide*, 30 April 1933, Magazines, RVC; "The New Rudy Vallée," *Radio Stars*, November 1932, 8–9, 48.

121. "As I Hear It, 3 July 1932, *Albany (NY) Knickerbocker Press*, Vallée Scrapbooks, vol. 63, RVC.

122. "The Listener," *Albany (NY) Knickerbocker Press*, June 1932, and *Louisville KY Courier Journal*, 14 February 1932, Vallée Scrapbooks, vols. 62 and 59, respectively, RVC. Both writers note a perceived change in Vallée's voice over the past year, which would be consistent with the microphone change.

123. Radio column "As I Hear It," 3 July 1932, *Albany (NY) Knickerbocker Press*, Vallée Scrapbooks, vol. 63, RVC.

124. *Radio Guide*, 31 March 1932, Periodicals, RVC.

125. For more on this shift in microphone technology, see chapter 6.

126. "Let's Gossip about Your Favorites," *Radio Stars*, February 1932, 16.

127. "Intimate Shots of Your Favorite Stars," *Radio Stars*, issues 1932–33.

128. See *Radio Stars*: Downey, February 1933, 5, 48–49; Columbo, October 1932, 42; and "Little Jack's Little Secret," September 1933, 16–17, 49. Mother love does still appear as an important motivator in some of these fan profiles, but it is increasingly rare and disappears almost entirely by the mid-1930s.

129. See all *Ramblin Round Radio Row* shorts on *Warner Bros. Big Band, Jazz and Swing Short Subject Collection*.

130. See, for example, *Second Fiddle, The Palm Beach Story, The Bachelor and the Bobby-Soxer*, and *Unfaithfully Yours*.

131. Vallée's last well-known role was in the stage and film musical *How to Succeed in Business without Really Trying*, playing his characteristic stuffed shirt and wearing his pince-nez.

Six "THE KIND OF NATURAL THAT WORKED"

1. See these typical examples: "The Sun Is Setting on the Original Crooner," *New Haven (CT) Journal-Courier*, 21 March 1932, Vallée Scrapbooks, vol. 60, Rudy Vallée Collection,

American Radio Archives, Thousand Oaks Library, Thousand Oaks, CA (hereafter RVC). "Are Crooners Doomed?," *Radio Guide*, 5 June 1932, 1.

2. *Radio Guide*, 5 June 1932, 1.

3. "Still Another Week for Bing," *Variety*, 1 December 1931, 19.

4. Giddins, *Bing Crosby*, 202–3.

5. See *Syracuse Journal*, 4 March 1932, Vallée Scrapbooks, vol. 60, RVC.

6. Crosby's short films for Mack Sennett are *I Surrender Dear* (1931), *One More Chance* (1931), *Blue of the Night* (1932), *Billboard Girl* (1932), *Dream House* (1932), and *Sing, Bing, Sing* (1933).

7. My discussion of Crosby's early life and career is derived from several biographies of him, most prominently Giddins, *Bing Crosby*, in addition to Shepherd and Slatzer, *Bing Crosby*; Crosby and Firestone, *Going My Own Way*; Crosby, *Call Me Lucky*; Osterholm, *Bing Crosby*.

8. Giddins describes the *Bugle* as a "broad parody of a hillbilly newsletter," containing "minstrel quips, mock ads, and hayseed caricatures" that appealed to the young Crosby's sense of humor (*Bing Crosby*, 39–40).

9. Giddins, *Bing Crosby*, 37.

10. "Crosby and Rinker," *Variety*, 6 October 1926, 56.

11. Paul Whiteman's Rhythm Boys (vocal group), "Mississippi Mud / I Left My Sugar Standing in the Rain," Victor VIC BVE 39271, 1927, record, YouTube, version posted by pax41, 26 November 2008. There were two further versions of this song from 1928, one with Frank Trumbauer's Orchestra on Okeh Records in which the banter dominates the vocals.

12. Brackett, *Interpreting Popular Music*, 56.

13. Bing Crosby with the Paul Whiteman Orchestra, "Ol' Man River," Victor, 1928, YouTube.

14. For New York City audience perceptions of Crosby and Rinker as "cocky," see Giddins, *Bing Crosby*, 154.

15. Bing Crosby, "I Kiss Your Hand, Madame," Columbia, 1929, YouTube. A mordent is "a type of ornament which, in its standard form, consists in the rapid alternation of the main note with a subsidiary note a step below" (Oxford Music Online, http://www .oxfordmusiconline.com). The mordent would become critically valued as a mark of Crosby's authentic Irish identity; Giddins, *Bing Crosby*, 169, connects Crosby's specific use of the mordent, "that wavering catch in the voice," to its traditional use in Irish folk singing, an example of how essentialist authenticity discourses established in the 1920s around "folk" music still persist as a way to culturally value some commercial music over other kinds (see Miller, *Segregating Sounds*). Similar discourses were employed to culturally legitimize the Italian American Frank Sinatra's pop singing in the 1950s because of his purported use of Italian bel canto.

16. "Rhythm Boys," *Variety*, 1 April 1931, 56.

17. *Zits*, 23 January 1932, Vallée Scrapbooks, vol. 59, RVC. The writer notes that Vallée is a public-made star, unlike the imitators who have been promoted by broadcasting companies in the wake of his success: "He is one star who was not pushed onto the public but the public pushed onto him."

18. *New York Sun*, 5 September 1931, Vallée Scrapbooks, vol. 32, RVC.

19. *New York Sun*, 5 September 1931, Vallée Scrapbooks, vol. 32, RVC.

20. *Variety*, 26 January 1932, 1, 34.

21. "Russ Columbo, 'Slob Ballad Singer,' Is Something Like Vallée but Lower," *New York World Telegram*, 29 September 1931, Vallée Scrapbooks, vol. 32, RVC.

22. *New York Sunday News*, 13 December 1931, Vallée Scrapbooks, vol. 34, RVC.

23. My understanding of early microphones has been helped enormously by my discussions with the Hollywood sound engineer and mixer and microphone historian Jim Webb, on 12 December 2009 and several times in September 2014, and Thomas Miller, chair of the Department of Professional Studies and Sound Recording Technology at DePaul University's School of Music, on 10 October 2007. For more on directional microphones and the proximity effect, see Nisbett, *The Sound Studio*. For descriptions of these early microphones, see Jim Webb's website, http://www.coutant.org/12mics/. Engineers of the time, like J. P. Maxfield, were unhappy with the proximity effect and considered it a "flaw" in microphone design, not as problematic as the high pitch perception from condenser mics but still a "distortion" that allowed thinner voices to sound fuller and richer. By the mid-1930s the industry had developed microphones with "roll-offs" set into them to allow singers to adjust the lower frequency sound, but they did not always do so, and the proximity effect remained an important characteristic of popular recordings; it is still employed in popular recording today.

24. Crosby, *Call Me Lucky*, 113.

25. See the introduction of the ribbon microphone by RCA and use by NBC in "The New Ribbon Microphone," *Radio News*, June 1931, 1067, 1096, 1118; "Directional Microphones Aid Programs," *Radio News*, July 1931, 18, 74.

26. Curiously, Crosby's biographers do not make any mention of this key technological shift in microphone technology and its defining impact on Crosby's career. Jim Webb explains that there is general agreement among engineers that Crosby took advantage of the directional mics' proximity effect and that it was an essential aspect of his rise to fame. Jim Webb, interview with the author, 12 December 2009.

27. Hilmes, *Only Connect*, 73–78.

28. Noted in Shepherd and Slatzer, *Bing Crosby*.

29. *Radio Guide*, 28 November 1931, 5.

30. *New York World-Telegram*, 23 December 1931, Vallée Scrapbooks, vol. 34, RVC.

31. *Pittsburgh Sun-Telegraph*, 12 January 1932; *New York Daily Mirror*, 12 January 1932; *New York Evening Post*, 14 January 1932; all in Vallée Scrapbooks, vol. 59, RVC. See also Crosby's denials reported in Crosby, *The Story of Bing Crosby*, 200.

32. Giddins, *Bing Crosby*, 281.

33. *Zits*, 7 November 1931, Vallée Scrapbooks, vol. 34, RVC.

34. "New Acts: Russ Columbo, Crooner," *Variety*, 8 December 1931, 35.

35. *New York World-Telegram*, 24 October 1931, Vallée Scrapbooks, vol. 32, RVC.

36. *Zits*, 7 November 1931, Vallée Scrapbooks, vol. 34, RVC.

37. See, for example, the description of Crosby's singing having "a torchier tone and sweet, sexy intonations" in *Zits*, 31 October 1931, Vallée Scrapbooks, vol. 32, RVC.

38. *Radio Guide*, 4 February 1932, 13.

39. *Pictorial Review*, April 1932, Vallée Scrapbooks, vol. 168, RVC.

40. *Radio Guide*, 6 November 1932, 1, Vallée Scrapbooks, vol. 168, RVC.

41. Friedwald, *Jazz Singing*, 38. Crosby concurs in his autobiography: "Jack was always trying to make me the top figure in recording. . . . He wouldn't let me get typed" (*Call Me Lucky*, 139). See also Giddins's detailed chapter on Crosby's relationship with Kapp and their song production, "Decca," in *Bing Crosby*, 365–93.

42. See Giddins, *Bing Crosby*, 593–606.

43. Bing Crosby, with the studio orchestra, "What Do I Care, It's Home!," Brunswick, 1932, YouTube; Bing Crosby, with Jimmie Grier and His Orchestra, "There's a Cabin in the Pines," Brunswick, 1932, YouTube; Bing Crosby, with Lennie Hayton and His Orchestra, "The Last Round Up," Brunswick, 1933, YouTube; Bing Crosby, with Lennie Hayton and His Orchestra, "Home on the Range," Brunswick, 1933, YouTube; Bing Crosby, with Lennie Hayton and His Orchestra, "Let's Spend an Evening at Home," Brunswick, 1933, YouTube.

44. On Crosby's minstrel-inflected early songs other than "Mississippi Mud," see Bing Crosby, with Paul Whiteman and His Orchestra, "Oh! Miss Hannah," Columbia, 1929, YouTube; "Southern Medley," Columbia Private Pressing, 1929, YouTube; Bing Crosby with studio orchestra, "Shine," Brunswick, 1932, YouTube; Bing Crosby, with Lennie Hayton and His Orchestra, "Cabin in the Cotton," Brunswick, 1932, YouTube.

45. Bing Crosby with Lennie Hayton and His Orchestra, "Brother, Can You Spare a Dime?," by E. Y. "Yip" Harburg and Jay Gorney, Columbia, 1932, YouTube.

46. Dyer, *Heavenly Bodies*, 1–18.

47. Attaching microphones to boom poles that moved with the speaker (but remained out of the frame) was common practice by 1930. Many film studios began using directional mics in place of condenser microphones when they became widely available in the summer of 1931, although Sennett's operation was smaller and his early Crosby shorts from 1931–32 seem to have relied more on playback and postproduction sound. As *Radio News* notes, the directional ribbon microphone was sometimes termed the "camera of sound" "in as much as it can follow the entertainer just as a camera or spotlight." "Directional Microphones Aid Programs," *Radio News*, July 1931, 74. See also Carl Dreher, "Talking Film Improvements," *Radio News*, July 1931, 16.

48. Giddins, *Bing Crosby*, 63, writes of Crosby's disinterest in women from childhood. Dixie Lee, Crosby's wife, affirmed in a 1937 interview with the fan magazine writer Gladys Hall, "Bing really doesn't like women. He's typically and entirely a man's man." *Radio Stars*, August 1937, 20–21. See also interview transcript, 13 May 1937, 6, Gladys Hall papers, Margaret Herrick Library, Academy of Motion Picture Arts and Sciences, Beverly Hills, hereafter MHL.

49. On the Code, see Maltby, "The Production Code and the Hays Office"; McGregor, *The Catholic Church and Hollywood*, 77–106; Mann, *Behind the Screen*, 121–60; Barrios, *Screened Out*, chapters 5–7.

50. Mann, *Behind the Screen*, 141–42.

51. *Variety*, 9 October 1934, 1.

52. Mark Rappaport's film *Silver Screen: Color Me Lavender* (1997) offers a lengthy discussion of the gay allusions in Crosby's *Road* films, in which he is paired with the sissy character Bob Hope as a buddy.

53. Bauer, *Bing Crosby*, 68.

54. Pleasants, *The Great American Popular Singers*, 136.

55. Friedwald, *Jazz Singing*, 48.

56. Friedwald, *Jazz Singing*, 190.

57. Whitburn, *Pop Memories*, 106; Giddins, *Bing Crosby*, 480.

58. Rogin, *Blackface, White Noise*, 14.

59. Jolson visited on the occasion of the release of *The Jolson Story*, the first biographical musical of his life, which helped spur a revival of his music. *The Jolson Story*, directed by Alfred E. Green, Columbia, 1946; Giddins, *Riding on a Blue Note*, 16.

60. See, for example, the three-part profile of Crosby, "Confessions of a Crooner," in *Tower Radio*, April, May, June 1934, Broadcasting Collection: Magazines, RVC; "The Secret of Bing Crosby's Greatness," *Photoplay*, October 1935, 72–73; "Mrs. Bing Crosby Gets Confidential," *Radio Stars*, August 1937, 20–21. See also these drafts of interviews with Crosby and Dixie Lee by Gladys Hall in the Margaret Herrick Library: "Secrets of the Stars," conducted 28 February 1934; "I Worry about My Children," conducted 21 February 1937, and several Paramount studio biographies, circa 1933 and 1934, Paramount Production files, MHL.

61. "Back to the Farm," *Photoplay*, October 1934, 26–27; "Down on the Ranch," *Photoplay*, September 1935, 8–9.

62. See *Radio Guide* articles from 31 March 1932, 1; 21 July 1934, 31; 4 August 1934, 5; and a three-part article, "The Beloved Loafer," 21 September–5 October 1935.

63. See, for example, *Liberty* magazine's review of Crosby's career in 1939: "It hasn't always been easy to be a crooner. Remember that song, 'Crosby, Columbo and Vallée'? It wasn't a very complimentary song. At the time, it sounded like the funeral dirge for all three of them. Something had to be done about it. Russ got Carole Lombard to fall in love with him. Bing Crosby had twins." *Liberty*, 25 March 1939, 57.

64. "Mother Gets Credit for My Success Says Bing Crosby," *L.A. Times*, 12 March 1935, MHL; "The Secret of Bing Crosby's Greatness," *Photoplay*, October 1935, 72–73.

65. Jack Lait, "Bing Crosby," *Radio Guide*, 21 July 1934, 31.

66. "Bing Crosby Rebels," *Radio Guide*, 22 February 1936, 20–21; "Secrets of the Stars," 28 February 1934, unpublished interview draft, Gladys Hall papers, MHL.

67. "Confessions of a Crooner," *Tower Radio*, April 1934, 22; "The Secret of Bing Crosby's Greatness," *Photoplay*, October 1935, 72–73.

68. Morris, *American Catholic*, 133.

69. See "Priest Asks Movie Actor to Be Backed Up," *Catholic Courier*, 2 February 1935; "Successful Protest," *Brooklyn Tablet*, 30 March 1935; both MHL. The notorious *Sailor Beware* was eventually adapted, loosely, into a 1936 Paramount film starring Lew Ayres and entitled *Lady, Be Careful*.

70. Morris, *American Catholic*, 197; McGregor, *The Catholic Church and Hollywood*, 54–55, 71.

71. Crosby, *Call Me Lucky*, 186.

CONCLUSION

1. Rudy Vallée and His Connecticut Yankees, "Deep Night," by Rudy Vallée and Charlie Henderson, Victor, 1929, reissued on *Heigh-Ho Everybody This Is Rudy Vallée*, ASV Living Era AJA 5009, 1992, CD; *My Own Private Idaho* (1991).

2. See, for example, Amy Taubin, "Film '91," *Village Voice*, 14 January 1992, 58; J. Hoberman, "Lowlife of the Mind" (review of *My Own Private Idaho*), *Village Voice*, 1 October 1991, 60. "Deep Night" is also played in full during the end credits.

3. Taubin, "Film '91," 58.

4. Sinatra's immature, asexual early crooner is most conspicuous in his early MGM films with Gene Kelly, *Anchors Aweigh* (1945), *Take Me Out to the Ballgame* (1949), and *On the Town* (1950); notably, he is paired in all three films with the comedian Betty Garrett, who avidly pursues him. Garrett's character also clearly functions as a comment on the inappropriate sexual assertiveness of the swooner-crooner fan.

5. Keightley, "Frank Sinatra, Hi Fi and the Formations of Adult Culture." See also McNally, *When Frankie Went to Hollywood*. It is worth noting that many of these teen idols were assimilated white ethnic Catholic or Jewish working-class young men who nevertheless needed to prove their adherence to middle-class white masculine norms. African American crooners became popular after World War II as well but were not marketed as teen idols and maintained a "gentlemanly," romantic, but asexual presence, as epitomized by Nat King Cole.

6. See Ehrenreich, *The Hearts of Men*, 14–28, for an analysis of the homophobic cold war pressure to "mature" and marry. See Terry, *An American Obsession*, 329–52, on sexual deviance and national security.

7. Travis, *The Handbook of Speech Pathology* (1957); the entry "The Physiology of Organic Voice Defects" appears in the chapter "Organic Voice Disorders," 658. This same entry, wording unchanged, appears in the 1971 *Handbook*, which has otherwise been considerably revised; see Travis, *The Handbook of Speech Pathology and Audiology*, 539–40.

8. Travis, *Handbook of Speech Pathology and Audiology*, 828.

9. Greene, *The Voice and Its Disorders* (1957), 122. This book went through several editions through 2001.

10. Greene, *The Voice and Its Disorders* (1957), 121, 126–27.

11. Greene, *The Voice and Its Disorders* (1957), 127–28.

12. See David Sedaris's memories of forced speech therapy in school in the 1970s, "Go Carolina," in *Me Talk Pretty One Day*, 3–15. For other accounts, see David Thorpe's documentary film *Do I Sound Gay?* (2015).

13. Koestenbaum, *The Queen's Throat*, 164. Tiny Tim's brief popularity, however devalued, did suggest that this more gender-queer, sexually liberal time in America allowed more room for such a sound in the mainstream.

14. See Eve Sedgwick's discussion of the diagnostic manuals and similar texts in her essay "How to Bring Up Your Kids Gay."

15. Hutchinson et al., *Diagnostic Handbook of Speech Pathology*, 210, 217; Lass et al., *Handbook of Speech-Language Pathology and Audiology*, 812; Greene, *The Voice and Its Disorders* (1980), 241–44; Greene and Mathieson, *The Voice and Its Disorders* (2001), 208–10. Puberphonia is still a recognized condition (often now called "mutational falsetto"); treatment focuses on helping adolescent boys adjust to their changing voices.

16. See, for example, Cartei and Reby, "Acting Gay."

17. Ron Smyth, associate professor of psychology and linguistics at the University of Toronto, interview with the author, 27 April 2014. This articulation and duration include sibilant frequency (the "hissy s" sound) and duration ("ssssew" rather than "sew") and aspiration duration (breathier sounds caused by opening the lips for longer periods of time on key consonants). Smyth notes that while voices vary culturally, associations between perceived homosexuality and "feminine" voices largely do not and are common across many cultures. See Smyth et al., "Male Voices and Perceived Sexual Orientation." See also Gaudio, "Sounding Gay," one of the earliest scholarly articles to question vocal essentialism.

18. See Binkley, *Getting Loose*.

19. Many of these fans consider his queerest album to be his first solo effort, the very successful *Off the Wall* (1979), which combined disco and rhythm and blues genres. See Wald, "Dreaming of Michael Jackson," 1–7; Royster, *Sounding Like a No-No*, chapter 4, "Michael Jackson, Queer World Making, and the Trans Erotics of Voice, Gender, and Age," 116–41.

20. On African American vocal production, see Heilbut, *The Fan Who Knew Too Much*, chapter titled "The Male Soprano."

21. Even on Broadway falsettos were sufficiently rare as to be conspicuous. When *Les Miserables* debuted on Broadway in 1987, many theatergoers considered the Irish star Colm Wilkinson's falsetto in "Bring Him Home" the highlight of the show. See Will Crutchfield, "The Falsetto Enjoying New-Found Attention," *New York Times*, 16 March 1987 (accessed online).

22. See Hilderbrand, "'Luring Disco Dollies to a Life of Vice.'"

23. Tom Sinclair, *Entertainment Weekly*, 3 September 2003, 148–50.

24. For example, see the following issues of *Entertainment Weekly*: 28 September 2012, 80; 20–27 September 2013, 158.

25. "Overly Attached Girlfriend," *Entertainment Weekly*, 31 December 2012, 26.

26. Dan Snierson, "Hitlist," *Entertainment Weekly*, 6 January 2012, 18.

27. The hugely popular boy band One Direction has provoked similar masculine anxieties and ridicule of its fervent fan base. See, for example, a *British GQ* cover-story portrait of the band and its audience that was widely critiqued on social media; Jonathan Heaf, "Pop Inc," *British GQ*, September 2013 (accessed online). For a fuller discussion of boy bands and their reviled female audiences, see Wald, "'I Want It That Way'"; Lipsitz, *Footsteps in the Dark*, 1–7.

28. For example, in 2003 the *American Idol* sensation Clay Aiken's soft voice and romantic appeal for millions of women (called "Claymates") made him so sexually suspect to critics and the media that he was forced to publicly address questions about his sexuality. The same questions were notably never asked of his *American Idol* peers, although they were later again asked—with even more urgency—of Adam Lambert in 2008–9.

29. This process of masculine rehabilitation has been applied to individual singers and boy bands over the years. On boy bands, see Wald, "'I Want It That Way.'"

30. Clark Collis, "Justin Timberlake," *Entertainment Weekly*, year-end special, 2006; Clark Collis, "Sexybeast," *Entertainment Weekly*, 9 February 2007.

31. Chuck Arnold, review of "Justin Bieber's 'Believe,'" *People*, 19 June 2012, 43.

32. Rae Votta, journalist and manager of social media for VH1, interview with the author, 10 April 2012.

33. Such intense affect has a long half-life, especially for young people. For many years I have begun one of my recurring classes by asking students who their childhood crushes were; invariably almost all the young women and some young men name boy band members.

34. Votta interview. On *American Idol*, see Meizel, *Idolized*.

35. I have previously published on *Glee*'s Kurt and Blaine: McCracken, "The Countertenor and the Crooner."

36. Note that I'm using the descriptive *countertenor* for Colfer because it has been widely used in the media and by Colfer himself as a way of describing his vocal range for a popular audience; he is not, however, a classically trained countertenor. My thanks to the classical countertenor Ian Howell for making this distinction for me in correspondence, 5 August 2011.

37. Michael Shulman, "The Many Hats of Chris Colfer," *New York Times*, 21 December 2012 (accessed online).

38. Criss is biracial (Filipino/Irish American), but this fact is rarely mentioned except by him. Since he passes as white on-screen, his racial difference is invisible and he remains an exemplar of contemporary white masculinity.

39. Racheline Maltese, "Big Life, Small Space," Tumblr post, 23 January 2013, http://lettersfromtitan.tumblr.com.

40. The intense popularity of the Kurt and Blaine characters internationally reflects, in part, the well-established industry and fan base for "soft masculinities" in other countries, particularly those in East Asia. See, for example, Sun Jung's discussion of young male pop-

ular idols in *Korean Masculinities and Transcultural Consumption*. The characters are currently very popular in Russia, where their homosexuality is viewed as subversive.

41. YouTube comments on the audio releases of Kurt's solo "As If We Never Said Goodbye," 21–25 April 2011, and Blaine's solo (sung to Kurt), "Somewhere Only We Know," 2–6 April 2011. These songs were performed in the same episode, "Born This Way," aired 26 April 2011. Blaine's song was available earlier as part of the *Glee Presents the Warblers* album; its tracks were also leaked before its 19 April 2011 release.

42. *The Voice*, 5 November 2012; my critique of the program is based on viewing all existing seven seasons through 2014.

43. *Pinocchio*, supervising directors Hamilton Luske and Ben Sharpsteen, Disney, 1940. Cliff Edwards and Chorus, "When You Wish upon a Star," by Leigh Harline and Ned Washington, Victor, 1940, http://itunes.com.

44. See, for example, Darren Criss's concert at the Garage, Islington, London, on 6 July 2011, http://www.youtube.com/watch?v=wm2hTgvvfY4.

BIBLIOGRAPHY

ARCHIVAL SOURCES

J. Walter Thompson Archive. The John W. Hartman Center for Sales, Advertising and Marketing History. Duke University, Durham, NC.

Margaret Herrick Library, Academy of Motion Picture Arts and Sciences, Beverly Hills (MHL).

Rudy Vallée Collection. Scrapbooks, Correspondence, Scripts, Periodicals, and Recordings. The American Radio Archives, The Thousand Oaks Library, Thousand Oaks, CA (RVC).

UCLA Film and Television Archive, University of California, Los Angeles

Wendall Hall papers, State Historical Society of Wisconsin, Madison.

RECORDINGS: A NOTE

I have noted in the text both the original recording dates of popular songs and the release date of the "best of" CD reissues of them in the 1990s, where I first heard them. Most of the early 1920s crooners were released on specialty imprints by English companies such as Living Era (ASV Records) and Flapper (Pavilion Records); small U.S. labels such as Audiophile Records (New Orleans), Diamond Cut Productions (Edison archive, Hibernia, NJ), and The Old Masters (George Morrow collection, San Mateo, CA); and specialty imprints from large multinational corporations such as Art Deco (Columbia, Sony Music). Since then, many of these songs have become available on streaming music channels such as Pandora and Spotify, as well as on YouTube (see especially the recording historian Tim Gracyk's constantly updated treasure trove of early crooner recordings on his YouTube channel).

FILMOGRAPHY

Note: I first saw many of these films on VHS copies passed around in graduate school or on nitrate in the UCLA Film and Television Archives. Fortunately, many films have since been released on DVD, which I have noted. For the collections, I have not listed all the shorts on the DVDS, just the ones relevant to this project.

Selected Shorts

Clinching a Sale (with Harry Richman). Directed by Ray Cozine. USA: Paramount, 1930. UCLA Film Archives. YouTube.

Crosby, Columbo, and Vallée (cartoon). Directed by Rudolf Ising. USA: Warner Bros., 1932. Private Collection. YouTube.

Metro Movietone Revue I (Harry Rose, Van and Schenck, The Capitolians, Grace Rodgers). Directed by Nick Grinde. USA: MGM, 1929. On *The Dawn of Sound II*. USA: MGM/UA Home Video, 1993. VHS. Also on *The Broadway Melody*. "Special Features." USA: Turner Entertainment, 2005. DVD.

Metro Movietone Revue II (Harry Rose, Johnny Marvin, George Dewey Washington, The Locust Sisters). Directed by Nick Grinde. USA: MGM, 1929. On *The Dawn of Sound II*. USA: MGM/UA Home Video, 1993. VHS. Also on *The Broadway Melody*. "Special Features." USA: Turner Entertainment, 2005. DVD.

Metro Movietone Revue I (Jack Pepper, Joseph Regan). Directed by Nick Grinde. USA: MGM, 1930. On *The Dawn of Sound II*. USA: MGM/UA Home Video, 1993. VHS. Also on *The Broadway Melody*. "Special Features." USA: Turner Entertainment, 2005. DVD.

Metro Movietone Revue II (Jack Pepper, Ella Shields, George Dewey Washington, Joseph Regan, The Ponce Sisters). Directed by Nick Grinde. USA: MGM, 1930. On *The Dawn of Sound II*. USA: MGM/UA Home Video, 1993. VHS. Also on *The Broadway Melody*. "Special Features." USA: Turner Entertainment, 2005. DVD.

A Movietone Divertissement (Tom Waring, Johnny Marvin). USA: MGM, 1928. On *The Broadway Melody*. "Special Features" (as *Movietone Revue #7*). USA: Turner Entertainment, 2005. DVD.

Our Gang: "Follies of 1938." Directed by Gordon Douglas. USA: Hal Roach Studios, 1937. Private Collection. YouTube.

Rudy Vallée and His Connecticut Yankees 771. Directed by Murray Roth. USA: Warner Bros. Vitaphone, 1929. Private Collection.

Swooner Crooner. Directed by Frank Tashlin. USA: Warner Bros., 1944. Private Collection.

That Goes Double (with Russ Columbo) 1495–6. Directed by Joseph Henabery. USA: Warner Bros. Vitaphone, 1933. Private Collection.

Selected Short Film Collections

Bing at Sennett, vols. 1–2. USA: Festival Films, 1995. VHS. Contains *One More Chance* (directed by Mack Sennett; Sennett Picture Corp., 1931); *Sing, Bing, Sing* (directed by Babe Stafford; Sennett Picture Corp., 1933); *Billboard Girl* (directed by Leslie Pearce; Sennett Picture Corp., 1932).

Hollywood Rhythm: The Paramount Musical Shorts, 1929–1941, Volumes 1–4. USA: Kino Video, 1997. VHS. Contains *Musical Justice* (directed by Aubrey Scotto; Paramount, 1931); *Radio*

Rhythm (directed by Joseph Stanley; Paramount, 1929); *I Surrender Dear* (directed by Mack Sennett; Sennett Picture Corp., 1931).

Hollywood Rhythm: The Paramount Musical Shorts, Volume 2: The Best of Big Bands and Swing. USA: Kino Video, 2001. DVD. Contains *Blue of the Night* (directed by Leslie Pearce; Sennett Picture Corp., 1932); *The Musical Doctor* (directed by Ray Cozine; Paramount, 1932); *Singapore Sue* (directed by Casey Robinson; Paramount, 1932); *Dream House* (aka *Crooner's Holiday*) (directed by Del Lord; Sennett Picture Corp., 1932).

The Jazz Singer Deluxe Edition. USA: Warner Bros. Home Video, 2007. DVD. Contains *Al Jolson: A Plantation Act 359* (1926); *Van and Schenck: The Pennant Winning Battery of Songland 395* (1926); *The Police Quartette 2320* (1927); *Adele Rowland: Stories in Song 2348* (1928); *Dick Rich and His Melodious Monarchs 2595* (1928); *Gus Arnheim and His Ambassadors 2585* (1928); *Paul Tremaine and His Aristocrats 742* (1929); *Baby Rose Marie: The Child Wonder 809* (1929); *Larry Ceballas' Roof Garden Revue 2627* (1928).

Vitaphone Cavalcade of Musical Comedy Shorts Collection. USA: Warner Bros. Home Video, 2010. DVD.

Vitaphone Varieties. USA: Warner Bros. Home Video, 2011. DVD. Contains *The Revelers, 483* (1927), *Morrissey and Miller Nightclub Revue 2293* (1927), *Earl Burtnett (Collegiate Jazz Artist) and His Biltmore Hotel Orchestra 2285* (1927), *Val and Ernie Stanton in "Cut Yourself a Piece of Cake" 2586* (1928), *Jimmy Clemons in "The Dream Café" 2242* (1927), *Gladys Brockwell in "Hollywood Bound" 2235* (1928), *Jay C. Flippen in "The Ham What Am," 2581* (1928), *Dick Rich and His Synco-Symphonists 2594* (1928), *Eddie White in "I Thank You" 2689* (1928), *Jack Waldron in "A Little Breath of Broadway" 2681* (1928), *Earl Burtnett (Collegiate Jazz Artist) and His Biltmore Hotel Orchestra 2295* (1928), *The Rangers in "After the Round Up" 2900* (1928), *Frank Whitman in "The Surprising Fiddler" 703* (1929), *Harry Fox and His Six American Beauties, 828* (1929), *Jack White "The Premiere Clown of Broadway" and His Montrealers 791* (1929), *Oklahoma Bob Albright and His Rodeo Do Flappers 810* (1920), *Mel Klee in "The Prince of Wails" 826* (1929), *The Gotham Rhythm Boys 832* (1929), *Poor Aubrey 3674–5* (1929), *Revival Day 367* (1926?).

Vitaphone Varieties. Vol. 2. USA: Warner Bros. Home Video, 2012. DVD. Contains *Hawaiian Nights, 422* (1927), *Waring's Pennsylvanians 427, 428* (1927), *The Happiness Boys 537* (1927), *Harry Wayman and His Debutantes 2261* (1927), *Earl Burtnett (Collegiate Jazz Artist) and His Biltmore Hotel Orchestra 2294* (1928), *Abe Lyman and His Orchestra 2338* (1928), *Eddie Peabody in Banjoland 2560* (1928), *Roy Fox "The Whispering Cornettist" 2819.*

Warner Bros. Big Band, Jazz and Swing Short Subject Collection. USA: Turner Entertainment Co., 2009. DVD. Contains *Rambling Round Radio Row 1–6, 1932–33 Season; Rambling Round Radio Row 1–2, 1933–34 Season; Rambling Round Radio Row 1934–35 Season.*

Feature Films

Anchors Away. Directed by George Sidney. USA: MGM, 1945. DVD.

Ann Carver's Profession. Directed by Edward Buzzell. USA: Columbia, 1933. Private Collection. DVD.

Anything Goes. Directed by Lewis Milestone. USA: Paramount, 1936. DVD.

Applause. Directed by Rouben Mamoulian. USA: Paramount, 1929. DVD.

The Bachelor and the Bobby-Soxer. Directed by Irving Reis. USA: RKO, 1947. DVD.

The Big Broadcast of 1932. Directed by Frank Tuttle. USA: Paramount, 1932. Private Collection.

Blessed Event. Directed by Roy Del Ruth. USA: Warner Bros., 1932. DVD.

Bondage. Directed by Alfred Santell. USA: Fox Film Corp., 1933. UCLA Film Archives.

Bonnie and Clyde. Directed by Arthur Penn. USA: Warner Bros., 1967. DVD.

The Broadway Melody. Directed by Henry Beaumont. USA: MGM, 1929. DVD.

Broadway thru a Keyhole. Directed by Lowell Sherman. USA: Twentieth Century Pictures, 1933. DVD.

The Call of the Flesh. Directed by Charles Brabin. USA: MGM, 1930. UCLA Film Archives.

Chasing Rainbows (excerpts). Directed by Charles Reisner. USA: MGM, 1930. UCLA Film Archives.

Close Harmony. Directed by John Cromwell and A. Edward Sutherland. USA: Paramount, 1929. UCLA Film Archives.

College Humor. Directed by Wesley Ruggles. USA: Paramount, 1933. UCLA Film Archives. DVD.

Crooner. Directed by Lloyd Bacon. USA: Warner Bros., 1922. UCLA Film Archives / TCM Channel.

Cuban Love Song. Directed by W. S. Van Dyke. USA: MGM, 1931. UCLA Film Archives.

Dames. Directed by Ray Enright and Busby Berkeley. USA: Warner Bros., 1934. DVD.

Devil May Care. Directed by Sidney Franklin. USA: MGM, 1929. UCLA Film Archives.

Devil's Holiday. Directed by Edmund Goulding. USA: Paramount, 1930. UCLA Film Archives.

Do I Sound Gay? Directed by David Thorpe. USA: IFC Films / Sundance Selects, 2015. Theater.

Double or Nothing. Directed by Theodore Reed. USA: Paramount, 1937. DVD.

Follow Thru. Directed by Lloyd Corrigan. USA: Paramount, 1930. UCLA Film Archives.

Footlight Parade. Directed by Lloyd Bacon. USA: Warner Bros., 1933. DVD.

42nd Street. Directed by Lloyd Bacon. USA: Warner Bros., 1933. DVD.

The Gay Divorcee. Directed by Mark Sandrich. USA: RKO, 1934. DVD.

George White's Scandals. Directed by Thornton Freeland, Harry Lachman, and George White. USA: Fox, 1934. TCM Channel / DVD.

Glorifying the American Girl. Directed by Millard Webb. USA: Paramount, 1929. TCM Channel.

Going Hollywood. Directed by Raoul Walsh. USA: MGM, 1933. DVD.

Going My Way. Directed by Leo McCarey. USA: Paramount, 1944. DVD.

Gold Diggers of Broadway (excerpts). Directed by Roy Del Ruth. USA: Warner Bros., 1929. UCLA Film Archives. On *The Dawn of Sound I*. USA: MGM/UA Home Video, 1992. VHS. Also on *The Jazz Singer Deluxe Edition*. USA: Warner Bros. Home Video, 2007. DVD.

Gold Diggers of 1933. Directed by Mervyn LeRoy. USA: Warner Bros., 1933. DVD.

Good News (excerpts). Directed by Nick Grinde. USA: MGM, 1930. UCLA Film and Television Archives.

Good News. Directed by Charles Walters. USA: MGM, 1947. DVD.

Hallelujah. Directed by King Vidor. USA: MGM, 1929. DVD.

Holiday Inn. Directed by Mark Sandrich. USA: Paramount, 1942. DVD.

The Hollywood Revue of 1929. Directed by Charles Reisner. USA: MGM, 1929. VHS Private Collection. DVD.

How to Succeed in Business without Really Trying. Directed by David Swift. USA: United Artists, 1967. DVD.

In Gay Madrid. Directed by Robert Z. Leonard. USA: MGM, 1930. UCLA Film Archives.

International House. Directed by A. Edward Sutherland. USA: Paramount, 1933. DVD.

The Jazz Singer. Directed by Alan Crosland. USA: Warner Bros., 1927. DVD.

The King of Jazz. Directed by John Murray Anderson. USA: Universal, 1930. DVD.

The Letter. Directed by Jean De Limur. USA: Warner Bros., 1929. DVD.

Love Me Tonight. Directed by Rouben Mamoulian. USA: Paramount, 1932. DVD.

Mississippi. Directed by Edward Sutherland. USA: Paramount, 1935. UCLA Film Archives. DVD.

Mother's Boy. Directed by Bradley Barker. USA: Pathé Exchange, 1929. UCLA Film Archives.

Moulin Rouge. Directed by Sidney Lanfield. USA: Twentieth Century Pictures, 1934. UCLA Film Archives.

My Own Private Idaho. Directed by Gus Van Sant. USA: New Line Cinema, 1991. DVD.

On the Town. Directed by Gene Kelly and Stanley Donen. USA: MGM, 1949. DVD.

The Palm Beach Story. Directed by Preston Sturges. USA: Paramount, 1942. DVD.

Paramount on Parade. Directed by Dorothy Arzner (10 others). USA: Paramount, 1930. Private Collection. VHS.

Pennies from Heaven. Directed by Norman McLeod. USA: Paramount, 1936. UCLA Film Archives. DVD.

Radio Days. Directed by Woody Allen. USA: MGM, 1987. DVD.

Rhythm on the Range. Directed by Norman Taurog. USA: Paramount, 1936. DVD.

Road to Morocco. Directed by David Butler. USA: Paramount, 1942. DVD.

Road to Singapore. Directed by Victor Schertzinger. USA: Paramount, 1940. DVD.

The Rogue Song. Directed by Lionel Barrymore. USA: MGM, 1930. UCLA Film Archives.

Sadie McKee. Directed by Clarence Brown. USA: MGM, 1934. DVD.

Second Fiddle. Directed by Sidney Lanfield. USA: Twentieth Century Fox, 1939. DVD.

The Show of Shows. Directed by John G. Adolfi. USA: Warner Bros., 1929. DVD.

The Singing Fool. Directed by Lloyd Bacon. USA: Warner Bros., 1928. DVD.

Song o' My Heart. Directed by Frank Borzage. USA. 1930. UCLA Film Archives. DVD.

So This Is College. Directed by Sam Wood. USA: MGM, 1929. DVD.

Stage Struck. Directed by Busby Berkeley. USA: Warner Bros., 1936. UCLA Film Archives.

Sweet Music. Directed by Alfred E. Green. USA: Warner Bros., 1935. TCM Channel.

Take Me Out to the Ballgame. Directed by Busby Berkeley. USA: MGM, 1949. DVD.

Three on a Match. Directed by Mervyn LeRoy. USA: Warner Bros., 1932. DVD.

Too Much Harmony. Directed by Edward Sutherland. USA: Paramount, 1933. UCLA Film Archives.

Top Hat. Directed by Mark Sandrich. USA: RKO, 1935. DVD.

20 Million Sweethearts. Directed by Ray Enright. USA: Warner Bros., 1934. TCM Channel.

Unfaithfully Yours. Directed by Preston Sturges. USA: Fox, 1948. DVD.

The Vagabond Lover. Directed by Marshall Neilan. USA: RKO, 1929. TCM Channel.

Waikiki Wedding. Directed by Frank Tuttle. USA: Paramount, 1937. DVD.

We're Not Dressing. Directed by Lewis Milestone. USA: Paramount, 1936. DVD.

Young at Heart. Directed by Gordon Douglas. USA: Warner Bros., 1954. DVD.

WRITTEN WORKS

Abbott, Lynn, and Doug Seroff. *Out of Sight: The Rise of African American Popular Music, 1889–1895*. Jackson: University Press of Mississippi, 2002.

————. *Ragged but Right: Black Traveling Shows, "Coon Songs," and the Dark Pathway to Blues and Jazz*. Jackson: University Press of Mississippi, 2007.

Abel, Richard. *Americanizing the Movies and "Movie-Mad" Audiences, 1910–1914*. Berkeley: University of California Press, 2006.

————. "The Most American of Attractions, the Illustrated Song." In *The Sounds of Early Cinema*, ed. Richard Abel and Rick Altman. Bloomington: Indiana University Press, 2001.

Abel, Richard, and Rick Altman, eds. *The Sounds of Early Cinema*. Bloomington: Indiana University Press, 2001.

Abelove, Henry. "Freud, Male Homosexuality and the Americans." In *The Lesbian and Gay Studies Reader*, ed. Henry Abelove, Michele Aina Barale, and David Halperin. New York: Routledge, 1993.

Acland, Charles, R., ed. *Residual Media*. Minneapolis: University of Minnesota Press, 2007.

Addison, Heather. *Hollywood and the Rise of Physical Culture*. New York: Routledge, 2003.

Adickes, Sandra. *To Be Young Was Very Heaven: Women in New York before the First World War*. New York: St. Martin's Press, 1997.

Adorno, Theodor. "On Jazz." *Discourse* 12, no. 1 (1989): 44–69.

————. *Sound Figures*. Stanford: Stanford University Press, 1999.

Albertson, Chris. *Bessie*. New Haven, CT: Yale University Press, 2003.

Allen, Frederick Lewis. *Only Yesterday: An Informal History of the 1920's*. New York: Harper-Collins, 2000.

Allen, Robert C. *Horrible Prettiness: Burlesque and American Culture*. Chapel Hill: University of North Carolina Press, 1991.

Altman, Rick. *The American Film Musical*. Bloomington: Indiana University Press, 1987.

———. "Cinema and Popular Song: The Lost Tradition." In *Soundtrack Available: Essays on Film and Popular Music*, ed. Pamela Robertson Wocjik and Arthur Knight. Durham, NC: Duke University Press, 2001.

———. *Silent Film Sound*. New York: Columbia University Press, 2004.

———, ed. *Sound Theory, Sound Practice*. New York: Routledge, 1992.

———. "The Technology of the Voice, Part One." *Iris* 3, no. 1 (1985): 3–20.

———. "The Technology of the Voice, Part Two." *Iris* 4, no. 1 (1986): 107–18.

American Academy of Teachers in Singing. "Reasons for Studying Singing." *Etude*, July 1931, 510.

———. *Singing, the Well-Spring of Music*. New York: American Academy of Teachers in Singing, 1933.

Anderson, Mark Lynn. *Twilight of the Idols: Hollywood and the Human Sciences in 1920s America*. Berkeley: University of California Press, 2011.

Anderton, Barries. *Sonny Boy: The World of Al Jolson*. London: Jupiter Books, 1995.

Antler, Joyce. *You Never Call! You Never Write: A History of the Jewish Mother*. New York: Oxford University Press, 2007.

Armstrong, Louis. *Swing That Music*. New York: Da Capo Press, 1993.

Arnheim, Rudolf. *Radio*. 1936. New York: Arno Press, 1971.

Baade, Christina L. *Victory through Harmony: The BBC and Popular Music in World War II*. New York: Oxford University Press, 2012.

Balio, Tino. *Grand Design: Hollywood as a Modern Business Enterprise, 1930–1939*. Berkeley: University of California Press, 1993.

Balk, Alfred. *The Rise of Radio: From Marconi through the Golden Age*. Jefferson, NC: McFarland, 2006.

Barkin, Elaine, and Lydia Hamessley. *Audible Traces: Gender, Identity, and Music*. Los Angeles: Carciofoli Verlagschaus, 1999.

Barnes, Ken. *The Crosby Years*. New York: St. Martin's Press, 1980.

———. *Sinatra and the Great Song Stylists*. London: Ian Allen, 1972.

Barnouw, Erik. *A History of Broadcasting in the United States*. Vol. 1: *A Tower in Babel: To 1933*. New York: Oxford University Press, 1966.

Barrios, Richard. *Screened Out: Playing Gay in Hollywood from Edison to Stonewall*. New York: Routledge, 2003.

———. *A Song in the Dark: The Birth of the Musical Film*. 2nd ed. New York: Oxford University Press, 2010.

Barris, Alex. *Hollywood's Other Men*. New York: A. S. Barnes, 1975.

Barthes, Roland. "The Grain of the Voice." In *Image, Music, Text*. Trans. Stephen Heath. New York: Hill and Wang, 1977.

————. *The Responsibility of Forms: Critical Essays on Music, Art, and Representation*. Trans. Richard Howard. New York: Hill and Wang, 1985.

Bauer, Barbara. *Bing Crosby*. Pyramid History of the Movies. New York: Pyramid, 1977.

Bean, Annemarie, James V. Hatch, and Brooks McNamara, eds. *Inside the Minstrel Mask: Readings in Nineteenth Century Blackface Minstrelsy*. Hanover, NH: Wesleyan University Press, 1996.

Bederman, Gail. *Manliness and Civilization: A Cultural History of Gender and Race in the United States, 1880–1917*. Chicago: University of Chicago Press, 1995.

Beebe, Roger, Denise Fulbrook, and Ben Saunders, eds. *Rock over the Edge: Transformations in Popular Music Culture*. Durham, NC: Duke University Press, 2002.

Bell, Anne Oliver. *The Diary of Virginia Woolf: Volume One 1915–1919*. San Diego: Harvest Books, 1977.

Bennett, Andy. *Popular Music and Youth Culture: Music, Identity, and Place*. New York: St. Martin's Press, 2000.

Bennett, Chad. "Flaming the Fans: Shame and the Aesthetics of Queer Fandom in Todd Haynes's *Velvet Goldmine*." *Cinema Journal* 49, no. 2 (2010): 17–39.

Bennett, Tony, with Will Friedwald. *The Good Life*. New York: Pocket Books, 1998.

Benson, Susan Porter. *Counter Cultures: Saleswomen, Managers, and Customers in American Department Stores, 1890–1940*. Champaign: University of Illinois Press, 1986.

————. *Household Accounts: Working-Class Family Economics in the Interwar United States*. Ithaca, NY: Cornell University Press, 2007.

Bergreen, Laurence. *As Thousands Cheer: The Life of Irving Berlin*. New York: Penguin Books, 1990.

Berlant, Lauren. *The Female Complaint: The Unfinished Business of Sentimentality in American Culture*. Durham, NC: Duke University Press, 2008.

Biddle, Ian, and Kirsten Gibson, eds. *Masculinity and the Western Musical Practice*. Burlington, VT: Ashgate, 2009.

Billman, Larry. *Fred Astaire: A Bio-Bibliography*. Westport, CT: Greenwood Press, 1997.

Binkley, Sam. *Getting Loose: Lifestyle Consumption in the 1970s*. Durham, NC: Duke University Press, 2007.

Biocca, Frank. "Media and Perceptual Shifts: Early Radio and the Clash of Musical Cultures." *Journal of Popular Culture* 24 (Fall 1990): 1–15.

Blake, Angela M. *How New York Became American, 1890–1924*. Baltimore: Johns Hopkins University Press, 2006.

Bodnar, John. *The Transplanted: A History of Immigrants in Urban America*. Bloomington: Indiana University Press, 1987.

Bookbinder, Robert. *The Films of Bing Crosby*. Secaucus, NJ: Citadel, 1977.

Bordman, Gerald. *American Musical Theatre: A Chronicle*. New York: Oxford University Press, 1986.

Bowlly, Al. *Modern Style Singing*. London: Henri Selmer, 1934.

Brackett, David. *Interpreting Popular Music*. Cambridge: Cambridge University Press, 1995.

————, ed. *The Pop, Rock, and Soul Reader: Histories and Debates*. New York: Oxford University Press, 2005.

Braun, Hans-Joachim, ed. *"I Sing the Body Electric": Music and Technology in the 20th Century*. New York: Wolke, 2000.

Brett, Philip, Elizabeth Wood, and Gary C. Thomas, eds. *Queering the Pitch: The New Gay and Lesbian Musicology*. New York: Routledge, 1994.

Brooks, Daphne. *Bodies in Dissent: Spectacular Performances of Race and Freedom, 1850–1910*. Durham, NC: Duke University Press, 2006.

————. "'Once More with Feeling': Popular Music Studies in the New Millennium." *Journal of Popular Music Studies* 22, no. 1 (2010).

————. "'The Voice Which Is Not One': Amy Winehouse Sings the Ballad of Sonic Blue(s)-face Culture." *Women and Performance* 20, no. 1 (2010).

Brooks, Tim. *Lost Sounds: Blacks and the Birth of the Recording Industry, 1890–1919*. Urbana: University of Illinois Press, 2004.

Brown, Jayna. *Babylon Girls: Black Women Performers and the Shaping of the Modern*. Durham, NC: Duke University Press, 2008.

Brundage, W. Fitzhugh, ed. *Beyond Blackface: African Americans and the Creation of American Popular Culture, 1890–1930*. Chapel Hill: University of North Carolina Press, 2011.

Bull, Michael, and Les Back. *The Auditory Culture Reader*. New York: Berg Press, 2003.

Burnim, Mellonee V., and Portia K. Maultsby. *African American Music: An Introduction*. New York: Routledge, 2006.

Burrough, Bryan. *Public Enemies: America's Greatest Crime Wave and the Birth of the FBI, 1933–34*. New York: Penguin Books, 2004.

Butler, Judith. *Undoing Gender*. New York: Routledge, 2004.

Butsch, Richard. *The Citizen Audience: Crowds, Publics, and Individuals*. New York: Routledge, 2008.

————. *The Making of American Audiences: From Stage to Television, 1750–1990*. New York: Cambridge University Press, 2000.

Caffin, Caroline. *Vaudeville: The Book*. New York: Mitchell Kennerley, 1914.

Calverton, V. F. *The Bankruptcy of Marriage*. New York: Macaulay, 1928.

Calverton, V. F., and Samuel D. Schmalhausen, eds. *The New Generation: The Intimate Problems of Modern Parents and Children*. New York: Macaulay, 1930.

Cantor, Eddie. *My Life Is in Your Hands*. New York: Harper and Brothers, 1928.

Cartei, Valentina, and David Reby. "Acting Gay: Male Actors Shift the Frequency Components of Their Voices towards Female Values When Playing Homosexual Characters." *Journal of Nonverbal Behavior* 36, no. 1 (2012): 79–93.

Carter, Julian B. *The Heart of Whiteness: Normal Sexuality and Race in America, 1880–1940*. Durham, NC: Duke University Press, 2007.

Cavanaugh, Jack. *Tunney: Boxing's Brainiest Champ and His Upset of the Great Jack Dempsey*. New York: Random House, 2006.

Cavicchi, Daniel. *Listening and Longing: Music Lovers in the Age of Barnum*. Middletown, CT: Wesleyan University Press, 2011.

Chafe, William Henry. *The American Woman: Her Changing Social, Economic, and Political Roles, 1920–1970*. New York: Oxford University Press, 1972.

Chanan, Michael. *Repeated Takes: A Short History of Recording and Its Effects on Music*. New York: Verso, 1995.

Charters, Ann. *Nobody: The Story of Bert Williams*. New York: Da Capo Press, 1983.

Chauncey, George. *Gay New York: Gender, Urban Culture, and the Making of the Gay Male World 1890–1940*. New York: Basic Books, 1994.

Chevigny, Paul. *Gigs: Jazz and the Cabaret Law in New York City*. 2nd ed. New York: Routledge, 2005.

Chude-Sokei, Louis. *The Last Darky: Bert Williams, Black-on-Black Minstrelsy, and the African Diaspora*. Durham, NC: Duke University Press, 2006.

Clement, Elisabeth. *Love for Sale: Courting, Treating, and Prostitution in New York City, 1900–1945*. Chapel Hill: University of North Carolina Press, 2006.

Coates, Norma. "(R)evolution Now? Rock and the Political Potential of Gender." In *Sexing the Groove: Popular Music and Gender*, ed. Sheila Whiteley. New York: Routledge, 1997.

Coben, Stanley. *Rebellion against Victorianism: The Impetus for Cultural Change in 1920s America*. New York: Oxford University Press, 1991.

Cockrell, Dale. *Demons of Disorder: Early Blackface Minstrels and Their World*. New York: Cambridge University Press, 1997.

Cohen, Lizabeth. *A Consumer's Republic: The Politics of Mass Consumption in Postwar America*. New York: Vintage Books, 2003.

——. *Making a New Deal: Industrial Workers in Chicago, 1919–1939*. New York: Cambridge University Press, 1990.

Coilin, Sid, and Tony Staveacre. *Al Bowlly*. London: Elm Tree Books, 1977.

Connell, R. W. *Masculinities*. 2nd ed. Berkeley: University of California Press, 2005.

——. "The Social Organization of Masculinity." In *Feminist Theory Reader: Local and Global Perspectives*, ed. Carol McCann and Kim Seung-Kyung. New York: Routledge, 2009.

Cook, Nicholas, and Anthony Pople, eds. *The Cambridge History of Twentieth-Century Music*. New York: Cambridge University Press, 2004.

Cooke, James Francis. *Great Singers on the Art of Singing: Educational Conferences with Foremost Artists*. Philadelphia: Theo. Presser, 1921.

Coontz, Stephanie. *Marriage, a History: From Obedience to Intimacy or How Love Conquered Marriage*. New York: Viking, 2005.

Cooper, Kim, and David Smay, eds. *Bubblegum Music Is the Naked Truth*. Los Angeles: Feral House, 2001.

Cott, Nancy F., ed. *History of Women in the United States: Historical Articles on Women's Lives and Activities*. Vol. 10: *Sexuality and Sexual Behavior*. New York: K. G. Sauer, 1993.

———, ed. *Public Vows: A History of Marriage and the Nation.* Cambridge, MA: Harvard University Press, 2000.

Couvares, Francis G., ed. *Movie Censorship and American Culture.* Washington, DC: Smithsonian Institution Press, 1996.

Coward, Noel. *Private Lives.* Garden City, NY: Doubleday, 1930.

Crafton, Donald. *The History of American Cinema.* Vol. 4: *The Talkies: America's Transition to Sound, 1926–1931.* New York: Simon and Schuster, 1997.

Craig, Maxine Leeds. *Sorry I Don't Dance: Why Men Refuse to Move.* New York: Oxford University Press, 2013.

Crosby, Bing. *Call Me Lucky.* 2nd ed. New York: Da Capo Press, 1993.

Crosby, Gary, with Ross Firestone. *Going My Own Way.* New York: Doubleday, 1983.

Crosby, Ted. *The Story of Bing Crosby.* New York: World, 1946.

Czitrom, Daniel J. *Media and the American Mind: From Morse to McLuhan.* Chapel Hill: University of North Carolina Press, 1982.

Davis, Angela Y. *Blues Legacies and Black Feminism: Gertrude "Ma" Rainey, Bessie Smith and Billie Holiday.* New York: Pantheon Books, 1998.

Davis, Janet. *The Circus Age: Culture and Society under the American Big Top.* Chapel Hill: University of North Carolina Press, 2002.

Davis, Katharine Bement. *Factors in the Sex Life of Twenty-Two Hundred Women.* New York: Arno Press, New York Times, 1972.

DeCordova, Richard. *Picture Personalities: The Emergence of the Star System in America.* Chicago: University of Illinois Press, 1990.

De La Pena, Carolyn Thomas. *The Body Electric: How Strange Machines Build the Modern American.* New York: New York University Press, 2003.

———. "Slow and Low Progress, or Why American Studies Should Do Technology." *American Quarterly* 58, no. 3 (2006): 915–41.

DeLong, Thomas A. *The Mighty Music Box.* Los Angeles: Amber Crest Books, 1980.

———. *Radio Stars: An Illustrated Biographical Dictionary of 953 Performers, 1920 through 1960.* Jefferson, NC: McFarland, 1996.

D'Emilio, John. "Capitalism and Gay Identity." In *Powers of Desire: The Politics of Sexuality,* ed. Ann Snitow, Christine Stansell, and Sharon Thompson. New York: Monthly Review Press, 1983.

D'Emilio, John, and Estelle Freedman. *Intimate Matters: A History of Sexuality in America.* New York: Harper and Row, 1988.

Denning, Michael. *The Cultural Front: The Laboring of American Culture in the Twentieth Century.* New York: Verso, 1996.

Deutsch, Sarah Jane. "From Ballots to Breadlines, 1920–1940." In *No Small Courage: A History of Women in the United States,* ed. Nancy Cott. New York: Oxford University Press, 2000.

Dimeglio, John E. *Vaudeville U.S.A.* Bowling Green, OH: Bowling Green University Popular Press, 1973.

Diner, Hasia R. *Erin's Daughters in America: Irish Immigrant Women in the Nineteenth Century.* Baltimore: Johns Hopkins University Press, 1983.

Doctor, Jennifer. *The BBC and Ultra-Modern Music, 1922–1936: Shaping a Nation's Tastes.* Cambridge: Cambridge University Press, 1999.

Doerksen, Clifford J. *American Babel: Rogue Radio Broadcasters of the Jazz Age.* Philadelphia: University of Pennsylvania Press, 2005.

Doherty, Thomas. *Hollywood's Censor: Joseph I. Breen and the Production Code.* New York: Columbia University Press, 2009.

———. *Pre-Code Hollywood: Sex, Immorality, and Insurrection in American Cinema, 1930–1934.* New York: Columbia University Press, 1999.

Donnelly, K. J. *The Spectre of Sound: Music in Film and Television.* London: British Film Institute, 2005.

Douglas, Ann. *Terrible Honesty: Mongrel Manhattan in the 1920s.* New York: Farrar, Straus and Giroux, 1995.

Douglas, George. *The Early Days of Radio Broadcasting.* Jefferson, NC: McFarland, 1987.

Douglas, Mary. *Purity and Danger: An Analysis of the Concepts of Pollution and Taboo.* New York: Praeger, 1966.

Douglas, Susan. *Inventing American Broadcasting, 1899–1922.* Baltimore: Johns Hopkins University Press, 1987.

———. *Listening In: Radio and the American Imagination.* New York: Random House, 1999.

———. *Where the Girls Are: Growing Up Female with the Mass Media.* New York: Random House, 1994.

Doyle, Peter. *Echo and Reverb: Fabricating Space in Popular Music Recordings, 1900–1960.* Middletown, CT: Wesleyan University Press, 2005.

———. "From 'My Blue Heaven' to 'Race with the Devil': Echo, Reverb and (Dis)ordered Space in Early Popular Music Recording." *Popular Music* 23 (2004): 31–49.

Dragonette, Jessica. *Faith Is a Song: The Odyssey of an American Artist.* New York: David McKay, 1951.

Drutman, Irving. *Good Company.* Boston: Little, Brown, 1976.

Duberman, Martin, Martha Vicinus, and George Chauncey Jr., eds. *Hidden from History: Reclaiming the Gay and Lesbian Past.* New York: New American Library, 1989.

Duchan, Joshua S. *Powerful Voices: The Musical and Social World of Collegiate a Capella.* Ann Arbor: University of Michigan Press, 2012.

Duggan, Lisa. "The Social Enforcement of Heterosexuality and Lesbian Resistance in the 1920s." In *Class, Race, and Sex: The Dynamics of Control*, ed. Amy Swerdlow and Hanna Lessinger. Boston: G. K. Hall, 1983.

Dunning, John. *On the Air: The Encyclopedia of Old-Time Radio.* New York: Oxford University Press, 1998.

Durand, Regis. "The Disposition of the Voice." In *Mimesis, Masochism, and Mime: The Politics of Theatricality in Contemporary French Thought*, ed. Timothy Murray. Ann Arbor: University of Michigan Press, 1997.

Dyer, Richard. *Heavenly Bodies: Film Stars and Society*. New York: St. Martin's Press, 1986.

———. *In the Space of a Song: The Uses of Song in Film*. New York: Routledge, 2012.

———. *Only Entertainment*. New York: Routledge, 1992.

———. *White*. Routledge: New York, 1997.

Echols, Alice. *Hot Stuff: Disco and the Remaking of American Culture*. New York: Norton, 2010.

Ehrenreich, Barbara. *The Hearts of Men: American Dreams and the Flight from Commitment*. New York: Anchor, 1987.

Ehrenreich, Barbara, Elisabeth Hess, and Gloria Jacobs. "Beatlemania: A Sexually Defiant Subculture?" In *The Subcultures Reader*, ed. Ken Gilder and Sarah Thornton. New York: Routledge, 1997.

Emerson, Ken. *DooDah! Stephen Foster and the Rise of American Popular Culture*. New York: Da Capo Press, 1997.

Ennis, Philip H. *The Seventh Stream: The Emergence of RocknRoll in American Popular Music*. Hanover, NH: Wesleyan University Press, 1992.

Erenberg, Lewis A. "From New York to Middletown: Repeal and the Legitimatization of Nightlife in the Great Depression." *American Quarterly* 38 (1986): 761–68.

———. *Steppin' Out: New York Nightlife and the Transformation of American Culture, 1890–1930*. Westport, CT: Greenwood Press, 1981.

———. *Swingin' the Dream: Big Band Jazz and the Rebirth of American Culture*. Chicago: University of Chicago Press, 1998.

Ericksen, Julia A., and Sally A. Steffen. *Kiss and Tell: Surveying Sex in the Twentieth Century*. Cambridge, MA: Harvard University Press, 1999.

Ewen, David. *The Life and Death of Tin Pan Alley: The Golden Age of American Popular Music*. New York: Funk and Wagnall, 1964.

Eyman, Scott. *The Speed of Sound: Hollywood and the Talkie Revolution, 1926–1930*. Baltimore: Johns Hopkins University Press, 1997.

Fass, Paula. *The Damned and the Beautiful: American Youth in the 1920s*. New York: Oxford University Press, 1977.

Faulkner, Howard J., and Virginia D. Pruitt, eds. *Dear Dr. Menninger: Women's Voices from the Thirties*. Columbia: University of Missouri Press, 1997.

Feld, Steven, and Keith H. Basso, eds. *Senses of Place*. Santa Fe, NM: School of American Research Press, 1996.

Felski, Rita. *The Gender of Modernity*. Cambridge, MA: Harvard University Press, 1995.

Finson, Jon W. *The Voices That Are Gone: Themes in 19th-Century American Popular Song*. New York: Oxford University Press, 1994.

Fischer, Claude A. *America Calling: A Social History of the Telephone to 1940*. Berkeley: University of California Press, 1992.

Fischer, Lucy, ed. *American Cinema of the 1920s*. New Brunswick, NJ: Rutgers University Press, 2009.

Fisher, Eddie. *Been There, Done That*. New York: St. Martin's Press, 1999.

Fishzon, Anna. *Fandom, Authenticity, and Opera: Mad Acts and Letter Scenes in Fin-de-Siècle Russia*. New York: Palgrave, 2013.

Fitzgerald, F. Scott. *This Side of Paradise*. [1920.] New York: Simon and Schuster, 1995.

Fleeger, Jennifer. *Sounding American: Hollywood, Opera, and Jazz*. New York: Oxford University Press, 2014.

Flinn, Caryl. *Brass Diva: The Life and Legends of Ethel Merman*. Berkeley: University of California Press, 2007.

———. *Strains of Utopia: Gender, Nostalgia, and Hollywood Film Music*. Princeton, NJ: Princeton University Press, 1992.

Floyd, Samuel A., Jr., ed. *Black Music in the Harlem Renaissance: A Collection of Essays*. Knoxville: University of Tennessee Press, 1993.

Foucault, Michel. *The History of Sexuality: An Introduction*. Vol. 1. Trans. Robert Hurley. New York: Vintage Books, 1990.

Fraiman, Susan. *Cool Men and the Second Sex*. New York: Columbia University Press, 2003.

Frayne, John George, and Halley Wolfe. *Elements of Sound Recording*. New York: John Wiley and Sons, 1949.

Freedland, Michael. *Jolie: The Al Jolson Story*. London: Comet, 1985.

Freud, Sigmund. *The Standard Edition of the Complete Psychological Works of Sigmund Freud*. Vol. 11: *Five Lectures on Psychoanalysis, Leonardo Da Vinci, and Other Works*. Trans. James Strachey; collaborator, Anna Freud. London: Hogarth Press, 1957.

Friedwald, Will. *Jazz Singing: America's Great Voices from Bessie Smith to Bebop and Beyond*. New York: Scribner, 1990.

Frith, Simon. *Performing Rites: On the Value of Popular Music*. Cambridge, MA: Harvard University Press, 1996.

———. "Pop Music." In *The Cambridge Companion to Pop and Rock*, ed. Simon Frith, Will Straw, and John Street. New York: Cambridge University Press, 2001.

———. *Sound Effects: Youth, Leisure and the Politics of Rock'n'Roll*. New York: Pantheon, 1981.

Frith, Simon, and Andrew Goodwin. *On Record: Rock, Pop, and the Written Word*. New York: Routledge, 1990.

Frith, Simon, Will Straw, and John Street, eds. *The Cambridge Companion to Pop and Rock*. New York: Cambridge University Press, 2001.

Fuller, Sophie, and Lloyd Whitesell, eds. *Queer Episodes in Music and Modern Identity*. Chicago: University of Illinois Press, 2002.

Gabbard, Krin. *Black Magic: White Hollywood and African American Culture*. New Brunswick, NJ: Rutgers University Press, 2004.

———, ed. *Jazz among the Discourses*. Durham, NC: Duke University Press, 1995.

Gabler, Neal. *Winchell: Gossip, Power and the Culture of Celebrity*. New York: Knopf, 1994.

Garafalo, Reebee. *Rockin' Out: Popular Music in the USA*. 2nd ed. Upper Saddle River, NJ: Prentice Hall, 2002.

Gaudio, Rudolf P. "Sounding Gay: Pitch Properties in the Speech of Gay and Straight Men." *American Speech* 69, no. 1 (1994): 30–57.

Gelatt, Roland. *The Fabulous Phonograph, 1877–1977.* 2nd ed. New York: Macmillan, 1977.

Gennari, John. *Blowin' Hot and Cool: Jazz and Its Critics.* Chicago: University of Chicago Press, 2006.

George-Warren, Holly. *Public Cowboy: The Life and Times of Gene Autry.* New York: Oxford University Press, 2007.

Gerhard, Jane F. *Desiring Revolution: Second-Wave Feminism and the Rewriting of American Sexual Thought, 1920 to 1982.* New York: Columbia University Press, 2001.

Gerstle, Gary. *American Crucible: Race and Nation in the Twentieth Century.* Princeton, NJ: Princeton University Press, 2001.

Giddins, Gary. *Bing Crosby: A Pocketful of Dreams. The Early Years 1903–1940.* Boston: Little, Brown, 2001.

———. Preface to *Call Me Lucky,* by Bing Crosby. 2nd ed. New York: Da Capo Press, 1993.

———. *Riding on a Blue Note: Jazz and American Pop.* New York: Oxford University Press, 1981.

Gilbert, Douglas. *American Vaudeville: Its Life and Times.* New York: Dover, 1940.

Giles, Peter. *The History and Technique of the Counter-Tenor: A Study of the High Male Voice.* Cambridge: Scholar Press, 1994.

Gitelman, Lisa. "How Users Define New Media: A History of the Amusement Phonograph." In *Rethinking Media Change: The Aesthetics of Transition,* ed. David Thorburn and Henry Jenkins. Cambridge, MA: MIT Press, 2003.

———. *Scripts, Grooves, and Writing Machines: Representing Technology in the Edison Era.* Stanford: Stanford University Press, 1999.

Gitelman, Lisa, and Geoffrey B. Pingree, eds. *New Media, 1740–1915.* Cambridge, MA: MIT Press, 2003.

Glenn, Susan A. *Female Spectacle: The Theatrical Roots of Modern Feminism.* Cambridge, MA: Harvard University Press, 2000.

Goldberg, Isaac. *Tin Pan Alley: A Chronicle of the American Popular Music Racket.* New York: John Day, 1930.

Goldman, Herbert, G. *Banjo Eyes: Eddie Cantor and the Birth of Modern Stardom.* New York: Oxford University Press, 1997.

———. *Jolson: The Legend Comes to Life.* New York: Oxford University Press, 1988.

Goldmark, Daniel, Lawrence Kramer, and Richard Leppert, eds. *Beyond the Soundtrack: Representing Music in Cinema.* Berkeley: University of California Press, 2007.

Goldsmith, Alfred, and Austin Lescarboura. *This Thing Called Broadcasting.* New York: Henry Holt, 1930.

Gomery, Douglas. *The Coming of Sound: A History.* New York: Routledge, 2005.

———. *Shared Pleasures: A History of Movie Presentation in the United States.* Madison: University of Wisconsin Press, 1992.

Gorbman, Claudia. *Unheard Melodies: Narrative Film Music*. Indianapolis: Indiana University Press, 1987.

Gottschild, Brenda Dixon. *Waltzing in the Dark: African American Vaudeville and Race Politics in the Swing Era*. New York: St. Martin's Press, 2000.

Gracyk, Tim. *Popular American Recording Pioneers, 1895–1925*. New York: Haworth Press, 2000.

Greene, Margaret. *The Voice and Its Disorders*. New York: Macmillan, 1957.

———. *The Voice and Its Disorders*. 3rd ed. Philadelphia: J. B. Lippincott, 1972.

———. *The Voice and Its Disorders*. 4th ed. Philadelphia: J. B. Lippincott, 1980.

Greene, Margaret, and Lesley Mathieson. *The Voice and Its Disorders*. 6th ed. Philadelphia: Whurr, 2001.

Gregg, Melissa, and Gregory J. Siegworth, eds. *The Affect Theory Reader*. Durham, NC: Duke University Press, 2010.

Gregory, James N. *Southern Diaspora: How the Great Migrations of Black and White Southerners Transformed America*. Chapel Hill: University of North Carolina Press, 2007.

Griffen, Clyde, and Mark C. Carnes, eds. *Meanings for Manhood: Constructions of Masculinity in Victorian America*. Chicago: University of Chicago Press, 1990.

Griffith, R. Marie. "Apostles of Abstinence: Fasting and Masculinity during the Progressive Era." *American Quarterly* 52, no. 4 (2000): 599–638.

Gross, Ben. *I Looked and I Listened: Informal Recollections of Radio and TV*. New Rochelle, NY: Arlington House, 1954.

Grossman, James R. *Land of Hope: Chicago, Black Southerners, and the Great Migration*. Chicago: University of Chicago Press, 1991.

Groves, E. R., and W. F. Ogburn. *American Marriage and Family Relationships: The Early Sociology of the Family*. Vol. 7. New York: Henry Holt, 1928.

Groves, Ernest R. *The American Family*. Chicago: J. B. Lippincott, 1934.

Groves, Robert W. "Americana as Revealed through Old Tin Pan Alley Era Songs." *Research in American Popular Music* 30 (1992): 25–42.

Gunning, Tom. "The Cinema of Attraction: Early Film, Its Spectator, and the Avant-Garde." In *Film and Theory: An Anthology*, ed. Robert Stam and Toby Miller. Malden, MA: Blackwell, 2000.

Halberstam, Judith. *In a Queer Time and Place: Transgender Bodies, Subcultural Lives*. New York: New York University Press, 2005.

Hall, Stuart. "Encoding/Decoding." In *Culture, Media, Language: Working Papers in Cultural Studies, 1972–1979*, ed. Stuart Hall et al. London: Hutchinson, 1980.

Hamm, Charles. *Irving Berlin: Songs from the Melting Pot. The Formative Years, 1907–1914*. New York: Oxford University Press, 1997.

———. *Yesterdays: Popular Song in America*. New York: Norton, 1979.

Handy, W. C. *Father of the Blues*. New York: Macmillan, 1944.

Hansen, Miriam. *Babel and Babylon: Spectatorship in American Silent Film*. Cambridge, MA: Harvard University Press, 1991.

Hanson, Ellis. *Decadence and Catholicism*. Cambridge, MA: Harvard University Press, 1997.

Harkins, Anthony. *Hillbilly: A Cultural History of an American Icon*. New York: Oxford University Press, 2004.

Harris, Charles. *After the Ball: Forty Years of Melody*. New York: Frank-Maurice, 1926.

Harrison, Scott D., Graham F. Welch, and Adam Adler, eds. *Perspectives on Males and Singing*. London: Springer, 2012.

Hatch, Kristen. *Shirley Temple and the Performance of Girlhood*. New Brunswick, NJ: Rutgers University Press, 2015.

Hawkins, Stan. *The British Pop Dandy: Masculinity, Popular Music and Culture*. Burlington, VT: Ashgate, 2009.

Heap, Chad. *Slumming: Sexual and Racial Encounters in American Nightlife, 1885–1940*. Chicago: University of Chicago Press, 2009.

Heilbut, Anthony. *The Fan Who Knew Too Much: Aretha Franklin, the Rise of Soap Opera, Children of the Gospel Church, and Other Meditations*. New York: Knopf, 2012.

Hemming, Roy, and David Hadju. *Discovering Great Singers of Classic Pop*. New York: Newmarket Press, 1991.

Hesmondhalgh, Desmond, and Keith Negus, eds. *Popular Music Studies*. New York: Oxford University Press, 2002.

Higashi, Sumiko. *Cecil B. DeMille and American Culture: The Silent Era*. Berkeley: University of California Press, 1994.

Higham, John. *Strangers in the Land: Patterns of American Nativism, 1860–1925*. 2nd ed. New Brunswick, NJ: Rutgers University Press, 1988.

Hilderbrand, Lucas. "'Luring Disco Dollies to a Life of Vice': Queer Pop Music's Moment." *Journal of Popular Music Studies* 25, no. 4 (2013): 415–38.

Hilmes, Michele. *Hollywood and Broadcasting from Radio to Cable*. Chicago: University of Illinois Press, 1990.

———. "Invisible Men: *Amos 'n' Andy* and the Roots of Broadcast Discourse." *Critical Studies in Mass Communication* 10, no. 4 (1993): 301–21.

———. *NBC: America's Network*. Berkeley: University of California Press, 2007.

———. *Only Connect: A Cultural History of Broadcasting in the United States*. Toronto: Wadsworth, 2002.

———. *Radio Voices: American Broadcasting 1922–1952*. Minneapolis: University of Minnesota Press, 1997.

Hirschhorn, Clive. *The Hollywood Musical*. New York: Portland House, 1991.

Hoberman, J., and Jeffrey Shandler. *Entertaining America: Jews, Movies, and Broadcasting*. Princeton, NJ: Princeton University Press, 2003.

Hoffman, Frank, Dick Carty, and Quentin Riggs. *Billy Murray: The Phonograph Industry's First Great Recording Artist*. Lanham, MD: Scarecrow Press, 1997.

Horn, David. "Torch Singer." In *Continuum Encyclopedia of the World Volume II: Performance and Production*, ed. John Shepherd. New York: Continuum, 2003.

Horning, Susan Schmidt. *Chasing Sound: Technology, Culture, and the Art of Studio Recording from Edison to the* LP. Baltimore: Johns Hopkins University Press, 2013.

———. "Chasing Sound: The Culture and Technology of Recording Studios in America, 1877–1977." PhD dissertation, Case Western University, 2002.

Horowitz, Daniel. *The Morality of Spending: Attitudes toward the Consumer Society in America, 1875–1940*. Baltimore: Johns Hopkins University Press, 1985.

Horten, Gerd. *Radio Goes to War: The Cultural Politics Propaganda during World War II*. Berkeley: University of California Press, 2002.

Hubbs, Nadine. *The Queer Composition of America's Sound: Gay Modernists, American Music, and National Identity*. Berkeley: University of California Press, 2004.

———. *Rednecks, Queers, and Country Music*. Berkeley: University of California Press, 2014.

Hutchinson, Barbara, Marvin Hanson, and Marlin Mecham. *Diagnostic Handbook of Speech Pathology*. Baltimore: Williams and Wilkins, 1979.

Huyssen, Andreas. *After the Great Divide: Modernism, Mass Culture, Postmodernism*. Bloomington: Indiana University Press, 1986.

Hyland, William G. *The Song Is Ended: Songwriters and American Music*. Oxford: Oxford University Press, 1995.

Hyman, Paula E. *Gender and Assimilation in Modern Jewish History: The Roles and Representation of Women*. Seattle: University of Washington Press, 1995.

Jacobs, Lea. *The Decline of Sentiment: American Film in the 1920s*. Berkeley: University of California Press, 2008.

Jacobson, Matthew Frye. *Special Sorrows: The Diasporic Imagination of Irish, Polish, and Jewish Immigrants in the United States*. Cambridge, MA: Harvard University Press, 1995.

———. *Whiteness of a Different Color: European Immigrants and the Alchemy of Race*. Cambridge, MA: Harvard University Press, 1998.

James, Rian. *All about New York: An Intimate Guide*. New York: John Day Guides, 1931.

———. *Crooner*. New York: Alfred H. King, 1932.

———. *Dining in New York*. New York: John Day, 1930.

Jansen, David. *Tin Pan Alley*. New York: Donald I. Fine, 1988.

Jarman-Ivens, Freya, ed. *Oh Boy! Masculinities and Popular Music*. New York: Routledge, 2007.

———. "Pitch Fever: The Castrato, the Tenor, and the Question of Masculinity in Nineteenth-Century Opera." In *Masculinity and Opera*, ed. Philip Purvis. New York: Routledge, 2013.

Jasen, David A., and Gene Jones. *Spreadin' Rhythm Around: Black Popular Songwriters, 1880–1930*. New York: Routledge, 2005.

Jenkins, Henry. *Textual Poachers: Television Fans and Participatory Culture*. New York: Routledge, 1992.

———. *What Made Pistachio Nuts: Early Sound Comedy and the Vaudeville Aesthetic*. New York: Columbia University Press, 1992.

Jennings, John J. *Theatrical and Circus Life or Secrets of the Stage*. St. Louis: M. S. Barnett, 1882.

Jessel, George. *So Help Me: The Autobiography of George Jessel*. New York: Random House, 1943.

Johnson, E. Patrick. *Appropriating Blackness: Performance and the Politics of Authenticity*. Durham, NC: Duke University Press, 2003.

Jones, Delilah. *Great Crooners: The Life, Times and Music Series*. New York: Friedman/Fairfax, 1996.

Jung, Sun. *Korean Masculinities and Transcultural Consumption: Yonsama, Rain, Oldboy, K-Pop Idols*. Hong Kong: Hong Kong University Press, 2011.

Kahn, Roger. *A Flame of Pure Fire: Jack Dempsey and the Roaring '20s*. New York: Harcourt Brace, 1999.

Kammen, Michael. *American Culture, American Tastes: Social Change and the 20th Century*. New York: Knopf, 1999.

Katz, Mark. *Capturing Sound: How Technology Changed Music*. Berkeley: University of California Press, 2004.

Kaye, Lenny. *You Call It Madness: The Sensuous Song of the Croon*. New York: Villard, 2004.

Keightley, Keir. "Frank Sinatra and the Hollywood Musical in Transition: *Young at Heart* (1955) and *Pal Joey* (1957)." Paper presented at the Cinema and Popular Song Conference, Iowa City, April 1999.

———. "Frank Sinatra, Hi Fi and the Formations of Adult Culture, 1948–1962." PhD dissertation, Concordia University, 1997.

Keil, Charles, and Steven Feld. *Music Grooves: Essays and Dialogues*. Chicago: University of Chicago Press, 1994.

Kelland, Clarence Budington. *The Great Crooner*. New York: Harper and Brothers, 1933.

Kendrick, Walter. *The Secret Museum: Pornography in Modern Culture*. New York: Viking, 1987.

Kenney, William Howland. *Recorded Music in American Life: The Phonograph and Popular Memory, 1890–1945*. New York: Oxford University Press, 1999.

Kenny, Nick. *Conducting a Successful Radio Column*. New York: Newspaper Institute of America, 1942.

Kibler, M. Alison. *Rank Ladies: Gender and Cultural Hierarchy in American Vaudeville*. Chapel Hill: University of North Carolina Press, 1999.

Kidd, Kenneth B. *Making American Boys: Boyology and the Feral Tale*. Minneapolis: University of Minnesota Press, 2004.

Kimmel, Michael S. *Manhood in America: A Cultural History*. New York: Free Press, 1996.

Kiner, Larry F. *The Rudy Vallée Discography*. Westport, CT: Greenwood Press, 1985.

Kinscella, Hazel Gertrude. *Music on the Air*. New York: Viking, 1934.

Kinsey, Alfred, et al. *Sexual Behavior in the Human Female*. Philadelphia: W. B. Saunders, 1953.

Kippax, Susan. "Women as Audience: The Experience of Unwaged Women of the Performance Arts." In *Culture and Power: A Media, Culture and Society Reader*, ed. Paddy Scannell et al. London: Sage, 1992.

Kitch, Carolyn. *The Girl on the Magazine Cover: The Origin of Visual Stereotypes in the American Mass Media*. Chapel Hill: University of North Carolina Press, 2000.

Klapper, Melissa R. *Jewish Girls Coming of Age in America, 1860–1920*. New York: New York University Press, 2005.

Kline, Wendy. *Building a Better Race: Gender, Sexuality and Eugenics, from the Turn of the Century to the Baby Boom*. Berkeley: University of California Press, 2005.

Knight, Arthur. *Disintegrating the Musical: Black Performance and American Musical Film*. Durham, NC: Duke University Press, 2002.

Koestenbaum, Wayne. *The Queen's Throat: Opera, Homosexuality, and the Mystery of Desire*. New York: Vintage Books, 1993.

Kraft, James P. *Stage to Studio: Musicians and the Sound Revolution, 1890–1950*. Baltimore: Johns Hopkins University Press, 1996.

Krasner, David. "The Real Thing." In *Beyond Blackface: African Americans and the Creation of Popular Culture, 1890–1930*, ed. W. Fitzhugh Brundage. Chapel Hill: University of North Carolina Press, 2011.

Kristeva, Julia. *Powers of Horror: An Essay on Abjection*. New York: Columbia University Press, 1982.

Lacey, Kate. *Feminine Frequencies: Gender, German Radio, and the Public Sphere, 1923–1945*. Ann Arbor: University of Michigan Press, 1996.

Lanza, Joseph. *Vanilla Pop: Sweet Sounds from Frankie Avalon to ABBA*. Chicago: Chicago Review Press, 2005.

Laqueur, Thomas. *Solitary Sex: A Cultural History of Masturbation*. New York: Zone Books, 2003.

Lass, Norman, Leija McReynolds, Jerry Northern, and David Yoder. *Handbook of Speech-Language Pathology and Audiology*. Philadelphia: B. C. Decker, 1988.

Lastra, James. *Sound Technology and the American Cinema: Perception, Representation, Modernity*. New York: Columbia University Press, 2000.

Latham, Angela J. *Posing a Threat: Flappers, Chorus Girls, and Other Brazen Performers of the American 1920s*. Hanover, NH: Wesleyan University Press, 2000.

Laurie, Joe, Jr. *Vaudeville: From the Honky-Tonks to the Palace*. New York: Henry Holt, 1953.

Lawrence, Amy. *Echo and Narcissus: Women's Voices in Classical Hollywood Cinema*. Berkeley: University of California Press, 1991.

Lears, T. J. Jackson. *No Place of Grace: Antimodernism and the Transformation of American Culture, 1880–1920*. Chicago: University of Chicago Press, 1994.

Lees, Gene. *Singers and the Song*. New York: Oxford University Press, 1987.

Lehman, Peter. *Roy Orbison: The Invention of an Alternative Rock Masculinity*. Philadelphia: Temple University Press, 2003.

Lenthall, Bruce. *Radio's America: The Great Depression and the Rise of Modern Mass Culture.* Chicago: University of Chicago Press, 2007.

Leonard, Neil. *Jazz and the White Americans: The Acceptance of an Art Form.* Chicago: University of Chicago Press, 1962.

Leppert, Richard, and Susan McClary, eds. *Music and Society: The Politics of Composition, Performance, and Reception.* New York: Cambridge University Press, 1987.

Lerner, Michael A. *Dry Manhattan: Prohibition in New York City.* Cambridge, MA: Harvard University Press, 2007.

Levine, Lawrence W. *Highbrow/Lowbrow: The Emergence of Cultural Hierarchy in America.* Cambridge, MA: Harvard University Press, 1988.

———. *The Unpredictable Past: Explorations in American Cultural History.* New York: Oxford University Press, 1993.

Lewis, Robert M. *From Traveling Show to Vaudeville: Theatrical Spectacle in America, 1830–1910.* Baltimore: Johns Hopkins University Press, 2003.

Lhamon, W. T., Jr. *Raising Cain: Blackface Performance from Jim Crow to Hip Hop.* Cambridge, MA: Harvard University Press, 1998.

Liebman, Roy. *Vitaphone Films: A Catalogue of the Features and Shorts.* Jefferson, NC: McFarland, 2003.

Lindsey, Ben B., and Wainwright Evans. *The Companionate Marriage.* Garden City, NY: Garden City Publishing, 1929.

Linn, Karen. *That Half-Barbaric Twang: The Banjo in American Popular Culture.* Chicago: University of Illinois Press, 1991.

Lipsitz, George. *Footsteps in the Dark: The Hidden Histories of Popular Music.* Minneapolis: University of Minnesota Press, 2007.

———. "Listening to Learn and Learning to Listen: Popular Culture, Cultural Theory and American Studies." *American Quarterly* 42, no. 4 (1990): 615–36.

Lockheart, Paula. "A History of Early Microphone Singing, 1925–1939: American Mainstream Popular Singing at the Advent of Electronic Microphone Amplification." *Popular Music and Society* 26 (October 2003): 367–85.

Loesser, Arthur. *Men, Women and Pianos: A Social History.* New York: Simon and Schuster, 1954.

Lombardo, Guy, with Jack Altshul. *Auld Acquaintance.* New York: Ballantine Books, 1975.

Lott, Eric. *Love and Theft: Blackface Minstrelsy and the American Working Class.* New York: Oxford University Press, 1993.

Loviglio, Jason. *Radio's Intimate Public: Network Broadcasting and Mass-Mediated Democracy.* Minneapolis: University of Minnesota Press, 2005.

Loviglio, Jason, and Michele Hilmes, eds. *The Radio Reader: An Anthology.* New York: Routledge, 2001.

Lystra, Karen. *Dangerous Intimacy: The Untold Story of Mark Twain's Final Years.* Berkeley: University of California Press, 2004.

Macdougall, Robert. "The Wire Devils: Pulp Thrillers, the Telephone, and Action at a Distance in the Wiring of a Nation." *American Quarterly* 58, no. 3 (2006): 715–41.

Macfarlane, Malcolm. *Bing Crosby: Day by Day*. Lanham, MD: Scarecrow Press, 2001.

MacLeod, David I. *Building Character in the American Boy*. Madison: University of Wisconsin Press, 1983.

Mahar, William J. *Behind the Burnt Cork Mask: Early Blackface Minstrelsy and Antebellum American Popular Culture*. Urbana: University of Illinois Press, 1999.

Maltby, Richard. "The Production Code and the Hays Office." In *Grand Design: Hollywood as a Modern Business Enterprise, 1930–1939*, ed. Tino Balio. Berkeley: University of California Press, 1993.

Mann, William. *Behind the Screen: How Gays and Lesbians Shaped Hollywood, 1910–1969*. New York: Viking Press, 2001.

Manring, M. M. *Slave in a Box: The Strange Career of Aunt Jemima*. Charlottesville: University Press of Virginia, 1998.

Marchand, Roland. *Advertising the American Dream, 1920–1940*. Berkeley: University of California Press, 1985.

Marks, Edward. *They All Sang: From Tony Pastor to Rudy Vallée*. New York: Viking Press, 1935.

Marks, Martin Miller. *Music and the Silent Film: Contexts and Case Studies, 1895–1924*. New York: Oxford University Press, 1997.

Marra, Kim, and Robert A. Schanke, eds. *Staging Desire: Queer Readings of American Theater History*. Ann Arbor: University of Michigan Press, 2002.

Marvin, Carolyn. *When Old Technologies Were New: Thinking about Electric Communication in the Late Nineteenth Century*. New York: Oxford University Press, 1988.

Mattfield, Julius. *Variety Music Cavalcade: A Chronology of Vocal and Instrumental Popular Music in the United States, 1620–1950*. New York: Prentice-Hall, 1952.

Mavor, Carol. *Reading Boyishly*. Durham, NC: Duke University Press, 2007.

May, Elaine Tyler. *Homeward Bound: American Families in the Cold War Era*. New York: Basic Books, 1988.

McBee, Randy D. *Dance Hall Days: Intimacy and Leisure among Working-Class Immigrants in the United States*. New York: New York University Press, 2000.

McBrien, William. *Cole Porter*. New York: Vintage Books, 1998.

McChesney, Robert W. *Telecommunication, Mass Media, and Democracy: The Battle for Control of U.S. Broadcasting, 1928–1935*. New York: Oxford University Press, 1994.

McClary, Susan. *Feminine Endings: Music, Gender, and Sexuality*. Minneapolis: University of Minnesota Press, 1991.

———. "Same as It Ever Was: Youth Culture and Music." In *Microphone Fiends: Youth Music and Youth Culture*, ed. Andrew Ross and Tricia Rose. New York: Routledge, 1994.

———. "Soprano Masculinities." In *Masculinity and Opera*, ed. Philip Purvis. New York: Routledge, 2013.

McCracken, Allison. "The Countertenor and the Crooner." Antenna (blog), 3, 10, and 17 May 2011. http://blog.commarts.wisc.edu/.

———. "'God's Gift to Us Girls': Crooning, Gender, and the Re-creation of American Popular Song, 1928–1933." *American Music* 17, no. 4 (1999): 365–95.

———. "Real Men Don't Sing Ballads." In *Soundtrack Available: Essays on Film and Popular Music*, ed. Pam Robertson Wojcik and Arthur Knight. Durham, NC: Duke University Press, 2001.

McElvaine, Robert. *The Great Depression: America 1929–1941*. New York: Random House Times Books, 1993.

McElya, Micki. *Clinging to Mammy: The Faithful Slave in Twentieth-Century America*. Cambridge, MA: Harvard University Press, 2007.

McFadden, Margaret T. "America's Boyfriend Who Can't Get a Date: Gender, Race, and the Cultural Work of the Jack Benny Program." *Journal of American History* (June 1993): 113–34.

McGovern, Charles F. *Sold American: Consumption and Citizenship, 1890–1945*. Chapel Hill: University of North Carolina Press, 2006.

McGreevey, John. *Parish Boundaries: The Catholic Encounter with Race in the Twentieth-Century Urban North*. Chicago: University of Chicago Press, 1996.

McGregor, Alexander. *The Catholic Church and Hollywood: Censorship and Morality in 1930s Hollywood*. New York: I. B. Tauris, 2013.

McLaughlin, Robert L., and Sally E. Parry. *We'll Always Have the Movies: American Cinema during World War II*. Lexington: University of Kentucky Press, 2006.

McNally, Karen. *When Frankie Went to Hollywood: Frank Sinatra and American Male Identity*. Chicago: University of Chicago Press, 2008.

Meehan, Eileen. "Why We Don't Count: The Commodity Audience." In *Connections: A Broadcasting History Reader*, ed. Michele Hilmes. Toronto: Wadsworth Press, 2003.

Meizel, Katherine. *Idolized: Music, Media, and Identity in American Idol*. Bloomington: Indiana University Press, 2011.

Melnick, Jeffrey. "Tin Pan Alley and the Black Jewish Nation." In *American Popular Music: New Approaches to the Twentieth Century*, ed. Rachel Rubin and Jeffrey Melnick. Amherst: University of Massachusetts Press, 2001.

Mercer, Kobena. *Welcome to the Jungle: New Positions in Black Cultural Studies*. New York: Routledge, 1994.

Merwin, Ted. *In Their Own Image: New York Jews in Jazz Age Popular Culture*. New Brunswick, NJ: Rutgers University Press, 2006.

Middleton, Richard. *Voicing the Popular: On the Subjects of Popular Music*. New York: Routledge, 2006.

Millard, Andre. *America on Record: A History of Recorded Sound*. New York: Cambridge University Press, 1995.

———. *Beatlemania: Technology, Business, and Teen Culture in Cold War America*. Baltimore: Johns Hopkins University Press, 2012.

Miller, Karl Hagstrom. *Segregating Sounds: Inventing Folk and Pop Music in the Age of Jim Crow*. Durham, NC: Duke University Press, 2010.

Miller, Neil. *Out of the Past: Gay and Lesbian History from 1869 to the Present*. New York: Vintage Books, 2005.

Mintz, Steven, and Susan Kellogg. *Domestic Revolutions: A Social History of American Family Life*. New York: Free Press, 1988.

Mizejewski, Linda. *Ziegfeld Girl: Image and Icon in Culture and Cinema*. Durham, NC: Duke University Press, 1999.

Modell, John. *Into One's Own: From Youth to Adulthood in the United States, 1920–1975*. Berkeley: University of California Press, 1989.

Moi, Toril. *Henrik Ibsen and the Birth of Modernism*. New York: Oxford University Press, 2008.

Moon, Krystyn. *Yellowface: Creating the Chinese in American Popular Music and Performance, 1850s–1920s*. New Brunswick, NJ: Rutgers University Press, 2005.

Mooney, Hughson F. "Songs, Singers, and Society, 1890–1954." *American Quarterly* 6, no. 3 (1954): 221–32.

Moorehead, Caroline. *Gellhorn: A Twentieth-Century Life*. New York: Henry Holt, 2003.

Mordden, Ethan. *Better Foot Forward: The History of the American Musical Theatre*. New York: Viking Press, 1976.

———. *Broadway Babies: The People Who Made the American Musical*. New York: Oxford University Press, 1983.

———. *Make Believe: The Broadway Musical in the 1920s*. New York: Oxford University Press, 1997.

———. *Sing for Your Supper*. New York: Macmillan, 2005.

Morris, Charles R. *American Catholic: The Saints and Sinners Who Built America's Most Powerful Church*. New York: Random House, 1997.

Morris, Mitchell. *The Persistence of Sentiment: Display and Feeling in Popular Music of the 1970s*. Berkeley: University of California Press, 2013.

Mukerji, Chandra, and Michael Schudson, eds. *Rethinking Popular Culture: Contemporary Perspectives in Cultural Studies*. Berkeley: University of California Press, 1991.

Murray, Matthew. "'The Tendency to Deprave and Corrupt Morals': Regulation and Irregular Sexuality in Golden Age Radio Comedy." In *The Radio Reader*, ed. Michele Hilmes and Jason Loviglio. New York: Routledge, 2002.

Nasaw, David. *Going Out: The Rise and Fall of Public Amusements*. Cambridge, MA: Harvard University Press, 1993.

Nash, Elizabeth. *Geraldine Farrar: Opera's Charismatic Innovator*. Jefferson, NC: McFarland, 2012.

Negra, Diane, ed. *The Irish in Us: Irishness, Performativity, and Popular Culture*. Durham, NC: Duke University Press, 2006.

Negus, Keith. *Popular Music in Theory*. Hanover, NH: Wesleyan University Press, 1996.

Newman, Kathy M. *Radio Active: Advertising and Consumer Activism, 1935–1947*. Berkeley: University of California Press, 2004.

Nicholson, Stuart. *Is Jazz Dead? (Or Has It Moved to a New Address)*. New York: Routledge, 2005.

Nisbett, Alec. *The Sound Studio*. 6th ed. Oxford: Focal Press, 1995.

Nolan, Frederick. *Lorenz Hart: A Poet on Broadway*. New York: Oxford University Press, 1994.

O'Brien, David. *Public Catholicism*. New York: Macmillan, 1989.

Odem, Mary E. *Delinquent Daughters: Protecting and Policing Adolescent Female Sexuality in the United States, 1885–1920*. Chapel Hill: University of North Carolina Press, 1995.

Ogren, Kathy J. *The Jazz Revolution: Twenties America and the Meaning of Jazz*. Oxford: Oxford University Press, 1989.

Oja, Carol. *Making Music Modern: New York in the 1920s*. New York: Oxford University Press, 2000.

O'Leary, Cecilia Elizabeth. *To Die For: The Paradox of American Patriotism*. Princeton, NJ: Princeton University Press, 1999.

Oliver, Paul. *Kings of Jazz: Bessie Smith*. New York: A. S. Barnes, 1959.

———. *Songsters and Saints: Vocal Traditions on Race Records*. New York: Cambridge University Press, 1984.

Olson, James S. *Catholic Immigrants in America*. Chicago: Nelson-Hall, 1987.

Orsi, Robert Anthony. *The Madonna of 15th Street: Faith and Community in Italian Harlem, 1880–1950*. New Haven, CT: Yale University Press, 1985.

Orvell, Miles. *The Real Thing: Imitation and Authenticity in American Culture, 1880–1940*. Chapel Hill: University of North Carolina Press, 1989.

Osterholm, J. Roger. *Bing Crosby: A Bio-Bibliography*. Westport, CT: Greenwood Press, 1994.

Pabst, Ralph M., and Gene Austin. *Gene Austin's Ol' Buddy*. Phoenix: Augury Press, 1984.

Pearson, Allison. *I Think I Love You*. New York: Knopf, 2011.

Pecknold, Diane. *The Selling Sound: The Rise of the Country Music Industry*. Durham, NC: Duke University Press, 2007.

Peiss, Kathy. *Cheap Amusements: Working Women and Leisure in Turn-of-the-Century New York*. Philadelphia: Temple University Press, 1986.

Peiss, Kathy, and Elizabeth Ewen. *Immigrant Women in the Land of Dollars: Life and Culture on the Lower East Side, 1890–1925*. New York: Monthly Press, 1985.

Peiss, Kathy, and Christina Simmons, eds. *Passion and Power: Sexuality in History*. Philadelphia: Temple University Press, 1989.

Penner, James. *Pinks, Pansies, and Punks: The Rhetoric of Masculinity in American Literary Culture*. Bloomington: Indiana University Press, 2011.

Peraino, Judith A. *Giving Voice to Love: Song and Self-Expression from the Troubadours to Guillaume de Machaut*. New York: Oxford University Press, 2011.

———. *Listening to the Sirens: Musical Technologies of Queer Identity from Homer to Hedwig*. Berkeley: University of California Press, 2006.

Peretti, Burton. *The Creation of Jazz: Music, Race, and Culture in Urban America*. Chicago: University of Illinois Press, 1992.

———. *Jazz in American Culture*. Chicago: Ivan R. Dee, 1997.

———. *Nightclub City: Politics and Amusement in Manhattan*. Philadelphia: University of Pennsylvania Press, 2007.

Pessen, Edward. "Two Kinds of Woman in the Tin Pan Alley Song of the 1920s and 1930s." *Research in American Popular Music* 30 (1992): 11–24.

Peters, John. *Speaking into the Air: A History of the Idea of Communication*. Chicago: University of Chicago Press, 1999.

Peterson, Richard A. *Creating Country Music*. Chicago: University of Chicago Press, 1997.

Pettegrew, John. *Brutes in Suits: Male Sensibility in America, 1890–1920*. Baltimore: Johns Hopkins University Press, 2007.

Picker, John M. *Victorian Soundscapes*. New York: Oxford University Press, 2003.

Pitts, Michael, and Frank Hoffman. *The Rise of the Crooners*. Lanham, MD: Scarecrow Press, 2002.

Pleasants, Henry. *The Great American Popular Singers*. New York: Simon and Schuster, 1974.

Pleck, Joseph, and Elizabeth Pleck, eds. *The American Man*. Englewood Cliffs, NJ: Prentice-Hall, 1980.

Poizat, Michel. *The Angel's Cry: Beyond the Pleasure Principle in Opera*. Ithaca, NY: Cornell University Press, 1992.

Pollack, Howard. *George Gershwin: His Life and Work*. Berkeley: University of California Press, 2006.

Potter, Dennis. *Seeing the Blossom*. London: Faber and Faber, 1994.

Potter, John, ed. *The Cambridge Companion to Singing*. New York: Cambridge University Press, 2000.

———. *Tenor: History of a Voice*. New Haven, CT: Yale University Press, 2009.

Pretor-Pinney, Gavin, and Tom Hodgkinson. *The Ukulele Handbook*. London: Bloomsbury, 2013.

Purvis, Philip, ed. *Masculinity in Opera: Gender, History, and the New Musicology*. New York: Routledge, 2013.

Rabinovitz, Lauren. *For the Love of Pleasure: Women, Movies, and Culture in Turn of the Century Chicago*. New Brunswick, NJ: Rutgers University Press, 1998.

Radano, Ronald. *Lying Up a Nation: Race and Black Music*. Chicago: University of Chicago Press, 2003.

Radano, Ronald, and Philip V. Bohlman, eds. *Music and the Racial Imagination*. Chicago: University of Chicago Press, 2000.

Railton, Diane. "The Gendered Carnival of Pop." In *The Gender and Media Reader*, ed. Mary Celeste Kearney. New York: Routledge, 2011.

Rapp, Rayna, and Ellen Ross. "The Twenties' Backlash: Compulsory Heterosexuality, the Consumer Family, and the Waning of Feminism." In *Class, Race, and Sex: The Dynamics of Control*, ed. Amy Swerdlow and Hanna Lessinger. Boston: G. K. Hall, 1983.

Razlogova, Elena. *The Listener's Voice: Early Radio and the American Public*. Philadelphia: University of Pennsylvania Press, 2011.

Reznik, Shiri, and Dafna Lemish. "Falling in Love with *High School Musical*: Girls' Talk about Romantic Perceptions." In *Mediated Girlhoods: New Explorations of Girls' Media Culture*, ed. Mary Celeste Kearney. New York: Peter Lang, 2011.

Richman, Harry, with Richard Gehman. *A Hell of a Life*. New York: Duell, Sloan and Pearce, 1966.

Riis, Thomas L. *Just before Jazz: Black Musical Theater in New York, 1890–1915*. Washington, DC: Smithsonian Institution Press, 1989.

Rodger, Gillian M. *Champagne Charlie and Pretty Jemima: Variety Theater in the Nineteenth Century*. Urbana: University of Illinois Press, 2010.

Rodgers, Richard. *Musical Stages: An Autobiography*. 2nd ed. New York: Da Capo Press, 1995.

Roediger, David R. *The Wages of Whiteness: Race and the Making of the American Working Class*. New York: Verso, 1991.

———. *Working toward Whiteness: How America's Immigrants Became White*. New York: Basic Books, 2005.

Rogers, Ginger. *Ginger*. New York: HarperCollins, 1991.

Rogin, Michael. *Blackface, White Noise: Jewish Immigrants in the Hollywood Melting Pot*. Berkeley: University of California Press, 1996.

Rose, Al. *Eubie Blake*. New York: Schirmer Books, 1979.

Ross, Andrew, and Tricia Rose, eds. *Microphone Fiends: Youth Music and Youth Culture*. New York: Routledge, 1994.

Ross, Steven J. *Working-Class Hollywood: Silent Film and the Shaping of Class in America*. Princeton, NJ: Princeton University Press, 1998.

Rotundo, E. Anthony. *American Manhood: Transformations in Masculinity from the Revolution to the Modern Era*. New York: Basic Books, 1993.

Royster, Francesca. *Sounding Like a No-No: Queer Scenes and Eccentric Acts in the Post-Soul Era*. Ann Arbor: University of Michigan Press, 2012.

Rubin, Martin. *Showstoppers: Busby Berkeley and the Tradition of Spectacle*. New York: Columbia University Press, 1993.

Rubin, Rachel, and Jeffrey Melnick, eds. *American Popular Music: New Approaches to the Twentieth Century*. Amherst: University of Massachusetts Press, 2001.

Rubin, Ruth. *Voices of a People: The Story of Yiddish Folksong*. Urbana: University of Illinois Press, 2000.

Russell, Ina. *Jeb and Dash: A Diary of Gay Life, 1918–1945*. Boston: Faber and Faber, 1993.

Russo, Alexander. *Points on the Dial: Golden Age Radio beyond the Networks*. Durham, NC: Duke University Press, 2010.

Russo, Mary. *Female Grotesques: Risk, Excess, and Modernity*. New York: Routledge, 1994.

Rustin, Nicolas T., and Sherrie Tucker, eds. *Big Ears: Listening for Gender in Jazz Studies*. Durham, NC: Duke University Press, 2008.

Sadie, Stanley, ed. *The New Grove Dictionary of Music and Musicians*. 2nd ed. New York: Oxford University Press, 2001.

Sanjek, Russell. *Pennies from Heaven: The American Popular Music Business in the Twentieth Century.* New York: Da Capo Press, 1988.

Santoro, Gene. *Highway 61 Revisited: The Tangled Roots of American Jazz, Blues, Rock, and Country Music.* New York: Oxford University Press, 2004.

Savran, David. *Highbrow, Lowbrow: Theatre, Jazz, and the Making of the New Middle Class.* Ann Arbor: University of Michigan Press, 2010.

———. *A Queer Sort of Materialism: Recontextualizing American Theater.* Ann Arbor: University of Michigan Press, 2003.

Saxton, Alexander. "Blackface Minstrelsy." In *Inside the Minstrel Mask: Readings in Nineteenth-Century Blackface Minstrelsy,* ed. Annemarie Bean, James V. Hatch, and Brooks McNamara. Hanover, NH: Wesleyan University Press, 1996.

Scanlon, Jennifer. *Inarticulate Longings: The* Ladies' Home Journal, *Gender, and the Promises of Consumer Culture.* New York: Routledge, 1995.

Scannell, Paddy. *Radio, Television and Modern Life.* Oxford: Blackwell, 1996.

Scheiner, Georganne. *Signifying Female Adolescence: Film Representations and Fans, 1920–1950.* Westport, CT: Praeger, 2000.

Schrum, Kelly. *Some Wore Bobby Sox: The Emergence of Teenage Girls' Culture, 1920–1945.* New York: Palgrave, 2004.

Schuller, Gunther. *Early Jazz: Its Roots and Musical Development.* New York: Oxford University Press, 1968.

———. *The Swing Era: The Development of Jazz, 1930–1945.* New York: Oxford University Press, 1989.

Schweitzer, Marlis. "Sex Acts: Reading the History of Female Sexuality through Art and Drama." *American Quarterly* 59, no. 2 (2007): 443–50.

Sconce, Jeffrey. *Haunted Media: Electrical Presence from Telegraphy to Television.* Durham, NC: Duke University Press, 2000.

S.D., Trav. *No Applause—Just Throw Money: The Book That Made Vaudeville Famous.* New York: Faber and Faber, 2005.

Sedaris, David. *Me Talk Pretty One Day.* New York: Back Bay Books, 2001.

Sedgwick, Eve. "How to Bring Up Your Kids Gay." *Social Text* 29 (1991): 18–27.

Senelick, Laurence. *The Changing Room: Sex, Drag, and Theatre.* New York: Routledge, 2000.

Shaw, Arnold. *The Jazz Age: Popular Music in the 1920s.* New York: Oxford University Press, 1987.

Shaw, Charles G. *Nightlife: Vanity Fair's Intimate Guide to New York after Dark.* New York: John Day, 1931.

Shepherd, Daniel, and Robert Slatzer. *Bing Crosby: The Hollow Man.* New York: St. Martin's Press, 1981.

Shepherd, John. *Music as Social Text.* Cambridge, MA: Polity Press, 1991.

Showalter, Elaine, ed. *These Modern Women: Autobiographical Essays from the Twenties.* New York: Feminist Press, 1989.

Siefert, Marsha. "The Audience at Home: The Early Recording Industry and the Marketing of Musical Taste." In *Audiencemaking: How the Media Create the Audience*, ed. James S. Ettma and D. Charles Whitney. Thousand Oaks, CA: Sage, 1994.

Simmons, Christina. "Companionate Marriage and the Lesbian Threat." In *Women and Power in American History*. Vol. 2: *From 1870*, 2nd ed., ed. Kathryn Kish Sklar and Thomas Dublin. Upper Saddle River, NJ: Prentice Hall, 2002.

———. *Making Marriage Modern: Women's Sexuality from the Progressive Era to World War II*. New York: Oxford University Press, 2009.

———. "Modern Sexuality and the Myth of Victorian Repression." In *Passion and Power: Sexuality in History*, ed. Kathy Peiss and Christina Simmons. Philadelphia: Temple University Press, 1989.

Sklar, Kathryn Kish, and Thomas Dublin, eds. *Women and Power in American History*. Vol. 2: *From 1870*. 2nd ed. Upper Saddle River, NJ: Prentice Hall, 2002.

Slobin, Mark. *Chosen Voices: The Story of the American Cantorate*. Chicago: University of Illinois Press, 2002.

———. *Tenement Songs: The Popular Music of Jewish Immigrants*. Chicago: University of Illinois Press, 1982.

Smart, Mary Ann, ed. *Siren Songs: Representations of Gender and Sexuality in Opera*. Princeton, NJ: Princeton University Press, 2000.

Smith, Jacob. *Vocal Tracks: Performance and Sound Media*. Berkeley: University of California Press, 2008.

Smith, Judith E. *Visions of Belonging: Family Stories, Popular Culture, and Postwar Democracy, 1940–1960*. New York: Columbia University Press, 2004.

Smith, Kate. *Living in a Great Big Way*. New York: Blue Ribbon Books, 1938.

Smith, Susan. *The Musical: Race, Gender, and Performance*. New York: Wallflower Press, 2005.

Smoodin, Eric. *Regarding Frank Capra: Audience, Celebrity, and American Film Studies, 1930–1960*. Durham, NC: Duke University Press, 2004.

Smulyan, Susan. *Selling Radio: The Commercialization of American Broadcasting 1920–1934*. Washington, DC: Smithsonian Institution Press, 1994.

Smyth, Ron, Greg Jacobs, and Henry Rogers. "Male Voices and Perceived Sexual Orientation: An Experimental and Theoretical Approach." *Language in Society* 32, no. 3 (2003): 329–50.

Snead, James. *White Screens / Black Images: Hollywood from the Dark Side*. New York: Routledge, 1994.

Snyder, Robert. *The Voice of the City: Vaudeville and Popular Culture in New York*. New York: Oxford University Press, 1989.

Soares, André. *Beyond Paradise: The Life of Ramon Novarro*. Jackson: University of Mississippi Press, 2010.

Socolow, Michael J. "Always in Friendly Competition: NBC and CBS in the First Decade of National Broadcasting." In *NBC: America's Network*, ed. Michele Hilmes. Berkeley: University of California Press, 2007.

Solie, Ruth A., ed. *Musicology and Difference: Gender and Sexuality in Music Scholarship.* Berkeley: University of California Press, 1993.

Sollors, Werner. *The Invention of Ethnicity.* New York: Oxford University Press, 1989.

Somerville, Siobhan B. *Queering the Color Line: Race and the Invention of Homosexuality in American Culture.* Durham, NC: Duke University Press, 2000.

Spaeth, Sigmund. *Fifty Years with Music.* New York: Fleet, 1959.

———. *A History of Popular Music in America.* New York: Random House, 1948.

Spigel, Lynn. *Make Room for TV: Television and the Family Ideal in Postwar America.* Chicago: University of Chicago Press, 1992.

Spring, Katherine. *Saying It with Songs: Popular Music and the Coming of Sound to Hollywood Cinema.* New York: Oxford University Press, 2013.

Staiger, Janet. *Interpreting Films: Studies in the Historical Reception of American Cinema.* Princeton, NJ: Princeton University Press, 1992.

———. *Media Reception Studies.* New York: New York University Press, 2005.

Stam, Michael. "The Sound of Print: Newspapers and Public Promotion of Early Radio Broadcasting in the United States." In *Sound in the Age of Mechanical Reproduction,* ed. David Suisman and Susan Strasser. Philadelphia: University of Pennsylvania Press, 2010.

Stamp, Shelley. *Movie-Struck Girls: Women and Motion Picture Culture after the Nickelodeon.* Princeton, NJ: Princeton University Press, 2000.

Stanfield, Peter. *Body and Soul: Jazz and Blues in American Film, 1927–1933.* Urbana: University of Illinois Press, 2005.

———. "An Excursion into the Lower Depths: Hollywood, Urban Primitivism, and *St. Louis Blues,* 1929–1937." *Cinema Journal* 41, no. 2 (2002): 84–108.

———. *Horse Opera: The Strange History of the 1930s Singing Cowboy.* Urbana: University of Illinois Press, 2002.

Stanley, Douglas, Norma Jean Chadbourne, and E. Thomas A. Chadbourne. *Singer's Manual.* Boston: Stanley Society, 1950.

Stanley, Douglas, and J. P. Maxfield. *The Voice: Its Production and Reproduction.* New York: Putnam, 1933.

Stanley, Douglas, and Alma Stanley. *The Science of Voice.* 2nd ed. New York: Carl Fischer, 1933.

Stanley, Douglas, and Alma Stanley. *The Science of Voice.* 3rd ed. New York: Carl Fischer, 1939.

Stansell, Christine. *American Moderns: Bohemian New York and the Creation of a New Century.* New York: Owl Books, 2000.

Staples, Robert. *The Black Male's Role in American Society.* San Francisco: Black Scholar Press, 1982.

Stark, James. *Bel Canto: A History of Vocal Pedagogy.* Toronto: University of Toronto Press, 1999.

Starr, Larry, and Christopher Waterman. *American Popular Music: From Minstrelsy to* MTV. New York: Oxford University Press, 2003.

Stecopolous, Harry, and Michael Uebel, eds. *Race and the Subject of Masculinities*. Durham, NC: Duke University Press, 1997.

Sterne, Jonathan. *The Audible Past: Cultural Origins of Sound Reproduction*. Durham, NC: Duke University Press, 2003.

Stowe, David. *Swing Changes: Big-Band Jazz in New Deal America*. Cambridge, MA: Harvard University Press, 1994.

Stowe, Harriet Beecher. *Uncle Tom's Cabin, or, Life among the Lowly*. New York: Penguin Books, 1981.

Strasser, Susan. *Satisfaction Guaranteed: The Making of the American Mass Market*. Washington, DC: Smithsonian Books, 1989.

Studlar, Gaylyn. *This Mad Masquerade: Stardom and Masculinity in the Jazz Age*. New York: Columbia University Press, 1996.

Suisman, David. *Selling Sounds: The Commercial Revolution in American Music*. Cambridge, MA: Harvard University Press, 2009.

Summers, Harrison B., ed. *A Thirty-Year History of Programs Carried on National Radio Networks in the United States, 1926–1956*. New York: Arno Press, 1971.

Susman, Warren. *Culture as History: The Transformation of American Society in the Twentieth Century*. New York: Pantheon Books, 1984.

Sutton, Allan. *Recording the Twenties: The Evolution of the American Recording Industry, 1920–1929*. Denver, CO: Mainspring Press, 2008.

Tatar, Elizabeth. *Strains of Change: The Impact of Tourism on Hawaiian Music*. Honolulu: Bishop Museum Press, 1987.

Tawa, Nicholas. *Supremely American: Popular Song in the Twentieth Century: Styles and Singers and What They Said about America*. Toronto: Scarecrow Press, 2005.

Taylor, Millie. *Musical Theatre, Realism and Entertainment*. Burlington, VT: Ashgate, 2012.

Taylor, Timothy D. *The Sounds of Capitalism: Advertising, Music, and the Conquest of Culture*. Chicago: University of Chicago Press, 2012.

———. *Strange Sounds: Music, Technology, and Culture*. New York: Routledge, 2001.

Terry, Jennifer. *An American Obsession: Science, Medicine, and Homosexuality in Modern Society*. Chicago: University of Chicago Press, 1999.

Théberge, Paul. *Any Sound You Can Imagine: Making Music/Consuming Technology*. Hanover, NH: Wesleyan University Press, 1997.

Thompson, Emily. *The Soundscape of Modernity: Architectural Acoustics and the Culture of Listening in America, 1900–1933*. Cambridge, MA: MIT Press, 2002.

Thorburn, David, and Henry Jenkins, eds. *Rethinking Media Change*. Cambridge, MA: MIT Press, 2003.

Tichi, Cecilia. *High Lonesome: The American Culture of Country Music*. Chapel Hill: University of North Carolina Press, 1994.

Toll, Robert C. *Blacking Up: The Minstrel Show in Nineteenth-Century America*. New York: Oxford University Press, 1974.

———. *On with the Show! The First Century of Show Business in America*. New York: Oxford University Press, 1976.

———. "Social Commentary in Late Nineteenth-Century White Minstrelsy." In *Inside the Minstrel Mask: Readings in Nineteenth-Century Blackface Minstrelsy*, ed. Annemarie Bean, James V. Hatch, and Brooks McNamara. Hanover, NH: Wesleyan University Press, 1996.

Tosches, Nick. *Where Dead Voices Gather*. New York: Random House, 2002.

Travis, Lee Edward, ed. *The Handbook of Speech Pathology*. New York: Appleton-Century-Crofts, 1957.

———. *The Handbook of Speech Pathology and Audiology*. New York: Appleton-Century-Crofts, 1971.

Tucker, Sherrie. *Swing Shift: All Girl Bands of the 1940s*. Durham, NC: Duke University Press, 2000.

Tucker, Sophie. *Some of These Days*. London: Hammond, 1945.

Turner, Patricia. *Ceramic Uncles and Celluloid Mammies: Black Images and Their Influence on Culture*. Charlottesville: University of Virginia Press, 1994.

Tyler, Don. *Hit Parade: 1920–1955*. New York: William Morrow, 1985.

Ulanov, Barry. *The Incredible Crosby*. New York: McGraw-Hill, 1948.

Ullman, Sharon R. *Sex Seen: The Emergence of Modern Sexuality in America*. Berkeley: University of California Press, 1997.

Utterson, Andrew, ed. *Technology and Culture: The Film Reader*. New York: Routledge, 2005.

Vallée, Rudy. *Let the Chips Fall*. Harrisburg, PA: Stackpole Books, 1975.

———. *Vagabond Dreams Come True*. New York: Grossett and Dunlap, 1930.

Vallée, Rudy, with Gil McKean. *My Time Is Your Time*. New York: Ivan Obolensky, 1962.

Valliant, Derek. *Sounds of Reform: Progressivism and Music in Chicago, 1873–1935*. Chapel Hill: University of North Carolina Press, 2006.

Van Der Merwe, Peter. *Origins of the Popular Style: The Antecedents of Twentieth-Century Popular Music*. New York: Oxford University Press, 1989.

Van de Velde, Th. H. *Ideal Marriage: Its Physiology and Technique*. New York: Random House, 1930.

Van Leeuwen, Theo. *Speech, Music, Sound*. New York: St. Martin's Press, 1999.

Van Vechten, Carl. *Nigger Heaven*. New York: Knopf, 1926.

Verma, Neil. *Theater of the Mind: Imagination, Aesthetics, and American Radio Drama*. Chicago: University of Chicago Press, 2012.

Vermoral, Fred. *Starlust: The Secret Fantasies of Fans*. London: Faber and Faber, 1985.

Vicinus, Martha. "The Adolescent Boy: Fin de Siècle Femme Fatale?" *Journal of the History of Sexuality* 5, no. 1 (1994): 90–114.

———. *Independent Women: Work and Community for Single Women, 1850–1920*. Chicago: University of Chicago Press, 1985.

Vinson, Jon. *The Voices That Are Gone: Themes in Nineteenth-Century American Popular Song.* New York: Oxford University Press, 1994.

Vogel, Shane. *The Scene of the Harlem Cabaret: Race, Sexuality, Performance.* Chicago: University of Chicago Press, 2009.

Wald, Elijah. *Escaping the Delta: Robert Johnson and the Invention of the Blues.* New York: HarperCollins, 2004.

———. *How the Beatles Destroyed Rock 'n' Roll: An Alternative History of American Popular Music.* New York: Oxford University Press, 2009.

Wald, Gayle. "Dreaming of Michael Jackson: Notes on Jewish Listening." *The Song Is Not the Same: Jews and American Popular Culture: The Jewish Role in American Life: An Annual Review* 8 (2011): 1–8.

———. "'I Want It That Way': Teenybopper Music and the Girling of Boy Bands." *Genders* 25 (2002). http://www.genders.org/g35/g35_wald.html.

———. "Women and Popular Culture: A Girl Issue?" Paper presented at the annual meeting of the American Studies Association, Montreal, October 1999.

Walker, Stanley. *The Night Club Era.* Baltimore: Johns Hopkins University Press, 1999.

Wallace, Michele. *Black Macho and the Myth of the Superwoman.* 2nd ed. New York: Dial Press, 1996.

Walsh, Frank. *Sin and Censorship: The Catholic Church and the Motion Picture Industry.* New Haven, CT: Yale University Press, 1996.

Ware, Caroline F. *Greenwich Village, 1920–1930.* Berkeley: University of California Press, 1963.

Ware, Susan. *Holding Their Own: American Women in the 1930s.* Boston: Twayne, 1982.

———. *Modern American Women: A Documentary History.* New York: McGraw-Hill, 1997.

Waring, Virginia. *Fred Waring and the Pennsylvanians.* Chicago: University of Illinois Press, 1997.

Warner, Michael. "Homo-Narcissism." In *Engendering Men: The Question of Male Feminist Criticism*, ed. Joseph A. Boone and Michael Cannon. New York: Routledge, 1990.

Waters, Ethel, with Charles Samuels. *His Eye Is on the Sparrow.* New York: Doubleday, 1951.

Watts, Jill. *Hattie McDaniel: Black Ambition, White Hollywood.* New York: HarperCollins, 2005.

Waugh, Thomas. "Posing and Performance: Glamour and Desire in Homoerotic Art Photography, 1920–1945." In *The Passionate Camera: Photography and Bodies of Desire*, ed. Deborah Bright. New York: Routledge, 1998.

Weheliye, Alexander. *Phonographies: Grooves in Sonic Afro-Modernity.* Durham, NC: Duke University Press, 2005.

Weisbard, Eric, ed. *Listen Again: A Momentary History of Pop Music.* Durham, NC: Duke University Press, 2007.

Weiss, Allen S. *Breathless: Sound Recording, Disembodiment, and the Transformation of Lyrical Nostalgia.* Middletown, CT: Wesleyan University Press, 2002.

Welch, Walter L., and Leah Brodbeck Stenzel Burt. *From Tinfoil to Stereo: The Acoustic Years of the Recording Industry, 1877–1929.* Tampa: University Press of Florida, 1994.

Whitburn, Joel. *Pop Memories: 1890–1954: The History of American Popular Music.* Menomonee Falls, WI: Record Research, 1986.

Whitcomb, Ian. *After the Ball: Pop Music from Rag to Rock.* Baltimore: Penguin Books, 1972.

———. "The Coming of the Crooners." In *The Rise of the Crooners*, ed. Michael Pitts and Frank Hoffman. Lanham, MD: Scarecrow Press, 2001.

White, Kevin. *The First Sexual Revolution: The Emergence of Male Heterosexuality in Modern America.* New York: New York University Press, 1993.

Whiteley, Sheila, ed. *Sexing the Groove: Popular Music and Gender.* New York: Routledge, 1997.

———. *Too Much Too Young: Popular Music, Age and Gender.* New York: Routledge, 2005.

Whiteley, Sheila, and Jennifer Rycenga. *Queering the Popular Pitch.* New York: Routledge, 2006.

Wilder, Alec. *American Popular Song: The Great Innovators, 1900–1950.* New York: Oxford University Press, 1972.

Wilentz, Sean, and Greil Marcus, eds. *The Rose and the Briar: Death, Love, and Liberty in the American Ballad.* New York: Norton, 2005.

Williams, Linda. *Playing the Race Card: Melodramas of Black and White from Uncle Tom to O.J. Simpson.* Princeton, NJ: Princeton University Press, 2001.

Williams, William H. A. *'Twas Only an Irishman's Dream: The Image of Ireland and the Irish in American Popular Song Lyrics, 1800–1920.* Chicago: University of Illinois Press, 1996.

Wilson, Carl. *Let's Talk about Love: A Journey to the End of Taste.* New York: Continuum, 2007.

———. *Let's Talk about Love: Why Other People Have Such Bad Taste.* New York: Bloomsbury, 2014.

Wilson, Elizabeth. *The Sphinx in the City: Urban Life, the Control of Disorder, and Women.* Berkeley: University of California Press, 1991.

Wilson, James. *Bulldaggers, Pansies, and Chocolate Babies: Performance, Race, and Sexuality in the Harlem Renaissance.* Ann Arbor: University of Michigan Press, 2010.

Wise, Gene. "Some Elementary Axioms for an American Culture Studies." In *Prospects 4*, ed. Jack Salzman. New York: Burt Franklin, 1979.

Witmark, Isidore, and Isaac Goldberg. *The Story of the House of Witmark: From Ragtime to Swingtime.* New York: Da Capo Press, 1976.

Wojcik, Pamela Robertson, and Arthur Knight, eds. *Soundtrack Available: Essays on Film and Popular Music.* Durham, NC: Duke University Press, 2001.

Wolfe, Charles. "On the Track of the Vitaphone Short." In *The Dawn of Sound*, ed. Mary Lea Bandy. New York: Museum of Modern Art, 1989.

Wondrich, David. *Stomp and Swerve: American Music Gets Hot, 1843–1924.* Chicago: A Cappella Books, 2003.

Wood, Sharon E. *The Freedom of the Streets: Work, Citizenship, and Sexuality in a Gilded Age City*. Chapel Hill: University of North Carolina Press, 2005.

Wurtzler, Steve J. *Electric Sounds: Technological Change and the Rise of Corporate Mass Media*. New York: Columbia University Press, 2007.

———. "The Social Construction of Technological Change: American Mass Media and the Advent of Electrical Sound Technology." PhD dissertation, University of Iowa, 2001.

Young, William H., and Nancy K. Young. *American History through Music: Music of the Great Depression*. Westport, CT: Greenwood Press, 2005.

INDEX

Page numbers in *italics* indicate illustrations.

emotion: audience affect and, 8, 17, 19, 65–73, 111–14, 123–24, 126–30, 136–59, 165, 168, 193–201, 209, 240–41, 251, 273–74, 306, 308, 322–24, 357n42; authenticity and, 12, 105, 122, 124, 251, 269–70; blues genre and, 96–99; cultural feminine and, 3, 6, 11, 13, 38–52, 66, 72, 151–59, 200–201, 208–11, 250–51, 317, 326–27; desire and, 19, 65–73, 176, 328–30; marriage ideals and, 143–46, 154–55; masculine coolness and, 6–7, 9–10, 19–20, 268, 271, 288–89, 303; maturity discourses and, 5–6, 8, 25–26, 34–35; psychopathology and, 229–30, 307; race and racialization of, 45; vulnerability and, 4, 6, 25–28, 107–8, 136–41, 155–59. See also audiences; crooners; immaturity; romance; voices; women

Endor, Chick, 74–75, 111, 113–14

Entertainment Weekly, 319, 321–22, 323

Erwin, Stuart, 291, 293, 295

ethnicities: affective attachments and, 5; assimilation and, 2, 70, 166–67, 298–310, 371n5; crooners and, 2, 210, 284–85, 341n42, 356n23; definitions of, 336n34; New York City and, 170–71. See also assimilation; race and racialization; urban environments; whiteness

Etting, Ruth, 103, 219

Eugene, 66

eugenics, 169

Evans, Madge, 299

Evening World, 164, 174–75

fairies. See homosexuality; pansy characters; queer(ing)

falsetto, 1, 10, 26, 30–31, 71, 165–66, 179, 235–36, 239–40, 282, 312–17, 324, 330

fans. See audiences; crooners; emotion

Farmer, Frances, *301*

Farrell, Billy, 58

Fass, Paula, 145

fellatio, 186, *186*, 353n39

feminine endings, 99, 101, 107–8, 175, 275–76, 331, 347n58

feminism, 33–34, 57, 132, 143, 151, 158, 328–30

Fisher, Eddie, 314, 336n35

Fitzgerald, F. Scott, 9, 157, 177–78, 215

flappers, 24, 74, 76, 94, 112, 122, 132–33, 141–42, *218*

Fleischmann Hour, The (radio show), 199, 241, 254–55, 257–58, 265, 365n103

Footlight Parade (film), 245

42nd Street (film), 245

Foster, Stephen, 60, 335n21

fox trot ballads, 62, 138, 213

"Frankie and Johnny" (Lyman), 112

Fred Allen Show (radio), 259

Fred Waring's Pennsylvanians, 103, 117, 121–22, *122*, *123*, 132–33, 137–38, 276

Freshman, The (Lloyd), 123

Freud, Sigmund, 28, 210–11, 230–31, 236, 242–43, 268, 315–16

Frey, Fran, 349n89

Friedwald, Will, 264, 286, 303

Frith, Simon, 77, 128, 146, 168

Fuhrman, Ivor, *145*

Fulton, Jack, 349n89

FutureSex/LoveSounds (Timberlake), 321

Gable, Clark, 299

Garland, Judy, 217

Garrett, Betty, 371n4

Garry, Al, 103–4

"Gay Love" (Crosby), 274

Gellhorn, Martha, 160, 175

gender: androgyny and, 24, 34, 181, 192, 217–23, 235; censorship and, 29–31, 179, 210–11, 223–26, 244, 298–310, 313–17, 341n51, 349n82; class identification and, 65–67, 149, 151–52, 224–26, 244–45, 254–55, 268, 285, 340n29; consumerism and, 4–5, 85, 181–92, 229–31; crooners' association and, 8, 31–35, 37–40, 64–73, 156, 181–92, 198–203, 208–11, 215–16, 218–23, 220, 226–38, 233, 242–63, 267–68,

Malin, Jean, 224, 240

Maltese, Racheline, 328

mammies, 16–18, 37–52, 56–58, 97, 219

"Mammy o' Mine" (Farrell and Hatch), 58, 59

"Mammy's Angel Chile," 56–57

"Mammy's Lit'l Choc'late Cullud Chile," 57

"Mammy's Little Alligator Bait," 46

"Mammy's Little Coal Black Rose," 57, 58

"Mammy's Little Pansy," 57

"Mammy's Little Pickaninny Boy" (Williams and Walker), 49, 50

"Mammy's Little Pumpkin-Colored Coons" (Hillman and Perrin), 46, 49, 51

"Mammy's Little Yaller Gal," 46

"Mammy's Sugar Plum" (song), 56–57

"Man I Love, The" (song), 156, 179

Mann, William, 299

Manners, David, 251, 365n99

"Mariana" (De Leath), 83

Marks, Edward, 67, 70

marriage: crooners' singing and, 24–25, 130, 144–45, 148–51; divorce and, 108, 129, 174, 282; gendered discourses of, 32–33, 241–42, 281–82, 285–87; home wrecker narratives and, 192–95; manuals for, 129–30, 187; psychology and, 14, 24; sexuality in, 13–14, 24, 125, 129–30, 143, 151–59, 243, 353n39

Martin, Quinn, 206

Martinelli, Giovanni, 103–4

Marvin, Johnny, 88, 90, 93–94, 103, 105, 106, 113, 125, 140, 270, 272, 287

masculinity: anxieties over, 2, 218–26; bodily activity and, 6–7, 73, 233–34, 254–63, 288–89, 300; boy singers and, 69–73; crooners and, 3–4, 8–15, 28–31, 103–4, 156–59, 181–92, 208–11, 216–17, 226–42, 244–45, 247–63, 267–68, 294–95, 363n79; Crosby's image and, 264–69, 288–300, 305–10; cultural feminine and, 6, 13, 38, 41–52, 72, 156, 208–11, 250–51, 317, 326–27; discipline and, 19–20, 78–80, 91, 140–41, 227–28, 231–32, 235–38; emotional detach-

ment and, 6–10, 19–20, 149–51, 268, 271, 273, 288–89, 303; humor and, 288–98; marriage manuals and, 143–45, 186, 286–87; modernity and, 13–15, 30–31, 171–72, 176–81; mothers and, 17, 71, 172–76, 239; psychology and, 230–31; singing and, 9, 78–80, 321–30; Vallée's audiences and, 130, 148–51, 154, 193, 200–201, 222–23, 260; vocal registers and, 1, 3–4, 8–15, 280, 313–17, 334n8. See also crooners; cultural feminine; gender; voices

mass media: Catholic invectives against, 226–28, 307–10, 362n42; collegiate type and, 117–18, 121–24, 131–33; consumers of, 14, 62, 258; crooner investments of, 5–6, 217; gendered divide in, 77–78, 134–35, 143–44, 208–11, 317–21; homogenization and, 85, 87–88, 93, 95–102, 167–69, 176–81, 305–10; nationalism and, 8, 224–26, 238–42; racial segregation and, 4, 7–15, 23, 56, 129–30, 178–79; radio's emergence and, 355n2; stardom and, 3–4, 61, 65–73, 76–78, 125, 135, 258, 276–77, 282–83, 350n97; tabloid industry and, 160–66, 181–95, 206–11, 218–23, 364n84; Tin Pan Alley and, 42–65, 340n28; variety shows and, 254–63. See also cinema; gender; modernity; radio

masturbation, 20, 151, 153, 158–59, 231, 234, 282

Matthews, A. E., 258

maturity. See crooners; gender; immaturity; masculinity

Maugham, Somerset, 258

Maxfield, J. P., 89, 236–37, 368n23

Mayer, John, 319

McClary, Susan, 1, 34, 99, 347n58

McCormack, John, 80, 135, 234–35, 269, 346n37

McCrea, Joel, 263

McDaniel, Hattie, 250

McIntyre, Lani, 304

McKenzie, Red, 238

McNamee, Graham, 202

"My Melancholy Baby" (Lyman), 74

"My Mother, My Sweetheart, and I" (Waring), 107

My Own Private Idaho (Van Sant), 311–12